Redefining Rape

Redefining Rape

*Sexual Violence in the Era of
Suffrage and Segregation*

Estelle B. Freedman

Harvard University Press

Cambridge, Massachusetts, and London, England | 2013

Library of Congress Cataloging-in-Publication Data

Freedman, Estelle B., 1947–
    Redefining rape : sexual violence in the era of suffrage and segregation /
Estelle B. Freedman.
    pages   cm
    Includes bibliographical references and index.
    ISBN 978-0-674-72484-6 (alk. paper)
    1. Rape—United States—History.   2. Women's rights—United
States—History.   3. Civil rights—United States—History.   I. Title.
    HV6561.F74 2013
    364.15'320973—dc23   2013002883

For Susan

Contents

Redefining Rape

Introduction

The Political History of Rape

"'Rape' is a word in flux," a *New York Times* editor acknowledged in 2011, after a spate of influential men—from priests to college athletic coaches to the president of the International Monetary Fund—denied accusations of assault, sexual harassment, or child sexual abuse. In the same year, congressional Republicans tried to tighten requirements for federal funding of abortions by changing the language of an exemption from "rape" to "forcible rape," prompting a journalist to ask, "What's behind the drive to redefine rape?" In 2012, when a Republican senatorial candidate justified his total opposition to abortion by claiming that victims of "legitimate rape" could not get pregnant, President Barack Obama told the nation that it did not make sense to "be parsing and qualifying and slicing" the subject because "rape is rape." Yet federal policy had only recently incorporated that view. A year earlier, members of the Women's Law Project told a national meeting of police officials that the narrow definition used by the Federal Bureau of Investigation in compiling the Uniform Crime Reports since 1927—"the carnal knowledge of a female, forcibly and against her will"—had led to the underreporting of rape. "You can't ignore the politics of crime," one police commissioner commented. Only in 2012 did the FBI revise its definition of rape to include any form of forced sexual penetration of a man or a woman as well as "non-forcible rape."[1]

The effort to redefine rape is not a recent phenomenon in American history. Generations of women's rights and racial justice advocates have contested the narrow understanding of rape as a brutal attack on a chaste, unmarried, white woman by a stranger, typically portrayed as an African American man. In the early nineteenth century, white women sought legal remedies to make it easier to prosecute coercive but nonviolent sexual relations with acquaintances. After emancipation, African American activists

1

insisted that black women could be victims of rape and that white men should be held accountable for assault. Suffragists claimed that women required equal political rights to ensure their public safety and fair rape trials. In the late twentieth century, feminists renamed nonconsensual sex with acquaintances and husbands as rape. Underlying all of their campaigns was the recognition that white men's freedom to be sexually violent or coercive lay at the heart of their political power.

These past contestations over the meaning of rape serve as reminders that sexuality, once viewed as a private matter, has proven to be thoroughly entwined with public life. Changing the definition and prosecution of rape has challenged the very meaning of citizenship in American history—that is, who was to be included in and who was to be excluded from privileges and obligations such as voting, jury duty, officeholding, and access to due process of law. On a practical level, the exclusion of African Americans and women from voting, lawmaking, and courtrooms (as jurors, lawyers, and sometimes even as observers) contributed to the immunities enjoyed by white men who seduced, harassed, or assaulted women of any race. On a rhetorical level, the constructions of black women as always consenting, white women as duplicitous, and black men as constant sexual threats all justified the very limitations on citizenship that reinforced white men's sexual privileges.

Redefinitions of rape occurred within a broader context of debates over the role of sexuality in the creation of what one historian has called a "stratified citizenry." The exclusion of foreigners who were deemed immoral from entering the country, or, until recently, of men and women considered to be homosexual from serving openly in the military, illustrate how sexual norms shape the American polity.[2] Yet the subject of rape rarely appears in accounts of American politics. The exceptions are telling: studies of lynching in the post-Reconstruction South and accounts of the trials of nine black youths convicted of interracial rape in Scottsboro, Alabama, during the 1930s.[3] Each of these historical touchstones underlines the centrality of race to the political history of rape. But they represent only part of a prolonged struggle over the meaning of sexual violence in the American past.

Political critiques of rape originated in the context of antebellum moral reform and women's rights movements. They intensified during a series of turbulent historical processes in the late nineteenth century. After Reconstruction, struggles to enfranchise women and to disfranchise black men coexisted, while the scourge of lynching helped implement Jim Crow segregation in the South. By the 1920s, women had won national suffrage, African Americans were abandoning the South, and lynching had declined markedly. Contributing to these transformations were a range of political actors—suffragists, free lovers, child-savers, African American journalists, anti-lynching crusaders, and interracial activists among them—who in diverse ways scrutinized the meaning of sexual violence. The expansion of civil rights and feminist politics in the late twentieth century fostered anti-rape campaigns that renewed the quest for female sexual self-sovereignty and helped transform both cultural interpretations and public policy concerning rape.

More than a social history of sexual violence told through the experiences of accusers and assailants, *Redefining Rape* asks how a series of distinctive political critiques of the construction and prosecution of sexual assault took shape in the United States. For almost two centuries a regionally, racially, and politically varied group of reformers has tried, in the face of formidable obstacles, to change legal understandings of rape. While we cannot know the actual extent of sexual violence or whether these reformers were effective in reducing it, we can begin to understand how these women and men formulated their ideas, how their influence on popular attitudes and public policies changed over time, and what legacies they left to later advocates of women's rights and racial justice.

AT ITS CORE, *rape* is a legal term that encompasses a malleable and culturally determined perception of an act. Different societies define which nonconsensual sexual acts to criminalize, which to condone, and how forcefully to prosecute the former. Indeed, the history of rape consists in large part in tracking the changing narratives that define which women may charge which men with the crime of forceful, unwanted sex, and whose accounts will be believed. The meaning of rape is thus fluid, rather than transhistorical or static. In contrast to those who view rape as a natural imperative resulting from male aggression and serving evolutionary ends, historians and feminist scholars ask how its definition is continually reshaped by specific social relations and political contexts.[4]

Legal definitions play an essential role in understanding the narratives of rape that vary over time. In British law, which provided the basis for most American statutes, the term *rape* originally referred to the nonsexual crime of violent theft (from the Latin *raptus* or *rapere*). That usage has continued in the present largely through metaphoric references to the "rape" of the land or of specific countries, such as "the rape of Belgium," signifying the violation of resources or of national sovereignty. By the fifteenth century, however, the legal definition of rape in England had narrowed to apply to the theft of a woman's virtue, either a daughter's virginity or a married woman's honor. Because the crime appropriated the sexual rights of a husband, his assurance of paternity, and family honor, the father or husband of a raped woman pressed criminal charges. By the time of the colonization of North America, however, women could bring rape charges themselves. As in England, early American law defined rape as the carnal knowledge of a woman when achieved by force and against her will by a man other than her husband. For a child under the age of ten, English common law did not require force or, in principle, raise the question of consent.[5]

Formally, the crime of rape was characterized not only by a lack of consent but also by the use of force and by a male perpetrator unrelated by marriage; in court it usually required as well both penetrative sexual intercourse and evidence of female resistance. In nineteenth-century America, an array of legal categories could also apply to sexual crimes. On a continuum of physical force, these acts ranged from coercive but presumably nonviolent offenses (such as seduction, criminal seduction, and abduction) to violent acts (such as attempted rape, assault with attempt to rape, aggravated assault, felony assault with intent to commit a rape, carnal knowledge and abuse of an infant, and rape). The terms incest and statutory rape could refer to noncoercive, coercive, or physically violent acts, as could sodomy, which was the only crime that applied to nonconsensual same-sex relations. Here, the terms rape, sexual assault, and sexual violence are used interchangeably to denote a broad set of acts, except when referring to a specific legal term, such as attempted rape, seduction, incest, or sodomy.

An important component of American understandings of rape has been the concept of consent, which lays at the heart of both Anglo-American law and the American ideal of liberal individualism.[6] Wives were not the only group lacking the right to withhold consent. Slave women could not refuse sex with their masters, a dictate that continued to haunt African American women long after emancipation. Though formally protected by law, in practice many servants also had little recourse when assaulted. Most formal statutes did not require chastity for a woman to charge rape, and jurists even debated whether a prostitute could be raped. But having had sexual relations, or even having a reputation for impurity, strongly disadvantaged women in the eyes of judges and jury members, who assumed that once a woman had consented she would consent again. These categorical restrictions flowing from marriage, enslavement, class, or reputation limited a woman's ability to withhold consent and influenced the prosecution of rape.

Conversely, the definition of the rapist depended strongly upon a man's class, race, or other social position. In the eighteenth century, the libertine, or rake, was typically an Anglo-American elite male who presumed the privilege of sexual access to women of any class, but he was rarely considered a criminal. In the South, the racialization of the rapist that accompanied the institutionalization of slave labor escalated after emancipation. Until the late nineteenth century, however, white tramps and strangers dominated much of the discourse on sexual assault. A common feature of these stereotypical rapists was the belief that (white) women would be unlikely to consent to have sex with men from these groups, making the "consent defense" less available to certain (nonwhite or marginal) men.

Along with these specifically American constructions, the highly variable representations of rape in western culture influenced understandings of sexual violence. One recurrent theme was the association of women with sexual duplicity, from the biblical account of Potiphar's wife falsely accusing Joseph of rape when he scorned her advances to later depictions of women who "cry rape." At the same time, rape has been linked to an ideal of female virtue, a crime against honor rather than a physical assault on a woman. The oft-cited story of the exemplary Roman matron Lucretia, who preferred suicide to living with the dishonor of having been raped, affirmed the belief that rape was a "fate worse than death." These two extremes, the seductress and the honorable woman, infiltrated both legal and cultural understandings of rape in America, casting doubt on rape claims and requiring an honorable reputation to support them.[7]

Narratives of conquest and empire, which tended to naturalize sexual violence as part of historical processes, also significantly influenced American definitions of rape. Depictions of the rape of the Sabine women treated assault as a nation-building episode in the establishment of Rome. Myths and tales conflated rape with the abduction or seduction of young women by powerful men, exemplified in the myth of the rape of Europa by the Greek god Zeus. While these heroic images continued to circulate, during the eighteenth century several writers made the conquest of women an object of satire or farce, as in Alexander Pope's "The Rape of the Lock" (a poem about the theft of a woman's beauty), or in the rape scenes in Henry Fielding's comic novels.[8]

References to rape have also communicated nonsexual political concerns, for rape has often functioned in an allegorical mode. With the rise of print culture in the eighteenth century, literary and artistic representations of rape increasingly used images of women under assault to protest violations of national sovereignty, as when a ravished woman stood for the colonists forced by the British to pay taxes on tea. Modern writers continued the practice, as did W. E. B. Du Bois when he invoked "Black Africa—frustrated, raped, and shamed" in his critique of colonialism.[9] A common theme running through all of these cultural representations, as well as the legal response to rape, was an ideal of female chastity that was more significant as a measure of family or national honor than as a form of female sexual sovereignty.

SINCE RAPE HAS LONG BEEN a powerful cultural and political symbol—one that has helped shape sexual, racial, and national ideals—why did concerted efforts to redefine sexual violence emerge in the nineteenth century? In part, a narrowing construction of rape provoked these reinterpretations, while recently established voluntary organizations intent on improving morality or extending rights provided structures for initiating legal reforms. Equally important, political ideas about gender, race, and sovereignty set the stage for rethinking sexual violence. In particular, the role of consent in western politics, along with more immediate concerns about the meaning of citizenship in the United States, explains the timing of the campaigns to redefine rape.

The Enlightenment ideas that influenced the American experiment in republicanism rested heavily upon a social contract that required the consent of the governed. The ability to consent was a prerequisite for autonomous personhood in nineteenth-century liberal thought, which idealized self-sovereignty. At their origins, both the social contract and classical liberalism intentionally applied only to white males. The flip side of the social contract was a sexual contract that gave ownership of women to their husbands. Only white men had the capacity to enter into civil society because women, like non-Europeans, were seen as particularly irrational, sexually unlimited, and bound to nature.[10] A central project of contemporary feminism has been the inclusion of women as fully human and autonomous beings, the "owners" of their own bodies rather than the instrumental objects of the needs of men. In the nineteenth century, however, only rare political writers insisted that self-sovereignty be extended to women of any race, including the right to determine when and with whom they had sexual relations.[11]

The implications of the sexual contract can be found in antebellum American links between legal capacity, political consent, and citizenship. In the early nineteenth century, newly written state constitutions bestowed rights upon citizens who had legal capacity. But the principle of coverture, by which male heads of households represented women and children, denied all women the right of political consent. Adopted from British common law, coverture meant that a husband governed over his wife, controlling her property, her earnings, and her person. Preserving the sexual entitlements of husbands required a dependent economic and legal identity for wives. In contrast to the independent male head of household—the ideal citizen—a woman remained dependent and thus unable to participate in republican government, apart from her role of inculcating virtue in her family.[12] Women's legal incapacity to refuse sexual, and thus reproductive, consent in marriage contributed to their political incapacity to exercise the rights of citizens, for they remained subjects, not sovereigns.

The issue of consent was central not only to rape but also to the entire struggle for women's rights. It was largely in response to the gap between ideals of consenting citizenship and the limitations of gender that beginning in the 1840s activists waged a series of campaigns against coverture. They succeeded in gaining married women's rights to property but encountered long term obstacles in the path to suffrage. Their efforts took on a new urgency after the Civil War, when more women entered public life as wage earners or sought higher education and professional lives. At the same time, the emancipation of slaves opened a discussion of women's rights. Freedwomen faced the possibility of being owned neither by a white master nor by a husband, while the postwar constitutional amendments promised to extend civil and political rights to all citizens. But the rights the Constitution now granted to freedmen were not extended to any women. Congressional debates made clear that the Fourteenth Amendment's guarantee of equal protection of the laws should apply to men across race lines but not fully to wives of any color, for they owed their services to their husbands. Nor did the Fifteenth Amendment include suffrage rights for women. In 1875 the Supreme Court affirmed that national citizenship did not entitle women to independent political identities, ruling unanimously that although women were citizens, states could curtail their right to vote.[13]

For freedmen, even the post–Civil War constitutional guarantees of the rights of citizens did not necessarily ensure self-sovereignty. Without the economic leverage of a secure livelihood, a requirement for insuring civil freedom, formal rights can be merely symbolic. And without access to justice through the rule of law, political rights remain fragile.[14] Although southern black men could now contract as free workers, coercive practices such as debt peonage and convict labor undermined their nominal free labor status. During the Jim Crow era, southern states devised mechanisms for disenfranchising African American men and reestablishing white rule, including the escalation of racial lynching, a form of political terror that made it difficult for southern blacks to resist the erosion of their rights. Key to national tolerance for vigilantism was the myth perpetrated by southern white politicians that lynching defended southern white womanhood against the sexual threat of black men. Even though most lynchings had nothing to do with sexual assault, rape accusations became central to the political strategy of disenfranchisement.

The specter of lynching suppressed dissent among African Americans and simultaneously reinforced white women's dependence.[15] In another political consequence, the southern rape myth represented "beastly" black sexual predators as incapable of the rational control required to exercise rights such as voting, officeholding, and jury duty. Again, beliefs about the capacity to control one's sexuality contributed to exclusion from citizenship. It is not a coincidence that a political discourse on rape emerged at the height of these controversies over restrictions on the rights of women and African Americans.

THE STRUGGLE TO REDEFINE RAPE in America has remained historically invisible, in part because the disparate critics considered here never formed a unified social movement. No single organization, such as those focused on achieving suffrage or temperance, addressed sexual violence. Thus there is no collection of national conference proceedings or a periodical devoted to the subject of exposing rape as a social and political problem. Nor was there a consistent set of local interventions, akin to the anti-vice commissions that addressed prostitution in American cities in the early twentieth century. A variety of legal sources and popular media help to document contestations over the meaning of rape in American history, including accounts of rape in the white and black press, in popular magazines, and in legal and medical journals. Appellate court decisions in seduction, rape, statutory rape, and sodomy cases provide insight into the interpretations of rape that helped limit rights based on race and gender.[16] While courtroom dramas offer important evidence of how Americans understood sexual violence, the writings of social purity, women's rights, free love, and anti-lynching reformers, and the work of organizations such as the Woman's Christian Temperance Union and the National Association for the Advancement of Colored People help document political interpretations of rape.

The initial responses to sexual violence, which were highly fragmented and regionally varied, occupied a very broad spectrum of American politics. At one extreme they included the nineteenth-century anarchist free love community, which condemned rape in marriage; at another extreme they included post-Reconstruction southern white supremacists who used rape fears to justify lynching. In between could be found an assortment of overlapping analyses of female sexual vulnerability and male aggression: among moral reformers who sought to protect white women from seduction; social purity and child protection advocates who argued for stronger statutory rape laws; white suffragists who condemned the male-dominated criminal justice system for its leniency to rapists; and African American women and men who attempted both to expose the myth of the black rapist and to condemn white men's sexual abuse of black women.

While diverse in membership and goals, each of these groups invoked the specter of rape to advance a political agenda: to reform or reject marriage; to sustain or undermine white supremacy; to empower or to protect women. Each group approached rape instrumentally and incrementally, only rarely challenging white male dominance directly. A racial divide, rather than cooperative efforts, characterized this history well into the twentieth century. Given their sometimes contradictory impulses, it is not surprising that no national group devoted its energies to the subject of reforming rape laws and criminal procedures. And given the range of actors and goals, this history does not have a singular narrative of social change. It is neither a story of unremitting progress through legal and cultural interventions nor a story of a failed reform movement. Changes in law and culture did result from the efforts chronicled here, though unevenly over time and across regions. Some campaigns were surprisingly effective, such as statutory rape reform. Others were painstakingly slow, as was the drive to end lynching. Even the most successful redefinitions of rape had either mixed, contradictory, or limited results, as so often happens within the history of reform. Taken together, however, these efforts testify to the role of sexual violence in sustaining white men's political privileges and in mobilizing challenges to those privileges.

Until recently, contestations over the rights of women and of African Americans have dominated the political discourse on sexual violence, overshadowing subjects of current concern, such as the sexual abuse of children by clergy, rape in prisons, wartime rape, and racial constructions beyond the black/white binary. Nineteenth- and early twentieth-century commentators on rape rarely pointed to prisons, religious institutions, or the military, nor did they look far beyond African American men as racialized sexual threats.[17] By the time that immigration from eastern and southern Europe peaked in the early twentieth century, the image of the black rapist had become so solidified that, with a few exceptions, it monopolized the cultural landscape. Certain immigrants did become associated with sodomy, however, especially when the sexual vulnerability of children outside the home attracted the attention of reformers. Along with race and gender, age provoked heated debates about the definition of sexual violence. At times children came close to dominating the discourse, even trumping the racial construction of rape, as when southern whites decried assaults on black girls. For any race, the ideal—that is, believable—victim became younger over time: from a woman, to an adolescent, to a girl. By the 1920s, the category included boys as well, an indication of the shift toward a gender-neutral legal approach to rape, one that developed more fully in the late twentieth century.

This narrative unfolds against a backdrop in which parallel white and black women's movements flourished, segregation and the disenfranchisement of African Americans solidified, and a national racial justice agenda took shape. For the history of feminism, the response to rape reveals how an initial emphasis on protective strategies that emphasized chastity and the reproductive family shifted increasingly to the championing of independent citizenship, including suffrage, jury service, and police authority. For the history of race relations, the discourse on rape shows not only how southern white polemics contributed to the deteriorating status of blacks but also how the anti-lynching campaign confronted the myths about race and rape, eventually converting some white liberals to their cause. For the history of sexuality, the redefinition of rape in the early twentieth century exposes the contradictions of sexual liberalism, which both empowered women to seek sexual sovereignty and masked coercive practices by presuming female consent.

Today *rape* remains a word in flux, and how we understand sexual violence continues to influence American politics. Contemporary debates over what constitutes sexual violence resemble conflicts that have recurred for almost two centuries. Women and their allies are still trying to expand the legal definition of rape to make it easier to prosecute men, whether or not they were strangers and whether or not the assault was physically violent. They continue to meet opposition from those who believe that only a narrower construction will protect men, whether from the fear of false accusation or from the loss of sexual privilege. African Americans and other ethnic minorities maintain their challenges to racial differentials in the prosecution of rape and to the heightened sexual vulnerabilities of women of color. As in the past, much more than the legal definition of rape is at stake. The history of repeated struggles over the meaning of sexual violence reveals that the way we understand rape helps determine who is entitled to sexual and political sovereignty and who may exercise fully the rights of American citizenship.

1

The Narrowing Meaning of Rape

From the settlement of the colonies in the seventeenth century through the early decades of the newly established United States, Americans expressed two seemingly contradictory responses to sexual assault. The laws harshly condemned the crime of rape but authorities hesitated to prosecute it fully. Persistent suspicions about female complicity discouraged convictions, with the notable exception of cases in which the defendants were not white men. Although these patterns differed between New England and the South, responses to rape in the seventeenth and eighteenth centuries increasingly heightened white men's sexual privileges.

In colonial America, rape was one of a number of sexual crimes—including fornication, adultery, and sodomy—that threatened to undermine the primacy of marital reproductive relations. British law, which was adopted in the colonies, defined rape as the "unlawful and carnal Knowledge of a Woman, by Force and against her will." Two features distinguished rape from other illegal sexual acts: the use of physical force and the lack of a woman's consent. These elements appeared in depictions of rape in popular culture as well. According to an advice manual published in Boston in the mid-eighteenth century, "Rape or Ravishment" was "a violent deflouring" [*sic*] of "a Woman who never consented thereunto."[1] The reference to deflowering hints at the common understanding that the crime robbed a young woman—and her family—of her virtue. The criminal definition did not apply to husbands, because wives could not retract their "matrimonial consent," nor did it not apply to same-sex relations, which typically fell under the category of sodomy.

On the surface, early Americans seemed to take rape and other nonreproductive sexual acts very seriously. Both northern and southern colonies listed rape as a capital offense, along with murder, treason, and sodomy (and, in early Massachusetts, adultery). The Puritans in seventeenth-century

New England were especially bothered by nonmarital sexual acts. Initially the Massachusetts Bay Colony limited the death penalty for rape to cases in which the victim was a married woman, but several assaults on young girls led to the extension of this penalty to single women. According to a 1699 Massachusetts law, either carnal knowledge of a girl under age ten or "committing Carnal Copulation" with any adult woman "by Force against her will" were felonies punishable by death. The Virginia General Court also made rape a capital offense but added the requirement of a unanimous verdict to apply this punishment.[2]

When they were prosecuted, early New England rape cases confirmed the view that Puritans considered the crime to be an atrocious offense. Seventeenth-century Connecticut courts usually convicted men who had been accused of sexual assault. Unlike their British counterparts, judges in New Haven Colony did not necessarily interrogate a woman's character when she brought rape charges. The courts in this colony even expelled a man who repeatedly made advances to young girls. Whether accused by single or married women, men convicted in early Connecticut were severely whipped, heavily fined, or sentenced to hang for rape or attempted rape. In other regions as well, courts sentenced men to death for the crime of rape. Of the seventy-three guilty verdicts for rape between 1700 and 1776 throughout the British colonies, all but five resulted in a death sentence. Those not executed (or pardoned) were whipped, fined, or exiled.[3]

Prosecution, however, could be weak, in part because many acts of coercion or assault were never officially reported, including unwanted sex during courtship. Equally important, the very severity of capital punishment meant that higher standards of evidence prevailed. The Massachusetts rape statute required that two witnesses testify to the act of penetrative sex. The Puritans more frequently prosecuted attempted rape, which was not a capital crime and did not require proof of penetration. In many colonies juries insisted on evidence of bodily harm to show that a woman had resisted physically to the fullest extent in order to prove that she had not consented. Throughout the colonies before 1800, when the death penalty remained typical, juries found guilty just under one-third of the white men tried for rape. If convicted, unless the victim was a child, a very young woman, or a married woman, the death penalty was unlikely.[4] Even when applied, courts often commuted the sentences. In 1676, after a master successfully appealed for leniency for his convicted black servant, a Massachusetts court substituted a severe whipping for the original sentence of hanging.[5]

Similarly, few cases of sodomy or bestiality reached the courts, in part because proving that intercourse had occurred could be difficult and in part because courts were reluctant to execute men for these offenses. In the early Chesapeake region, despite the uneven sex ratio that might encourage same-sex relations, only one man was executed for sodomy—a ship's captain who assaulted his servant. The rare prosecutions for same-sex assaults in the colonial era typically involved children. In the seventeenth-century Dutch colony of New Netherlands, one slave was strangled and burned after he confessed to "sodomy by force" with a ten-year-old identified as a Negro.[6]

Along with underreporting and reluctance to impose capital punishment, early Americans' understanding of sexuality helps explain the low conviction rates for rape. Complicating the task of proving consent was the thin line between what was then considered coercive, rather than consensual, sex. Men often employed some level of aggression when they approached women sexually. Virginia gentleman William Byrd recorded in his diary that he would have "ravish't" one woman "if her timely consent had not prevented the Violence." The assumption that women who fought back simply feigned resistance while in fact desiring sex encouraged other men to persist. The subtitle of an eighteenth-century poem defending another elite man—"The Agreeable Rape"—insinuated that women wished to be taken by force. These beliefs about women's responsibility for their own assaults reverberated within court cases. Some women who reported rape found themselves accused of fornication and punished by whipping. Other women simply did not reveal assaults by family members or masters, knowing they would not fare well in the courts.[7]

The rare criminal convictions for rape followed distinctive social patterns. Indians and men of African descent (whether slave or free) were more likely to be prosecuted and convicted of rape than were white men. Two-thirds of those indicted for sexual assault in eighteenth-century Connecticut, and the half-dozen sentenced to death, were either African Americans, Indians, foreigners, or transients. In all colonies prosecutors dropped charges much more frequently if the defendant was white. No white men were convicted of rape in seventeenth-century Virginia. In colonial North Carolina, none of the fourteen white men charged with rape were found guilty, whereas all twelve of the accused black men were executed. Acquittals were more likely when single women—rather than children or married women—accused men of rape, with the notable exception of black men convicted of assaults on single women. The disparity rested in part on class and racial understandings of consent and of character. Presumptions about elite white men's sexual desirability and their honesty worked in their favor when they claimed that women had agreed to have sexual relations with them. Similarly, free white women who charged men with rape fared better in court than did female indentured servants. Indeed, in 1670 two Virginia servants who testified that their master raped them were punished themselves with extra years of service.[8]

Enslaved women had even less chance of protesting assaults. The commoditization of Africans as chattel property required a dehumanization that denied bodily integrity to all slaves. For women, reproductive labor belonged to masters. Early in the history of slavery in the Americas, white owners recognized the economic value of pregnant bondswomen and did not necessarily care how they came to be mothers. Evidence of forced breeding reinforced the vulnerability of slave women and their lack of control over their bodies. In seventeenth-century Massachusetts, when Samuel Maverick was "desirous to have a breed of Negroes," he forced an enslaved African woman to have sex with a "Negro young man." When "she would not yield by persuasions," the owner insisted that she comply "will'd she nill'd she"—whether or not she consented. The woman complained bitterly but in the end she had no recourse.[9]

These clear patterns—strong penalties, weak prosecution, beliefs that women desired aggressive sex, and racial and class distinctions in prosecution and conviction—persisted throughout the long colonial era. By the late eighteenth century, however, American ideas about rape were undergoing subtle transformation. Evidence of women's sexual vulnerability during the Revolutionary War made rape a topic of public concern.[10] In addition to assaults by British soldiers, rising rates of premarital pregnancy and bastardy in the growing commercial cities raised fears of sexual and social disorder. Two other trends point toward an emerging understanding of rape that would become influential in the early republic. New ideas about sexuality, gender, and citizenship helped to strengthen the protections enjoyed by white men accused of rape, while the social distinctions in colonial-era prosecution of sexual assault increasingly took the form of a racial, rather than a class, divide.

British influences helped shape the ways Americans defined consent and thus the prosecution of rape. In late eighteenth-century London, a libertine subculture celebrated male conquests of women, a theme that resonated from the novels of Samuel Richardson to popular bawdy songs. These texts, which built upon earlier depictions of sexually insatiable women, portrayed seduction as a kind of game. Publications in colonial American cities incorporated jokes about women's vulnerability to seduction by libertines and rakes. "That I promised to wed you, and love you,' tis true/But I've tried you, my Doll, and I find you won't do," read a poem in a 1774 Philadelphia almanac.[11] Elements of the libertine culture could also be found in late eighteenth-century Boston and New York, where wealthy gentlemen openly visited brothels.

At the same time, men blamed women for seducing them and expressed fears that women would inhibit men's sexual pursuits by blackmailing them with false claims of rape. In this period the earlier writings of the British jurist Lord Matthew Hale attained widespread influence. In his oft-quoted definition, rape was "a most detestable crime," but it was also "an accusation easily to be made and hard to be proved, and harder to be defended by the party accused, tho never so innocent." American legal manuals reiterated Lord Hale's suspicions about the veracity of women who claimed they had been sexually assaulted.[12] A new scrutiny of women's complaints replaced the earlier Puritan approach to sexual crime. In the late seventeenth century, the governor of New Haven Colony had stated that "a young girle [would not] bee so impudent as to charge such a carriage upon a young man when it was not so." Yet a century later, Connecticut courts increasingly questioned or dismissed women's rape accounts. The older Puritan emphasis on the sinfulness of both men and women had been supplanted by a narrative of male conquest of willing female partners. As images of the female temptress or seductress gained prominence throughout the early republic, women who charged rape seemed more complicitous, and their claims of resistance could be discounted more easily.[13]

Contributing to the new climate were popular texts that warned men about the power of deceitful and unscrupulous women who were at best responsible for losing their virtue and at worst seductresses of men. Hannah Foster's 1797 novel *The Coquette*—based on the case of a woman impregnated by her suitor—described the heroine as "the victim of her own discretion." More explicit depictions of female desire appeared in popular accounts of working-class women, such as "The Longing Maid," depicting a woman who sought "some jolly brisk man," and "The Orange Woman," depicting a woman whose strategy for outwitting male rakes was to emulate them by rejecting marriage and "kiss whene'er I find 'em."[14] At a time when urban men considered poor and working women fair game for sexual adventures, these attitudes provided them with a measure of legal impunity.

The trial of the wealthy New Yorker Harry Bedlow, accused in 1793 of raping seventeen-year-old seamstress Lanah Sawyer, illustrates the sense of entitlement expressed by elite men. Bedlow had at first appeared to be a protective gentleman who escorted Sawyer to her home and then called on her to go out walking. But she claimed that he forced her into a brothel and ignored her repeated refusals of his sexual advances. The defense attorney cast doubts on Sawyer's character, citing her willingness to go out walking with Bedlow as "a strong presumption of her consent." Echoing Lord Hale, the attorney referred to rape as an offense "easily charged by the woman." Significantly, he warned the jury that the accusation of rape placed "the life of a citizen in the hands of a woman." In the early years of the republican experiment, this reference to citizenship as a gendered privilege clearly resonated with the all-male jury, which deliberated for only fifteen minutes before acquitting Bedlow. The verdict ignited a riot among working men, revealing their belief that Bedlow's class, as well as male, privilege had allowed him to get away with rape.[15]

In contrast to men, women could not claim the rights of citizens, in part because of the belief that they lacked the self-control that was prerequisite for a virtuous citizenry. Like the Enlightenment philosopher Jean-Jacques Rousseau, who wrote that women's inability to control their "unlimited desires" posed grave temptations to men, Thomas Jefferson disqualified women, along with children and slaves, from the possibility of citizenship. Women, Jefferson suggested, "could not mix promiscuously in the public meetings of men" without the risk of the "depravation of morals and ambiguity of issue."[16] In other words, allowing women to participate in the affairs of state could unleash a kind of sexual anarchy. Jefferson's concern, however, was not that women would be sexually vulnerable but rather that men would lose their virtue, along with the guaranty of paternity that marriage presumably provided.

The eighteenth-century view that women lacked sexual self-control and that they posed a threat of seducing men created a cultural disadvantage for those women who claimed they had been raped. Ideas about sexual violence in turn reinforced men's political advantages. Whether they were virtuous women who had to be protected by men or sexual temptresses, women remained dependents and thus unsuitable for citizenship.[17]

PRESUMPTIONS OF FEMALE COMPLICITY, combined with the entitlements of male citizens, shaped the meaning of rape for all women; but for groups in which men had weak or no claims to citizenship, female vulnerability intensified. The riot after the Bedlow acquittal revealed a class dynamic in which working men felt that their rights to protect female kin had been disregarded. This disparity deepened along with the emerging notion of race—a legal and cultural construction based partly on skin color, partly on relations of conquest, and partly on the ways individuals performed social roles. Like gender ideology, the view that race determined one's character, and subsequently one's rights, permitted exceptions to the republican ideal of self-government. Racial ideology constructed a social hierarchy that relegated darker-skinned peoples to a lower status. Race, like class, marked certain women as being even less virtuous than their elite white counterparts. In addition, the denial of citizenship to men of conquered groups weakened their ability to protect female kin.

One good example of this dynamic is the plight of Native American women during the conquest of the Americas. Before the arrival of Europeans, women captured in warfare between indigenous North American peoples were sometimes viewed as sexually available slaves, but they might also be integrated into families as wives or concubines.[18] In contrast, when European men encountered local populations throughout the Americas, they often portrayed native women as willing prostitutes in order to justify sexually coercing or assaulting them. In the mid-eighteenth century, Choctaw and Creek leaders protested white men's "debauching" or fondling native women in the southern British colonies. On the northern Mexican frontier, Spanish soldiers treated indigenous women as fair game for rape, the "spoils of war" awarded to victorious armies.[19] "Let us go to the pueblos to fornicate with the Indian women," one Spaniard exclaimed, for "only with lascivious treatment are Indian women conquered." Priests at the Spanish missions lamented the pervasive abuse of indigenous women by soldiers as an obstacle to their efforts to convert the local populations to Christianity. Even when the Catholic Church condemned rape and military officers attempted to curtail it, soldiers felt entitled to sexual access to native women. In addition, when conquered Pueblo women were required to perform labor for Spanish employers, they became vulnerable to sexual assault. As one priest explained in 1761, too many of them returned home "deflowered and crying over their dishonor or pregnant."[20]

These patterns continued on later frontiers. After American annexation of Spanish and Mexican territories in the nineteenth century, Anglo western migrants treated native and Mexican women as if they were prostitutes. When white miners in California failed to induce native women to have sex for money, the men used force. Even if women filed complaints, California law held that the testimony of an Indian was not enough to convict a white person. In other parts of the West, settlers and soldiers took advantage of their legal impunity. After George Armstrong Custer won a battle against the Cheyenne, he allowed his officers to "avail themselves of the services of a captured squaw," as he did himself. Depending on the extent to which they had been subdued, native men might try to retaliate, but episodes during the settlement of the Northwest hint at the costs of resistance. In the 1840s, prospectors in Oregon killed the native men who tried to prevent them from assaulting women in an Indian encampment.[21] Racial double standards did not go unnoticed. When a Mexican woman was hanged in California for killing a drunken man who had forced his way into her home "for the vilest of purpose," a local newspaper pointed out that "had she been of the Anglo-Saxon race, instead of being hung for the deed, she would have been lauded" for defending her virtue.[22]

Another product of conquest, slavery, both encouraged and condoned rape. From the time of their transportation across the Atlantic through their settlement in the colonies, enslaved African women were vulnerable to sexual assault. A study of one slave-trading firm found that "systematic rape and sexual abuse of slave women were part of the normal practice" of both the men who directed the company and the planters who purchased slaves. Once in America, slaves had no legal recourse because they could not testify in court against their owners. Furthermore, because slaves in southern colonies could not legally marry, many of their owners considered enslaved women to be fair game. Southern white men's access to black female slaves was common knowledge in the South.[23] As a contemporary of Thomas Jefferson acknowledged, "In gentleman's houses every where, we know that the virtue of unfortunate slaves is assailed with impunity." In the rare instances when free black women accused white men of rape, courts assumed that they had consented, so deeply had all women of their race been marked by the sexual availability of slaves.[24]

In addition to distinguishing which women could be raped, race increasingly influenced popular and legal notions of who would be prosecuted. Although colonists initially considered Native American men to pose a sexual threat, the rape of white captives was in fact rare. Whether in British or Spanish colonies, some women captured by Indians were sexually abused, but the majority could be integrated into Native cultures as wives, albeit without great choice in the matter. With conquest, the threat of Indian attack diminished, as did fears about the rape of white women.[25] In the meantime, however, tales of black rapists began to fuel the image of racial savagery. The fear of slave rebellion during the American Revolution included the specter of the retaliatory rape of white women by former slaves. By then the process of racialization had already been set in motion in colonial statutes. As early as 1765, for example, an index to the laws of Maryland read: "RAPE: See Negroes."[26]

Admittedly, not all colonists identified rape as a racial crime, nor did southerners express widespread fears that black men threatened the purity of white women, an accusation that would emerge during the late nineteenth century. Throughout most of early America other frameworks still dominated interpretations of rape, including Puritan beliefs in original sin and assumptions about lower-class immorality. When New England ministers preached on the occasion of the execution of rapists, their sermons treated condemned sinners equally, whether black or white. In depictions of rape during the Revolution, British soldiers, as often as slaves, were represented as sexual threats to colonial women. Although southern colonies outlawed interracial sex, well into the nineteenth century local communities often tolerated consensual unions. Even when a white woman charged a black man with rape, neighbors might be suspicious of her claim and presume consent, especially if she was poor or disreputable.[27]

At the same time, however, a range of legal evidence suggests that racial distinctions began to solidify in the late eighteenth century. In some colonies the law prescribed castration for black but not white men convicted of rape, although this punishment was rarely employed. An eighteenth-century Pennsylvania statute imposed castration upon any free or enslaved black man convicted of attempting to rape a white woman. Several other colonies also set harsher penalties for enslaved men than for free white men, treating the rape of white women as an expression of slave rebellion against white mastery. Differential punishment deepened after the American Revolution. When the newly formed states established their criminal codes, they eliminated the death penalty for all but a few crimes, usually retaining it only for murder or treason. Many states substituted long prison terms as punishment for convicted rapists. This reform, however, largely benefited white defendants. Particularly in the South, black men could still be executed or castrated for the rape or even the attempted rape of a white woman. Prosecution patterns continued to differ by race, as well. Black men were more likely to be charged with rape, white men with the lesser crime of attempted rape. Standards of evidence were higher when white men stood trial, leading to a higher rate of acquittal. If convicted, black men were four times more likely than white men to receive death sentences.[28]

Both continuity and change characterized the response to rape in the colonial and revolutionary eras. Rape remained a serious crime, but one that was underreported and underprosecuted. Social status continually influenced which women would be believed if they charged rape and which men would be convicted. By the time of the establishment of the United States, however, the understanding of rape reflected the paradox at the heart of the republican political ideology that shaped the new nation: The expansion of white men's rights at the end of the eighteenth century paralleled a contraction of opportunities for others who were defined as being outside the democratic polity.[29] The principles of self-government embodied in the founding documents of the republic applied to free white men and not to slaves, free blacks, Native Americans, or women. Ideologies of race and gender difference justified these exclusions by placing white men at the top of interlocking social hierarchies, allowing them to rule over those deemed to lack the intelligence and the virtue required of citizens. Legal and cultural understandings of rape contributed to this process by emphasizing the freedom of white men and the threats posed to male citizens by nonwhite men and all women. These trends would continue during the decades between the Revolution and the Civil War, when popular and legal constructions of rape continued to narrow to require a chaste, white female victim and a nonwhite male perpetrator for conviction. In short, the definition and prosecution of rape in the early republic shows that the sexual prerogatives of white men—like their rights to citizenship—rested upon the legal disabilities of African American or Native American men and all women.

IN THE NEW REPUBLIC, the crime of rape continued to be defined as the carnal knowledge of a woman by force and against her will, but nineteenth-century American case law and legal treatises refined the meanings of both *force* and *consent*. Despite variations across states and regions, two major conditions emerged as key determinants of whether a sexual act constituted rape: the character of the woman and the evidence of her resistance. On both counts the definition of rape continued to tighten along lines first evident in the late eighteenth century. To protect the rights of a man accused of rape, a woman (who was identified in court records as the complainant or the prosecuting witness) had to have a reputation for chastity—that is, not having had sexual relations outside of marriage. She also had to be able to prove that she had exercised the utmost resistance during an assault.

Historically the value of a woman's purity strongly influenced the response to rape. In societies in which prospective husbands sought virginal brides, virtue had a calculable worth when fathers negotiated marriages for their daughters. Sexual assault undermined both the honor of the family and a daughter's marriageability. For this reason medieval British laws allowed a man to escape execution if he married the woman he had raped. This option diminished with the evolution of common law after the twelfth century, but the importance of a woman's virginity persisted. For a married woman, rape represented the appropriation of a husband's sole sexual access to his wife, compromising his paternity. A wife, too, had to be beyond reproach. In either case, the crime concerned fathers and husbands as much as the women who had been assaulted. By the time of the establishment of the United States, rape statutes recognized the woman rather than her male relatives as the injured party, but the requirement of female chastity remained critical.

The American republican experiment rested upon the concept of a virtuous citizenry, capable of honest self-government. In the more mobile and commercial world of the early nineteenth century, however, both familial control and familial protection waned. Individuals needed to regulate morality themselves to achieve a virtuous society. Americans began to believe that although women could not be citizens themselves, as wives and mothers they played a crucial role in influencing men's characters, the morals of children, and thus the future of the nation. Within the emerging white middle class, ideals of female modesty, decorum, and even passionlessness competed with earlier images of the temptress and the seducer.[30] The decline of parental control over courtship and marriage, along with new ideas about the political value of female purity, placed a burden on these new guardians of national morality. Women were now expected to internalize virtue to supplant the protection once provided by male kin. At the same time they became responsible for improving the morals of men.

These ideological shifts had important implications for the meaning of rape. The ascendant middle-class ideal of female purity served to heighten social distinctions between pure women and those who fell from the chastity ideal. The former deserved protection from assault but the latter did not. A woman's chastity, even more than the use of force by an assailant, became a key legal precondition for prosecuting rape. Beliefs about

African American immorality affected free black women in the North as well as slaves. The antebellum penny press, for example, included no stories of sexual assaults against black women by white men.[31] Poor, working-class, immigrant, and Indian women also fell outside the ideal of female purity, so they too found it hard to be viewed as believable victims.

Even middle-class white women had to overcome the grave doubts about their characters when they complained to authorities about sexual assault. The fluidity of social status in an increasingly mobile society made Americans extremely vigilant about an individual's reputation. At a time when reliance on self-regulation replaced the earlier social sanctions imposed by close-knit communities and kin, suspicions about duplicitous characters were magnified. The counterparts to the virtuous citizen and the citizen's wife were the "confidence men and painted ladies" who peopled American fiction and advice literature. Like the earlier female temptress, the "designing woman" might allege rape in order to force a marriage or to bargain for a financial settlement.[32] Within this framework of suspicion, lawyers and doctors closely scrutinized women's accounts of assault to be sure that the complainant had a pure character.

Concerns about false accusations echoed both biblical-era fears of vengeful accusations and Lord Hale's more recent caveats about rape charges. Medical and legal texts throughout the nineteenth century reiterated these themes, including Hale's criteria for rape prosecution that a woman had cried out, resisted, and reported the assault immediately. In the 1830s a physician wrote in *A Manual of Medical Jurisprudence* that "of the long catalogue of human crimes, there is no one perhaps, which has given rise to so many false accusations as that of rape." In an 1842 ruling, New York Supreme Court Judge Greene C. Bronson reasoned that a woman who had been seduced by a man—in this particular case, she had succumbed after repeatedly refusing him—might feel so much shame for having submitted that she retroactively claimed rape. Judge Bronson warned that in rape cases "there is much greater danger that injustice may be done to the defendant, than there is in prosecutions of any other character."[33]

Some medical and legal writers went even further to suggest that innocent men had been executed for the crime of rape on the basis of women's false accusations. In fact, capital punishment for rape had been eliminated in most American states, with the notable exception of black men convicted of the rape of white women. Yet doctors and lawyers circulated unsubstantiated claims that women's unreliable testimony had sent men to the gallows. A number of British texts published in the United

States asserted that young girls falsely accused their fathers of incest. "I assure you a multitude of persons have been hanged by such a mistake," a physician wrote in the 1830s.[34] Although inaccurate, these hyperbolic statements suggested the depth of men's fears of false testimony and help explain the extensive legal protections that allowed white men to exercise their sexual prerogatives.

To ascertain whether an accusation might be false, legal authorities asked whether a woman had in truth consented and whether she had resisted sufficiently to prove lack of consent. Key to the former was the sexual reputation of the prosecuting witness. What has since been labeled the "chastity requirement" presumed that once a woman had consented to have sex with one man, she lost not only her honor but also her credibility as a witness. The logic regularly employed by defense attorneys was that if she had a sexual history, a woman had by proxy granted consent to all other men. An 1838 opinion from New York's highest court used classical allusions to contrast the promiscuous wife of a Roman emperor with the woman who would rather die than dishonor her family. Justice J. Cowen asked rhetorically, "Will you not more readily infer assent in the practiced Messaline, in loose attire, than in the reserved and virtuous Lucretia?"[35] His point was that past experience mattered in a rape case.

Antebellum courts regularly allowed extensive character evidence to be introduced by defense attorneys. Casting doubts about a woman's sexual history implied that she could not have been raped. Even in cases with abundant evidence, or when a man had confessed that rape had taken place, impugning a woman's reputation could lead to a lighter sentence or a better chance that he would receive a pardon. Character counted even when young girls reported sexual assaults. The author of a textbook on medical jurisprudence suspected that evidence of a child's ruptured hymen resulted not from rape but because "young girls of erotic temperament will use foreign bodies for gratification."[36] In balancing the protection of men from false accusations of rape with the protection of girls and women from false accusations of promiscuity, the scales often tipped toward the former.

Technically, even a prostitute should have been able to bring rape charges, but defense attorneys and judges regularly cast doubts on the veracity of complaining witnesses by implying that they habitually sold their bodies. According to Justice Cowen, the jury should carefully distinguish "between one who would prefer death to pollution, and another who, incited by lust and lucre, daily offers her person to the indiscriminate embraces of the opposite sex."[37] Many states made a distinction between admissible evidence of a woman's general character and inadmissible evidence of specific prior sexual acts. New York courts allowed questions to be raised about a woman's past experience in order to determine whether she might be a common prostitute and thus less believable as a prosecuting witness. Not all jurists agreed, including a Vermont justice who wrote in 1864, "It is no defence that she was a common strumpet, if a rape was actually committed upon her."[38] More often, however, that very defense effectively enabled men to rape with impunity.

The second key question in nineteenth-century rape trials was whether the woman had fought back sufficiently to overcome doubts that she really wanted to have sex. The view that sexual relations required male aggression and female surrender continued to circulate throughout the nineteenth century. Judge Bronson of New York, for example, warned that even if a woman seemed to resist, "it may still be that she more than half consented to the ravishment."[39] His language practically negated the possibility of rape. A later New York appellate court ruling explained the importance of proving resistance: "Can the mind conceive of a woman, in the possession of her faculties and powers, revoltingly unwilling that this deed should be done upon her, who would not resist so hard and so long as she was able?" If she did not resist fully, the decision continued, "must it not be that she is not entirely reluctant?" After acknowledging exceptions in cases in which a woman had been drugged, or did not have the mental capacity to resist, or encountered multiple assailants, the New York Court insisted that "she must resist until exhausted or overpowered, for a jury to find that it is against her will." An 1876 criminal law treatise made the point vividly, stating that a woman "ought to defend her virtue with as much force and energy as she would her money. Nature has given her hands and feet with which she can strike and kick, teeth to bite and a voice to cry out—all these should be put in requisition in defense of her chastity."[40]

For this reason, a woman enhanced her legal claims considerably if her body revealed the physical signs of violence and her resistance to it. The absence of these signs could temper the treatment of a defendant. In 1801 a formerly enslaved man from the East Indies was sentenced to death in Massachusetts for the rape of a ten-year-old white girl. His successful petition to be deported instead of hanged, signed by dozens of supporters, argued that "no other mark of violence appeared on her body" other than signs of intercourse, which could have been "voluntary or involuntary." A New York court ruled that a man convicted of rape deserved a new trial after he claimed that the woman accusing him had inflicted wounds upon herself to provide evidence that he had assaulted her.[41]

The chastity and resistance requirements were the major but not the only obstacles to conviction. Some states also required evidence of complete penetration and seminal emission in order to prosecute a man for rape. Furthermore, if a woman failed to resist and then became pregnant, persistent beliefs that conception required female orgasm led juries to assume that the woman had enjoyed the act and thus had consented. Although most doctors abandoned these views about impregnation by the mid-nineteenth century, some did not, and juries continued to act on them. In 1862 Dr. Edmund Arnold testified in court that it was "very improbable" that pregnancy could result from rape. He believed that "in truly forcible violations . . . the uterine organs cannot well be in a condition favorable to impregnation."[42] This erroneous theory periodically resurfaced for well over a century.

Given these constraints, it is not surprising that most men tried for rape were not convicted, although patterns differed by state. In Vermont, where postrevolutionary legal reforms eliminated the requirements that a victim had to have cried out for help and reported the assault immediately, 65 percent of the men prosecuted for rape were found guilty. In contrast, New York State continued to require evidence of a cry for help, immediate reporting, and the "utmost resistance." The stricter standards may explain the lower conviction rates in that state, where one county acquitted 67 percent of men prosecuted for rape or attempted rape. In both states the chances for conviction improved if the charge was attempted rape.[43]

The prosecution of rape both reflected and reinforced men's control of women in their families. Married women who had been raped by strangers had a better chance of winning their cases than single women, for rape threatened a husband's ownership of his wife's sexuality. A survey of incest trials before the Civil War reveals that it was almost unprecedented for a daughter to pursue rape charges against her father, given the expectation that children should submit to patriarchal authority within the family. The outstanding exception was the conviction of Ephraim Wheeler of Massachusetts in 1805 after his thirteen-year-old daughter Betsy reported that he had raped her. Equally unusual was her mother's willingness to support the daughter in court. Ephraim Wheeler denied the crime, claimed that Betsy was lying, and then tried to portray her as a willing accomplice to incest (which, unlike rape, was not a capital crime). Nonetheless, the court sentenced him to death and, failing to receive a pardon, he was executed.[44]

The hanging of Ephraim Wheeler is historically significant for its rarity, but it points to the more usual pattern. For a single woman, even a child, to convince a jury that she had been raped required a chaste past, a violent assault, and a valiant but unsuccessful struggle that culminated in penetrative sex but did not result in pregnancy. For all of these reasons, filing a rape charge could be daunting for white women. For black women, the task was even more challenging.

The influence of the South on the ways Americans understood rape in the nineteenth century cannot be overstated. After the American Revolution, slavery gradually died out in the North, but with the rise of a cotton economy it became more entrenched in the South. Sustaining white mastery required widespread cultural and legal support. Nothing better exemplified the dynamic of racial dominance than the response to rape. While northern women faced heightened scrutiny when they charged men with sexual assault, at least they could testify in court. Few southern black women had this option. When northern states eliminated capital punishment for rape, southern states retained it for black men convicted of assaulting white women. In the antebellum South, race began to define rape. Legal disparities in prosecution would deepen after the Civil War. By the late nineteenth century, two sets of southern racial beliefs strongly shaped definitions of rape throughout the nation: first, that black women could not be raped, and second, that black men threatened white female virtue.

As in early America, the fact that white men could legally own black women greatly expanded the sexual privileges of slaveholders. Some owners bought young black women for the explicit purpose of having sexual relations with them, while others coerced or assaulted already enslaved women. In either case they had little fear of legal consequences. The British heritage that constructed rape within the context of patriarchal authority supported these practices. Because female slaves belonged to their owners, not to their male kin, sexually violating these women was not considered rape. A husband's forced sexual relations with his wife broke no laws, and like husbands, slave owners implicitly claimed this exemption. Antebellum southern legal culture interpreted sexual assaults on slaves in these terms. As one lawyer explained, "The violation of the person of a female slave, carries with it no other punishment than the damages which the master may recover for the trespass upon his property."[45] In this view, the rape of an enslaved woman by a man other than her owner was a property offense against the master.

Southern laws made explicit the exclusion of enslaved, or even free, black women from legal protection. Several states revised the wording of their rape statutes after the 1830s by adding "white" before "woman" in the definition of this crime. In other states legal practices precluded prosecution, for a slave could not testify in court against a master. Only if a white witness corroborated her account could an enslaved woman turn to the law.[46] In antebellum Missouri, even though the rape law applied to "any woman," its limits became clear in the case of a teenage slave named Celia, who was executed for murdering the master who repeatedly raped her. Because women could plead self-defense when they killed an assailant, Celia's attorney argued that she had killed her master to prevent further sexual assaults. The judge, however, refused to instruct the jury that the homicide could have been legally justifiable. To do so would have granted women like Celia the right to resist rape by their masters.[47]

There were exceptions to these patterns, for in some southern states black women could charge white men with rape. Even then, though, the crime did not merit the same punishment as did assaults on white women. In Tennessee the law applied across race lines, but rape was a capital offense only if the person assaulted was white. A Georgia statute outlawed the rape of slaves by white men, but the penalties were more lenient than if a white woman had been assaulted. When the Georgia legislature amended its rape law in 1861 to include "free or slave" women, it left the punishment in such cases to the discretion of the court, in contrast to the prescribed prison terms for men convicted of raping white women.[48]

Along with these legal constraints, popular understandings of race and sexuality meant that white men did not necessarily define their sexual relationships with slaves as rape. Instead, the perception of black women as sexually lascivious provided an excuse for imagining that they always consented. That slaves could not legally marry in the South reinforced the view that black women were disreputable. Some southerners even defended slavery on the grounds that the sexual availability of black women protected white women from assault, akin to northern arguments that prostitution was a "necessary evil" for preserving the purity of respectable women. The pro-slavery writer William Gilmore Simms drew on this analogy in excusing the rape of slaves. Too many slaveholders made "their slaves the victims . . . of the most licentious passions," Simms admitted, but he preferred this practice to the commercial prostitution in northern cities because, he believed, female slaves lacked "consciousness of degradation."[49]

Slave owners had economic incentives, as well as ideological justifications, for retaining their sexual privileges. Like forced breeding among slaves, sex with enslaved women often resulted in an increase of human property: the children who were born into slavery. Mixed-race children followed the legal status of their mothers, so the owners profited from impregnating slaves. To abolitionist Lydia Maria Child, the legal practice that a child born to a slave followed her mother's status "furnishes a convenient game to the slave-holder—it enables him to fill his purse by means of his own vices."[50] Some owners manumitted their concubines and the children born to them, following their sentiments rather than their economic interests. But many of these children remained enslaved.

White southern women did not like the ubiquitous presence of mixed-race children on southern plantations, for it reminded them of their husbands' infidelities. According to South Carolina diarist Mary Chesnut, "any lady is ready to tell who is the father of all the mulatto children in everybody's household but their own. Those she seems to think drop from the clouds." For the most part, planters' wives expressed more concern about the characters of their male kin than the plight of slave women. "The institution of slavery degrades the white man more than the Negro," Gertrude Thomas wrote in her diary after bemoaning the sale of light-skinned women who became the concubines of their owners. Rather than accuse male kin of rape, many southern white women blamed enslaved women by portraying them as willing partners.[51]

The psychological effects of sexual abuse took a heavy toll on female slaves. Sexualized and harassed by men, they also endured the jealous rages of white mistresses. Even when they actively resisted, they remained vulnerable. Enslaved women who successfully fought off white assailants risked execution, severe physical punishment, or being sold away from family. A Virginia slave named Peggy refused to have sex with her owner, who was also her father, even after he threatened to rape her. For participating in his murder Peggy was sentenced to death, but she was sold to slave traders after white men petitioned for clemency. Sukie Abbott's master assaulted her while she was making soap in the kitchen, so she shoved him into the hot pot, a story long recalled by other slaves. At the time, however, the result was the sale of Sukie.[52]

Not all interracial sexual relationships constituted forcible sex, although it can be difficult to isolate the element of consent in relationships that were so inherently coercive. Since the colonial era some slaves had long-term relationships with their owners, as did Sally Hemings with Thomas Jefferson.

In the nineteenth century, former slave Harriet Jacobs wrote that she resisted the sexual advances of her master but later willingly engaged in a relationship with another white man. In her words, it seemed "less degrading to give one's self, than to submit to compulsion." Some enslaved women no doubt made a calculated decision to improve their life circumstances by becoming the concubines of their owners. The abolitionist Sarah Grimké, who had grown up in a slaveholding family, sympathized with the dilemma faced by female slaves. In 1837 she lamented, "If amid all her degradation and ignorance, a woman desires to preserve her virtue unsullied, she is either bribed or whipped into compliance." Grimké condemned the market in light-skinned women who were sold as concubines and deplored as well the way slavery contaminated the morality of southern white women by their complicity in the "crimes of seduction and illicit intercourse."[53]

Other opponents of slavery deplored white men's access to enslaved women's bodies. Harriet Beecher Stowe alluded to rape when she claimed in the 1850s that "the worst abuse of the system of slavery is its outrage upon the family." Lydia Maria Child acknowledged that the sexual vulnerability of slave women "has generally been kept veiled" and vowed to make public "its monstrous features" for the sake of "my sisters in bondage, who are suffering wrongs so foul, that our ears are too delicate to listen to them." The radical abolitionist newspaper *The Liberator* was more direct in its critique when it published graphic exposés of the rape or sexually sadistic beatings of female slaves. "South Carolina," Henry C. Wright wrote to the paper in 1858, "is one great legalized and baptized brothel." Here and elsewhere in abolitionist literature, prostitution referred to forced sex.[54]

The sexual privileges that slave owners enjoyed affected enslaved men as well. Husbands and fathers could not prevent assaults upon female kin, a reminder of their own status as property. Some men did retaliate, even murdering whites who raped black women, but the costs were enormous. Enslaved men themselves could not necessarily escape sexual advances from their white owners or overseers. In writing about sexual mastery, Harriet Jacobs stated that white men sometimes "exercise the same authority over the men slaves." White women, too, could coerce their male slaves to have sex with them. At the same time, enslaved men could try to exercise male privilege when they assaulted black women, particularly if they were in positions of authority over other workers. Both southern law and antislavery literature, however, largely ignored the possibility of rape among slaves.[55]

In contrast, when black men assaulted white women, the southern legal response was formally severe, although unevenly applied. A black man convicted of the rape or attempted rape of a white woman or girl faced the death penalty; a white man could expect a prison term. Yet antebellum southern courts did not always convict or execute slaves for rape. In parts of the South, capital punishment of slaves was more likely for the crimes of murder or insurrection than for rape. When convicted, a slave had a good chance of successfully appealing the decision. Appellate courts in the antebellum South overturned almost 60 percent of convictions of the black men for the rape or attempted rape of white women. If the accuser came from a common, rather than an elite, background, the appeal had better chances. In ordering a new trial for a black man convicted of raping a white woman, the Florida Supreme Court explained in 1860 that even though she had not consented, the jury could take "into consideration the degraded character of the witness."[56] As in the North, presumptions that poor women would consent to sex influenced the courts.

An additional influence on the process of appeals and requests for pardons was the support of elite white men, for owners knew that execution or long imprisonment would deprive them of valuable laborers. That white men also defended some free blacks accused of rape suggests that male privilege as well as economic interest could be at stake. In some cases, class divisions among whites meant that plantation owners supported a black man's petition for pardon while poorer whites opposed it. An 1859 protest in North Carolina illustrated these tensions. Poorer whites wrote that "our wives and daughters are to be insulted and injured by every Buck Negro upon the high ways [because of] a few *speculators who care* more for a few *hundred dollars* than they do for the safety of the females of their county."[57] Their sentiments recall those of the working men who rioted after the acquittal of Harry Bedlow in New York City; in both cases, poorer men defended the reputations of women of their class.

For all of these reasons, even when a white woman accused a black man of rape in the antebellum South, the charge did not necessarily lead to a death sentence. Neither did it regularly incite white men to take vigilante action, for lynching remained rare. The crises precipitated by the Civil War, however, would soon deepen the racial, and diminish the class, distinctions in the meaning of rape. During the war, although white southern women also experienced rape by Union soldiers, black women bore the brunt of wartime sexual violence, including cases in which black men had to witness their female relatives being raped.[58] Race also influenced the prosecution of rape. When the military tried either Union or Confederate men for wartime rape, African Americans were disproportionately convicted and executed. Still, black soldiers accused of rape faced trials, not lynch mobs. By the end of the war, courts began to treat slaves differently and fewer slaves convicted of rape received pardons, signaling the harsher climate that would prevail in interracial rape cases after Reconstruction.[59]

Taken together, the response to rape in both the North and the South helped sustain the political divides that privileged white male citizens over both white women and African Americans. Even more so than in the colonial era, nineteenth-century courts protected white men accused of rape—whether by distrusting white women who brought rape charges, denying the possibility of the rape of black women, or identifying the crime of rape with black men. Requiring a reputation for prior chastity and visible signs of physical injury limited the chances for successful prosecution of rape charges brought by any woman.

When southern states defined rape as a crime against a white woman, they gave masters sexual immunity and eliminated legal recourse for the most vulnerable victims. The cultural silence about the rape of enslaved women lay at the heart of the deepening national stereotype of African American women as inherently immoral. The identity of the rapist further reinforced white male privilege. When rape trials led to convictions, for white defendants the crime tended to be a lesser one of attempted rape with relatively short prison sentences. In contrast, convicted black men faced capital punishment or long prison terms. After emancipation, white assaults on black women and the manipulation of sexual fears about black men would produce not only physical terror but also ideological grounds for limiting the rights of freed people. By portraying African Americans as sexually promiscuous and aggressive, white southerners could claim that former slaves and their descendants lacked the virtue necessary for exercising the rights of citizens.[60]

The sexual prerogatives of white men, like their rights to citizenship, thus rested upon the legal disabilities of African American men and both black and white women. Over the course of the nineteenth century, popular and legal constructions of rape had narrowed to imagine a chaste white female victim and a nonwhite male perpetrator. These constraints set the stage for a series of efforts to redefine rape. Initially intended to protect white women, the struggle against sexual assault would become central not only to female empowerment but also to the debates over race and citizenship in the decades after the Civil War.

2

The Crime of Seduction

The British feminist Mary Wollstonecraft, best known for her 1792 treatise *A Vindication of the Rights of Woman,* died before she could complete a fictional sequel to her influential critique of the social limitations on women's lives. The novel she had been writing, *Maria,* subtitled *The Wrongs of Women,* made concrete the devastating effects of inequality on two central characters: Maria, a middle-class woman confined to a madhouse by her husband, and the working-class servant Jemima, who attended Maria there. One of the major "wrongs" depicted throughout the life histories of these two women was sexual assault. As a married woman, Maria had to submit to whatever sexual demands her husband placed upon her. She also learned that before their marriage he had dismissed a young servant girl whom he had seduced and impregnated. Jemima's own mother had been seduced when a fellow servant promised marriage; once pregnant, however, she realized "that she was ruined" because he refused to wed her. By age sixteen Jemima had entered service herself, where she had to avoid the "disgusting caresses" of a master who eventually, by "blows and menaces," compelled her "to submit to his ferocious desire." Pregnant and destitute, Jemima resorted to an abortifacient and then became a common prostitute. "I have since read in novels of the blandishments of seduction," she reflected, "but I had not even the pleasure of being enticed into vice." The protagonist Maria eventually rejects the constraints of marriage in favor of the free-love principle that only sentiment, and not duty, justified sexual relations.[1]

Published posthumously in London in 1798, the novel *Maria* appeared in the United States the following year. At the time, few Americans contemplated the rights or the wrongs of women, and the book attracted little notice. Soon, however, the growth of female academies and women's literacy, along with a new emphasis on female virtue, prepared the ground for women's gradual entry into public life. By the 1830s, white middle-class women in the northern states were joining the burgeoning social reform efforts to improve American society by opposing intemperance, vice, and slavery. In the process, some women began to question the limits on their public authority. At midcentury they forged a women's rights movement that called for full citizenship, including suffrage, for women. Some of these reformers and suffragists would eventually adopt Mary Wollstonecraft's concerns and attempt to redefine rape beyond forcible assault to include coercive or forcible "seduction."

For generations, individual women had been protesting sexual assault each time they reported a rape and whenever they braved the courtroom to testify in criminal cases. After the 1830s the first public critics spoke out. At a time when American courts narrowed the definition of rape to apply largely to a chaste, single white female victim, especially by a black predator, women reformers and their male allies campaigned to expand legal remedies against white men and to diminish white women's sexual vulnerabilities. In the antebellum decades, northern moral reformers targeted men who seduced single women but did not marry them. After the Civil War, suffragists decried both rape and the double standard of criminal justice, demanding enfranchisement and jury duty for women in order to ensure fair prosecution in rape cases. In the late nineteenth century, radical free lovers questioned the limits of these reforms and first articulated a woman's right to refuse marital sex.

These overlapping campaigns to question the meanings of sexual consent and coercion took place in the context of heightened attention to female virtue and to the greater sexual vulnerability of young white women. In colonial America most courting couples could engage in sexual relations with the presumption that marriage would follow, especially if the woman became pregnant. Clergy and family members would enforce the union, in part so the community would not have to support offspring born out of wedlock. Although fornication was a sin, it did not connote a woman's moral demise. In the early nineteenth century, just as church authority and parental control over morality declined, new opportunities for travel and labor in the growing commercial cities and mill towns expanded the possibilities to be seduced and abandoned.[2] Increased danger and weaker external protections created pressures on middle-class women to internalize morality. In sermons and advice literature influential Americans celebrated female virtue for its own sake, not only as a way to avoid the risk of pregnancy but also for the social good. Only a pure woman could raise virtuous children and, through her domestic influence, foster morality within her husband, the experts explained.

With these new responsibilities came higher moral standards. If sullied through sexual relations before marriage, a woman's reputation was ruined.[3] Along with a loss of honor for her parental family came an economic cost. Given her lowered prospects for marriage and lack of opportunities to be self-supporting, her family would have to support her. The prediction that a once-ruined woman might become a prostitute loomed large in this cautionary literature. Chastity became a survival strategy for those women who embraced middle-class ideals, seduction a threat to maintaining it.

As young women assumed greater responsibility for their own morality, a social reform movement began to decry obstacles to female virtue. In the early nineteenth century a range of voluntary associations coalesced to address perceived threats to public morals, including intemperance and prostitution. Formed in the wake of religious revivals that stressed human perfectibility, these groups thrived among the middle classes in growing commercial towns and cities of the northeastern states, where class and gender relations were in flux. The motives of these moral reformers included the conversion of sinners and the maintenance of a stable and sober working class. Although instigated by Protestant clergy, the membership increasingly included churchwomen. Along with decrying intemperance and vice, they began to focus on white men who seduced women under the false promise of marriage. By midcentury, legislators responded to their calls to strengthen state sanctions and protect women from unscrupulous seducers. The resulting laws both constrained white male sexual privilege and reinforced the centrality of chastity and marriage for women.

MORAL REFORM GREW OUT of broader concerns about the growth of prostitution, which became increasingly visible in European and American cities over the course of the nineteenth century. Once tolerated as a necessary evil that protected respectable women from men's sexual demands, prostitution now troubled public health officials and moralists. By midcentury a small movement to rid the nation of this sin had emerged. Rather than blaming the "fallen woman" who sold her body to men, female moral reformers reversed earlier seduction tales that attributed women's fall from virtue to innate female lust. They popularized instead the view that libertines, male employers, and acquaintances often drove women into prostitution. This narrative built upon earlier Anglo-American depictions of the libertine. In *A Vindication of the Rights of Woman* (1792), Mary Wollstonecraft expressed compassion for the many innocent girls "*ruined* before they know the differences between virtue and vice" who, lacking other means of support, turned to prostitution as their "only refuge."[4] Wollstonecraft also incorporated this critique in the story of the servant Jemima in *Maria*.

Early American fiction employed the seduction tale as well. The popularity of literary tales about the seduction of innocent women by dissolute elite men reflected broader concerns about the dangers that aristocratic behavior posed for the innocent new nation. They also drew attention to female vulnerability. In Susanna Rowson's *Charlotte Temple* (1794), a man promises marriage to convince an innocent young woman to engage in sexual relations and then abandons her when she becomes pregnant. Popular songs and magazine stories written by male and female authors began to depict men as deceitful betrayers and to emphasize the importance of women protecting themselves.[5] These counternarratives contested both the earlier cultural depictions of lascivious women and the legal opinions that exonerated white men while blaming the women they seduced or assaulted.

Taking this message as a call to action, the New York Female Moral Reform Society instigated a public movement to diminish tolerance for the practice of seduction. Founded in New York City in 1834, the Society initially set out to provide refuge for the growing number of prostitutes and to provide moral uplift in the process. When these efforts proved daunting, the group shifted attention to "the licentious man" who victimized women. They explained that male deceivers destroyed women's virtue, leading them into a life of sin; outcast women, rather than their seducers, paid the price. In their periodical *The Friend of Virtue,* moral reformers described the danger of tolerating the libertine: "Who among us can tell that our sisters and daughters are safe while the seducer is unhesitatingly received into our society and treated with that attention which virtue alone can claim."[6]

By the 1840s hundreds of female moral reform associations had formed in small towns as well as cities in New York State and New England. Their members employed whatever means were available to women to transform public attitudes toward seducers and their victims. Along with publishing seduction narratives, the *Friend of Virtue* in Boston reported on trials related to men's sexual misconduct. New Yorkers took more radical steps when they tried to shame men they considered licentious by publishing their names in *The Advocate of Moral Reform*. Further defying gender conventions that relegated women to domestic space and influence, some moral reformers monitored the entrances to brothels to get their evidence. That their critics accused moral reform newspaper exposés of inciting vice rather than containing it suggests that not only association members read these articles.

Along with publicizing men's transgressions, the moral reformers took action. In Utica, New York, they pledged to train their sons in purity and rebuked them if they sinned. Occasionally they helped working women press charges against employers who sexually exploited them. They urged women to shun licentious men rather than ostracize the women who fell from virtue. "Level your artillery at the head and heart of the debauchee," advised the New York City group. "Fix an eternal stigma upon . . . every man who will sport with female virtue." Groups in Boston and New York criticized the limited economic opportunities that drove women to prostitution, and they established homes for "friendless" pregnant women in the hope of preventing their entry into the trade.[7]

Female moral reformers were not alone in their campaign against male licentiousness. Protestant clergy called attention to the sexual risks faced by women in cities such as New York and Boston. One minister wrote to the *Advocate of Moral Reform* to condemn "the prowling tiger in human form" who "may make havoc of the innocence and loveliness of female youth." He explicitly complained that these men could retain "all the privileges of a free citizen," including the vote and eligibility for "the highest offices in the land."[8] In 1848 a group of New England clergymen, alarmed at the increase in licentiousness, blamed men for a range of sexual affronts, from incest to seduction to rape. Pondering the plight of rural migrants, the clergy explained that some young women who arrived in the city unchaste "probably were seduced from purity at home." Others had previously "permitted familiarities without yielding virtue" but found it harder to resist "the artful machinations of the profligate" in the city. Still other "entirely innocent" women fell prey to men who deceptively lured migrants to work in brothels or sexually ruined domestic servants in their households. Even a woman who earned wages at a trade, they warned, risked the false attentions of the villainous young man who, through flattery and gifts, "gains her trust with expectations of marriage" but abandons her once the "horrid seduction is achieved." Now ruined and unable to return to her family home, she might well commit suicide or enter a life of prostitution.[9]

With the weakening of familial and church sanctions against seducers, female reformers turned to the state to enforce morality. Several legal remedies were already in place. Seduction and breach of promise laws applied when men enticed women to consent to premarital sex on the false promise of marriage or by using other duplicitous means, such as a drugged drink. These laws differentiated between the civil offense of seduction, when a woman had consented to have sex, and rape, defined as a criminal act committed by force and against a woman's will. The civil statutes presumed that instead of violence seducers used nonphysical coercion or fraud to achieve their goals. They punished the seducer for destroying a woman's chastity, circumventing the issue of her consent. As a remedy the laws permitted financial compensation for the family of a seduced woman, particularly if she became pregnant.[10]

Although these civil statutes addressed the economic plight of young women abandoned by the men who impregnated them, they also bolstered patriarchal authority and retained the centrality of marriage as woman's vocation. Echoing biblical precepts and earlier European practices, the seduction laws gave a man the option of marrying the young woman rather than paying financially for her "ruin." Mary Wollstonecraft described this kind of union as a "*left-handed* marriage" and understood it as less than ideal. She accepted the practice only as long as women had to "depend on man for a subsistence, instead of earning it by the exertion of their own hands or heads."[11] Even if these marriages provided nominal respectability, they did not always guarantee support. In 1810 a young woman in New England complained about male libertines who were "well skill'd in the arts of seduction"; one of them seduced another woman on promise of marriage and then, to avoid paying for maintenance of the child born as a consequence, "he married her, and left her, friendless, without money, the very Morning after the ceremony was performed."[12] In other cases, however, the threat of a seduction suit might persuade an errant suitor to make good on his promise of marriage.

Merely seducing and impregnating a woman who was still living in her father's home could provoke a civil seduction suit, whether or not a man had promised marriage. Because the pregnancy deprived him of his daughter's household labor, it was the father and not the daughter who filed suit as the aggrieved party. The grounds for this action originated in the master/servant relationship as applied to a patriarchal family economy. Daughters who lived at home owed their services to their fathers, who stood as masters in relation to them. When a daughter became pregnant, her father was entitled to sue the seducer for damages for her lost labor. Working-class fathers could use this mechanism to demand compensation when employers seduced and impregnated their daughters, such as those employed as servants. A wealthier man who had no intention of marrying the young woman might make a cash settlement to her family to avoid going to court.[13] Over the nineteenth century more fathers filed these suits and won financial compensation for lost services, and not only when a daughter became pregnant. One New York court ordered that an employer pay the considerable sum of five hundred dollars to a father whose daughter he had "debauched" and infected with venereal disease. Another court awarded damages to a father whose seventeen-year-old daughter had committed suicide when she found out that the lover who had promised to marry her already had a wife.[14]

Some families measured the cost of seduction not in lost services but in lost honor. As an eminent Georgia jurist acknowledged in an 1852 ruling, even though seduction law derived from the labor relationship of master and servant, paternal outrage could also influence a decision. In the case in point, the defendant had appealed an award of $1,049 to a father whose twenty-one-year-old daughter he had seduced, claiming that the judge should have limited the amount to actual lost services. Justice Joseph Henry Lumpkin declared dramatically, "Never, so help me God, while I have the honor to occupy a seat upon this bench, will I consent to control the Jury, in the amount of compensation which they may see fit to render a father for the dishonor and disgrace thus cast upon his family; for this atrocious invasion of his household peace." While family honor carried particular weight in the South, Lumpkin's concern signaled a broader trend over the century as a woman's chastity alone came to dominate seduction cases. Increasing numbers of northern fathers filed seduction suits, even though the commercializing economy meant that they depended less on the labor of daughters in the home. They knew that seduction, even without pregnancy, seriously reduced a young woman's marital prospects by undermining her qualifications to become a virtuous wife and mother. As in Justice Lumpkin's opinion, northern courts awarded punitive damages to fathers who had suffered mentally for the loss of a daughter's reputation and the family honor, and not merely for the financial loss of her labor.[15]

Seduction suits not only reinforced the patriarchal authority of fathers but also shored up the chastity ideal. Either by civil statute or through court interpretation, to make the case that a woman had been wrongfully seduced, her reputation had to be beyond reproach. In another iteration of the cost of past experiences, a woman who had already sullied her reputation could not, by definition, be trusted in court. Whatever her past, a woman's word alone did not suffice, for the laws required that supporting evidence be presented in court.[16] These limitations may have dissuaded some families from filing seduction charges and meant that others who did so lost their suits.

Even with the growing popularity of civil seduction suits, some families continued to defend female honor on their own through extralegal violence. Nineteenth-century newspapers publicized the murder trials of fathers and brothers around the country who acted to avenge the honor of their female kin by killing seducers. Bemoaning one such case, the *New York Times* recommended harsher legal punishment for seducers and the abolition of "the antiquated barbarisms" that recognized only loss of service and not the "moral injury" of seduction. To achieve an acquittal or diminish the penalties for the murder of a seducer, defense attorneys invoked the "unwritten law," a precursor of the insanity defense. This popular belief held that a man was justified when, in a fit of passion, he killed the scoundrel who had debauched his wife or daughter (or in the case of adultery, if the defendant had killed his wife and her lover). So familiar was this doctrine that one Washington, D.C., judge cut short a rape trial, arguing that the "matter should have been settled outside of court by the brother or father."[17]

Some women avenged seducers themselves. When southerner Amelia Linklaw killed the traveling salesman who impregnated but would not marry her, the defense attorney justified the act because the man had "robbed her of all that was dear to her—her virtue."[18] In New York, public opinion divided over whether Maria Barberi, a fifteen-year-old Italian immigrant who murdered the man who had seduced and abandoned her, should die for this crime. "So long as it is the unwritten law of this land that no man can be punished for killing the seducer of his wife, his sister or his daughter," a St. Louis paper editorialized, "it is strange that a jury should find a verdict of death against a woman for killing her own seducer." The *New York Tribune* recognized the racial contours of this defense, as well. The paper pointed out that while an "unwritten jury-made law" allowed a white woman to kill the man who had seduced and betrayed her, "it is not yet established that she can do this with impunity if she is black, brown or yellow, while her seducer is accounted white." Typically, however, the unwritten law reinforced the expectation of patriarchal authority over women in cases when familial or individual protection had failed. As the *Tribune* put it, the victim's male kin "may act as her proxy."[19]

In contrast to legal and extralegal remedies that centered on male authority, moral reformers questioned the patriarchal foundations of seduction law in ways that anticipated later, more radical arguments for women's independent legal rights. Women's rights advocates explicitly objected that civil seduction statutes presumed male ownership of a woman's chastity and labor. Abolitionist Lydia Maria Child wrote indignantly that under state seduction laws "the woman must acknowledge herself the *servant* of somebody, who may claim *wages* for her lost time!" She compared the legal plight of women to that of slaves; in either instance the notion of woman as chattel property offended her deeply. Foreshadowing the mass women's movements that would follow, Child suggested that "had we not become the slaves we are deemed by law, we should rise *en masse* in the majesty of moral power, and sweep that contemptible insult from the statute book." Child's was also a rare voice questioning the underlying assumption of the laws that once a woman had been seduced, her life had been ruined, for she believed that any woman could recover her virtue, even if she had once fallen.[20]

Moral reformers did point out the limits of denying women the standing to sue. Because only fathers could bring seduction suits, they warned, seducers could prey upon fatherless girls with impunity. Writing in the *Friend of Virtue,* one woman imagined a libertine plotting the ruin of a chambermaid: "She is an orphan too, and that is in my favor."[21] Some complained that the juries hearing seduction cases were not made up of a woman's peers. Short of calling for female jury service, they raised the question of courtroom gender bias by asking how women could expect fair trials when some of the jurors themselves might be dissolute men. Later in the century suffragists renewed critiques of the patriarchal framework of seduction statutes and called for including the rights of mothers. Surveying laws that discriminated against women, Matilda Joselyn Gage questioned why a "father can recover damages against a man who seduces his daughter, but a mother can not recover for the seduction of a daughter," even though, in her opinion, a mother's love exceeded that of the father. This legal disability related to other limits of coverture. Only after the passage of married women's property laws and when mothers had gained legal responsibility for their children could they bring seduction suits on behalf of daughters.[22]

The argument against allowing a young woman herself to bring a seduction suit rested in part on her having consented to sex, which negated any grounds to complain, and in part on men's fears of female duplicity and female authority. For women to have this standing, one court explained, would empower "the female sex to become seducers in their turn, and to prefer false claims for a pretended violation of their chastity."[23] Nonetheless, some single women did gain this right, beginning with an 1851 Iowa statute that allowed a woman to bring suit if she had been coerced to consent to sex because of force or fraud. In the process of reforming their legal codes in the late nineteenth century, over a dozen states—including several in the South—redefined the wronged party from a father who sought compensation for lost services to a woman who had been personally injured. Thus, in the 1890s sixteen-year-old Jessie Marshall could bring a civil seduction suit against her older, married employer, southern California hotel owner Jacob Taylor, who had impregnated her. "Until I met Mr. Taylor I was a chaste and virtuous girl," Marshall testified in court. Then one evening he gave her a glass of wine, she became incapacitated, and he convinced her to have intercourse. Noting Taylor's wealth, a California court awarded her damages of twenty-five thousand dollars.[24]

Granting women the ability to bring suits marked a departure from the patriarchal origins of seduction law. It had broader political implications, as well. Legal dependence on men provided one rationale for excluding women from voting. Gaining independent standing to bring seduction suits pointed toward a society in which women, legally viewed as individuals rather than as familial dependents, represented themselves. Just as the extension to women of the rights to control their own wages and property undermined the principle of coverture, so too the revision of seduction laws had the potential to expand the principle of self-sovereignty.[25]

Seduction laws could enhance women's legal capacities in a practical way by allowing redress for far more than merely breach of promise. Victims of forcible assault could use them to circumvent the narrow requirements for prosecuting rape by acquaintances. Seduction presumed female consent, in contrast to the legal definition of rape as a sexual act accomplished against her will. The boundary between seduction and rape, however, was not always a clear one. The term *seduction* could serve as a code for rape, as it often did in the best-selling novels read by many middle-class women. Like other euphemisms, such as *ruin,* it could refer to forced sex with a suitor, employer, or other acquaintance. The Massachusetts Supreme Court affirmed in an 1872 case that a seduction suit could involve physical force.[26] Imagine a continuum that ranged from a mutually consensual sexual act, to one in which a man persuaded a reluctant or unwilling woman to engage in sex through verbal coercion (including deceit, promise of marriage, or emotional manipulation), to a purely physical coercion (or conquest) despite verbal resistance, to a violently aggressive sexual assault. A woman might ultimately consent in all but the last of these scenarios. Seduction laws, though primarily concerned with consensual sex, could also be applied in those cases when a woman had not consented but had not experienced the level of physical violence required to prove rape.

In some cases, then, seduction represented a "legal fiction" that stood for the act of forcible sex, with plaintiffs and lawyers agreeing to file a civil seduction suit rather than a criminal rape complaint.[27] This option was particularly appealing if a woman feared that a jury might acquit a male acquaintance who was likely to claim that she had consented. Seduction law took the question of consent off the table. Some judges reinterpreted rape complaints as cases of seduction. Given the often thin line between consent and coercion and the reluctance of juries to convict men of rape, successful seduction suits offered a legal tool to punish assailants and warn other men that they could not necessarily get away with the rape of an acquaintance.

IN THE LATE 1830S both moral reformers and suffragists began to argue that civil seduction statutes did not punish men sufficiently for the sexual ruin of women. They called for the addition of criminal sanctions that would mandate imprisonment as well as fines. A key argument invoked throughout the century compared seduction to the crime of theft. "Why was the theft of every item except a woman's chastity considered a crime," moral reformers wondered in 1844. A later writer complained, "A man who would be subject to arrest and imprisonment if he should rob a girl or woman of her pocket book, may with comparative legal impunity seduce her and despoil her person."[28] In this analogy, chastity was a commodity that was as valuable to women as money. Calling for the elevation of seduction to a criminal offense implied an egalitarian move of extending comparable legal protection to both sexes. But the value of the commodity was gender-specific, for it rested upon an ideology that required a higher standard of female morality.[29] Some reformers held that purity was even more valuable to women than property. In the context of women's limited economic options, they had a point. As Wollstonecraft understood, economic dependence on men made marriage critical for women's survival.

To achieve criminal penalties for seduction, female moral reformers overcame an initial resistance to engaging in public activism. In New York they set out to gather petitions urging the state legislature to pass a criminal seduction law, eventually collecting forty thousand signatures. At first male lawmakers treated their effort with "contempt or indecent humor" and passage seemed unlikely. Just as they had worried about dissolute jurors in seduction trials, moral reformers now wondered about the morality of lawmakers. Perhaps, they insinuated, an antiseduction bill would pass only if it exempted members of the legislature. They were not without male allies, though. Early suffrage supporter and attorney E. P. Hurlbut denounced the civil remedy of paying a family for the loss of a daughter's honor when the act, in his view, was more harmful to society than the theft of property. Conservative clergy also argued for punishing the "male fiends" who seduced women, as did men who were concerned about the growth of prostitution. To gain further male support, reformers appealed to "the broken hearted father" who could do no more than sue for damages.[30]

These arguments succeeded in several states. In 1844 both Pennsylvania and Michigan enacted criminal seduction laws, and in the same year a New York State legislative committee approved a bill "to combat the double standard of sexual conduct and male libertinism." The New York legislators acknowledged the similarity of some seductions to rape when they referred to women who were "compelled to yield to superior brute force." Their language nicely illustrates the redefinition of rape beyond the narrow confines of a fight to the death, suggesting that a woman could be forced to consent. To ensure passage of the bill, moral reformers published the names of legislators who opposed it and urged male voters not to reelect "the libertine and his associates." Though initially defeated, the bill passed in 1848, the year in which the Seneca Falls Convention, held in upstate New York, approved an agenda for achieving legal rights for women. Instead of rights, however, the New York legislators invoked their duty to protect women from the specter of the "heartless libertine" who ruined the lives of his victims.[31] Similarly, when suffragists in Massachusetts celebrated the passage of an antiseduction bill in 1886, they stressed protection. If "properly enforced by the courts," they predicted, it would "save hundreds of young girls from ruin."[32]

Opponents of the laws worried that the criminalization of seduction would limit the sexual privileges enjoyed by white men. Some feared that the statutes would allow a woman to blackmail a man with the threat of a false seduction claim that could lead to imprisonment. But others simply did not believe that the practice of seduction, as opposed to rape, merited criminal penalties. The lawyer Simon Stern, for example, wanted to keep the distinction between the felony of rape and the morally wrong but not criminal act of seduction. The former constituted the theft of property through violence, he wrote in 1868, insisting that the "animal" who committed the act deserved jail or the hangman. But seduction was a mere fraud, Stern explained, not a theft. He acknowledged that a man might falsely promise marriage, or claim that sex would not lead to pregnancy, or otherwise persuade a woman to give in to his desires. To treat this behavior as a crime, he feared, would "open the door to countless prosecutions of persons for offences . . . the perpetration of which it has been thought neither expedient nor just to deprive men of their liberty for a long term of years." Invoking liberal political ideals, Stern held that criminalization was out of step with the age of reason and the principle of "non-interference of government with matters purely moral."[33] His desire to preserve men's traditional liberty to engage in coercive acts short of violent rape without criminal penalties epitomized a persistent strain in the response to sexual assault in American history.

Despite such opposition, state after state enacted laws establishing criminal liability for seduction, almost twenty states by 1900 and thirty-five by 1935. Increasingly women gained standing to sue and to recover damages in their own names. The laws enlarged the opportunities for prosecuting sexual coercion, imposing penalties that were not inconsequential. The New York statute mandated a prison term of up to five years and a fine of up to a thousand dollars for any man who was convicted of seducing a woman of previously chaste character into having intercourse under the promise of marriage. By comparison, New York State could sentence a convicted rapist to up to twenty years in prison. Although conviction rates under the New York seduction law remained low—only 16 percent of cases in the late nineteenth and early twentieth centuries—that figure was twice as high as the conviction rate for rape cases. Because removing consent from the picture made conviction easier, charging seduction may have seemed a preferable course to women who were reluctant to prosecute rape.[34]

In some ways these seduction laws represented an expansion of the legal definition of rape. Along with suitors who "seduced and abandoned" with promises of marriage, acquaintances who coerced women into sex were now put on guard by the threat of both criminal penalties and financial restitution. At times the laws allowed working women to complain of what would later be termed sexual harassment, as did an Iowa cheese factory worker, Eliza Brown, who testified that her boss told her that "if I would not consent to his wishes he would turn me off, and hire someone who would." Brown became pregnant, had a child, and sought her employer's financial support. Although she initially won a large settlement in her seduction suit, the Iowa Supreme Court overturned it for lack of corroborating evidence. In this case and others, criminal seduction laws allowed women to prosecute forceful unwanted sex, especially if they became pregnant, but they could not guarantee the outcome.[35]

Even when states did criminalize seduction, the laws by no means signaled a triumph for female legal independence. The New York law engaged the state to protect women from ruin in the name of family stability. The conditions for conviction included prior chastity, the promise of marriage, and corroboration beyond the testimony of the woman. The corroboration requirement remained problematic. Suffragist lawyer Samuel E. Sewall recognized the pitfalls of what would later be termed the "he said/she said" scenario. "I doubt very much the wisdom of this provision," Sewall commented on the 1886 Massachusetts law, for "where the main fact of a case is usually known only to two persons, such a rule as this is especially likely to impede the course of justice." Sewall implied that a woman's testimony should suffice. And, like medieval rape laws and earlier civil seduction statutes, many of the laws stated that marriage was a "bar to prosecution." Thus a man could avoid prosecution by marrying the woman he had seduced—Wollstonecraft's left-handed version. This option continued in New York and elsewhere into the twentieth century.[36]

At the same time, defendants found ingenious ways to use the laws to their advantage. Just as the term *seduction* could redefine consensual sex as a crime, it could also redefine an act of rape as a less serious offense, providing an escape route for white men who forced themselves on women. In 1868 the Wisconsin Supreme Court overturned the criminal seduction conviction of a man named Croghan, who complained about the way the jury instructions at his trial compared rape and seduction. The court recognized that Croghan had forced himself on his wife's niece, who was between fifteen and sixteen years old. He had "treated the girl roughly at first, and actually threatened to kill her," acting in ways that might have constituted a crime "of greater atrocity." But because he succeeded in persuading her to have sex, the crime was not rape. Justice Orasmus J. Cole explained, "If she afterwards freely consented to the sexual intercourse, being enticed to surrender her chastity by means employed by him, then the offense is seduction." Justice Cole's final comment suggests the limits of the legal process. "It is probably as important for the protection of female character that the true distinction between the crime of seduction and rape should be maintained, as that criminal justice should be properly administered in this case." He sent the case back for retrial.[37]

Other court rulings illustrate how legal efforts to redefine rape could simultaneously challenge and strengthen white male sexual privilege. In 1892 a twenty-two-year-old Georgia woman brought a criminal seduction charge against a Mr. Jones, who had courted her for eight years. On the promise of marriage she had "yielded" to him—initially "by force," on the seat of a buggy, but subsequently "for love." For years he kept postponing the wedding, but after she bore his child she took him to court. Jones claimed that he could not be guilty of seduction because that crime required consent, and she had resisted him when they first had intercourse. He was not the only man who appealed a conviction for a lesser sexual crime on the procedural grounds that the charge should have been the more serious one of rape. While Jones seemed to be putting himself in jeopardy of more severe penalties, he no doubt realized that it would have been much harder to prove rape, given the subsequent consensual relations. In one sense his conviction for seduction was a retroactive punishment for a rape that was not followed by marriage. But the decision affirming Jones's conviction denied that the initial act had been rape, in terms that contributed to the belief that "no" meant "yes." The paternalistic Justice Lumpkin interpreted the young woman's initial resistance as part of her "maidenly modesty." "No modest girl or woman," he explained, "upon the occasion of her first carnal contact with a man, will readily submit to the intercourse without some reluctance and some show of resistance." Lumpkin quoted Lord Byron's poetry ("And whispering, 'I will ne'er consent'—consented") to support his point that women feigned resistance.[38]

Criminal seduction laws could reinforce racial as well as gender ideologies. Because they applied almost entirely to white women, the statutes contributed to the racialization of rape in the nineteenth century. African Americans rarely appeared in press reports or court cases concerning seduction. After Reconstruction eight southern states passed criminal seduction laws, but few black women brought charges under them. When they did, racial stereotypes about black licentiousness could lead southern courts to assume that African American women did not have the moral standing to protect their own chastity. Some black families did try to use seduction laws to enforce marriage by a reluctant suitor. In the 1890s a white male jury sentenced a black teacher named Ben Parks to four years in prison for seducing a woman of his own race. On appeal, however, the Texas Supreme Court overturned the conviction because the trial judge had overruled objections to inflammatory comments made to the jury describing Parks as a scoundrel, villain, and brute. In this case the higher court affirmed the right of a black man to defend his reputation at the expense of the young black woman he had seduced and refused to marry.[39]

Interracial seduction cases were also rare. Where antimiscegenation laws prohibited marriage between the races, a white man's promise of marriage to a nonwhite woman had little meaning. Even a mixed-race woman had weak legal standing, given the tightening racial boundaries exemplified by the "one-drop rule" that determined black or white identity. In Louisiana, Edward Slattery successfully defended himself from a seduction suit brought by his concubine of ten years, Lilly Carson, who had a mixed racial heritage. When he left the relationship, she wanted him to provide payment for herself and their young daughter. But because she was "not a person of the white race," Slattery successfully contended, they could not have wed and thus he could not have seduced her under promise of marriage. Antimiscegenation laws did not, of course, outlaw nonmarital sexual relations between white men and women of color. But because seduction law did not apply, these women had no additional legal remedy when coerced. This exclusion buttressed the understanding that African American women were not respectable; though fair game for sex, they were not marriageable.[40]

Besides excluding black women from protection, the seduction laws exacerbated the differential treatment of black and white men, contributing to the racially two-tiered system for prosecuting rape. Antiseduction laws increasingly applied to nonconsensual sex between a white man and a white woman. White men accused of rape were more likely to be charged with either attempted rape or criminal seduction, terms that could obscure the use of force. If convicted, they served relatively short prison terms. In contrast, the crime of coercive, violent sex was increasingly associated with black men, who faced long prison terms, execution, and, by the late nineteenth century, the threat of lynching.

Although the white women's rights movement did not question the racially exclusive application of seduction laws, suffragists did take issue with other limitations. They were not satisfied with disparities in penalties, noting that in some states the sentence for seduction was lighter than that for larceny.[41] Courts sometimes interpreted the laws in ways that angered suffragists. In 1889 the Iowa Supreme Court ruled that women who remained on the streets late at night lost their protection against seduction. The ruling hinted at late-nineteenth-century concerns about the working women who increasingly appeared on the streets of American cities. Anticipating later feminist demands for safe access to public space for women, the Iowa suffrage newspaper protested the ruling as leaving a license for assault. The court effectively announced, according to the *Woman's Standard,* that "if you can catch a girl upon the streets after a certain hour at night you can consider her fair prey."[42]

The most problematic feature of the laws, however, was the chastity requirement. To bring a criminal seduction charge, a woman had to have a previous "chaste character"; some statutes, by their wording, applied only to "virtuous unmarried females," that is, virgins. This requirement encouraged defendants to raise the same questions in court about a woman's purity that pervaded rape cases. Had she ever allowed "familiarities" with other men? Was her family considered immoral? If so, she might not be chaste enough for the state to protect her purity. One suffragist pointed out, "Of all the fragile things in this world, a woman's good name is about the most defenseless." Women's rights advocate Genevieve Lee Hawley criticized the legal requirement that "previous good repute must be proved." In a variation on the theft analogy, she appealed to the sanctity of property by pointing out that the man who was robbed did not have to prove that he had possessed what had been stolen, yet a woman had to show that she had possession of her chastity.[43]

Hawley was right. As in rape trials, defendants in seduction cases regularly tried to undermine the credibility of their accusers by casting doubts about the woman's virtue. Again, men tried to turn the law to their advantage. In southern California, Miguel Samonset convinced his fiancée to have sex with him because they would soon be married, but he failed to appear for the wedding, having sailed off to France. Samonset defended himself from seduction charges on several grounds, including the claim that his health required a sea voyage. In a feat of circular reasoning he also argued that the fact that his (unnamed) fiancée had agreed to have sex with him proved that she was not chaste, and thus she had no standing to sue for seduction. To support the point he called on witnesses to testify that she had "deported herself as a lewd woman." In this case, however, the effort to undermine the very basis of seduction law, with its focus on the initial ruin of a woman's virtue, failed. The court enforced a fine of one thousand dollars against Samonset.[44]

In other courts and regions, even a virgin could be disqualified from charging seduction if the defendant successfully disparaged her family's reputation as immoral. In Georgia, Emma Chivers won a seduction case against the Reverend Myron Wood, who had enticed her to have sex by promising that when his ailing wife died, he would marry her. Wood admitted having sex with Chivers but portrayed her as a loose woman by insinuating that her mother ran a brothel and had consorted with an African American man. His strategy played to both class and race prejudices by associating Chivers with groups considered outside the realm of respectability. On appeal the court redefined virtue in a way that granted Reverend Wood his freedom. Even if Chivers herself had never been guilty of fornication or adultery, she could have been "burning with lust." If so, she could not be seduced, for "the man who, by promise and persuasion, gets her to break the law, has only violated the last clause of this statute. . . . The woman is not a victim."[45]

This 1873 ruling remained in effect in Georgia until overturned in 1892, when the court held that a woman should be considered virtuous unless proven to have had "illicit intercourse" with other men. Courts in other states also affirmed that chastity referred to virginity ("so long as that woman has not surrendered her virtue she is not put without the pale of the law," a California court explained). Nonetheless, legal writers continued to cite the Wood case to show that a woman need not engage in sexual intercourse to be impure, if her mind was "defiled by lustful desires and unchaste wishes."[46] Legal redress for seduction continued to rest heavily upon the ideal of female purity, limiting the use of the laws primarily to white middle-class women whose reputations were beyond reproach.

INITIALLY A REMEDY for loss of services due to pregnancy, over the course of the nineteenth century seduction suits increasingly addressed the loss of a woman's chastity, a key determinant of her opportunities for marriage or respectable employment. Antiseduction laws thus fortified a gender ideology that defined women by their purity, even as reformers questioned the double standard that allowed men to escape the moral penalties imposed on women who had premarital sex. In this sense the moral reformers were protectionists who accepted Victorian-era constructions of woman's unique role as a virtuous mother whose well-being depended on the support of a husband. If a woman consented to sex because she expected to marry the man, the state should enforce a respectable status or make the seducer pay. At the same time, though, seduction law provided some leverage for women to rein in white male sexual privileges. Families could sue employers who sexually exploited working women or suitors who used deceit or coercion to obtain sex. Given the potentially devastating consequences of bearing a child out of wedlock or losing a virtuous reputation, the laws allowed some single women to hold men accountable when they falsely promised to marry. When reformers questioned a father's sole right to sue, they contributed to the growing critique of coverture and inched toward legal independence for women.

The prosecution of seduction provided a limited response to the sexual vulnerability of women in nineteenth-century America, a remedy that flowed from a framework of inequality.[47] Without economic independence, women could experience "ruin" if impregnated or merely "debauched." When physically assaulted, women were reluctant to charge rape, knowing that they would not face juries of their peers. In these contexts they might opt to bring charges of seduction rather than rape. Broadly defined, rape denied a woman's right of sexual consent, but in court she would be portrayed as a consenting partner, either in fact or because her reputation had negated the right to withhold consent. Antiseduction laws broadened the definition and prosecution of sexual assault by removing consent from the agenda. The statutes rested upon the view that because men put women in the position of losing their virtue, men should share the moral and financial costs of that loss.

Seduction law would fall out of favor by the mid-twentieth century, but for several generations it signified a growing concern about the sexual coercion of white women by acquaintances. At a time when states imposed stiff evidentiary standards for plaintiffs and lesser penalties for convicted rapists, and when medical and legal experts approached victims with heightened suspicion, women and their families employed whatever means they could to prosecute sexual assault or sexual irresponsibility on the part of men. Moral reformers who championed the criminalization of seduction called on the state to fill in the gap when churches and families could no longer enforce marriage. Like Mary Wollstonecraft, women's rights advocates accepted the strategic value of seduction laws, given women's lack of economic opportunity and legal equality. By the late nineteenth century, however, suffragists expanded upon this initial mobilization against women's sexual vulnerability to embrace women's rights as citizens.

3

Empowering White Women

In 1869 the *New York Tribune* reported that a Chicago woman had committed suicide after being abandoned by the man who had seduced her with promises of marriage. To prevent such tragedies, the paper recommended, keeping a brothel should be made a felony, because so many seductions led women to these "haunts of sin." One of America's leading advocates of woman suffrage, Elizabeth Cady Stanton, disagreed. In the suffrage newspaper *The Revolution* she suggested instead "that every young girl should be taught the use of firearms, and always carry a small pistol for her defense. Moreover, that she should be accompanied by an immense Newfoundland dog whenever she is in danger of meeting her *natural protector.*" Stanton was far more radical than most women of her day, but her tongue-in-cheek comment in favor of female self-possession rather than male protection revealed a critical strain in the feminist response to seduction and rape. Empower women and they would use their wits—and their rights—to prevent sexual assault.[1]

Suffragists, who typically embraced liberal political principles, believed that expanding women's rights as citizens would allow them to hold legislators and judges responsible for the treatment of rape. Free lovers took the argument even further. Steeped in anarchist politics, they rejected state authority over individuals and boldly expressed their view that the rape of wives by husbands revealed the hypocrisy of marriage. Although they differed on the marriage question, each group recognized that sexual assault—often referred to as "outrage"—undermined women's self-sovereignty. Each group championed the rights of women in ways moral reformers and most Americans did not. Both suffragists and free lovers drew analogies between race slavery and white men's domination of white women; free lovers and anarchists, such as Victoria Woodhull, first used the phrase "sexual slavery" to critique gender relations.[2] Like moral reformers, however, neither suffragists nor free lovers paid attention to the sexual vulnerability of African American women, nor did they take note of the escalating racial violence linked to rape accusations against black men. Rather, suffragists and anarchists sought to empower white women to resist rape by expanding their political or their sexual rights.

THE FORMAL WOMEN'S RIGHTS MOVEMENT that coalesced in the northern states after the Seneca Falls Convention in 1848 shared many concerns with the moral reformers who initiated the criminalization of seduction. Both groups chafed against the privileges enjoyed by white men and deplored the legal challenges women faced in court. Some suffragists enthusiastically supported the prosecution of seducers. Like the moral reformers who targeted men who failed to protect—or who even betrayed—women, suffragists insisted that male behavior and man-made laws left women legally and sexually vulnerable. Yet the post–Civil War woman suffrage movement diverged from the antebellum emphasis on protection by further rejecting women's dependence on men. Responding to antisuffrage arguments that women needed male protection, Julia Ward Howe asked how women could depend on chivalry when the "greatest danger of woman lies in the brutal sexuality of man." Or as another suffrage advocate put it in 1868, "the only protection that will shield woman from the 'wrongs' she suffers is to protect her in her 'rights.' "[3] As a remedy to sexual assault, suffragists sought not the enforcement of marriage by the state but rather the goal of formal legal equality and an end to the principle of coverture.

During the last third of the nineteenth century, woman suffrage was a highly unpopular cause. Mainstream editors and politicians ridiculed the notion of women asserting public authority. The specter of female voters clearly threatened a white, middle-class gender system in which men ideally supported women economically and represented them politically. Most suffragists focused attention on women's limited educational and economic opportunities or the denial of property rights to married women. References to sexuality often remained veiled. At times, however, national and regional woman suffrage groups did address the physical and sexual abuse that women suffered at the hands of men. They blamed these wrongs against women on male domination of legislatures, juries, and the judiciary. The sexual abuse of women and the double standards perpetuated by courts during rape trials provided grist for the suffragists' mill. Only full citizenship, they insisted, would end these injustices. Suffragists agreed with moral reformers that the definition of rape should include sexual coercion short of violent assault, but they went further to envision a fundamental restructuring of women's status. As voters and as members of juries, women would undermine rape by influencing the law and commanding greater respect from men.

The *Woman's Journal,* the weekly publication of the American Woman Suffrage Association (AWSA), provided a major vehicle for articulating these views. Formed in 1869, the AWSA represented the more moderate branch of the women's rights movement to emerge from an ideological and strategic split after the Civil War. AWSA leaders such as Lucy Stone and Henry Blackwell accepted the postwar amendments to the U.S. Constitution that extended suffrage to black men but not yet to women of any race. In contrast, National Woman Suffrage Association (NWSA) founders Susan B. Anthony and Elizabeth Cady Stanton, who briefly edited the *Revolution* (1868–1871), felt betrayed by former abolitionist colleagues who did not press for simultaneous black and female suffrage.[4] Each group publicized the problem of sexual assault, but Stone and Blackwell's "Crimes against Women" column in the *Woman's Journal* provided the most extensive coverage linking sexual assault and domestic violence to women's legal disabilities.

Stone and Blackwell had been committed abolitionists before the Civil War and ardent supporters of woman suffrage. Each had a deep personal as well as political history of questioning the legal principle of marital coverture, which included a husband's right to his wife's sexual services. The couple used the occasion of their own marriage in 1855 to register a protest against these patriarchal assumptions. Before they wed, Henry Blackwell had assured Lucy Stone, "I wish, as a husband, to *renounce* all the privileges which the law confers upon me, which are not strictly *mutual.*" Their wedding-day protest rejected legal powers that gave the husband "an injurious and unnatural superiority . . . which no man should possess." Reflecting their beliefs in the independent identities of spouses, Stone retained her family name rather than take that of her husband, a unique protest in the nineteenth century.[5]

During the 1870s and 1880s, Stone and Blackwell collected reports from around the country in the style of the crime columns typical of daily newspapers. Their "Crimes against Women" column included accounts about men who assaulted their wives, their daughters, or other women. One 1875 compilation reported an attack by two men on a Long Island woman, who was "outraged and left insensible"; the conviction of and fourteen-year sentence meted out to a Pennsylvania man for the rape of a ten-year-old girl; the impregnation of a fourteen-year-old servant by her master (settled by a payment of eight hundred dollars after she gave birth); and the plight of a boarding school girl who "was outraged in a sleeping car" when a man in the compartment placed a handkerchief soaked with chloroform over her (he escaped prosecution because the girl had not reported the assault promptly). Contributors to the column regularly targeted judges who dismissed sexual assault charges or treated rapists lightly. Like other suffrage publications, the *Woman's Journal* proselytized the explicit political message that only full citizenship for women would remedy these crimes and injustices. "[At present] assailants of women are either acquitted or subjected to very insufficient penalties," a state that would continue "until women are voters." Rather than relying on the protection of male kin, male clergy, or male judges, one writer explained, "women should have increased power, social, civil, legal, political, and ecclesiastical."[6]

Not surprisingly, given their roots in an abolitionist movement that criticized slavery for encouraging the sexual abuse of black women, Stone and Blackwell invoked an analogy between atrocities committed by slave owners and the cruelty of "brutal husbands" to their wives. Abolitionists such as Sarah and Angelina Grimké and Lucretia Mott had initially drawn the comparison between slaves and wives, on the one hand, and masters and husbands, on the other hand. Suffragists continued to do so after emancipation. "A dominant sex is productive of as much human suffering as a dominant race," Blackwell explained in 1874. Like slaves, he pointed out, wives were treated as if they existed to serve their male masters. Though concentrating on domestic violence, Blackwell subtly acknowledged rape in marriage. Most "outrages against women," he claimed, took place within the seclusion of the home. He imagined that when a woman resisted her husband's sexual advances, he felt justified, as did the slaveholder, in using force against her. Like emancipated slaves, women required citizenship to free themselves from violence, for "while they remained a disfranchised and subject class, so women, to-day, are left without adequate legal protection." Blackwell reiterated his solution to the vulnerability of both blacks and women: "Equal Rights and Impartial Suffrage are the only radical cure for these barbarities."[7]

At the time, the American press often applied terms such as *barbarities* in a racially specific way to refer to black men, who were increasingly demonized as sexual threats to white women. Some suffragists adopted this racist discourse. When the *Revolution* reprinted accounts of rape, it included southern newspaper reports of black men accused of assaulting white women.[8] Incorporating the evolutionary concepts being used to rationalize white supremacy, Elizabeth Cady Stanton claimed that "as you go down and down in the scale of manhood the idea strengthens at every step, that woman was created for no higher purpose than to gratify the lust of man." In granting suffrage to all men, she complained in 1869, the Fifteenth Amendment would give men from the "lower orders" political power over "educated matrons." Stanton warned educated, refined (white) women that without suffrage, "Chinese, Africans, Germans and Irish, with their low ideas of womanhood" would be making laws "for you and your daughter." This threat implied the perpetuation of women's sexual vulnerability as well as their legal inequality.[9]

In contrast, Henry Blackwell and Lucy Stone almost exclusively named white men as sexual threats, at times comparing them to slave owners. In doing so they countered the trend of racialization that masked white men's crimes. At the same time, however, the *Woman's Journal* remained silent about the escalating violence against black men accused of rape, dozens of whom were lynched annually in the 1880s and 1890s. The paper was also silent about the continuing sexual exploitation of freed black women. For the most part the racial analogy worked in one direction only, to extend citizenship to white women, without recognizing the use of rape to deny black citizenship, a problem that African Americans would have to address on their own.

Along with invoking the analogy with race to argue for equal rights, the *Woman's Journal* incorporated another political theory of rape, one that took culture into account to reject biological and patriarchal justifications for sexual violence. In an article titled "Women's Deprivation of Rights the Source of Men's Crimes," the anonymous author rejected the view that men's "animal passion" alone could explain "the ruthlessness with which a man purchases the satisfaction of a passing lust." Nor was woman's physical incapacity to defend herself the root of her vulnerability. Rather, a culture that treated women as less valuable than men contributed to gender violence. Whether "consciously or unconsciously," the man who assaulted or killed a woman had learned that "the inferiority of the victim permits his indulgence." Denying women equal rights contributed to this belief. Only full equality could counter the contempt that enabled "outragers and murderers" to destroy women's lives. Suffrage could help transform this contempt by granting women the status of self-possessing citizens.[10]

Suffrage supporters insisted that the vote could reduce women's sexual vulnerability, not only by elevating their rights, but also by providing a practical tool for expediting political change. Some writers claimed that educated white women would prevent political corruption by counteracting the votes of foreign-born and black men; others believed that as mothers they would oppose war. Less frequently articulated was the instrumental effect suffrage might have in preventing violence against women and children. Enfranchisement would allow women to hold elected officials accountable for the ways the state responded to rape. In 1877, when the governor of New York pardoned a man who had been imprisoned for rape, Lucy Stone lamented the fact that women could not vote him out office, elect someone who would not pardon rapists, or serve as "judges nor even jurors in such cases." The following year, when the governor of Massachusetts pardoned several men convicted of rape, Stone reiterated her complaint in terms that both invoked and rejected female dependence on men: "What protection have the women of Massachusetts, either for themselves or for their young daughters, when this worst of all crimes which can be committed against us, is so frequently pardoned by Governor Rice?"[11]

Stone took comfort when the governor of Pennsylvania declined to pardon a man sentenced for "a revolting and unnatural crime," but she did not want to rely on the goodwill of officials when only men could elect them. Even male voters "who outrage their daughters," she pointed out, enjoyed the "political power to vote for the man who pardons them." They could elect legislators who would pass laws abolishing punishment "for crimes like theirs." A reader named Pearl Parsons echoed this dismay over the power of corrupt men in a letter to the *Woman's Journal* about the involvement of police officers in the brutal rape of a young woman in Delaware. Parsons decried the mayor of Wilmington because he "cannot quite decide what mild punishment to dole out to these *voting criminals*." As Stone later put it, rather than acting indirectly through their "silent influence" on men, women voters could take responsibility for the passage and enforcement of laws related to sexual assault.[12]

Amid this talk of political rights, suffragists occasionally employed the rhetoric of female chastity, whether strategically or from deeply held beliefs in the value of sexual purity. At a time when women remained economically and politically dependent, sex outside of marriage still connoted male privilege, not female emancipation. Both moral reformers and suffrage proponents favored a single, female standard of chastity before marriage and fidelity within it. Yet suffragists took the defense of women's

purity beyond antebellum calls for the state to protect women from seduction. According to the *Woman's Standard,* "When men will deliber-
ately refuse to pass laws to protect the most sacred thing on earth, the
chastity of woman, it is time the mothers of men arise in the might of
outraged justice and wrest the scepter from the hands of power. . . . God
hasten the day of woman's political emancipation for this cause alone, if
for nothing else!"[13] The preservation of women's virtue thus served as an
argument for enfranchisement.

The suffrage press condemned not only male legislators but also male
judges who either enforced a double standard of justice or seemed too
sympathetic to men accused or convicted of rape. A writer in the *Woman's
Exponent,* the pro-suffrage Mormon women's newspaper, compared the
outcomes of two cases: first, the lenient eighteen-month sentence received
by a saloon keeper who had outraged a young woman, and second, the
three-year sentence imposed on a mother who abandoned a child she
could not support. "These are the fruits of men's laws for men," she concluded. In Lucy Stone's words, "The only way to have these crimes against
women punished as they deserve, is to have women share the law-making
power." When an Iowa judge overturned a conviction for attempted rape
on the grounds that a fifteen-year-old girl had not resisted sufficiently,
state suffragists called for a petition campaign to demand women's rights
as the only recourse to "the votes of the rakes and libertines of the state."[14]
The need to curtail the sexual privileges granted male citizens by courts
provided yet another justification for political equality.

Voting was not the only solution. Lenience toward rapists could be tempered, and justice for women more frequently achieved, if women could
serve on juries, a goal that remained elusive long after women gained the
vote. The inequity of excluding women from hearing sexual assault cases
irritated suffragists. "A Case for Women Jurors" was the title the *Woman's Journal* placed over a letter to the paper about a military court that
had dismissed incest charges against a former soldier. Like early women's
rights advocates and some moral reformers, postbellum suffragists often
complained that women had a fundamental right to trial by a jury of their
peers. "Women alone are the peers of women," insisted a writer in the
Woman's Standard, with a slightly veiled reference to sexual assault: "In
certain criminal proceedings women alone can understand what has been
committed and what resisted."[15]

The case of the young domestic servant Hester Vaughan exemplified
the problem. "Seduced" (possibly raped) and then abandoned by her

lover, Vaughan had been found lying next to her dead infant soon after giving birth. In 1868 a Pennsylvania court convicted her of murder and imposed the death penalty. The *Revolution* editorialized that Vaughan was a product of society, "seduced by it, by the judge who pronounced her sentence, by the bar and jury, by the legislature that enacted the law (in which, because a woman, she had no vote or voice)." Suffragist orator Anna Dickinson lectured about Vaughan's plight, and the Working Women's Association called a mass protest meeting that issued a resolution demanding that women be tried by their peers. The *Revolution* published extensive accounts of the protests against the verdict and questioned whether women jurors would not have extended sympathy "to a woman who kills a child, the fruit of an outrage perpetrated upon her?" According to Elizabeth Cady Stanton, who personally lobbied Pennsylvania governor John Geary in the Vaughan case, even "His Excellency" agreed that "justice would never be done in cases of Infanticide, until women were in the jury-box." Governor Geary pardoned Vaughan.[16]

Suffragists also drew on maternalism—the strategy of invoking motherhood as a justification for female authority outside of the home—to further the cause of achieving justice in criminal courts. At the 1891 convention of the recently merged National and American Woman Suffrage Association, Lillie Devereux Blake of New York suggested that in cases involving seduction and infanticide, women jurors "could better understand the temptations than could men," and she called for more "maternal influence" in the courtroom. Commenting on stories about assaulted women who were forced to testify in public, including one woman who committed suicide, a suffrage paper insisted that "the mother element is needed in the judicial department of government as in all others." In one instance an immigrant woman was held in jail for over a month before testifying against her assailant, who had remained free on bail. The *Woman's Tribune* labeled this story "Legal Outrage on a Woman" and predicted that "if the mother brain had anything to do with the judicial part of our government," an assaulted woman would not be detained among criminals.[17]

Whatever comforts the mother element might bring female victims, woman's voice in government could impose harsh penalties on those found guilty of sexual assault. Some suffragists wished to expand capital punishment, which most states had eliminated for white, though not for black, men found guilty of rape. For them, imposing the death penalty for rape would signal that the crime was worthy of this severe punishment. Henry Blackwell made this argument to counter those who expressed "maudlin sympathy" for men who committed assault. To drive home his point, he detailed an extreme case in which six white ruffians bound and "outraged" a woman, who later died from the attack. "No wild beast, or venomous reptile, is so dangerous or so deadly as are such persons," Blackwell wrote in the *Woman's Journal*. Women's influence on trials, he argued, would lead to harsher sentences for such crimes.[18]

Although they could not elect judges or serve on juries, women reformers sought interim means to counteract the disadvantages faced by their sex in court. They often combined the protective approach of moral reformers with calls for women's rights when they monitored courtrooms during trials of sensitive cases. In 1895 Sarah Sanford, an agent of the Humane Society of Oakland, California, tried to keep curious male spectators at bay during an incest trial by packing the courtroom with "grey haired women." In the trials of women who had murdered the men who had seduced them, suffragists and temperance activists reached out to the accused, went to the courtroom, and wrote letters to the press in their support. Henry Blackwell called attention to the trial of Maria Barberi, the fifteen-year-old Italian immigrant who killed her seducer, which he considered to be "an object lesson for woman suffrage" because the defendant "has had not trial by a jury of her peers." To compensate for this imbalance, women petitioned for commutation of Barberi's sentence and helped her get a new trial.[19]

Women's simple act of attending trials could challenge prevailing notions of decency. One argument against admitting women to the bar as lawyers, articulated most clearly by the Wisconsin Supreme Court in 1875, was that it was "revolting to all female sense of the innocence and sanctity of their sex" that women should hear courtroom discussions that were "unfit for female ears," including cases of sodomy, incest, rape, seduction, and fornication. Showing that women could attend to such cases without panic undermined that exclusionary argument. In Los Angeles, when women packed the courtroom during the 1888 trial of Hattie Woolsteen for the murder of the dentist who had seduced her, the local press questioned the propriety of their hearing "all the prurient details" of the case. In response a letter writer to the *Los Angeles Times* protested. If a poor woman like Woolsteen "must give in public the unhappy and indelicate details of her situation," the writer asked, was it not "a thousand times more fitting that women should be there, by their mere presence, to bear her up than that men, many of them beastly and cruel, should, by mere right of masculine superiority and protection, add to her misery by their presence?"[20]

Aiding victims took more institutional forms, as well. The Protective Agency for Women and Children, which grew out of the Woman's Club of Chicago, mirrored an earlier group in England, the Society for the Protection of Women and Children from Aggravated Assaults. As one member explained, the Chicago agency formed in 1886 in response to reports of "grossly inadequate punishment inflicted upon the dastardly criminals" who committed "crimes upon women and children." This protective enterprise was one of a number of reform institutions created by urban middle-class women seeking to alleviate the impact of industrial capitalism upon working women. The Protective Agency exposed a range of unfair labor practices, such as employers who withheld wages. Members identified sexual abuse, whether in the family or in the workplace, as another injustice suffered by working women. Board member Caroline M. Brown referred to the "blackest and worst of crimes committed against little children and young girls," while the annual report explained that the agency reached out to the "unhappy girls who have been deceived by those whom they most trusted or the outraged victims of brute strength and brutal lust."[21] Using the euphemisms of their time, they spoke out against child abuse, seduction, domestic violence, and rape.

To enforce punishment of these assailants, the Protective Agency raised funds to maintain both a lawyer and female agents to assist young women who had been sexually harmed or financially exploited. In 1888 a stepmother sought help when the justice of the peace released her husband after she had him arrested for sexually assaulting his daughter. An agent persisted in prosecuting the father until he was eventually sent to prison. Protective Agency board members recognized that many women were reluctant to press charges because they risked the shame of public exposure, not only of the crime committed against them but also because defense attorneys would ask "dreadful and insulting questions" about their characters in the courtroom. Witnessing the "offensive publicity and scurrilous cross-examination," Brown reported, "you would feel that the machinery of justice was all set in motion to defend the guilty and browbeat the innocent." For this reason the agency sent a "delegation of reputable women" that could change "the moral tone of the Police court." Club members followed up after trials to ensure that "those human blood hounds, with wolfish eyes" who threatened girls and young women would not return to drive them to a life of prostitution. They established a home for self-supporting women to prevent sexual or economic exploitation. Although these middle-class reformers initially spoke the language of defending women's purity, they came to believe that even "sinful" women were "victims of an environment of poverty."[22]

In addition to providing legal aid, the Chicago Protective Agency for Women and Children lobbied to change state laws. Its members drafted a criminal seduction statute and, after a decade of work, secured its passage in 1899. They also successfully influenced laws to raise the age of consent and to prosecute acts of seduction that led to prostitution. At a moment when women first gained access to law schools and the legal profession, the Protective Agency provided a model of legal advocacy. The Chicago women were less successful when they tried to expand their enterprise, for they could not inspire the National Council for Women to replicate their legal service project throughout the country. In 1905 the Protective Agency merged with the Illinois Bureau of Justice, a private group that provided legal aid to both women and men.[23]

The Chicago agency illustrates the persistence of the protective services that characterized nineteenth-century reform while pointing toward the public advocacy roles for women that expanded during the early twentieth century. For the most part, however, the solution to the problem of rape proposed within the late nineteenth-century women's rights movement called for empowering women through suffrage. This measure of full citizenship would elevate women's status and thus discourage disrespectful treatment. It would also provide leverage within the criminal justice system, as would jury service. Ensuring fairer prosecution of sexual predators would in turn undermine men's sense of sexual entitlement. Above all, allowing women to vote would hold judges and legislators accountable for the laws defining and prosecuting sexual assault.

Elizabeth Cady Stanton pointed out in the late 1860s that the root of sexual outrages "will be found in the idea that woman was made for man," citing as shameful the practice of teaching young girls to consider men "the source of light and wisdom." On this point *Woman's Journal* contributor Thomas Wentworth Higginson agreed, writing in 1880 that "if men were systematically taught by church and state to regard women as their equals," fewer of these crimes would occur.[24] Revising ideas about gender, however, never carried the import of enfranchisement. For suffragists, sexual assault remained an instrumental issue, another weapon in the rhetorical arsenal of those visionaries who imagined equal citizenship for women. The vote, proponents insisted, would solve all forms of sexual inequality. Once they were politically empowered, women could change laws and improve prosecution in order to punish and deter rape.

By overstating the power of suffrage and of legal reform more generally, they underestimated broader obstacles, including economic and racial inequalities and deeply ingrained gender norms. Their inflated expectations set the stage for disappointment once women gained the vote.

ALTHOUGH THEY PROPOSED the radical goal of enfranchisement, suffragists remained conventional in their views of marriage. Apart from the exceptional public marital vows exchanged by Lucy Stone and Henry Blackwell, the women's rights movement largely avoided the topic of a husband's right to his wife's sexual services. In the *Woman's Journal,* Blackwell merely alluded to rape in his discussions of domestic abuse. Rarely did the suffrage press directly question the marital exemption—the legal definition of rape as a crime committed against a woman by a man other than her husband.

At the time, the principle of marital unity, or coverture, not only overrode a woman's right to make contracts, own property, and vote but also ensured a husband sexual access to his wife. In the influential reasoning of seventeenth-century British jurist Sir Matthew Hale, "The husband cannot be guilty of a rape committed by himself upon his lawful wife, for by their mutual consent and contract the wife hath given up herself in this kind unto her husband, which she cannot retract."[25] American jurists agreed, as illustrated by an 1845 divorce case decided by the Connecticut Supreme Court. Emmeline Shaw complained that her husband, Daniel Shaw, took her by force and "compelled her to occupy a bed" with him, despite her ill health. According to Chief Justice Thomas Scott Williams, because his intent was not to endanger his wife's health, Daniel Shaw's actions did not constitute the "intolerable cruelty" necessary for a divorce. The ruling is telling in its endorsement of men's sexual rights: "Are we to allow nothing to the frailty of human nature, excited by passion? Are we to couple an act of this kind with an act where a violent blow was given, which must greatly injure or endanger, and which was so intended? In a case of so delicate a nature, the court ought not to interfere." Not until the early twentieth century would courts begin to consider such behavior a form of cruelty that justified marital dissolution.[26]

That the marriage contract legally negated a woman's right to withhold consent to sexual relations had important implications for the meaning of citizenship. Republican government rested upon the consent of the people, but in marriage women lost that right. A husband's control over the body of his wife was central, and not merely incidental, to the principle of coverture that denied married women rights to enter into contracts or own property. English legal treatises argued that if a wife broke a contract, she might be imprisoned, which meant that her husband would no longer have access to her body.[27] Preserving the sexual entitlements of husbands thus required a dependent economic and legal status for wives, which in turn denied their claims to political identities as full citizens.

Early women's rights advocates regularly opposed coverture when it applied to property or to voting, but they less frequently addressed the issue of sexual consent within marriage. Within antebellum feminist circles, Elizabeth Cady Stanton and Susan B. Anthony periodically tried to raise "the marriage question" in discussions of a woman's right to divorce her intemperate or abusive husband, terms that could imply sexual assault. In a letter to Anthony, Stanton wrote, "It is in vain to look for the elevation of woman so long as she is degraded in marriage." Privately Lucy Stone agreed that unwanted sex in marriage was "perfectly appalling." Writing to Stanton, she recounted the story of a woman whose husband "gave her no peace either during menstruation, pregnancy, or nursing." Stone later expressed her view that suffrage and property rights meant little "if I may not keep my body, and its uses, in my absolute right." Yet Stone feared that raising the marriage question would damage the suffrage cause, so she cautioned against public discussion of marital abuse. Even as postbellum suffragists escalated their demands for equality within marriage, they shied away from confronting the sexual rights of husbands.[28]

Elizabeth Cady Stanton came closest to questioning the marital exemption when she insisted on a woman's fundamental right to control her own person. In 1857 Stanton compared "the present false marriage relation" to "legalized prostitution" and publicly approved of a woman's right to divorce. But her effort to introduce a divorce resolution at the 1860 National Woman's Rights Convention met strong resistance. Although Stanton framed the problem in terms of conserving marriage as a virtuous institution against the threat of "violence, debauchery, and excess," suffragists feared being tainted by the label "free lover." Stanton's insistence that women have control of their own person recurred in the postwar decades, particularly in the pages of the *Revolution*. As a male physician wrote to the paper in 1868, "Every woman possesses the inherent right to the full and perfect control of her own person, in or out of the marriage relation. This is Revolution."[29]

In England some liberals and radicals did question the marital exemption. In the late eighteenth century, Mary Wollstonecraft had included the wrong of unwanted marital sex in her novel *Maria*. The philosopher Jeremy Bentham referred to a woman's inability to divorce a man she detested as "a species of slavery." He believed that "to be constrained to receive his embraces" in marriage was "a misery too great to be tolerated." In 1869 John Stuart Mill bemoaned the fact that a wife owed sexual services to her husband, "however brutal a tyrant she may unfortunately be chained to." No matter how she felt toward him, he had the authority to "enforce the lowest degradation of a human being, that of being made the instrument of an animal function contrary to her inclinations."[30] Short of calling this behavior rape, these liberal theorists extended to wives the individual right to consent to sex.

In the United States, the few writers who addressed marital sex often emphasized the physical well-being of women and their potential offspring. Health reformer Eliza Duffey wrote in the 1870s that unwanted marital sex exhausted women and damaged their bodies. In one of her health treatises for women she complained that neither "disinclination, weariness, [nor] ill health" were considered to excuse a wife if "her husband's inclinations" required her to have sex. Duffey found it "strange" that the law recognized rape as a punishable crime yet "there is no recognition whatever of a married woman's right to a control over her own person." She noted that even brutal conduct by a husband was not grounds for divorce. According to Duffey, a wife should be "no more bound to yield her body to her husband after the marriage between them, than she was before, until she feels that she can do so with the full tide of willingness and affection."[31]

Anticipating later birth-control arguments that every child should be wanted, some nineteenth-century feminists insisted on a woman's right to determine when to become a mother. In her 1871 speech to the National Woman Suffrage Association, Paulina Wright Davis alluded to the fruits of unwanted marital sex when she protested "compulsory maternity." The alternative principle of voluntary motherhood granted wives the right to refuse sex with their husbands. Nineteenth-century suffragists preferred it to the practices of contraception or abortion, which remained linked to prostitution and connoted promiscuity. Voluntary motherhood was an early form of reproductive choice and reflected the emerging eugenic theory that children conceived during forced intercourse might be diseased or severely impaired.[32] The argument that bringing healthy children into a family required consensual sex could simultaneously reinforce women's maternal identities and empower wives within their marriages.

A more radical critique of marital sex emerged within the anarchist free-love movement. The free-love ideology originated in the early nineteenth century within utopian socialist communities in Europe, such as those established by followers of Charles Fourier in France and of Robert Owen in England. In contrast to liberal reformers, who applied the language of individual rights or maternalism to strengthen women's position within the family, utopian (and later Marxian) socialists questioned the family as an institution in which women became the property of men. Fourier believed that all forms of sexuality should be acceptable as long as they were consensual; some of his followers referred to marriage as "legalized rape."[33] In the United States a small but vocal band of women and men embraced free love, established utopian communities, and published tracts and journals that proselytized their views.

The term *free love* did not necessarily refer to promiscuity, although some utopians accepted multiple sexual partners. Rather, most of them preferred committed, egalitarian unions based on mutual affection and unfettered by the laws of church or state. Many free-love tenets overlapped with the women's rights movement, but free lovers took the feminist analysis of inequality in marriage to its logical extreme. Moral reformers wanted to protect women from being abandoned by men who had promised to marry them, and suffragists wanted equal rights for women within marriage. In contrast, free lovers blamed marriage for most of the problems these other groups identified. Despite their shared distaste for coerced sex, suffragists such as Henry Blackwell did not defend the free lovers, for fear that association with these radicals would further damage the image of the already unpopular women's rights cause.[34]

The response to seduction provides a good example of the distinctive politics of free lovers. Seduction laws literally enforced marriage by encouraging a man to choose between making good on his promise to marry or paying a fine and possibly serving a prison term. Free lovers argued that if men did not claim ownership of women, the crime of seduction would not exist. As Thomas Nichols and Mary Gove Nichols wrote in 1854, in a society in which "women are no longer considered as property to be guarded, and liable to be stolen, like a horse, or a negro," women would freely enjoy sexual relations whether initiated by the man or the woman. As long as both parties consented, no one—and especially not the state—would have a right "to interfere." Doing away with marriage, the Nicholses explained, meant the emancipation of women from the constraints of chastity. Under these ideal conditions, seducers would become as rare as would the detestable "negro-stealers"—and even the abolitionists—after the end of slavery. Tennessee Claflin, sister of the notorious free-love advocate Victoria Woodhull, also attributed the "clamour about seduction" to the necessity of marriage. She further argued that women posed the greater threat of seduction because their financial and political dependence led them to "entrap men" in order to marry and be supported. Only enfranchisement "with full opportunity for development" would allow mutual love between men and women. In the meantime Claflin wanted the law to protect not only women but also "male ninnies" seduced by young girls and grown women.[35]

Most free lovers in the United States agreed that either a woman or a man should be able to consent to sex outside of marriage without penalties. They also forcefully denounced the converse condition of a husband's right to have sex with a nonconsenting wife. At a time when marriage represented the core of Victorian social order, free lovers began to name unwanted marital sex as a form of rape. Just as the Grimké sisters and Henry Blackwell compared the plight of slaves and women, free lovers used the term *sexual slavery* to describe women's obligation to have sex within marriage. They urged husbands to reject that form of male privilege. In some of the small utopian communities founded at midcentury, men who adopted free-love principles tried to practice sexual constraint and to defer to women's sexual and reproductive desires. Those who wanted to influence the broader society outside their utopian worlds expounded upon this understanding of marriage in books, pamphlets, and newspapers.

At midcentury, Mary Gove Nichols articulated the free-love opposition to obligatory marital sex when she insisted that women had a right to control their own bodies. Nichols derived this view from her own disastrous first marriage, which she referred to as "an abyss of evil" beyond description because of the repeated unwanted sex she had endured. Her second husband, Thomas Low Nichols, agreed with her in condemning "lustful men" who would "compel their wives to submit to their embraces," especially at times that could damage a woman's health. In *Marriage: Its History, Character, and Results* (1854) the Nicholses complained that "the rape or ravishment of a married woman by her husband, accomplished by whatever violence and outrage," was not considered a crime. The marriage contract thus destroyed a woman's "personal rights." Rape was a serious crime, sometimes punished by death. But once "a few words have been said by the priest," they complained, "not only does the law justify the outrage, but she is severely blamed by a virtuous society for not submitting to the man, to whom her person, her whole being forever belongs!"[36] To diminish the brutal crime of rape "in marriage or out of it," the act deserved to be punished.

These arguments circulated in the late nineteenth century through the work of a small but vocal band of sexual radicals. One of the best-known, the flamboyant and popular lecturer Victoria Woodhull, was a political gadfly who in 1872 ran for the presidency of the United States on the Equal Rights ticket. Woodhull called marriage "a license for sexual commerce" and insisted that sexual freedom meant "the abolition of prostitution both in and out of marriage." Her ideal went beyond the freely chosen monogamous unions advocated by most free lovers, for Woodhull justified a woman's choice of a series of sexual partners. She shared the Nicholses' view of obligatory marital sex and deplored a husband's rights in explicit language. "Night after night," Woodhull claimed, "there are thousands of rapes committed under cover of this accursed license . . . millions of suffering wives are compelled to minister to the lechery of insatiable husbands." Like other free-love advocates she rejected forced reproduction, arguing that when a woman loathed a man, she should not have to bear his child.[37]

Although Woodhull embraced free love only briefly before adopting a more conventional morality, other anarchists continued to redefine rape as an act committed within marriage. In the anarchist journal *Liberty,* Lillian Harman questioned the limitation of rape laws by pointing out that a husband "can go to the brothel and commit a crime which will, if he is prosecuted, send him to the penitentiary; but, if he comes home the same night and commits the same crime on his wife, he will not be troubled by the law." Legal treatises, she complained, held that *"the prostitute can be raped but that the wife cannot."* In their journal *The Word,* Ezra and Angela Heywood echoed the interpretation of marriage as a form of prostitution, adding that husbands could force their wives not only to have sex but also to bear children, whether or not they wished to do so. For Angela Heywood, unwanted reproduction was a form of sexual abuse. "Women do not like rape and have a right to resist its results," she wrote.[38]

The Heywoods took the concept of voluntary motherhood much further than did reformers and suffragists, for the couple questioned recently enacted state laws that criminalized contraception and abortion. Angela Heywood's satirical response to anticontraception statutes illustrates the direct language and unconventional views characteristic of her writing. In imagining an empowered female citizenry, she wrote that "as well might women vote that man shall flow semen only when she says; that he must keep his penis tied up with 'continent' twine. . . . Which, if he is found without, he shall be liable, on conviction by twelve women, to ten years in prison and $5000 fine." Although the Heywoods considered abortion an "unnatural" act, they blamed men "who freight a woman with offspring" for requiring it and then for punishing her for "the results of their own lascivious indiscretion."[39]

Free-love literature took to its extreme, as well, the complaints of doctors who feared that unwanted marital sex undermined the health of mothers.[40] Moses Harman's journal *Lucifer the Light-Bearer* carried sensationalistic stories about the sexual abuse of wives, not only on their wedding nights but throughout their marriages. One such account recalled the "brutal outrages, morning, noon and night" imposed on a pregnant wife by her husband. Perhaps the most controversial exposé appeared in a letter from a physician detailing the damage inflicted on a wife who was recovering from postchildbirth gynecological surgery. Her husband forced himself upon her sexually despite her condition. "Did this man rape his wife?" asked Dr. W. G. Markland. "If a man stabs his wife to death with a knife does not the law hold him for murder? If he stabs her to death with his penis, what does the law do?"[41] Letters to free-love papers described wives whose husbands beat them if they tried to refuse sexual relations. One writer summarized men's presumptions: *"That is what I got you for, and I am going to have it."* While many of these comments intended to expose the hypocrisy of marriage, some writers also called for legal reform. "Give us a hand at law making," wrote Mrs. M. C. Gurney of Kansas in 1886. She welcomed "an opportunity to wipe from the statute books such infamous laws as the one that a married man can not rape his wife."[42] These free lovers explicitly linked marital rape to the limitations on female citizenship.

Far from being sexual prudes, the free lovers bemoaned the fact that forced relations destroyed women's natural desire for sexual pleasure. Victoria Woodhull censured a minister whose "brutal approaches" to his wife "made sexual reciprocity impossible for her." Woodhull affirmed women's capacity to enjoy sex but suggested that wives who had to rebel against male ownership were less likely to be able to respond positively.[43] Other free-love advocates wrote explicitly about what they considered to be the best means to achieve sexual pleasure for women and men. "We are related sexually; let us face the glad fact with all its ineffable joys," wrote Angela Heywood in one of her tamer statements. For free-love advocates, however, only when both parties consented to intercourse could sex truly be fulfilling. Ida Craddock rejected the sexual techniques "commonly practiced among married people today—methods which involve loss of sexual self-control, tigerish brutality, persistent rape of the wife's person, and uncleanness." As an alternative she counseled a spiritual sexual union and provided detailed instructions for intensifying pleasure through prolonged and gentle intercourse.[44]

The free-love prescription of long-term, committed, and mutually enjoyable unions that respected the individual rights of women to determine when to have sex may now seem rather tame. At the time, however, this advice enraged moralists. In addition to rejecting organized religion and using explicit sexual language in their publications, free lovers challenged a husband's absolute authority over his wife when they named rape in marriage. They condoned women like Mary Gove Nichols who left unhappy marriages. So threatening was their radical critique of marriage that local censors tried to suppress free-love publications and silence their writers.

The most vigilant of these moralists, Anthony Comstock, was an agent of the New York Society for the Suppression of Vice. He sounded an alarm that the circulation of obscene materials threatened to corrupt the nation's youth, leading them to indulge in masturbation and young men to consort with prostitutes. Comstock's definition of obscenity included not only racy literature and nudity in art but also information about contraception, abortion, and anything else that challenged the primacy of marital reproductive sexuality. He was the driving force behind the 1873 federal law, known as the Comstock Act, which prohibited the circulation of obscene materials through the U.S. mail. Working for the post office, he personally arrested several thousand men and women and claimed that during the first decade after passage of the law he had destroyed tons of "villainous literature." Free lovers provoked some of his harshest attacks because of their explicit descriptions of sex and their rejections of both marriage and religion. Comstock warned the public of the "blasphemy and filth commingled" in free-love publications, claiming that they "ruthlessly trample under feet the most sacred things" and sought "to overthrow every social restraint."[45]

Comstock began his drive against free lovers in 1872 when he unsuccessfully prosecuted Victoria Woodhull for publishing details of an extramarital affair between a prominent clergyman and a parishioner. Passage of the Comstock Act the following year gave him broader powers for pursuing the publishers of free-love newspapers and pamphlets. He would write to them under an assumed name, order copies of their literature, and then arrest them for sending the materials to him through the mail. His relentless pursuits led to the imprisonment of Moses Harman for publishing explicit letters from doctors and wives who complained of unwanted sex in marriage. Comstock hounded Ida Craddock for circulating her sexual advice pamphlets, such as *The Wedding Night,* through the U.S. mail. She had recently served several months in jail when Comstock rearrested her. In 1902 a jury found Craddock guilty, but before she could be sentenced she committed suicide, attributing her act to Comstock's efforts to reimprison her. Ezra Heywood faced four different trials for obscenity before Comstock succeeded in having him sentenced to two years at hard labor. Heywood died within a year of his release from prison.[46]

Naming marital rape was not the sole or even the primary reason for Comstock's persecution of free lovers. Their explicit references to sexual organs and the elaboration of sexual pleasures in print offended the anti-vice crusader just as much. By shutting down the most radical sexual critics, however, Comstock effectively closed off the discussion of rape in marriage. The problems broached by Lillian Harman, Ezra Heywood, and Angela Heywood could no longer be addressed in print. Even if Comstock had not suppressed the free-love message, it is unlikely that it would have found a wide sympathetic audience, for marriage remained a central economic and social institution in late nineteenth-century America. But Comstock helped draw boundaries around sexual discourse that influenced more moderate camps, including those who advocated the individual rights of women. In the early twentieth century, as they began to achieve their goals of full citizenship, suffragists still did not confront coverture in the form of the marital exemption in rape law. By then Americans were beginning to rethink marriage as a companionate rather than patriarchal institution. Still, few writers broached the problem of rape within marriage as directly as did the anarchists who had first insisted that women should not have to give blanket sexual consent upon marriage.

IN THE 1890S Elizabeth Cady Stanton lamented, "You can scarcely take up a paper that does not herald some outrage on woman; from the dignified matron on her way to church to the girl of fourteen gathering wild flowers on her way to school." Like the press, Stanton attributed most of these assaults to lower-class men, but she also insisted on holding "men in high places responsible for the actions of the lower orders." Her particular targets among the elites were "clergymen and legislators" who should be molding American morals. "So long as the Church and the State in their creeds and codes, make woman an outcast, she will be the sport of the multitude," Stanton concluded.[47]

To some extent both suffragists and free lovers agreed with Stanton's views. Both groups favored voluntary motherhood, but some free lovers supported contraception as well. Free lovers insisted on an independent female sexuality unfettered by formal marriage, whereas suffragists, who largely avoided the question of a husband's sexual rights, condemned physical violence against wives. Each set of northern activists confronted the sexual privileges that allowed white men to rape with impunity. Suffrage and free-love analyses of rape also shared serious limits. In scope, each remained race-bound. This oversight may seem historically odd, given that both groups included former members of the abolitionist movement, which had condemned the rape of slave women. In the more conservative postwar era, however, when suffragists divided bitterly over the priority of black male versus universal suffrage, and as white supremacist theories dominated American politics, reformers and radicals alike lost sight of the sexual plight of former slaves.

In their gender analysis, too, suffragists and free lovers expressed a narrow vision, emphasizing their respective legal strategies for undermining coverture rather than promoting structural critiques of inequality. To contest sexual violence, suffragists wanted the state to expand citizenship rights to include women. Free lovers wanted to reject the state's power to regulate personal life. Yet broader contexts, beyond the law, seriously undermined women's ability to withhold sexual consent, within or outside or marriage. As long as women remained economically dependent on men, neither suffragists nor free lovers could achieve even their limited goal of empowering white women. During the nineteenth century the protective strategy embodied in antiseduction laws, which reinforced marriage, proved to be far more influential. Few states enacted woman suffrage, the marital exemption in rape law held firm, and the goal of female self-sovereignty as a defense against rape remained elusive.

4

Contesting the Rape of Black Women

In August 1874, a young African American woman named Julia Hayden, who had recently arrived in western Tennessee to open a school, heard several men shouting for her to let them come inside her home. According to the press, the drunken white youths assumed that she would "admit them and submit to their wishes." Fearful, Hayden locked the door. As they walked away, one of the men fired his pistol into the house. The bullet killed Julia Hayden. Local African Americans held "indignation meetings" throughout Tennessee to protest the murder of Hayden and the recent lynchings of black men. The Hayden tragedy also attracted the attention of northern journalists, who had disparate opinions about its significance. The liberal magazine *Harper's Weekly* condemned the murder as a form of white resistance to the education of freed blacks, a contested issue in Tennessee at the time. In contrast, the *New York Tribune* considered the shooting merely an unfortunate case of mistaken identity, given black women's reputation for "wanting in chastity." The publication of the African Methodist Episcopal Church, the *Christian Recorder,* declared the *Tribune's* comments "insulting to every colored husband, father, and brother, in the land."[1]

We do not know the outcome of the trial of the two white men accused of the murder of Julia Hayden, but the press controversy reveals how politically charged the sexual respectability of black women had become in the aftermath of emancipation. Southern white men still deemed all black women to be sexually available, a view that some northerners shared. Even if the men who approached her knew that Hayden was an educated, middle-class woman, they may have targeted her sexually because her school threatened to disrupt the local racial hierarchy. That the black press extended the insult to men and not only to women reflected aspirations that African American husbands, fathers, and brothers should be able to provide the kind of patriarchal protection that slavery had denied them. Reactions to the Hayden murder vividly display the political as well as personal stakes underlying contestations over the sexual rights of black women.

The Hayden tragedy also illustrates the conflicting goals of former slaves and former owners for coexisting in the postemancipation South. White southerners wanted to maintain a cheap and docile agricultural labor force and to reestablish political mastery in the face of black male enfranchisement. African Americans looked forward to claiming sovereignty over their labor, their families, and their bodies. The constitutional amendments that outlawed slavery, established equal protection, and granted suffrage to freed men gave them the legal status to do so, but their former owners resisted these political entitlements. The sexual integrity of black women played a key role in this postemancipation struggle. As one form of control, southern whites deepened the association of rape as an act committed by a black (not a white) man against a white (not a black) woman. In addition to using rape charges to justify lynching, they treated all black women as acceptable sexual outlets for what a northern journalist critically referred to as "the licentious passions of Southern white men."[2] Rather than define their assaults as rape, these men presumed that black women either welcomed them or had no moral purity to defend.

Southern blacks waged a counteroffensive to these ideas. They asserted their newly gained rights in order to achieve sexual respectability and physical safety. Freedom gave black women greater leverage to resist the sexual demands of white men, who were no longer their owners. As voters African American men could elect representatives to office who could revise state laws to include black women as victims of sexual assault. Although black women could not vote, they seized rights to sexual self-sovereignty where they could. They turned to the federal government to expose white assailants. Now able to testify in court, they reported rape to authorities. They accused men of their own race of rape, even though these charges resonated with white southern constructions of the black rapist. Hindered by political and racial constructions of black immorality, freedwomen and freedmen waged an uphill battle against white male sexual privilege. Their efforts revealed the centrality of sexuality, along with economic opportunity and political rights, to achieving the goal of full citizenship after emancipation.[3]

THE CHALLENGES TO SEXUAL self-sovereignty for African American women had deep roots in the antebellum South. Neither enslaved men nor enslaved women had legal ownership of their own bodies, so masters who controlled slave labor could exercise their sexual prerogatives without facing legal consequences. Aside from their formal power over enslaved women, many southerners justified their behavior in cultural terms, presuming that female slaves lacked sexual morality and would always consent. This belief fueled the notion that enslaved women were little more than prostitutes, trading sex for better treatment by their masters. After emancipation, former slaves hoped to end white men's unlimited sexual prerogatives by redeeming black women's reputations and ensuring their safety. In the words of James T. White, an African American minister from Indiana who served in the Arkansas legislature during Reconstruction, "The white men of the south have been for years indulging in illicit intercourse with colored women, and in the dark days of slavery this intercourse was in a great majority of cases forced upon the innocent victims; and I think the time has come when such a course should end."[4] Ending this practice meant that rape would be redefined to include black women as victims.

That task proved to be fraught with impediments. After the defeat of the Confederacy some southern men tried to retain their mastery by having sex with their former slaves or other freedwomen. Although they now had the right to refuse, and at times fought back successfully, these women and their kin faced retaliatory violence. White Texan Tilman Curloo threatened former slave Virginia Harrison, and when she refused to "yield to his desires," he made good on his promise and killed her. In one night a mob of white Texans rampaged against black women, sexually assaulting three of them, attempting to rape a black child, and beating or robbing twenty others. When the husband of one of the women tried to defend his wife and home, three of the white assailants shot and killed him.[5] After a white man twice raped his wife, freedman Cuff Canara of Louisiana fought back, but the assailant shot at the enraged husband and pursued him with hounds as Canara fired back in self-defense. The Freedmen's Bureau noted that local observers seemed to think that the former slave "had committed the greater crime by killing the dogs, than the man who shot him."[6] In this climate, exercising the right to refuse sex or to defend female kin remained as risky as under slavery, a message that the assailants no doubt intended to convey.

Political motives clearly inspired one of the most extensive uses of rape as a weapon of terror. In 1866 white citizens in Memphis, Tennessee, rioted for three days, burning black houses, churches, and schools and killing dozens of freed men and women who had settled there after being displaced by the war. Fearful of "negro domination" in the wake of national civil rights legislation, local whites wanted to limit the geographic and economic mobility of former slaves. They began with attacks on African American men who had served in the Union Army, some of whom now patrolled Memphis streets. They also assaulted black women, treating all of them as if they were disreputable prostitutes. White men solicited or coerced sex and, when rebuffed or resisted, used force. Armed men, including some police officers, brutally raped black women in their homes. Former slave Lucy Smith recalled that when she refused to have sex with the men who had broken into her home, they "drew their pistols and said they would shoot us and fire the house if we did not let them have their way with us." After the first man raped her, several others choked and punched her, leaving her for dead.[7]

Rape in the postwar South clearly represented not only an assault on black women but also a contestation between white and black men. The white men who stripped, tied up, and then brutally raped Rhoda Ann Childs in Georgia in 1866—she told a congressional investigation that one of them "ran his pistol into me" and threatened to pull the trigger—objected to her husband's service in the Union Army. Anonymous masked night riders, such as members of the newly formed Ku Klux Klan, burned black churches and schools, subjected African American men to severe whippings and sometimes castration, and targeted whites who supported equal rights. They also sexually assaulted black women and employed gang rape against families known to vote for Republicans. Before they "ravished" Harriet Simril, white neighbors told her that they wanted her "old man to join the Democratic ticket." In Georgia, night riders attacked the wife and daughter of a black Republican leader. These rapes were intended to humiliate husbands, to discourage them from political participation, or to punish them for their successes.[8]

In response to these continuing risks, African Americans protested against sexual assault. When they felt that their communities were threatened, some black men organized to protect women, as did the Sons of Benevolence in Savannah, Georgia, in 1865. In Virginia and Alabama they issued complaints about white police officers or jail keepers who sexually assaulted black women. Turning to federal authorities, African American women told the Freedmen's Bureau and northern military officials about the "outrages" committed against them. In 1868 Jenny Wychie of Georgia reported that a white man overtook her on a road, drew his pistol, and took her into the woods with the intent to rape her. Sarah Martin of Tennessee could not report the attack on her, but others told the Freedmen's Bureau when this fourteen-year-old "poor girl" was "Raped & murdered & no clue to the perpetrators of this diabolical out-rage."[9] During congressional hearings on the Klan in 1871, southern blacks testified about both sexual violence and their efforts to resist it. Only a few night riders went to prison as a result of these investigations, but the willingness to publicize sexual terror during these hearings gave support to Reconstruction efforts to protect former slaves and constrain the Klan.[10]

The national response to southern violence included a number of laws to protect freed people. Elected with the help of newly enfranchised black male voters, Republican members of Congress (some of whom were Afri-can American themselves) chipped away at white political domination. A series of enforcement acts granted federal courts the power to rule on cases concerning the intimidation of local voters. The Ku Klux Klan Act of 1871 allowed federal prosecution or intervention against conspiracies to deprive citizens of their rights. In 1875 the federal Civil Rights Act outlawed discrimination in public accommodations, a locus of sexual risk for black women when they traveled. As John R. Lynch, an African American congressman from Mississippi, argued during the debates, white women "of an admitted immoral character" enjoyed first-class rail-way accommodations to which no black woman, even a "refined colored lady," could aspire.[11] Social class, not race, Lynch implied, should deter-mine who merited protection from sexual insults and attacks.

As former slaves began to assert greater control over their own persons, and armed with the right to testify in court, at least some black women took the unprecedented step of turning to state authorities to prosecute sexual assailants. They could do so because southern state legislatures began to remove the term *white* from rape statutes when they rewrote their legal codes, effectively criminalizing sexual assaults on black women. Although never widespread, the scattered evidence of interracial rape tri-als revises the view that black women never charged white men with sex-ual assault. Against great odds some tried to use the law to dispute the sexual privileges these men exercised.

It is difficult to estimate how many black women attempted to file rape charges after emancipation. The only survey of late nineteenth-century courts throughout the South looks at appellate decisions, limiting cases to those in which a conviction had already been made. Two white men

convicted of interracial rape appealed their guilty verdicts, and both succeeded in having them overturned. Local studies reveal tantalizing evidence of efforts to report rape that did not go to appeals courts. In a
North Carolina county between 1865 and 1886, twelve black women and
twelve lower-class white women (and no elite white women) went to court
to prosecute men for rape or attempted rape. Most of these cases involved
intraracial rape, however, and most of the men received short prison
terms. One white-on-black rape charge in this county was taken seriously
by the local court and local press, although a lack of evidence allowed the
defendant to go free. Still, turning to the state to prosecute a white man
for rape testified to black women's expectations for respectability and
citizenship.[12]

Some members of the educated black middle-class, who often differentiated themselves from the rural masses, may have shunned the publicity of trials. They did, however, expect to be treated as upstanding
and moral citizens. "White men make us respect white ladies," a black
newspaper editor wrote in 1882, "and they must make white men respect ours." The editorial referred to an educated young woman named
Laura Lomax who successfully prosecuted Doc Jones, a white man who
had "insulted and struck" her on the street in Charlotte, North Carolina, while she was walking with her suitor, Jim Harris. In addition to
his conviction, Jones suffered a pistol-whipping from Harris and then a
beating from a group of black men that included Lomax's brothers.
When a white news report of the incident referred to Lomax as "a colored girl," the local black press took issue and reminded the editor that
she was "a respectable young lady" who came from a prominent family.[13] Once again social class might elevate black women to the status of
those protected by law.

Evidence from the press also speaks to a new sense of legal entitlement immediately after emancipation. White newspaper coverage of rape,
which included police reports that did not go to trial as well as acquittals
that did not go on to appellate courts, provide an intriguing indicator of
change. In a sample of four regionally diverse white newspapers from
1870 to 1900, only a small proportion of all sexual assault reports involved black women, but the coverage increased from 4 percent of rape
stories in the 1870s to 10 percent in the 1890s. The *Atlanta Constitution*
sample contained no reports of white-on-black rape in the 1870s, but
these stories constituted 4 percent of all rape reports in that paper in the
1890s.[14] Though sparse, this newspaper coverage suggests that readers

might be aware that black women could be raped. Like the local court cases, most of the news stories involved intraracial rather than interracial assaults on black women. In exceptional cases, however, the press reported African American women who accused white men, particularly when the victims were children.

Both the white news reports and known court cases frequently concerned mothers who acted to protect young daughters from sexual assault. In 1869 a poor black mother in North Carolina filed charges against a white man who had exposed himself to her children and attempted to rape her daughter. In 1878 a white man in North Carolina was formally accused, though never convicted, of raping a twelve-year-old black girl. A black mother in Atlanta who saw a young white man attempting to rape her nine-year-old daughter went to the police and identified the man. Though most white men escaped punishment, the public references to them alerted southerners that black families intended to protect girls. Courts even convicted some white men. In one highly unusual trial in 1897, an all-white male jury in Alabama imposed life imprisonment on a white man named Will Clark for the rape of a fourteen-year-old black girl. Concluding its brief account of the verdict, the *Atlanta Constitution* commented that the trial had been fair and claimed that the verdict was well received "by the people of the county in which the outrage was perpetrated."[15] The paper did not point out that the case was an exception, while the rule remained impunity for white men who assaulted African American girls or women.

Young black victims may have seemed more sympathetic to white judges and jurors, especially at the end of the nineteenth century, when a growing child-saving movement led to heightened protections for youths. During the 1890 trial of a white man for the attempted rape of a fourteen-year-old African American girl, a North Carolina prosecutor told the jury that "this thing of outraging innocent girls, white or black, must be stopped by the Courts." If not, he continued, referring to the growth of vigilantism in the South, "Judge Lynch will stalk through the land unmolested." In a rare white critique of the racialization of lynching, the prosecutor speculated, "If the color of the parties was reversed, no doubt the jury would neither have the pleasure, nor displeasure, of trying the defendants." Although the court sentenced the defendant to five years in prison, the appellate court overturned the decision on a legal technicality concerning the wording of the indictment.[16] Like other efforts to prosecute white men for assaults on black women, this case revealed both black claims to the rights of citizens and the formidable southern resistance to their efforts.

SEXUAL VIOLENCE against black women had clearly entered the political discourse on the rights of African Americans. But these postemancipation moves toward redefining black women as rape victims pale in comparison with the cases of rape as a weapon of political terror and the more quotidian assaults on black women by white men that never reached the press, police, or prosecutors. Long-standing white sexual privileges persisted, facilitated by the reversals in the African American quest for citizenship and the deepening ideological resistance to granting moral status to black women.

One barrier to protecting black women from assault was political. The initial inroads through courts and federal laws proved to be short-lived. National politics, southern culture, and the economic dependence of freed people all undermined the quest for respectability and safety from assault. The demise of Radical Reconstruction after 1877 and the gradual "redemption" of southern state governments by Democrats ensured the reestablishment of white political and economic dominance. At the end of the century, as southern states disenfranchised black men and institutionalized racial segregation, the continued rape of black women by white men strengthened white supremacy. Part of white resistance to African American citizenship consisted of a rhetorical attack on the morality of former slaves in which black men were cast as dangerously aggressive and black women as unconditionally promiscuous.

In the decade before she became the leading African American critic of lynching, black journalist Ida B. Wells put her finger on the problem posed by these views. "Among the many things that have transpired to dishearten the Negroes in their effort to attain a level in the status of civilized races," she wrote in 1886, "has been the wholesale contemptuous defamation of their women." Wells made this statement in a letter to a white newspaper in Memphis whose editor, former Union army officer G. P. M. Turner, had defended "respectable colored people" by commenting that black women were no longer, "as it had been," harlots whose virtue "was a thing of jest." After emancipation, he believed, they had the opportunity to be as decent as white women.[17]

Elaborating on Turner's historical argument, Wells alluded to the rape of slave women when she explained that "our enslavement with all the evils attendant thereon was involuntary." No longer enslaved, black women now insisted on being admitted to the realm of moral purity. For Wells, no accusations "sting so deeply and keenly as the taunt of immorality; the jest and sneer with which our women are spoken of, and the utter incapacity or refusal to believe there are among us mothers, wives and maidens who have attained a true, noble, and refining womanhood."[18] Implicit in her statement was a class divide, between those black women who had attained this vision of womanhood and those who had not. For any black woman, however, the goal of achieving morality encountered increasingly harsh opposition in the final decades of the nineteenth century, for southerners grouped all African Americans in one moral class.

As Wells understood, the spread of cultural representations of lascivious black women in the late nineteenth century facilitated white men's continued sexual entitlements. After emancipation, the weight of southern imagery of black women shifted from the more positive, if paternalistic, Mammy figure to the more dangerous and despised black seductress. For decades visual arts and literature had incorporated images of the sexualized bodies of African or slave women and linked them to prostitution. Now social commentators promulgated theories of racial depravity that extended these depictions to freed women.[19] One of the strongest proponents of this view, Virginia historian Philip Bruce, claimed that since emancipation, the morals of former slaves had declined. "Chastity," he wrote in 1889, "is a virtue which the parents do not seem anxious to foster and guard in their daughter; she has no abiding sense of personal purity." These judgments found expression in the ideas of conservative mixed-race writer William Hannibal Thomas. Admittedly an unrepresentative figure, Thomas endorsed the opinions of southern white men when he labeled most black women "lascivious by instinct and in bondage to physical pleasure."[20]

White women in the South reinforced their race superiority by demeaning the sexual morality of all black women. Mrs. L. H. Harris, who would become a prolific novelist in the early twentieth century, depicted black men and women as morally irresponsible creatures who lived in a "cesspool of vice." She compared the "savage nature" of black men to that of "wild beasts" and refused to consider even churchgoing black women to be respectable. Harris proclaimed that "the most prominent women in their religious enthusiasms are oftenest public prostitutes." Although Harris blamed white men who seduced young black girls as one source of their immorality, she still insisted that "prostitution is the rule."

Implying that black women were to blame for the moral failings of black men, Harris concluded that as long as "Negro Womanhood" lacked virtue, so too would black men.[21] With few exceptions, southern white women adhered to the views expressed by one writer that "negro women evidence more nearly the popular idea of total depravity than the men do. . . . I cannot imagine such a creation as a virtuous black woman." This construction gave white men free sexual rein and limited the ability of African American women of any class to refuse sexual consent.[22]

While these assessments denied black women a sense of sexual sovereignty, the limited economic options for former slaves created conditions that made them more sexually vulnerable. In towns and cities where rural blacks migrated after the war, many freed women could find jobs only as domestic workers in white households. The sexual risks of this labor were widely known. One former servant who spent thirty years working for white families in the South explained, "A colored woman's virtue in this part of the country has no protections . . . nearly all white men take undue liberties with their colored female servants—not only the fathers, but in many cases the sons also." There were serious dilemmas for a servant whose employer made sexual advances. If she refused, or if she reported, she might lose her job. Further, she might well be blamed for having instigated any sexual relations. Outside of domestic work, as well, black women experienced sexual pressures. A "Southern colored woman" recalled a series of insults—from the clerk in a store who took her hand and uttered "some vile request," to the man in a crowd who laced his hands around her, to the school director who assured her a job "if I did his bidding."[23] White working women might also experience these forms of coercion, and they too might remain silent to maintain their jobs. For black women, however, the options were narrower, for they were constrained not only economically but also by the racial and sexual filters through which their complaints would have been viewed.

The goal of ending the "dark days of slavery," when white men could claim ownership of black women's bodies, faced enormous political, cultural, and economic obstacles. Without the political standing that would enable them to prosecute whites, some former slaves contemplated the option of leaving the South. As one man asked the American Colonization Society in 1891, "Can we Raise our Doughters hear with no law to pretec them [?] [sic]."[24] His question revealed the frustration felt by free black men who could not exercise their rights as male heads of households to secure the safety of their families. For them, full citizenship included access to the patriarchal role long available to white men. For black women the consequences were deeply personal as well as political. Those who came of age at the end of the nineteenth century learned early in their lives that race alone was "sufficient invitation to the Southern white man."[25] Despite African American attempts to shape and use the law, and despite evidence of sympathies toward young black victims, southern whites largely refused to elevate black women to the protected, respectable class of "ladies." That goal would require long-term campaigns. But in one way, some African American women were able to gain the standing to charge rape in court, albeit primarily against men of their own race.

IN HIS 1904 POEM "The Black Woman's Burden," Daniel Webster Davis acknowledged the dual sexual threats that shadowed women of his race. Along with the sinful white men who preyed on their virtue, they also had to battle "the lust / Of thine own blood, whose lecherous men / So oft thy truth would try." Several years later an African American nurse made a similar observation in more direct language. "We poor colored women wage-earners in the South are fighting a terrible battle," she wrote. "On the one hand, we are assailed by white men, and, on the other hand, we are assailed by black men, who should be our natural protectors."[26] While such direct references by African Americans to intraracial rape are rare, newspaper reports, court cases, and Freedmen's Bureau records support these observations. We know about black men's assaults because black women and girls reported them in the decades after emancipation. In doing so they claimed the mantle of respectability, creating a crack in the race-bound definition of female moral purity. Like non-elite white women who accused men of rape, these witnesses had to endure the scathing treatment of attorneys who maligned them in these cases in order to defend black men.

For most of the century, southerners and other Americans largely ignored intraracial black rape.[27] During the slave era, southern courts did not necessarily recognize it as a crime. As one lawyer argued successfully in an 1859 Mississippi case, "the crime of rape does not exist in this State between African slaves." The very next year, however, the Mississippi legislature filled one gap in the law by making it a crime punishable by death or whipping for a black man to rape or attempt to rape a black female who was under the age of twelve, setting a cultural, if not legal, precedent that the youth—and not only the race—of a victim mattered in the definition of rape. In 1861 Georgia criminalized the rape of free or slave women of any age, although the penalties were more lenient than if the victims were white.[28] After emancipation, local authorities sometimes identified black men who committed intraracial assault. In 1866 a justice of the peace in Georgia authorized a manhunt for "a Negro" who "had committed a rape on his daughter."[29]

Another indicator of the awareness of intraracial rape appeared in newspaper reports of black victims of sexual assault. From the 1870s to the 1890s, black-on-black rape reports increased in national newspapers, especially in the *Atlanta Constitution*.[30] Reports of these assaults largely explain the expanded coverage of black victims of rape in this paper. The stories included an 1882 account of a "colored girl" named Carrie Ross who broke away from an attack by John Thompson, "a negro man." The subheadline of a police roundup column in 1887 read: "A Negro Makes a Brutal Assault—Upon a Girl of His Own Race." Elaborating on a court-room drama, the *Constitution* reported that a black man tried to commit suicide after being sentenced to a year in prison for the rape of a "negro girl." When a "mulatto" was jailed in rural Alabama for attempting to rape a thirteen-year-old girl from an educated family, the *Constitution* claimed that blacks might lynch the assailant.[31] In this article and other accounts, the Atlanta paper used intraracial black rape as an occasion for reinforcing the legitimacy of lynching. Although the white press ac-knowledged that black women could be raped, limiting coverage to black assailants protected white men's sexual entitlements. Nonetheless, the spike in attention to black-on-black assaults at the end of the century rep-resents a small shift in white southern definitions of rape.

The fledgling African American press also began to take note of intra-racial rape. These accounts remained rare at the end of the century, for pointing them out could reinforce stereotypes about black rapists and contradict the goal of achieving patriarchal authority within black fami-lies. One report in the *Christian Recorder* handled the conflict by por-traying black men as both attackers and defenders of women of their race. A "young colored man" named Charles Webb had tried "to outrage a colored girl named Alberta Howard" after returning from church in Maryland. A companion named Vance Sharp heard her cries and struck Webb, fractur-ing his skull. As if to assure readers of Howard's propriety, or perhaps to grant her an active role in the case, the article noted that she had followed proper procedures by reporting the assault to authorities.[32]

While the white and black press both began to acknowledge intraracial assaults, most white southerners remained highly skeptical that black women could be raped. For them, contesting the redefinition of black women as rape victims buttressed the defense of white supremacy. In 1886, for example, a white observer commented that a black man in Florida had been "charged with a crime that I believe is almost impossible to commit (that of raping another negro)." Granting sexual morality to any black woman could undermine white men's sexual access to them. Commenting on intraracial rape, influential southern white writers continued to insist that innate immorality characterized the race. In 1895 a white Kentucky physician explained the rarity of intraracial black rape as follows: "The reason for this is the natural complaisance of the females of his own race, the male being able to easily satisfy his desire without violence."[33] In a vicious circle, the lack of prosecution of intraracial black assaults contributed to stereotypes that in turn affected legal outcomes. Thus, the white supremacist Philip Bruce took the scarcity of intraracial rape charges as evidence that the crime did not occur and thus proved the immorality of black women:

> The rape of a negress by a male of her own color is almost unheard of, a fact that is a strong proof of the sexual laxness of the plantation women as a class; for if they attached any importance to sexual purity, and strenuously resisted all improper encroachment upon it, the criminal records of the negro men would contain details of many such assaults.[34]

Despite these views, black women did go to court to charge black men with attempted rape and with sexual assault. Like non-elite white women, who found it hard to win rape convictions, these black women had to meet community standards of morality—no reputation for drinking or sleeping around, no out-of-wedlock children in their families. Propriety was fundamental in intraracial rape trials because black defendants typically raised doubts about the chastity of their accusers. White women faced character attacks in court as well, but the prevailing perceptions of black women's sexual immorality made convictions even more unlikely and harder to sustain. Southern appellate courts often overturned guilty verdicts against black men accused of intraracial rape. In the late nineteenth century these courts sustained only one-third of the convictions for black-on-black rape or attempted rape, while they sustained just over half of the convictions for black-on-white rape or attempted rape.[35]

A Virginia appellate decision illustrates how convicted black men benefited from the chastity requirement. In 1873 the Supreme Court of

Virginia reversed the lower-court conviction of Henry Christian for the attempted rape of Martha Mallory. After taking Mallory to a performance, Christian had tried to overcome her resistance to having sexual intercourse by pushing her down on the ground, choking her, and trying to remove her clothing. She resisted and filed attempted rape charges. Along with finding a technical problem in the language of the indictment, the court considered the character of each person. The decision noted that Christian "had wooed her pretty roughly in a way that would have been horrible and a shocking outrage toward a woman of virtuous sensibilities." But the fact that Mallory admitted to being "the mother of two bastard children" showed that she "had yielded to others before." That fact, along with her failure to cry out, meant that although his conduct was "extremely reprehensible," it did not constitute attempted rape.[36]

In the Christian case the character requirement for victims overrode the racialization of black men as rapists, but the same argument failed for twenty-six-year-old Butler Hall of Florida. In appealing his conviction, Hall tried to portray his accuser, nineteen-year-old Ida Franklin, as a common prostitute with whom he had prior relations. He attributed the rape charge to her desire to get paid for sex. White men had used this strategy successfully, often invoking the term *prostitute* to refer to poor white women who had prior sexual experiences. But Franklin had reported the assault promptly and several witnesses testified to her agitated state at the time, so the court accepted her version of events. In 1886 the jury convicted Hall and the judge sentenced him to life imprisonment.[37]

The outcome of the Hall case was exceptional. Black men typically served shorter prison terms for intraracial than for interracial rape, for even when black women won convictions, doubts about their chastity influenced sentencing. White defendants regularly impugned the sexual morality of their accusers, but black men could rely on both sexual and racial biases to diminish their own culpability. Confessed rapist Edward Powell of Virginia petitioned for early release in 1882 by claiming that because his victim had born children out of wedlock, she had a *"loose, depraved character."* He succeeded in convincing the governor to release him five years before his original sentence expired. Racial stereotypes and a strong sense of paternalism influenced sentencing in an 1876 case when a Georgia appeals court ordered a new trial for a sixteen-year-old black youth who had been convicted of the rape of a ten-year-old black girl. The twenty-year prison term, the court decided, seemed "rather severe" in light of the fact that "the parties all belong to the colored population of our state, who, owing to their ignorance, as a general rule, should have justice administered to them tempered with much mercy."[38] Such mercy would have been highly unlikely if the victim had been a white child.

Even very young black girls faced vilification as seductresses and prostitutes. In 1897 the state of Florida tried William Golden for the rape of eight-year-old Hattie Dargan; both of them were African American. The defense tried to impugn the child's moral character and described her as "filthy," a code for her class status. Although Golden was convicted and sentenced to death, white community members petitioned the governor to commute the sentence or pardon him. Hattie Dargan, they claimed, was "a hoar [sic] and a girl of immoral character" who had previously traded sex for candy. These prominent white male citizens crossed lines of class—as well as race—to plead for clemency for the illiterate Golden. Accepting the arguments about the child's character, and sustaining an earlier pattern of white paternalism, the governor commuted the sentence from death to one year at hard labor.[39]

Despite these reversals on appeal, the willingness to bring charges for intraracial assaults upon young black victims reflects a pattern in which age mattered in the successful prosecution of rape. Young women dominated all late nineteenth-century rape cases in newspaper reports, including those involving African Americans. The press and the courts may have been more sympathetic to young women, whether black or white, in this era of increased concern about preserving childhood innocence. In over two hundred newspaper accounts that indicated the age of a victim, that age declined for all girls from an average of nineteen years during the 1870s to an average of thirteen years in the 1890s. Significantly, however, African American girls had to be younger than their white counterparts to be identified in the press as the victims of rape; their average age in these accounts was thirteen and a half years, compared to sixteen and a half years for white victims.[40] This age gap highlights a racial difference in cultural understandings of childhood innocence. African American girls lost that innocence at a younger age, the press implied, making them more vulnerable not only to assault but also to courtroom claims that they had consented to sex.

IN THE FACE of escalating racial violence that could target them sexually, African American women attempted to assert rights to ownership of their own persons in the postemancipation South. They reported assaults to the Freedmen's Bureau, accused both white and black men of rape, turned to the state to prosecute these men, and defended their own morality in court. The attention to black women and girls as victims of rape presented a potential wedge into the strict racialization of rape as a crime committed only against white women. Identifying young girls as victims of assault showed that age could trump race in establishing female respectability. Like class, age could mediate doubts about credibility in the eyes of blacks or whites. For black girls and women, however, the legacy of slavery strongly shaped the outcome of rape cases. To be female and African American remained an obstacle to being a believable rape victim and a challenge to attaining the full rights of citizenship, including sexual self-sovereignty.

MARIA:

OR, THE

Wrongs of Woman.

A

POSTHUMOUS FRAGMENT.

BY

MARY WOLLSTONECRAFT GODWIN.

AUTHOR

OF A

VINDICATION OF THE RIGHTS OF WOMAN.

PHILADELPHIA:

PRINTED BY JAMES CAREY,
No. 16, *Chesnut-street.*

1799.

Beginning with British writer Mary Wollstonecraft *(above)*, early women's rights advocates decried white men who seduced servants and working women or who persuaded young girls to consent to sexual relations under false promise of marriage.

In addition to addressing seduction in *A Vindication of the Rights of Woman* (1792), Wollstonecraft provided a rare critique of unwanted sex in marriage in her posthumously published novel, *Maria: Or, The Wrongs of Woman* (1798). (Library of Congress)

Lucy Stone and Henry Blackwell, who were both suffragists and abolitionists, crafted an egalitarian marriage in which he renounced any privileges bestowed by law upon him as a husband that were not shared by his wife. In the 1870s and 1880s, Blackwell and Stone coedited the "Crimes against Women" column in the suffragist *Woman's Journal,* in which they compiled accounts of sexual violence and exposed judicial practices that they believed condoned assault. (Their daughter, Alice Stone Blackwell, stands behind them.) (Library of Congress)

Helen H. Gardener, later a suffrage activist, initially campaigned in the 1890s to increase the legal age at which a young woman could consent to have sexual relations. Gardener helped persuade state legislators to raise the age, set by common law at ten years, to between sixteen and eighteen years. (Library of Congress)

THE BLACK LIST OF STATES.

Below we give the black list of states, showing the limit at which fathers, brothers and husbands have placed the age at which *a little girl may consent to her ruin:* —

TEN YEARS.
Alabama, North Carolina, South Carolina.

TWELVE YEARS.
Kentucky, Louisiana, Texas, Wisconsin.

THIRTEEN YEARS.
Iowa, New Hampshire, Utah.

FOURTEEN YEARS.
Arizona, California, Connecticut, Georgia, Idaho, Illinois, Indiana, Maine, Maryland, Michigan, Minnesota, Missouri, Nevada, New Mexico, North Dakota, Ohio, Oregon, Vermont, West Virginia.

FIFTEEN YEARS.
Delaware, Montana.

SIXTEEN YEARS.
Arkansas, Colorado, District of Columbia, Massachusetts, Mississippi, New Jersey, New York, Pennsylvania, Rhode Island, South Dakota, Tennessee, Washington.

SEVENTEEN YEARS.
Florida.

In 1895 Helen H. Gardener compiled the "Black List" of states where statutory rape laws still set the age of consent below eighteen. She published the list in the national magazine *The Arena*.

The nineteenth-century American press typically portrayed rape victims as pure, young white women and their assailants as violent strangers, including white tramps and desperados. Vigilante mobs often targeted men of any race who assaulted children. *Above:* "Food for Judge Lynch" (*National Police Gazette*, 1889) shows armed men chasing three tramps who have ravished a young girl in her home in the presence of her father, who lies helpless on the floor. *Below:* "Tragic Retribution Visited Upon the Rape Fiends" (*National Police Gazette*, 1879) illustrates the lynching in Colorado of two white men awaiting trial for attempted assault on a four-year-old girl. (Reprinted with permission from images produced by ProQuest LLC, www.proquest.com)

After the end of Reconstruction, the association of black men with the crime of rape deepened. By the end of the century, southerners were justifying lynching as a means of protecting the sexual honor of white women and calling for the disenfranchisement of black men. The *National Police Gazette* reported far more accounts of white than of black rapists, but the paper emphasized the brutality of black men.

Right: "The Negro Crime" (1878). *Below left:* "No Negro Outrage for Her" (1882). *Below right:* "Lynched in Court" (1887). (ProQuest LLC)

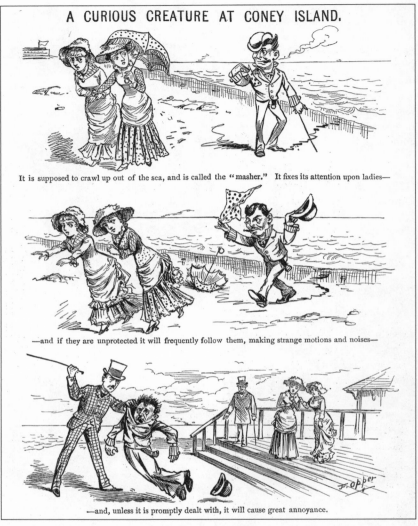

A CURIOUS CREATURE AT CONEY ISLAND.

It is supposed to crawl up out of the sea, and is called the "masher." It fixes its attention upon ladies—

—and if they are unprotected it will frequently follow them, making strange motions and noises—

—and, unless it is promptly dealt with, it will cause great annoyance.

As white women increasingly entered public space, they encountered men known as mashers, who annoyed, insulted, or harassed them. The press initially treated mashers as quasi-comic figures, as in this 1882 cartoon, which emphasized the need for male protectors. (ProQuest LLC)

In the early twentieth century, urban women increasingly complained about men who harassed them as they traveled on city streets to get to their jobs or to go shopping. In 1906 the *Chicago Tribune* targeted men who loitered outside downtown hotels and department stores, asking, "What can be done to rid the Palmer House block of Mashers?" Along with calls for more policemen, the *Tribune* and other newspapers featured stories of women defending themselves through physical prowess and extolled the appointment of the first policewomen. (ProQuest LLC)

As the woman suffrage movement gathered momentum, fears of women's public authority prompted political humor, such as this 1913 cartoon in *Life* magazine. A parody of a Roman tale, "The Rape of the Sabine Men" imagined enfranchised women abducting and presumably assaulting emasculated men. (ProQuest LLC)

5

The Racialization of
Rape and Lynching

Looking back at the late nineteenth century, African American scholar
W. E. B. Du Bois captured a complex political process that was central
to the reestablishment of white supremacy in the South. "The charge of
rape against colored Americans was invented by the white South after
Reconstruction to excuse mob violence," he explained. Since then it had
become "the recognized method of re-enslaving blacks." Building upon
the earlier image of the black man as a sexual threat, southerners created a "moral panic" that revived the politics of the post–Civil War Ku
Klux Klan.[1] In the past, interracial rape charges had not meant an automatic death sentence for black men, for the class and reputation of the
accuser helped determine whether the relationship had been consensual
or coercive. By the 1880s, however, southerners had begun to deny the
possibility of consensual interracial unions. Soon they portrayed all African American men as a constant, and monstrous, threat to all white
women.[2]

As Du Bois noted, the panic over the black rapist played a central role
in allowing lynching to flourish in the South after the 1880s. By justifying the summary, and brutal, executions of African Americans as a means
of protecting white women from rape, lynch mobs gained immunity from
prosecution for their crimes. The process that enabled this mechanism
involved the redefinition of rape through a tightening of the racial categories of both assailant and victim. The racialization of rape and lynching
took several decades to solidify. It built upon political realignments and
emerging racial ideologies and was greatly facilitated by the press. Once
established, the redefinition of rape provided a powerful political weapon
for undermining African American civil rights and reinforcing white supremacy. Lynching not only destroyed thousands of lives; it also served to
disenfranchise African American men and to intimidate southern blacks

from speaking out against the erosion of their political identities as citizens.

ALTHOUGH THE RACIALIZATION of sexual assault originated in early America, only in the closing decades of the nineteenth century did rape become widely regarded as "The Negro Crime." Antebellum southerners did not issue dire warnings about black male sexual aggression. Even during the Civil War they seemed more concerned about slave insurrections than the threat of rape. "During all those long four years of terrible conflict," Frederick Douglass claimed in 1894, "when the Negro had every opportunity to commit the abominable crime now alleged against him . . . [h]e was never accused of assault, insult, or an attempt to commit an assault upon any white woman in the whole South." Some white women who remained on farms and plantations felt protected by their slaves from the possibility of violence by Union soldiers.[3]

In the first decades after the war, rape remained a crime associated as much with class as with race. Newspapers frequently blamed rape on white tramps and desperados who invaded the sanctity of the rural home. A product of the economic depression of the 1870s, the "tramp problem" troubled Americans who feared not only the wandering unemployed but also the specter of class warfare. Tramps often dominated the press coverage of rape in the 1870s and 1880s, when several *New York Times* headlines referred to their "brutal outrages." So frequent were reports of sexual assaults by tramps that the *National Police Gazette* used the phrase "The Tramp Terror" as a code for rape. In 1889 that paper published a drawing of three white tramps who "ravish" a young white woman in her father's presence. Reflecting the racially inclusive targets of vigilantes, the *Gazette* titled this illustration "Food for Judge Lynch."[4]

By the 1890s, however, the image of black men as sexual threats had deepened, and they began to bear the brunt of mob violence. A changed national political context accelerated this transition. The gradual return of power in southern states to Democrats who had supported slavery and the Confederacy followed the end of federal enforcement of Reconstruction policies in 1877. The U.S. Congress soon began to retract formal protections for freed people. In 1883 the Supreme Court overturned the prohibitions on discrimination in public transportation in the Civil Rights Act of 1875; in 1894 Congress repealed the Force Act, which allowed federal troops to protect black voters. Then in the 1890s a third party, the Populists, threatened to achieve a political alliance between black and poorer white voters in the South. In response to Republican and Populist electoral successes, Democratic politicians sought ways to undermine the black vote. They found that rape fears could be an extremely useful tool for gaining and sustaining power, and for undermining local civil rights.

A key argument used by southern Democrats was that the political authority of black men would lead to sexual access to white women. First they accused their opponents of supporting interracial marriage; next they invoked the image of the black rapist. By the end of the century even Populist politicians were accusing their political opponents of condoning interracial rape. In North Carolina, Democrats claimed that the rape of white women by black men had increased in the years since the Republican Party had come to power in the state. By promising to defend the "safety of the home," they helped eliminate black men from state politics at the end of the century.[5]

In a political script replayed throughout the South, Democrats stirred up fears of black lust, promising to protect the purity of white womanhood and guarantee future racial purity. Whites were determined, in the words of Virginian Thomas Nelson Page, "to put an end to the ravishing of their women by an inferior race." White politicians began to build their careers on the defense of lynching. Although Georgian Tom Watson had condemned lynching in 1892, he learned that the route to election as governor and then senator was to endorse mob violence. Similarly, journalist Hoke Smith, who offered rewards to lynchers, rode to victory as governor and then senator from Georgia.[6]

The political implications of these appeals to southern whites went further than single campaign victories. Depicting African Americans as natural rapists allowed Democrats to maintain that blacks were incapable of the self-control and morality required for citizenship. This exclusionary construction in turn justified the disenfranchisement of black male voters, achieved through devices such as literacy tests, poll taxes, and all-white primary elections. Accusations about black voters who had sold their franchise to corrupt Republican politicians merged with accusations about vicious black sexual criminals. Henderson M. Somerville, a former associate justice of the Alabama Supreme Court, articulated this conflation when he claimed that most interracial rapes occurred where the black "exercise of the right of suffrage becomes a vendible article, leading to the corruption not only of the ballot, but equally of the public morals. . . . Political equality breeds ambition for social equality, with its train of evils."[7] Justice Somerville clearly linked black citizenship with sexual access to white women, implying that disfranchisement would reduce rape, a formula repeated by other southerners.

Such arguments helped white supremacist politicians win elections, and once in power these officials further strengthened the association of rape and race. They installed sheriffs and a judiciary that viewed black men as sexual predators, black women as inherently immoral, and white women as in need of protection. These stereotypes infused the criminal justice system. Arrest data from Savannah, Georgia, reveal that for years the police pursued only black, and not white, men accused of rape or seduction, reinforcing the myth of the black male rapist and enabling white men to escape punishment for interracial or intraracial rape. A black man on trial for rape had once benefited if his white accuser had a questionable reputation for chastity. In contrast, in 1887 an Alabama court sentenced a black man to life in prison on the uncorroborated testimony of a white prostitute. However just the elevation of this woman's credibility may have been, the fact that the defendant was black, not white, may well have influenced the decision. Although state laws no longer mandated separate punishments for whites and blacks, southern courts circumvented formal equality. When they had the option of imposing either capital punishment or prison terms for convicted rapists, these courts sent white men to prison and ordered the execution of black men.[8]

Southern politicians also exploited sexual fears to justify the policy of racial segregation, a regime that gradually spread through the former Confederate states and that would be affirmed in 1896 by the U.S. Supreme Court's ruling in *Plessy v. Ferguson*. One argument for separating the races on public transportation was that the proximity in railway cars and other modes of transport provided opportunities for sexual contact between black men and white women. In a related reaction to the public presence of former slaves, some whites argued that if African American men gained authority over white southerners—as public school teachers or as police officers, for example—they would abuse their access to white women.[9] The power of these warnings allowed Democratic politicians to discredit Republican or Populist candidates for office by associating them not only with support for black political rights but also with the goal of "social equality"—a code for practices that could lead to interracial marriage.

Concerns about interracial marriage and its effect on racial purity fueled the preoccupation with black-on-white rape. In the antebellum period, despite legal prohibitions, southerners often accepted these unions if the white woman came from a common rather than an elite background. Toleration diminished after black citizenship replaced slavery. Over time, southern white authorities redefined rape to include voluntary unions; in the process they denied white women the possibility of consenting to sexual relations with black men. Signs of the tightening social space for these interracial unions appeared during the Civil War, when Democratic opponents of black enfranchisement accused Republicans of favoring *miscegenation,* a new term they employed to imply that political equality would result in the social equality of intermarriage. Emancipation and black citizenship escalated the process. A system of dominance based not on servitude but on race alone required a tighter boundary to protect white racial identity. Sexual relations between black men and white women raised fears that their offspring would dilute the dominant race. In contrast, children born to black women by white fathers inherited the race of the mother and thus remained black.[10]

Promoting anxiety about amalgamation proved highly effective in arguing against extending rights to African American men. Vigilantes first introduced the rhetoric of defending southern white women, regardless of their class backgrounds, against the threat of black rapists. In the late 1860s Ku Klux Klan members often framed their acts of violence against former slaves as a necessary defense of the safety of their own homes. As one member explained, "Rapes were already being committed in the country. . . . We felt that we must at any cost protect ourselves, our homes, our wives and children from outrage."[11] These accusations infiltrated mainstream political discourse after the end of Reconstruction, when Democrats increasingly linked black men's rights as citizens to their access to white women. Concerned that black enfranchisement would encourage sexual mixing, southern state legislatures began to outlaw interracial marriage. In the process, court rulings delegitimized consensual unions between black men and white women, claiming that they were an "unnatural" and illicit form of sexuality. This shift from toleration to persecution to criminalization contributed to the association of the crime of rape with any such unions. If discovered in an interracial relationship, a white woman might now decide to declare herself a rape victim, possibly under pressure from kin or community members. In Arkansas a non-elite white woman charged the black man with whom she had been intimate for over a year with raping her. She was encouraged, if not forced, to do so by other whites, who then lynched her black lover.[12]

It is impossible to know how many of the black men accused of rape in this era had been involved in consensual unions with their white accusers. The influence of this redefinition on the law was clear, however. In 1880 a Georgia prosecutor argued before a jury that "the defendant was a negro, and the prosecutrix a white woman, and that they ought to put a stop to miscegenation as there was no telling where it would stop if it were not cut off."[13] In an 1899 decision the same court articulated a doctrine that would influence later cases concerning the role of race in determining criminal intent: "Where a negro is charged with assault with intent to commit a rape upon a woman of the white race, no inference that he reasonably presumes to think that a white woman will consent to his lustful embraces will ever arise in his favor, unless the circumstances are such that no other inference can be possibly drawn."[14] In short, any sexual relations between a black man and a white woman could be defined as rape.

Along with converting consensual relationships into coercive ones, late nineteenth-century constructions of rape drew a firm line between black men and the contemporary ideal of civilized white manliness, which embodied self-control and respectability. In making this distinction, southern whites employed somewhat contradictory ideas about both nature and culture. On the one hand, they naturalized black men as innate sexual predators; on the other hand, they blamed the historical event of emancipation for freed people's descent into sexual immorality.

Popular theories of "scientific racism" influenced this construction by proposing that evolutionary progress culminated in the superior civilization of white Europeans. The notion of racial "degeneracy" referred to the primitive characteristics of other groups, including their alleged propensity toward sexual depravity. Late nineteenth-century laws that restricted immigration drew on these ideas to prevent certain foreigners, such as the Chinese, from becoming potential citizens. The literature on degeneracy portrayed black men as primitive, animalistic, and characterized by an innate sexual aggression. According to Dr. William Lee Howard, "attacks on defenseless white women are evidences of racial instincts." Unlike whites, who could rationally control their impulses, Howard proposed, in "the full-blooded negro" intellectual development ceased at puberty, when sensuality took over. Northern writers also adopted dehumanizing references to "animal-like" and murderous blacks who reverted to "savagery." University of Pennsylvania anthropologist Daniel G. Brinton considered African Americans lower on the evolutionary ladder than Europeans but higher than the apes. To ensure racial purity, he argued, white women should not mate with black men.[15]

At the same time, southerners pointed to changing historical contexts to justify their views. The emancipation of slaves, they argued, had unleashed black sexual desires for white women, partly as retribution against the former powerlessness of enslaved men, who had not been able to protect their female kin from assault. Philip Alexander Bruce wrote that black men took "fiendish delight" in degrading white women as a form of revenge "upon one whom he has hitherto been compelled to fear . . . the white woman in his power is, for the time being, the representative of that race which has always over-awed him." Thomas Nelson Page believed that interracial rape had been rare under slavery. The problem originated, he believed, "in the teaching of equality and the placing of power in the ignorant negroes' hands." Drawing a class distinction not shared by many of his fellow southerners, Page granted that the "intelligent negro" understood the limits of "social equality." For "the ignorant and brutal young negro," however, social equality signified "but one thing: the opportunity to enjoy, equally with white men, the privilege of cohabiting with white women." These ideas reached wider audiences through images of former slaves ravishing southern white womanhood in literary depictions of Reconstruction, such as Thomas Dixon's 1905 novel, *The Clansman*.[16]

The late nineteenth-century white press reflected these racial views. Although newspapers continued to report rapes by white men, the language used to describe racial groups differed. White rapists appeared as individual criminals, often identified as hobos or desperados who were not representative of their race. In contrast, accounts of accused black men associated sexual assault with an entire race, reflecting the contemporary theories of racial primitivism that deepened the "white racist imagination" of the period in both the North and the South. When a mob in upstate New York attempted to lynch a black man accused of rape, the *Atlanta Constitution* seized upon the event to lecture northerners about the dangers of granting full citizenship to African Americans. If given political and social privileges, the *Constitution* warned, "the hereditary slave and semi-brute . . . will not forget his barbarian instincts at once." Lest northerners miss the lesson, the paper reasserted that natural tendencies led black men to commit rape: "There is a heap of nature in this. The Northerner never saw nature in it as a Southern affair. Perhaps he will now."[17]

That this attempted lynching took place in New York State reminds us that northerners did not necessarily require instruction from the southern press, for they too propagated the image of the innate black rapist. The *New York Times* described rape as "a crime to which negroes are particularly prone." The *National Police Gazette*—the sports and crime weekly geared toward working-class men—usually reported sexual assaults committed by white men, but it carried some of the earliest and most vicious rhetoric concerning African Americans. The phrase "The Negro Crime" reoccurred in *Gazette* accounts of the rape of white women in the late 1870s. The paper identified rape as a "characteristic crime" of black men and used this view to justify vigilantism. Condemning the "ridiculously mild punishment" of nine years' imprisonment for the rape and robbery of a white woman by a black man named Ponsley in Pennsylvania, the *Gazette* expounded, "At a time like this, when the crime of rape, which, it may be said without prejudice, the records of current events exhibit as the characteristic crime of Ponsley's race, is so frightfully rife throughout the land, we turn with relief from this disgusting display of mawkishness . . . to the more effective, adequate and virile justice dealt out in the court of Judge Lynch."[18] That solution was precisely what southerners embraced by the end of the nineteenth century.

LYNCHING—THE MURDER of those accused or convicted of crime by extralegal mobs—had long been practiced in America. Originally a means of enforcing order or morality in the absence of an established criminal justice system, it flourished in recently settled or sparsely populated areas such as the West. Victims were predominantly white, ranging from horse thieves and desperados to abolitionists and politicians. Even after courts were established in the West, mobs continued to exercise "frontier justice," as they did when Mexicans or Indians were accused of theft or of murdering whites. Nationally, men of any race who were accused of sexually assaulting white women or girls might face lynch mobs. Southern blacks were not initially the primary targets. Because killing a slave deprived them of valuable property, slave owners preferred severe punishment, such as whipping, for serious crimes. In the decade before the Civil War the lynching of slaves did increase in parts of the South, but Mexicans in the West still faced a higher risk of lynching than did blacks in the South.[19]

After the Civil War, mobs continued to lynch white men accused of particularly egregious crimes, such as the rape and murder of a girl or young woman. Lynching revived at the end of the century as a tool of racial terror, driven in part by rape accusations. In central Texas, few black men had been lynched prior to the 1880s, and rarely in response to rape charges. In contrast, between 1884 and 1897, mobs in this region lynched ten black men for allegedly sexually assaulting white women, in one instance for the charge of a man's "laying his hands" on a white farm wife.[20] Rape was being redefined as any action by a former slave that struck whites as overly assertive.

By the 1890s lynching came to be associated primarily with the South, the intimidation of former slaves, and the charge of rape. Multiple historical contexts help explain why the practice expanded while its focus narrowed to target African American victims. The "scientific" ideas that placed blacks at a lower evolutionary stage equated them with beasts, and this dehumanization made their torture and murder more imaginable. Yet the extent of lynching in the South fluctuated over time, correlating with economic conditions. During the deep agricultural depression of the 1890s, the practice peaked, suggesting that hard times made poorer whites more likely to attack blacks.[21]

Changes in southern politics and laws influenced this process. Where Republicans held local power, southern whites who feared that these officials would be lenient toward black criminals sometimes took the law into their own hands. In addition, the reform of southern legal codes after the war formally placed whites and blacks on an equal footing and sometimes eliminated capital punishment for rape and attempted rape. Lynching effectively reinstated a racially specific death sentence for sexual assault, without the niceties of due process. In the past, elite southerners had intervened to protect some black men accused of rape because they had been valuable laborers. This form of white protection eroded when former owners no longer had either a self-interested or a paternalistic stake in blacks' welfare. Now the intimidation of black men through the threat of lynching helped maintain informal control over the labor force of sharecroppers and tenant farmers.[22]

Whatever the sources, the consequences of the epidemic of lynchings, primarily in the South, were horrendous. Between 1882 and 1929, mobs seized more than three thousand African Americans who had been accused or convicted of crime. They took them from their homes or from jails and publicly killed them, often brutally. At the peak of vigilantism in 1892, lynch mobs murdered 230 people; of these, 161 were black. The practice became so widespread that Mark Twain referred to the country as the "United States of Lyncherdom." Although most lynching occurred in the South, newspapers throughout the nation reported in detail the hanging, shooting, and burning alive of black men and women. Some of the eighty or more victims who were female died at the hands of mobs after defending themselves from white rapists, or when their male relatives intervened to protect them from sexual assault. Lynch mobs not only murdered but also sadistically tortured, mutilated, and burned the bodies of black men, in some cases castrating them. These "symbolic rapes" constituted a form of white men's physical control of black men.[23]

White women played an important role in this terror. Elite southern women both embraced white supremacy and, like northern moral reformers, valued female chastity. Some of them urged men to participate in lynch mobs, others sought to uplift the moral standards of white and black men to reduce rape. Their views on lynching as a response to rape were not always consistent. Georgia temperance advocate Rebecca Latimer Felton, who championed women's public activism, at first denounced lynching. Over time, however, she came to sanction the mob. In an 1897 speech in which Felton blamed white southern men for failing to protect their women, she particularly chided corrupt politicians. By supplying black male voters with alcohol, she claimed, they put white women at risk of assault. Felton's larger point was that both rape and lynching would continue unless white politicians supported temperance, along with educational and economic progress for women. But the rhetorical flourish she employed left a more lasting mark: "If it takes lynching to protect women's dearest possession from drunken, ravening human beasts, then I say lynch a thousand a week if it becomes necessary." The white southern press heralded Felton's statement as an endorsement of the mob. Even when she professed that she was misunderstood, she reinforced the point by insisting that the "brutal lust" of black men accounted for almost all of the rapes of white women in the South. Within a year Rebecca Felton was defending the lynching of "the black fiend who destroys a white woman in her home or on the highway" as the "unwritten law" of the state.[24]

Other southern white women not only justified lynching as a means of protecting themselves from rape; they also participated in vigilante mobs. The accuser might be asked to identify the man who assaulted her and given the choice of whether he would be shot or set on fire. At times groups of women gathered to encourage men to kill, but women could be active themselves. "His Victim Heads the Mob" one newspaper titled an account of a lynching in 1900. Female as well as male kin of the accuser participated in the torture of the lynched man. In 1892 the *New York Times* reported that in Arkansas, Mrs. Henry Jewell was "accorded the privilege" of lighting the "funeral pyre" of the man she accused of assaulting her—a man whom others suspected had been her consensual sexual partner.[25] As they concentrated their fears upon black men, southern white women said little about the threat of intraracial rape, in contrast to the northern moral reformers who were trying to contest white men's sexual privileges.

The racialization of rape and lynching was widespread but it was never complete. Juries still convicted white men for the rape of white women, and courts rather than mobs might determine the fate of black men accused of sexual assault. Where rape remained a capital offense, black men were not always executed. In 1899 a jury in Georgia acquitted an older black man charged with rape, and in another case a judge sentenced two young black men found guilty to life imprisonment. If convicted in the North, where most states had eliminated rape as a capital offense, black and white men served prison terms.[26] Southern appellate courts could protect the rights of accused black men, as did the Georgia Supreme Court in 1879. A "negro man" identified only as Johnson appealed his conviction for the attempted rape of Sarah Cole, a white woman. Although Johnson had confessed to the crime, the court found "no evidence in the record" that he had "attempted to have carnal knowledge of Sarah Cole." His confessions, the court ruled, had been "extorted by threats and fear." Twenty years later the same court unanimously reversed the conviction of a young black man, explaining that there was "no overt act done by the accused to effectuate the criminal design which would amount to an assault upon the girl."[27]

Outside the South lynch mobs continued to target other groups, such as Asians and Mexicans in the West, for a range of alleged crimes. Those who enjoyed some political rights, as did the Hispanic men who might serve on juries in New Mexico, were less likely to be demonized as rapists. White men in the South, Midwest, and West continued to face lynch mobs if they were known to have sexually assaulted children, committed incest, or perpetrated extremely violent acts such as mutilation and murder. Continuing suspicions about white tramps appeared in the press, as illustrated by a *New York Times* article in 1897. When the body of a young white woman was discovered in Alabama, the paper speculated that "the girl was assaulted, either by a white tramp seen in the neighborhood or a negro," predicting that in either case the "murderer will certainly be lynched if caught."[28]

It is also true that not only white men joined lynch mobs. In exceptional cases, African Americans responded to intraracial rape or murder with lynching, particularly during the 1890s. Some of these vigilantes punished accused thieves; some retaliated against black men who cooperated with white lynch mobs. Most, however, reacted to murder, rape, incest, or assault, as did a black mob in Arkansas in 1892 when it seized and hung a man who was in custody for the rape of his stepdaughter.[29] White southerners sometimes encouraged these lynchings. In rural Louisiana in 1896, white men successfully urged blacks to lynch an African American man accused of the rape of two black children. The white press reported these murders, sometimes approvingly. "Negroes Lynch a Negro" headlined one of several northern accounts of black-on-black lynchings that appeared in 1900, most of which involved assaults on young black girls.[30]

Despite these variations in the patterns of southern legal and extralegal justice, the lynching of black men by white mobs in the South emerged as the archetypal vigilante event, quantitatively and qualitatively more extreme than other forms of lynch law. In Georgia, of sixty-three victims of lynchings who had been accused of rape between 1880 and 1930, sixty were black and three were white. In the same period over 80 percent of those lynched in Virginia were black. Throughout the South white men were only 10 to 20 percent of the victims but predominated as members of lynch mobs. Whites who were lynched were accused of having committed particularly heinous crimes, and they did not suffer the sadistic torture experienced by many black victims. Moreover, the lynching of white, but not black, men provoked public calls for due process of law. Criminal charges against vigilantes were more likely outside the South, whatever the race of the victim, but these charges seldom resulted in arrests and convictions.[31]

In possibly the sole exception to these racial dynamics, in 1888 a group of five African American men in Charleston, South Carolina, lynched a white man for "criminal assault upon a young colored girl" after the child's death as a result of the attack. In response to a petition campaign, the governor pardoned the two black men convicted of the murder. That the victim was a child, and that she died, seemed to justify the passionate mob response by these African American men.[32] For the most part, white men preempted legal processes by killing black men and women for a range of alleged crimes. What gave them the liberty to do so was the racialization of rape.

Although the majority of these murders had nothing to do with sexual assault, southerners justified lynching as a defense of the purity of southern white womanhood. They considered it a form of swift revenge for rape, one that did not require a white woman to endure the personal exposure of courtroom testimony where her chastity might be called into question. Mississippi governor James Vardaman summarized this logic: "The man whose daughter, wife or friend is outraged will not consent to have the victim brought into court before the gaping crowd."[33] As a warning to blacks not to "insult" white women, lynching rested upon the same unwritten law used to defend those who murdered seducers and adulterers in a fit of passion. In 1887 a New Orleans newspaper explained that "the South has chosen to regard the protection of woman as the supremest importance. Hence, its code on this point is severe; its unwritten lynch laws are more so." In this view, lynching was a crime of passion. The people who burned alive a black man in Texas in 1893, one white writer insisted, "were for the time insane," so horrifying was the possibility of a white woman losing her virtue to a black man. A frenzied mob might breach the rule of law with community approval. "No law of God or man can hold back the vengeance of our white men upon such a criminal," Atlanta editor John Templeton Graves wrote, implicitly justifying the random murder of blacks: "We will hang two, three, or four of the Negroes nearest to the crime until the crime is no longer done or even feared in all this southern land we inhabit and love." Even as the proportion of lynchings linked to allegations of sexual assault declined over time, southerners continued to use this inflammatory language.[34]

By framing their terrorist acts as a defense of female purity—"lynching as the remedy for rape," as one southern columnist wrote—white supremacists effectively immobilized much of their opposition and gained broad extralegal powers. When northerners questioned the practice, southerners invoked the defense of womanhood. "The Northern people are not here," wrote "Georgia" to the *New York Times*. "If they were, the first time one of their daughters was assaulted they would head the mob." Similarly, the *Savannah News* commented, "If the north had the black population of the south and as many assaults on white women were committed by black brutes as there are in the south," then lynching would be just as frequent in that region. The rape defense successfully disarmed most critics to leave lynching beyond reproach. As a southern white critic of mob rule pointed out, "It is only because lynching for rape is excused that lynching for any other crime is ever attempted."[35] Invoking sexual assault thus protected vigilantes from prosecution, whoever they targeted, for to question lynching was to risk accusations of endorsing rape.

These views of rape had not always permeated the South. A driving force behind the lynching frenzy was the white press. The *Virginia Register* editorialized, "When a brute in human form criminally assaults a woman speedy death is the only proper penalty." Even when the *St. Louis Globe-Democrat* wrote that "it is always better to let justice be enforced by regular means than to resort to violent measures," the paper excused lynching in the case of "outrages upon white women," explaining that "there is nothing more revolting than an offense of this kind; and it is no wonder that white men hasten to hang black ones who are guilty of it." When the *Los Angeles Times* criticized lynching, southerners labeled the paper a "defender of negro rape fiends." The southern white press insisted that blacks were "responsible for terrible provocations for lynchings." One Texas newspaper proposed that "the best way to cure the evil is to remove the cause."[36]

Along with aggressive editorials, the formulaic news reports of lynching contributed to making the practice familiar and acceptable. Hundreds of stories followed a pattern: Learning that a black man had been accused of or arrested for rape, a mob of vigilantes numbering from dozens to thousands located the suspect, if necessary breaking into a jail before trial or disrupting the transport of the prisoner; sheriffs and other public officials professed that they did their best to fend off the mob before surrendering the prisoner; the hanging or shooting proceeded, and no one was arrested for the murder. At times southern papers competed with each other in establishing the process of vigilante justice and, indeed, in inciting whites to lynch accused black men. The detailed press coverage illustrates well one historian's characterization of lynching narratives as "a kind of acceptable folk pornography in the Bible Belt." Repeated gruesome scenarios helped routinize vigilante violence, including images of black men hanged by mobs and burned at the stake, the female accuser or her husband at times urged to "apply the match." Perhaps the basest comment in the press appeared in the sensationalistic *National Police Gazette,* which titled one lynching report "Another Coon To Roast."[37]

The press seized on the exceptional black mobs to suggest that former slaves defended lynching as a response to rape. In 1882, the *National Police Gazette* reported that a group of "greatly excited" blacks had to be restrained from taking out of jail the assailant in the intraracial rape of an eight-year-old girl, purporting their view to be that "if it had been a white child outraged the prisoner would have been lynched and that they must defend their own race." The same year the *Atlanta Constitution* assured readers, after the rape of the ten-year-old daughter of "a respectable colored man," with the headline "He Will Be Lynched," adding "The Negroes Have the Rope Ready, and are hunting the villain down."[38]

These black rape victims, however, only rarely elicited the kind of press outrage reserved for white women. Fewer than 10 percent of the lynching reports in white newspapers concerned assaults on black women. All but one of these, like the 1882 stories, involved young women. Again, the age distinction is telling, for intraracial rape cases that involved children led to particularly strong reactions. Indeed, the Atlanta paper insinuated that lynching was an appropriate response to the rape of children, regardless of their race. Still, in the exceptional South Carolina lynching of a white man by a black mob, an editorial in the local white paper questioned whether the fourteen-year-old black girl he attacked was "respectable" enough to warrant the defense of her honor.[39]

THE LABELING OF RAPE as "The Negro Crime" and the racialization of lynching emerged within the context of rapid social change in late nineteenth-century America, but the destabilization of the racial hierarchy lay at the heart of the southern panic over rape. The prospect of former slaves exercising their rights as citizens—including economic mobility as free laborers and political influence as voters—triggered strong reactions among whites. The loss of mastery, exacerbated during hard economic times and restated through popular biological notions, contributed to the hardening of earlier cultural associations of race and rape. In this climate, southerners found that accusations of black sexual degradation could justify not only the rape of black women but also the murder and political intimidation of newly enfranchised black men. Only a small proportion of southerners joined lynch mobs, but the broader culture showed widespread support for the mob actions, largely because of the manipulation of sexual fears. Rape thus played a central role in the era of lynching and segregation. Only by confronting the racialization of rape could African Americans hope to implement their rights as citizens.

6

African Americans
Redefine Sexual Violence

In 1895 the radical journalist Ida B. Wells published a pamphlet titled *A Red Record* in which she detailed the horrors of lynching and exposed the contradictory views of rape that supported them. "Humanity abhors the assailant of womanhood, and this charge upon the Negro at once placed him beyond the pale of human sympathy," she explained. Even those who considered lynching a crime remained silent lest others "mistake their plea and deem it an excuse" for sexual assault. Yet this southern sensitivity to women's honor, Wells pointed out, "confines itself entirely to the women who happen to be white." She refused these racial boundaries: "Virtue knows no color line, and the chivalry which depends upon complexion of skin and texture of hair can command no honest respect."[1] Wells's bold rejection of both the racialized assailant and the racialized victim helped mobilize African Americans to protest lynching and to expose the rape of black women by white men.

At the end of the nineteenth century, African American journalists and northern women's club members attempted to undermine the racialization of rape. They challenged the designation of rape as "The Negro Crime," an association that justified lynching as a means of punishing or preventing all interracial sexual relations. Lynching, they began to argue, had little to do with rape; the association was merely a screen to protect the mob from prosecution. Simultaneously, these writers and editors employed a range of arguments to defend the respectability of black women, including an insistence that white men should be held accountable for interracial assaults. African American women took a leading role in rejecting the dual southern myths about black male sexual predators and unchaste black women. At a time when southern black men risked lethal retribution for speaking out politically, black women often operated in subtle political capacities. Taking care neither to offend whites nor to upstage black

104

men, these women forged a sexual politics that acknowledged the intersections of racial and sexual injustice.[2] In contrast to those white reformers who interpreted rape as a problem rooted in gender inequality and women's exclusion from full citizenship, black women viewed sexual assault as a problem rooted in racial injustice that affected both men and women.

Both class and race dynamics shaped this discourse on sexual assault. Members of a small but influential black elite, journalists and activists often used language that differentiated themselves from those African Americans who did not share their social standing or sexual values. Sometimes agreeing with southern whites, they tried to substitute class for race when they condemned poor, rural blacks for committing rape. In a similar move, black club women who claimed their right to sexual respectability often contrasted their own morality with that of lower-class black women. Temperance advocates, for example, tried to align with middle-class white women who shared their mission of uplifting poorer blacks. Yet middle-class African Americans faced great difficulty in attracting white allies by invoking class or gender affinities. For the most part, black club women and journalists waged a racially isolated battle to expose the faults in white constructions of black sexuality and of sexual violence. Their critique would flourish in the next generation, when the migration of southern blacks to northern cities began to provide a stronger political base. In the meantime they initiated protests against the manipulation of sexual fears and the use of sexual assault to enforce white supremacy.

AS LYNCHING ESCALATED in the late nineteenth-century South, black politicians and journalists waged a countercampaign to the sensationalized and often sympathetic coverage of lynching in the white press. They condemned vigilante mobs and questioned the rape accusations used to justify them. A few black editors called for violence against whites in response to lynchings, warning white men that they were ready to avenge the fallen through armed resistance. More moderate voices called for self-improvement in African American communities, suggesting that black crime was the cause of lynching. Outspoken critics like Wells exposed the rape myths at the heart of lynching and explicitly linked the lynching of black men to white men's assaults on black women. As one northern black paper explained, it was time to put a stop "to the debauching of colored women, and the murdering of colored men who dare assert their rights and endeavor to protect their wives and daughters."[3]

Addressing the sexual underpinnings of lynching became increasingly risky, and African American writers had to be cautious. Jesse Duke, who had recently established the Montgomery, Alabama, *Herald,* suggested in 1887 that a consensual relationship had led to the lynching of a young black man accused of rape. The "appreciation of the white Juliet for the colored Romeo," he predicted, would increase as African Americans became "more intelligent and refined." For expressing these views Duke had to leave town to escape lynching at the hands of a mob. While northern black editors supported Duke, opinions in the southern black press were mixed, with some writers (like some local black leaders) distancing themselves from his words. A decade later, North Carolina newspaper editor Alexander Manly similarly suggested an alternative scenario to claims that lynching responded to rape: White women were attracted to black men, he explained, but when "the white women's infatuation or the man's boldness" called attention to the consensual union, "the man is lynched for rape." Manly went further by issuing a warning to white men to desist from their assaults on black women in terms that implied sexual revenge: "Don't think ever that your women will remain pure while you are debauching ours." In response, white mobs burned Manly's press during a violent uprising that left much of the black leadership of Wilmington, North Carolina, either dead or in exile.[4]

The most powerful and sustained critique of lynching came from Ida B. Wells, whose rejection of the rape justification for lynching led to her exile from the South in 1892. Born into slavery a few years before emancipation and largely self-educated, Wells broke with contemporary reporting techniques to detail the injustice and incivility of lynching, both quantitatively and qualitatively. Her writings and speeches inspired the first national anti-lynching movement. Like Dukes before her and Manly after, Wells recognized the role of rape charges in undermining African American rights. She exposed the fallacy that vigilantes killed black men to avenge the rape of white women. Lynching, she warned, served to "stamp us a race of rapists and desperadoes." By portraying black men as sexually uncontrollable and thus "incapable of self-government," whites could justify the denial of suffrage and civil rights to African Americans. Wells was not able to end mob murders or to undercut southern white attitudes, but her campaign helped make lynching symbolic of the escalating racial injustice of the era.[5]

Wells was already an activist when lynching escalated. As a young woman she had resisted physically when denied her seat in a first-class railway car, biting the hand of the white conductor who tried to remove her. Although she successfully sued the railroad company over the segregated seating, the ruling was later overturned. While she never publicly condoned lynching, Wells wrote in her diary in 1887 that if a man had really taken "a woman's reputation . . . one is strongly tempted to say his killing was justifiable." Then in 1892, when she was editing a newspaper in Memphis, Tennessee, a white mob lynched several black businessmen who were her close friends. Their grocery store had competed with a nearby white business, and during a brawl between owners several white men had been shot. The murdered black men, she later wrote, "had committed no crime against white women." But lynching gave an "excuse to get rid of negroes who were acquiring wealth and property," and it served to "keep the race terrorized." In protest, Wells urged African Americans to boycott white businesses or relocate outside of the South.[6]

The editorial that Wells published infuriated local whites, who attacked her press and threatened her life. Turning the white view of interracial sex on its head, she wrote, "Nobody in this section of the country believes the old thread bare lie that Negro men rape white women. If Southern white men are not careful, they will over-reach themselves and public sentiment will have a reaction; a conclusion will then be reached which will be very damaging to the moral reputation of their women." Wells referred to white women who had clandestine interracial unions and then redefined these relations as rape. Her acknowledgment of consensual unions incited death threats against Wells, who was traveling at the time and could not return to the South. As the *New York Times* later put it, she became "a refugee because she had imputed unchastity to the victims of negro outrages in the South."[7]

Banished to the North, Wells proceeded to initiate a systematic study of lynching. She collected each reported episode, culling stories from black newspapers and statistics from the *Chicago Tribune,* the white paper that had begun compiling data on lynching in 1882. Wells noted the alleged causes as well as the frequent revelations of false accusations of rape. To give one of her many examples, she wrote about the discovery by a white reporter that

the Afro-American who was lynched in Chestertown, Md., in May for assault on a white girl was innocent; that the deed was done by a white man who had since disappeared. The girl herself maintained that her assailant was a white man. When that poor Afro-American was murdered, the whites excused their refusal of a trial on the ground that they wished to spare the white girl the mortification of having to testify in court.[8]

In a crusade to expose the myth of the black rapist, Wells published her results in newspapers, magazines, pamphlets, and books. She lectured throughout the North and in England and inspired others to hold the nation responsible for the terrorism of lynching in the South. Her reporting, the eminent black activist Frederick Douglass observed, was "a revelation of existing conditions" that showed that lynching had nothing to do with any "increased lasciviousness on the part of Negroes." Rather, Wells proposed, racial double standards embodied in southern law and culture created myths about black rapists. When white men were accused of sexual assault, they could, and usually did, employ some variation of the consent defense by claiming that their accusers had been willing partners. But the emerging views of white women as unequivocally undesiring of interracial sex meant that black men could never invoke consent. Whether they had assaulted a white woman, engaged in a consensual interracial union, or—more typically, as Wells argued—constituted an economic or political threat to white supremacy, impugning white female purity gave lynch mobs free rein.[9]

Wells stood out as the most radical critic of lynching for her thorough rejection of the rape justification and her calls for black self-defense ("a Winchester rifle should have a place of honor in every black home," she wrote, to be used "for that protection which the law refused to give"). Not all black writers agreed with her. The former abolitionist, temperance advocate, and suffragist Frances Ellen Watkins Harper told a reporter from a white newspaper that she did "not approve of Miss Wells' vehemence in dealing with the subject." Harper did not "believe lynchings of negroes who assault girls are brought about alone by the color of the criminals," noting that some white men had also "had summary punishment meted out to them."[10] The African American press usually took a far more cautious stance than did Wells. Black journalists in the late nineteenth century took pains to condemn rape with an almost formulaic acknowledgment that it was a "beastly" act regardless of the race of the assailant. One editorial in the *Savannah Tribune* commented almost sympathetically about a lynching in which a "colored man" helped capture the "Negro fiends" who had been accused of assaulting a white woman while threatening her husband with a gun. In 1897, when Dr. M. A. Majors commented on the torturous lynching of Henry Smith for the alleged rape and murder of a three-year-old white girl in Paris, Texas, he insisted that both the lynchers and the lynched were outlaws. Majors condemned "the damnable, nefarious and blighting outrage of rape upon the female sex of any race."[11]

Like Majors, other black writers called for severe punishment for sexual assault. "No violator of the chastity of women, white or colored, should ever be allowed to run at large," the manager of a black paper wrote. "His place is on the gallows or in prison for life." The "Negro race condemns the crime of rape, as much as the white people do," explained another black journalist. Whatever the race, he continued, "no guilty man should be allowed to escape." The salient point here was guilt. The problem was that black men did not have the opportunity to prove their innocence of what all agreed was a terrible crime. As a black Floridian wrote to the *Christian Recorder* in 1897, "there is nothing lower than rape," adding that when a black man "pleads not guilty to such a low act, then give him a trial and let him prove himself innocent if he can."[12] By endorsing severe but legal punishment for rape, the black press aligned with white critics of rape and tried to undercut one set of arguments in favor of lynching.

Such forceful denunciations of black rapists seemed to be directed as much at white as at black audiences. Writing in the magazine of the Congregationalist Church, Tuskegee Institute founder Booker T. Washington opened his discussion of lynch law by stating clearly, "I have not the slightest sympathy with any one who commits, or attempts to commit, an outrage upon the person of a woman." He, too, believed that "when the truth of such a crime is ascertained . . . death in a lawful manner should follow." A black clergyman from Mississippi wrote a letter to a white newspaper to condemn the rapes "committed by individual members of the negro race." If white men would "take the time to read negro journals and converse with negro leaders," he continued, they would learn that "the negro is outspoken in denouncing the rapist and all other classes of law-breakers."[13]

A number of black critics of lynching tried to align themselves with whites when they drew class distinctions between educated race leaders and illiterate black masses. Class, rather than race, some writers insisted, best explained these criminals. Their views echoed those of educated African Americans who adopted a white middle-class definition of manhood in order to obtain political rights. The black press contrasted the beastly men who assaulted women and the better sort of blacks who condemned them. "A few brutes among us who may attempt to rob, steal, or rape, are no more to us than the same classes are to others," explained one writer, who went on to request that "a jury, duly sworn, be allowed to pass upon the guilt or innocence of all criminals or supposed criminals, be they black or white." In a letter to the editor of the *Savannah Tribune,* Thomas B. Lillard argued that "the rapist is no more to be found among the intelligent and peaceful Negro than among the same class of any other citizens." At the same time Lillard urged "the colored ministers of Savannah" to condemn rape severely in order to "reach the lower stratas of the race from which comes this class of criminals."[14]

A variation on the appeal to class appeared in the views of Mary Church Terrell, a leader of the National Association of Colored Women. Terrell identified with the better-educated members of her race, who distanced themselves from poor, rural southern blacks. Writing for a white audience, she pointed out that the educated blacks whom southerners often ridiculed for their class aspirations where not the ones who committed rape. Rather, she held, the "illiterate negroes" whom southerners lauded for their docility and loyalty as "what a really good negro should be" were, Terrell insisted, "the only ones contributing largely to the criminal class." The "best negroes," Terrell assured whites, would never sympathize with a rapist. While more moderate writers like Terrell and Washington left standing the southern assumption that some black men posed an ongoing sexual threat to white women, they also suggested that educational and other uplift activities for rural blacks would reduce the risk of rape. In Washington's terms, the remedy for lynching was "Christian education for the white man and the black man." Both, he implied, were capable of threatening women sexually.[15]

However cautious the black press may have been in assuring whites that rape was an abominable act, the overriding message was that lynching was equally problematic. "We abhor and condemn mob law and lynchers as we do the rapist," a typical report stated in 1897. Both kinds of criminals were "monsters" who deserved the death penalty. Like their white counterparts, black papers ran articles describing gruesome burnings and mutilations of black men that dwelled on the suffering of the victims as they died. Unlike white papers, however, these accounts emphasized the fact that white men got away with murder when they lynched blacks. One headline in the *Savannah Tribune* clearly illustrated this theme: "Murderers Burn the Body."[16]

At a time when southern whites portrayed black men as primitive rapists, the critics of lynching emphasized the barbarism of mobs that burned and tortured black victims. According to the *Florida Sentinel,* lynching called into question "the boasted civilization of this country." After a mob lynched two black men who were on trial for rape in 1896, the *Savannah Tribune* began with the formulaic acknowledgment that the crime of rape was one of the "most detestable known in the law of civilization." Still, though, it provided no excuse for "people making barbarians of themselves" rather than letting the law take its course.[17]

Some white southerners agreed that lynch mobs were barbaric, undermined the rule of law, and sacrificed the reputation of the South. Georgia passed an anti-lynching bill in 1893, as did several other southern and northern states, but local tolerance for the mob made it hard to enforce these laws. In 1895 Governor William Atkinson, an opponent of mob rule, called on the Georgia legislature to empower him to remove from office any law enforcement officers who failed to prevent lynchings. The following year Atkinson offered a reward of five hundred dollars each for the capture of the white men who hanged and shot two black men being tried for rape. "Oh! For a thousand such men as Governor Atkinson," the *Savannah Tribune* exclaimed. As during Reconstruction, some African Americans turned to northern allies to secure protection. In 1894, inspired by Ida B. Wells, New Hampshire representative Henry W. Blair introduced a bill into Congress that would authorize a federal investigation into all attempts over the prior decade at "unlawful violence" in response to "alleged assaults by males upon females." Members of the Woman's Loyal Union of New York and Brooklyn and the Woman's Era Club of Boston were "energetically pushing" petitions in support of the bill.[18] Though unsuccessful, the effort pointed toward later strategies that involved northern pressure and called for federal intervention.

Short of legal redress, a key to undermining the widespread support for vigilante mobs was the project of dismantling the labeling of rape as "the Negro crime." Ida B. Wells initiated a critique by tabulating the *Chicago Tribune* reports of lynchings between 1884 and 1892 to show that "only *one-third* of the 728 victims to mobs have been *charged* with rape, to say nothing of those of that one-third who were innocent of the charge." Most lynchings responded to accusations of murder, not rape. When the Tuskegee Institute began to issue semiannual reports on lynchings, black newspapers published the results and repeatedly observed that only a minority of the episodes involved rape accusations. Other black leaders also invoked the data, as did Mary Church Terrell, who attempted to refute white writers who blamed lynching on rape. "In the first place," Terrell began, "it is a great mistake to suppose that rape is the real cause of lynching in the South." She cited the fact that fewer than one-quarter of lynchings involved rape accusations.[19]

Critics also sought to identify the deeper springs that gave rise to lynching. Wells pointed to the social and political control intended by the threat of the mob. In some cases, she noted, blacks were "lynched because they were saucy" to white people, a clear signal that survival in the Jim Crow South required racial deference. At times black newspapers repeated this complaint, identifying the South's "fad" for the "cry of 'rape' when it is deemed desirable to put offensive Negroes out of the way." Terrell attributed lynching to regional lawlessness and the race hatred that had been directed at former slaves. These same forces, she recognized, underlay "the disfranchisement acts, the Jim Crow Car laws, and the new slavery called 'peonage.' "[20]

Terrell's reference to the indebtedness of southern tenant farmers and sharecroppers hinted at the economic intent of linking rape and lynching. Aside from the murder of individual competitors, like the Memphis grocers, some white politicians tried to exploit the fear of sexual assault to keep former slaves and their children in menial jobs. They invoked the image of the black rapist, for instance, in debates about state funding for black schools. A member of the Alabama House of Representatives from Tuskegee tried to block an appropriation to build a black school in Montgomery by accusing Booker T. Washington of producing students who had been "legally hanged for rape." His logic implied that education empowered black men to assert their claims to white women. Although the bill passed by a narrow two-vote margin, the opposition illustrated the way sexual fears could be manipulated to restrict the mobility of southern blacks and the broader usage of rape as a political tool during the lynching era.[21]

African American writers pointed out another political function of the association of race and rape: the protection it afforded white men who committed rape. When a white writer insisted that lynching would continue until "black brutes learn to stop committing rape," the *Savannah Tribune* parsed the statement for its racial insinuations: "We surmise from this sentence that a white man can commit rape to his heart's content and no attention will be paid him, but that it is certain death to a Negro to do so." In a letter to Booker T. Washington written in 1903, the African American novelist Charles Chesnutt noted that given the "hysterical" focus on black rapists, "one would almost be inclined to believe that rape committed by a white man upon a white woman was scarcely any offense at all in comparison."[22] Their comments anticipated a strategy that would flourish in the early twentieth century, when the black press openly publicized sexual assaults committed by white men.

In the late nineteenth century, some southern white women did call attention to sexual assaults committed by white men, especially if the victims were young girls. And occasionally an exceptionally brutal lynching—as when Georgians tortured Sam Hose and burned him alive in 1899—provoked a few white women to speak out against the "barbarism" of the mob. Eliza E. Mell called on other white club women in Georgia to "rise up in indignant protest" and bring "woman's influence" to bear on ending "such brutal violence." But the organized white women's movement did not share African Americans' sense of urgency about lynching. Both southern and northern white women's clubs opposed lynching because it circumvented the law, but their members rarely questioned the guilt of accused black men. One spokeswoman for the Georgia Women's Federation gave a tepid critique of lynching on the grounds that it did not prevent rape. The mob, she complained, made martyrs of criminals; better that the law provide "some sure, dreaded physical punishment" as a deterrent to rape. Nor were northern women more responsive. Although the liberal magazine *The Nation* suggested in 1893 that as women sought greater legal rights for their sex they would be "the last to ask for the services of roving mobs for their protection against any form of outrage," the organized suffrage movement did not join the African American protest against lynching.[23]

Inspired largely by Ida B. Wells, critiques of lynching by both women and men articulated an alternative to the white supremacist analysis of rape. Wells took the most radical stance, acknowledging consensual interracial sexual relations, issuing unconditional condemnations of lynching, and endorsing direct action such as boycotts and self-defense. Moderate reformers such as Mary Church Terrell and many black male journalists often drew class distinctions between respectable and criminal elements in the black community when they spoke out against both rape and lynching. Over time the black press would embrace Wells's strategy of undermining the rape defense used to justify the crime of lynching. In the process of condemning lynching, all of these writers highlighted white men's crimes, whether as sexual assailants or as vigilantes.

IN THE PROCESS of defending black men accused of rape, African American women addressed their own sexual vulnerability. In 1886 Ida B.

Wells deplored the blanket accusations of immorality that denied the accomplishments of those black "mothers, wives and maidens who have attained a true, noble, and refining womanhood." She recognized that countering sexually demeaning images was central to the African American quest to be included among the "civilized races."[24] Wells's insight into the connection between racial status and female virtue makes sense in the context of nineteenth-century American beliefs that a virtuous citizenry required a virtuous womanhood. Because this ideal enabled middle-class women to perform as citizens even when they could not participate fully in politics, the disregard for African American women's virtue served to reinforce the secondary status of their race.

After emancipation, southern black women had very limited success in defending themselves from white men, especially as the rise of lynching and Jim Crow segregation disempowered their race. Some of them adopted a "politics of silence" about rape, lest any discussion of sexuality contribute to negative depictions of their morality.[25] In northern states, though, middle-class black women began to counteract the pervasive stereotypes of promiscuity that erased their ability to refuse sexual consent. Inspired by Ida B. Wells, they insisted that African American women could be as virtuous as white women. Their analysis interwove gender-specific concerns about the costs of sexual violence to women with a vision of uplifting the status of the race. Like journalists, they often drew distinctions between the respectable black middle class and those lower-class black women whose sexual behavior, they suggested, discredited the race.

This dialogue about black women's sexuality could be couched in rather discrete language. When educator Anna Julia Cooper expressed her concern in *A Voice from the South* (1892), she referred to the promising "Colored Girls of the South" who lived "in the midst of pitfalls and snares, waylaid by the lower classes of white men." Speaking at the 1893 Columbia Exposition in Chicago, Cooper told of the "painful, patient and silent toil of mothers to gain a fee simple title to the bodies of their daughters." In plainer words, she was acknowledging that white men raped black women with impunity. Writing anonymously, one African American woman told the readers of a white magazine that "few colored girls reach the age of sixteen without receiving advances." Black writers such as Pauline Hopkins wove moral tales about the legacies of rape into their fiction. One backstory in Hopkins's 1899 novel *Contending Forces* involved a rape that led to the birth of a mixed-race child whose origins were then kept secret. Hopkins did not directly portray rape, but she used a prolonged description of the whipping of the black female protagonist as a displaced representation of sexual assault. While subtle, these references to rape nonetheless exposed the personal consequences of violence for black women.[26]

The black women's club movement provided a major forum for directly addressing the quest for sexual respectability. In the 1890s, in parallel with the racially exclusive white women's club movement, middle-class black women established dozens of civic groups, including the Ida B. Wells Club in Chicago and the New Era Club in Boston. Their members pledged to address not only women's issues such as suffrage but also race problems such as lynching and the particular liabilities faced by African American women. The initial impetus for the founding of a national federation of black women's clubs was the damaging, pervasive cultural stereotype of black female immorality. In 1895 Josephine St. Pierre Ruffin, president of the New Era Club, issued a call for a national conference, in part to refute a white journalist's "denouncement of the morality of the colored women of America." In a defense of lynching, J. W. Jacks had compared the value of white women's chastity (worthy of a man's life) to that of black women, who so lacked sexual virtue, he believed, that they could be easily seduced.[27] Ruffin circulated Jacks's comments to women's clubs around the country, urging them to respond and calling them together in a national union.

From its origins, the group that became the National Association of Colored Women (NACW) confronted the stereotypes that made black women more vulnerable to sexual assault and impeded their coalition with white women. "Year after year," Ruffin lamented, "southern women have protested against the admission of colored women into any national organization on the ground of the immorality of these women." One reason to create a national women's organization, Mary Church Terrell told members at the first conference of the NACW, was to "set in motion influences that shall stop the ravages made by practices that sap our strength, and preclude the possibility of advancement."[28] Her words clearly referred to assaults on women, but they also alluded to the diminution of the race by women's having to bear the costs of both rape and tarnished reputations.

Members of African American women's clubs often combined their critique of lynching with a condemnation of white men's sexual abuse of black women. In doing so they expanded the tentative discourse on rape that had emerged within the predominantly white moral reform and women's rights movements at midcentury, both of which had largely ignored the plight of black victims of rape. In her 1904 article "Lynching from a Negro's Point of View," Terrell expressed amazement at the false charge that the crime of rape characterized her race. "Throughout their entire period of bondage," she wrote in a white magazine, the *North American Review*, "colored women were debauched by their masters. From the day they were liberated to the present time, prepossessing young colored girls have been considered the rightful prey of white gentlemen in the South, and they have been protected neither by public sentiment nor by law." Pauline Hopkins exposed the hypocrisy of southern white men claiming to protect women's purity, given their own complicity in rape, when she indicted *"The men who created the mulatto race, who recruit its ranks year after year by the very means which they invoked lynch law to suppress."*[29]

Like the lynching critiques that distinguished between black criminals and law-abiding black citizens, so too club women sometimes defended the virtue of elites at the expense of poorer black women. When they insisted on their moral equality with whites, they usually meant educated, middle-class white women. Reacting to the statements of white women that denied black women's virtue, Sylvanie Francaz Williams insisted that "educated virtuous colored women" were "trying to lift their race out of the mire of sin, away from the temptation which allures them onward through the immorality of the superior race." Along with blaming immorality on whites, Williams also blamed poverty, and not simply race, for whatever sinful behaviors that rural southern blacks adopted. Reiterating the theme of class, she compared the brutalization of the "Negro" to that of poor whites in England and around the world.[30]

Ida B. Wells drew some class distinctions as well. In her 1886 letter to white newspaper editor G. P. M. Turner she explained that she wrote in the name of "the virtuous colored women of this city." Her wording could imply that not all black women fell into that category. Those who did, Wells suggested, certainly deserved the privileges of respectability, including the right to withhold consent to unwanted sexual relations. In another iteration of the theme, she repeated her insistence that "Virtue knows no color line" when she condemned the acquittal of several white men who had been accused of raping a "respectable colored girl" in Baltimore. Again, while her intent was no doubt to include African Americans within the realm of the respectable, her language could suggest that not all black girls qualified. "Our race is no exception to the rest of humanity, in its susceptibility to weakness," Wells acknowledged. She added pointedly, though, that even elite whites could behave badly. Her larger theme was that if the members of the white race would simply grant to blacks the capacity for morality, it would be "a great incentive to good morals" for those who might fall prey to temptation.[31]

Black journalists and women's club members agreed that white men deserved most of the blame for the sexual degradation of women of their race. Since the 1860s the African American press had been exposing "insults" to black women, as did the *Christian Recorder* in a complaint that even in the tolerant setting of Philadelphia, "the very lowest and most vulgar language that ever any human being uttered, is addressed to our wives and daughters." Black papers carried stories of white men accosting black women on steamer ships or in railroad cars, often editorializing about the double standard of justice that allowed these white men to escape the fate of black men accused of sexual assault. When a court dismissed charges of attempted rape against two white men who had repeatedly tried to enter the railway berth of Mrs. Moses S. Jones, the *Savannah Tribune* drew this analogy: "When we think how any Negro who is just suspected of fooling with a white woman, is summarily delt [*sic*] with and to see these fellows given their freedom, it galls us deeply." Another writer advised black women that "every precaution should be taken" when they traveled, including having male kin accompany them in order "to witness any attack." The same journalist advised husbands to teach their wives to use firearms, in case a "scoundrel" of any race threatened their honor.[32]

Even more than the black press, African American women activists defied contemporary sexual taboos by redefining rape to include assaults on black women by white men. In her political attacks on lynching, Ida B. Wells first exposed the hypocrisy of white concern about female purity by detailing cases of white men who got away with the rape of black women and girls. In *Southern Horrors* (1892), she condemned a series of judicial decisions, including the acquittal of three white ruffians who had attacked a "young Afro-American girl, while out walking with a young man of her own race"; the light sentences or release of white men who "outraged" black girls; and the refusal of grand juries to indict white men for rape. Why, Wells asked rhetorically, did lynch mobs not target these rapists? To southerners who invoked chivalry as a motive for lynching, Wells insisted, "True chivalry respects all womanhood."[33]

In *A Red Record* (1895) Wells elaborated on the double standard of justice that rested on the defamation of the character of black women. A South Carolina writer had repeated indignantly the claim that white men who assaulted black women were not comparable to black men who assaulted

white women "because the colored woman had no finer feelings nor virtue to be outraged!" Wells pointed out that "colored women have always
had far more reason to complain of white men in this respect than ever
white women have had of Negroes." Wells was more outspoken than
most, but other northern black club women also publicized the impunity
with which white men raped black women in fairly blunt terms. In 1894
Josephine Ruffin's daughter, Florida Ruffin Ridley, wrote in the movement's journal, the *Woman's Era,* that "we read with horror of two different colored girls who have recently been horribly assaulted by white men
in the south. We should regret any lynchings of the offenders by black
men, but we shall not have occasion," she added, lamenting that "should
these offenders receive any punishment at all it will be a marvel." Educator and club woman Nannie Burroughs directly addressed white hypocrisy about rape in a pamphlet in which she exhorted white men to stop
"making excursions into the Negro race, depositing white offspring and
then crying out against social equality."[34]

Club women differed in their political rhetoric and their willingness to
antagonize whites, but most agreed on the importance of defending the
respectability of black women. As Jim Crow segregation engulfed the
South, endorsed by the Supreme Court decision in *Plessy v. Ferguson*
(1896), club women revived Reconstruction protests over the particular
hardship they faced in having to travel in second-class railway cars. In
these settings, they explained, "the womanhood of the race" faced "every
outrage and insult." The moderate reformer Margaret Murray Washington, whose husband Booker T. Washington led the Tuskegee Institute,
spearheaded a campaign to repeal separate car laws in the name of protecting black women's honor.[35]

Other middle-class club women invoked history and culture to refute
charges that the women of their race lacked innate virtue. Any immorality,
they held, had been forced upon them by white men. Educator and social
reformer Addie Hunton defended "Negro Womanhood" by recalling "an
almost unmentionable history" of "compulsory immorality" under slavery. That legacy explained in part the moral failings of vulnerable black
women. "It is not strange," she wrote, "that those whose prey she had
been for so long should have followed her into her new environments."
While white men had "used cruel force when it was their right," Hunton
believed, they now used more subtle forms of seduction to defeat the morality of the black woman by seeking "to subvert her with glittering bau-
bles." Hunton admitted that poverty, lack of education, and the low

wages they earned may in fact have led some women astray. She assured her readers, however, that the majority of black women were establishing virtuous Christian homes and uplifting others through education.[36]

A range of club women recognized the sexual dangers faced by wage-earning black women and sought protective measures. One northerner went south to expose the sexual exploitation of young black women by employment agencies. NACW member Fannie Barrier Williams reported that she frequently received letters from "the still unprotected colored women of the South" asking her help placing their daughters in jobs "to save them from going into the homes of the South as servants, as there is nothing to save them from dishonor and degradation." Like the antebellum moral reformers who had established refuges for women, African American club women sought to aid young rural migrants who did leave the South. Northern clubs provided social services and established residences for women arriving in cities, such as the Phyllis Wheatley Home in Chicago and the White Rose Mission in New York. NACW members also sought racial uplift through temperance and education, aligning at times with the Woman's Christian Temperance Union and the broader social purity movement. Like white groups, black women's clubs resolved to "require the same standard of morality for men as for women," calling on mothers to "teach their sons social purity as well as their daughters."[37]

One subject stands out for its absence in black women's articulation of their vulnerability—intraracial rape. By the end of the nineteenth century, their efforts to redefine rape focused almost entirely on naming white men as assailants and black women as unwilling victims. Given white panic about the black male rapist, it is not surprising that middle-class black women who defended men of their race from rape charges would be reluctant to include them in their critique of male behavior. Their protective stance constituted a "culture of dissemblance" that could silence those assaulted or those concerned about rape.[38] In a sense, both white and black middle-class women who publicly condemned rape in the nineteenth century agreed that white men should be held accountable. They disagreed, however, over black men's culpability, a strategic difference that impeded alliance across race lines.

BECAUSE BLACK CLUB WOMEN KNEW that speaking only to their own communities would not deter rape or lynching, they envisioned a role for white women. In contrast to Ida B. Wells, whose editorials and pamphlets confronted whites with the truths about lynching, many club women employed a milder strategy of moral suasion in an attempt to win white allies. They implored white social purity activists to acknowledge the sexual vulnerability of black women. One club member explained in 1897, "We need their assistance in combating the public opinion and laws that degrade our womanhood." They also needed quite practical aid. NACW officer Frances Ellen Watkins Harper hinted at white women's complicity in the degradation of black women in her poem, "A Double Standard," in which a female servant has been seduced and abandoned by a man's wiles. The servant complains that the world brands her with shame yet still honors him, and directs her voice at the female kin of her seducer: "Within your homes you press the hand / That led me down to hell."[39] White women could try to prevent the sexual exploitation by male kin in the homes in which black domestic servants worked.

Black club women tried to engage white women in the common mission of undermining white men's sexual privileges by appealing to both gender and class affinities. They argued that white women who ignored crimes against black women, or forgave the men who committed them, were colluding in protecting these men from being prosecuted for rape, with consequences for all women. Nannie Burroughs wrote that concealing "Anglo-Saxon vice" helped keep the white race "on the throne of virtue," but at the same time it made white women vulnerable. Burroughs posed the question more pointedly than some: "Why is it that we do not 'hear' of the white men of the United States committing outrages upon white or black women?" She called on white women to break their own silence about sexual assault: "Let the thousands of white women whose mouths are shut by pride speak out."[40]

Although black club women urged their white counterparts in the women's movement to publicly oppose the lynching of black men and the rape of black or white women, few white women answered Nannie Burroughs's call. The post–Civil War split among women's rights advocates over the exclusion of woman suffrage in the Fifteenth Amendment had left a deep scar. When the National American Woman Suffrage Association (NAWSA) reunited the two branches in 1890, few remnants of the antebellum interracial alliances among abolitionists remained and theories of white racial superiority flourished. NAWSA officials played to the racial prejudices of southern members to keep them in the fold, reinforcing these conflicts. Other reform organizations, like most American institutions, remained racially segregated. Black women joined the Women's

Christian Temperance Union (WCTU), and WCTU president Frances E. Willard professed that she would welcome black women in the same societies as white women, but white southern members would not accept mixed-race chapters. Willard then justified the separate racial organization of the WCTU on the grounds that "coloured women, as a class, much prefer to affiliate with those of their own race."[41] An interracial anti-lynching movement would not emerge for another generation.

The realignment of southern politics at the end of the century, when the specter of lynching contributed to disfranchisement and segregation, made interracial coalitions unlikely. The few white women who opposed lynching tended to accept southern myths about rape. One prominent southern suffragist who argued that vigilantes did not effectively deter rape offered the alternative of legally castrating rapists. Northern suffragist Alice Stone Blackwell (the daughter of Lucy Stone and Henry Blackwell) disagreed on this remedy, pointing out that most lynchings were not even in response to rape. Yet Blackwell still predicted that "when women have a voice in making the laws," they would likely enact castration for rapists "of whatever race or nationality." Occasionally a white southern woman did empathize with black women's vulnerability. Quaker educator Martha Schofield played to class sympathies when she told a Purity Congress in 1895 that white women "cannot conceive the feelings of modest, retiring, educated and refined colored women who know they are never safe from the insults of white men," even men from respectable families. As much as white women tried to uplift "colored women," Schofield advised, they should turn their attention to educating boys so that they would learn "to respect *all women*." Hers was a rare voice, however, in its attention to white men's responsibility for the rape of black women.[42]

The public conflict between Ida B. Wells and WCTU president Frances E. Willard exemplified these racial tensions. Wells wanted white reformers such as Willard to condemn without equivocation not only lynching but also the false charges of rape that fueled vigilantism. Yet when Willard addressed the WCTU in 1893, she reinforced the southern rape myth by claiming that intoxicated black men posed a threat to the safety of womanhood. Willard later referred to lynched men as "devourers of women and children" and, of particular irritation to Wells, wrote that it was unfair that illiterate southern blacks, whom she depicted as frequenting grog shops and saloons, "should be entrusted with the ballot." At the organization's 1894 conference, Ida B. Wells and sympathetic WCTU members failed in their effort to pass a strong anti-lynching resolution. Instead, the

WCTU condemned lawless acts but at the same time incorporated the southern defensive rhetoric by referring to "the unspeakable outrages which have so often provoked such lawlessness."[43]

When she tried to respond to Wells's call to condemn the rape of black women, Willard equivocated. In one address she amended an earlier statement about "the nameless outrages perpetrated upon white women and little girls" to add that "the immoralities of white men in their relations with colored women are the source of intolerable race prejudice and hatred." Despite her use of the present tense, Willard went on to claim that the curse of attacks on "the helpless bondwoman" had "largely ceased" in the South. Her nod to the respectability of black men and the vices of white men emphasized temperance but left the rape fears in place. "An average colored man when sober is loyal to the purity of white women," Willard told the 1894 national convention, continuing that "under the influence of intoxicating liquors . . . the ignorant and vicious, whether white or black, are most dangerous characters."[44] Willard's comments echoed earlier black clergy who pointed to habits of class, rather than to race, as the source of sexual violence. But they did not constitute the condemnation of lynching that Wells sought.

Black club women felt the need to distinguish between attitudes toward temperance and lynching, two social problems that Willard had conflated by blaming rape on drunkenness. While lecturing in England, Wells had learned that British women regarded Willard highly for her temperance campaign and they assumed that she would be an ally in the anti-lynching campaign. Wells corrected that view and publicly chastised Willard for her collusion in the construction of the myth of the black male rapist, as well as for maintaining a racially segregated temperance organization. In response, Willard attacked the credibility of Wells's statements about consensual unions of black men and white women. African American women's clubs implicitly defended Wells when they, too, targeted Willard, calling her an apologist for lynching (even as they politely applauded her temperance work).[45]

Both Willard and Wells advocated temperance and formally opposed lynching, but the distinctive sexual politics of black and white women underlay the conflict between these two reformers. Willard feared for the safety of white women in the South, but she did not extend her critique of rape to black victims and she failed to question the validity of southern rape charges against black men. Refusing to accept the possibility of consensual unions across race lines, she attributed all interracial sexual relations to male violence. In contrast, Wells believed that southern white women could not only consent to interracial sexual unions but could also seduce and then betray black men when they accused their lovers of rape.[46]

While Wells reversed the dominant contrast between black promiscuity and white innocence, her depiction of interracial unions had to overlook both the will of some black women and the vulnerability of some white women. Consider her statement that "the miscegenation laws of the South only operate against the legitimate union of the races; they leave the white man free to seduce all the colored girls he can, but it is death to the colored man who yields to the force and advances of a similar attraction in white women."[47] In this formulation, white men and women are seducers, black men and women their victims. White men did in fact "seduce" black women, and white women "seduced" black men. But to make this case Wells had to ignore forms of consensual interracial sex. Nor did Wells or most of her colleagues draw attention to the possibility of coercive intraracial sex among blacks. This was an understandable political strategy at the time, but it perpetuated the masking of black-on-black rape.

The defense of African American womanhood in the late nineteenth century overlapped with both white female and black male political analyses of rape. Like their white counterparts, black female reformers simultaneously sought justice and protection when they named sexual assault as an affront to their personhood. Like their male allies in defense of their race, black women activists looked beyond the racial construction of rape when they condemned lynching itself as a form of outrage and recognized that the myth of "the Negro crime" served to preserve the sexual prerogatives of white men. But African American women wrote about rape and lynching from a distinctively gendered as well as racial perspective. They viewed rape from the intersection of their identities, as women and as black Americans. In their writing and speaking, women such as Frances Ellen Watkins Harper, Pauline Hopkins, Mary Church Terrell, Ida B. Wells and others made public both the trauma of assault and the need to claim for their race the moral capacities for citizenship.[48]

THE SOUTHERN WHITE DISCOURSE on rape was only one of the means of enforcing white supremacy and symbolizing black dispossession during the Jim Crow era. Economic practices such as sharecropping, the lack of state support for black education, and the denial of civil rights and suffrage all operated simultaneously to achieve that racial hierarchy. Yet rape was not simply another item in this list, for it had implications for each of these practices. Denying the virtue of black women and demonizing black men as sexual threats to white women provided powerful ideological support for these southern economic and political practices, while lynching effectively suppressed the possibility of widespread protests against them.

Rape was deeply constitutive of the broad racial discourse that denied black manhood and citizenship, but it was a particular affront to black women. For all of these reasons, a range of critics tried to provide a counter-discourse on rape. In the late nineteenth century the black press and club women often privileged class in an effort to diminish the racialization of rape. By the end of the century they increasingly pointed to legal double standards and the culpability of white men. At a time when their ability to exercise formal political power was diminishing, African Americans employed a variety of rhetorical strategies to resist the southern white construction of rape. They were unable to make much headway in undermining support for lynching, which grew ever more vicious. Only in the next generation, with the expansion of a northern black public sphere, would the groundwork laid by Ida B. Wells, the black press, and the black women's clubs begin to persuade some white Americans of the injustice of lynching and the respectability of black women.

7

Raising the Age of Consent

In a short opinion issued in 1894 by the Supreme Court of Georgia, Justice T. J. Simmons reversed the conviction of a man named Pounds who had been tried for the rape of "a female between the ages of ten and eleven years." The issue at stake was not whether Mr. Pounds (presumably a white man) had sexual relations with the girl, for the court acknowledged that "it appeared that sexual intercourse was accomplished." Rather, the question to be decided at the appellate level was "whether the female was in fact capable of consenting to the act or not." At the time, the Georgia rape statute set the age below which a female could not consent to sex at ten years. The child was just over that threshold, but the jury had been instructed that if "they believed from her age and appearance that she was incapable of consenting," they could still convict. Pounds's attorney complained that the jury should also have been told that they could have acquitted him "if they believed she was capable of consenting and did actually consent." Justice Simmons agreed, ordering a new trial. Equally telling, though, was another complaint in the appeal, which suggested that not all Georgians were comfortable with the low age of consent in their state. During his concluding argument to the jury in the original trial, the solicitor-general had referred to a contemporary movement to revise rape statutes around the nation and in Georgia. Over the objection of Pounds's counsel, he had commented that "the age of consent in many States is higher than in this State, and should be made higher here; and a committee of ladies waited on the judiciary committee of the last house of representatives and urged that the age of consent be raised to twelve years in this State."[1]

Not until 1918 would Georgia raise the age of consent, and then to age fourteen, but the ruling in the *Pounds* appeal reveals a constellation of concerns about sexual crimes against girls in the late nineteenth century.

125

Throughout the country, as in Georgia, judges, lawyers, doctors, and social reformers deliberated the age at which a girl had the understanding and capacity to consent to sex; women engaged in state and national politics by urging legislators to protect girls; and Americans disagreed over the validity of the movement to revise statutory rape laws. Resistance to change may have been steeper in Georgia than nationally, for southerners opposed most legal reforms that might empower women or African Americans. As the history of lynching illustrates, southerners concentrated their sexual fears on black men, while redefining statutory rape could put white men at greater risk of prosecution.

The age-of-consent movement resembled the earlier effort to criminalize seduction. In each case critics attempted to revise state laws, undermine the consent defense, and problematize a range of sexual acts not covered by the narrow legal definition of rape. Moral reformers redefined seduction as a felony; social purity, temperance, and suffrage advocates wanted to extend the statutory meaning of childhood (and sexual maturity) beyond the age of ten. Each group argued that terms like *seduction* and *statutory rape* covered a range of sexual acts, from voluntary to coercive to forceful. As one age-of-consent advocate observed, most delinquent (by which she meant sexually active) girls had "the experience which today is called betrayal, but which ought to be called rape."[2] Both campaigns juxtaposed constructions of young women as dependents in need of protection with claims about women's rights.

In the late nineteenth century, statutory rape reform attracted far more attention than the criminalization of seduction, largely because of the growing attention to child-saving in a range of social movements. Concerns about immigration, urban poverty, and prostitution spawned efforts to protect children, including new laws ranging from compulsory education and child labor restrictions to a higher minimum age for marriage. By the end of the century, the term *adolescence* denoted a critical period that preceded full adulthood, a time when older boys and girls required particular guidance. In this climate, warnings about the sexual vulnerability of adolescent girls reached a receptive audience. At the same time, statutory rape reformers could flex stronger political muscles than could earlier critics of seduction. Through organizations like the Woman's Christian Temperance Union, middle-class women's maternal authority was expanding well beyond the private family and into the public arena. Even though most women could not vote, run for office, or serve on juries, they were able to wage a national campaign that convinced male legislators to make it easier to prosecute men who persuaded young girls to have sex. By 1920 every state had raised the age of consent, typically to sixteen or eighteen.[3]

Although their memberships overlapped, the temperance and suffrage movements had less success in the late nineteenth century than the age-of-consent advocates. The emphasis on protection, and not only women's rights, may have made statutory rape reform seem less threatening than giving women the vote. But the absence of an organized protagonist also advantaged this cause. The "liquor interest" had economic motives for rallying men's opposition to both temperance and suffrage in order to prevent the passage of prohibition. White men could openly claim drinking as a privilege worth defending, but few of them would openly identify with the sexual assailant. Even those men who exercised their sexual prerogatives within marriage, frequented brothels, or defended themselves from rape charges by portraying their accusers as seductresses were unlikely to mobilize publicly to defend the right to have sex with young women. Though unorganized, male critics did resist statutory rape reform and they forced legislative compromises that tempered the new laws. They also identified problems with the criminalization of consensual sex that even proponents had to acknowledge. The debates over raising the age of consent revealed persistent tensions between the goals of protecting girls and protecting white men's sexual privileges. They also pointed toward the construction of rape as a crime committed primarily against youth.

IN THEIR STATUTES concerning rape, American states generally incorporated English criminal codes that differentiated between forcible rape, in which a woman's resistance indicated her lack of consent, and statutory rape, when the state deemed a woman or girl incapable of granting consent. The mentally incompetent, for example, did not have to prove resistance because they did not have the capacity to understand or defend themselves against sexual assault. Minors—"infants" in the law—were the major group covered by the concept of statutory rape. According to laws against "carnal knowledge and abuse of an infant female," under a certain age a girl was incapable of agreeing to sexual relations. If the complainant was underage, she did not have to prove that force had been used. In 1576, English law had set the age of consent at ten years. American states typically adopted age ten or twelve as the threshold of capacity to consent. This "age of consent" initially coincided with the age at which a woman could be married, and some jurists associated it with the onset of puberty. As with other American rape laws, the penalties for statutory rape varied according to race. In the South, a white man convicted of raping an underage girl could be sentenced to five to twenty years in prison, while a black man could be castrated or executed.[4]

Whether prosecuted as rape or statutory rape, sexual assaults on children and youth frequently appeared in police and court records, increasingly so in the late nineteenth century. Popular concerns about youth, along with the establishment of protective agencies, helped draw greater attention to the sexual vulnerability of children. Of the prosecutions of rape or attempted rape in New York City, those that involved girls under age eighteen increased from approximately 40 percent in 1790–1876 to almost 90 percent in 1886–1901. Similar patterns held in other regions. In one Iowa county, 85 percent of the charges for rape or assault with intent to rape in 1880–1910 concerned girls who were younger than fifteen.[5]

Measured by prosecutions, press accounts, or levels of community outrage, the sexual assault of girls unsettled the public more than did the rape of adult women. In court proceedings, adult women who filed rape complaints could expect to be interrogated about their complicity and portrayed as seductresses. Hypothetically, notions of childhood sexual innocence made young girls more believable accusers, and in practice even those who were over the statutory age of consent fared better in court if they appeared to be immature and naive.[6] Not all observers shared these sentiments—physicians and judges expressed greater skepticism—but the press remained especially sympathetic to children's accounts of assault. A large majority of newspaper reports of rape in New York, Atlanta, and Los Angeles either identified victims as "young" women or gave their ages as under fifteen years. The average age of white victims in these stories fell from almost twenty years in the 1870s to around thirteen and half years in the 1890s.[7]

Newspapers typically portrayed girls as helpless victims and labeled their attackers as beasts, an approach exemplified by a *New York Times* headline, "Fiendish Outrage on a Child." Stories about white men who faced lynch mobs typically involved assaults on girls. In 1879 the *National Police Gazette* reported that a band of "solid business men" in Colorado removed two white male "rape fiends" from the jail where they awaited trial for attempting to assault a four-year-old girl. An illustration showed the men hanging from a makeshift gallows. Other stories reveal the depth of community reactions and served to warn men of the wrath they might expect from both men and women. In Nebraska a mob tarred and feathered a white man who had assaulted "a little girl." An Arizona man who took "indecent liberties" with an eight-year-old girl was advised to leave town to avoid lynching; while he fled, a group of local women "attacked him with rawhides and lashed him out of town for over a mile." Where the rule of law prevailed, moral outrage found expression in courtrooms. The *Los Angeles Times* wrote approvingly when a judge sentenced "Tom Gormley, the brutal ravisher of little Maggie Sweitzer," to San Quentin prison for fifty years. Two newspapers reported a dramatic scene in which a mother seized a chair during a trial to attack the man accused of assaulting her ten-year-old daughter.[8]

The press and the public reacted even more strongly to interracial accusations. A report of a seventeen-year-old black youth in South Carolina, accused of enticing his white employer's five-year-old daughter into an attic and unsuccessfully trying to "outrage" her, was labeled "one of the blackest crimes ever known in this section." Entire immigrant communities could suffer after child assault accusations. In 1889 thousands of white male citizens rioted against the small Chinese population in Milwaukee, Wisconsin, because of accusations that two Chinese men had lured white girls aged eight to thirteen into their laundry with treats in exchange for sex.[9] Though racially specific, these episodes shared much with reports of white assailants, including expressions of sympathy for victims and vengeance toward the accused.

In contrast to journalists, medical and legal authorities tended to question accounts of child rape. At a time when new scientific expertise enabled the medical profession to expand its public authority, courts increasingly turned to physicians to provide testimony in rape cases. Even a child under the age of consent might be scrutinized before or during a trial, with doctors weighing in about whether physiological evidence proved that an assault had occurred. Implementing the advice of both European and American medical writers, doctors often sought alternative explanations for the injuries displayed by children. The British physician Michael Ryan claimed that vaginal damage did not necessarily mean that a child had been assaulted. Another doctor concluded that an eleven-year-old girl could not have been raped because when he tried to insert his little finger into her discolored labia "the complaint of pain was so great" that he could not proceed. An assailant, he implied, could not have accomplished the act.[10]

At times doctors seemed more concerned about the men accused of assault than the children they examined. One writer defended the man suspected of assaulting a girl by arguing that because he was married he had "abundant means for the indulgence of passion" and thus had no need to gratify himself "upon a child." Even Dr. Jerome Walker, who reported the extent of child rape to the Society for the Prevention of Cruelty to Children (SPCC), worried about applying medical evidence to convict men. "It will not do to give the child the benefit of doubts," he wrote in 1886, "for that is injustice to the alleged assailant, who may be a deserving and innocent man." By the late nineteenth century most American physicians followed the view of the pioneering German sexologist Richard von Krafft-Ebing, who wrote in a text translated into English in the 1890s that it was "incomprehensible that an adult of full virility, and mentally sound, should indulge in sexual abuses with children."[11]

When consulted about incest, medical authorities reiterated these views. For most of the nineteenth century, the legal term *incest* referred to consensual relations among close relatives. Rape charges could be filed if force had been used, but these cases remained rare. Doctors were reluctant to investigate familial sexual abuse even when young girls showed symptoms of venereal infection. They typically insisted that the disease could have been contracted from unsanitary linens rather than from sexual intercourse within the family. Dr. John C. Cook, president of the Chicago Pediatric Society, pondered the possibility that in "a family of educated and refined people" a father had infected his four-year-old daughter with gonorrhea. "I am glad to hear it restated," Cook continued, "that it is possible to contract the disease in a water-closet." So unthinkable was incestuous transmission that doctors ignored the possibility when fathers and daughters shared the same bed and had symptoms of the same disease. When they did acknowledge the sexual abuse of children in families, medical writers tended to focus on immigrant and working-class fathers. Like Cook, they exempted those from middle- and upper-class homes.[12]

Nineteenth-century judges also were usually disinclined to believe that men assaulted their daughters. A Texas justice wrote in 1849, when the court reversed a conviction for incest, that the charge was "so shocking to the moral sense of every civilized being, so degrading and humiliating to human nature" that it seemed hard to "believe it possible to have been committed in this age and country." Given such doubts, judges looked skeptically at children's claims and imposed high standards of evidence. A unanimous opinion issued in 1900 by the Georgia Supreme Court illustrates the higher standard for review in incest cases. The court ordered a new trial for a man who had been convicted of "incestuous adultery" after he impregnated his stepdaughter, whom he had coerced into having an ongoing sexual relationship. The justices acknowledged that if the stepfather had committed the crime, "his offense against a female of tender years, under his protection was most odious and heinous," and he deserved "severe punishment." However, the decision continued, the fact that the charge was "so well calculated to excite indignation" required a higher standard of scrutiny to ensure "that the trial is in every respect free from material error." Unconvinced that the conviction met this standard, the court ordered a new hearing.[13]

The scarcity of incest trials in the nineteenth century makes it hard to detect patterns, but the records do provide clues. A survey of incest appeals in southern states revealed that even judges who condemned the practice were reluctant to prosecute fathers. Nationally judges reversed almost half of the convictions in over one hundred appellate court decisions between 1800 and 1900. Aside from appeals, men convicted of incest found ways to avoid severe punishment. In a controversial plea bargain, a man charged in San Bernardino County, California, "with incest of the lowest type" served only three months in county jail by confessing to simple assault rather than assault to rape. This sentence irritated not only local citizens but also a judge, who called for stronger penalties. Men sent to prison often sought pardons and in some cases appealed for release on the grounds that their daughters and wives should not have been believed in court.[14]

When girls accused men outside of their families, court rulings varied widely. Ohio, which did not follow British common law, had no statute addressing consensual underage sex. In the 1860s the Ohio Supreme Court overruled the convictions of several men who had assaulted girls under the age of ten, on the grounds that the children had voluntarily consented to have sex. At least one judge expressed his regret that Ohio law did not punish "carnal knowledge of a young child." Elsewhere corroboration requirements in rape laws made it difficult for girls to prove they had been assaulted. A Minnesota court reversed the conviction of a priest who had been accused of raping a seventeen-year-old girl because her word did not suffice legally. In the opinion of the court, "even young girls, like older females, sometimes concoct an untruthful story to conceal a lapse from virtue."[15]

The tension between the goal of protecting girls and disbelief that men assaulted them ran throughout the appellate decisions issued by the

Georgia Supreme Court in the late nineteenth century. The court considered itself the protector of innocent youths. In the opinion of Justice James Jackson, writing in 1876, the law was "an invisible but all jealous and watchful guardian" of a girl, "equal to the arm of her father at her home." In the absence of parental protection, the law "would shield her from danger, or vindicate her when wronged." In the following decades the court sometimes affirmed convictions of men accused of the rape of girls, particularly if the child had not yet entered puberty, the age at which, the court believed, "passion or sexual desire moves a female." Or as an 1899 opinion put it, the common-law age of ten years was "arbitrary" and could be rebutted, depending on the child's "apparent physical development" and her demeanor as a witness.[16] But when a girl was not considered a competent witness, or if there was no corroborating evidence, the court reversed convictions in language that reinforced doubts about female veracity. In the 1898 case of a "young girl" who testified that she had been thrown on a bed and raped by the man in whose house her family boarded, the court cautioned that "the testimony of the person alleged to have been raped should always be scrutinized with care." Even though the girl had cried and "told him not to do it," she had not called out to attract others, she had no witnesses, and she had not reported the event immediately. The court reversed the man's conviction.[17]

The reluctance of medical witnesses and judges to condemn men accused of sexual crimes against children contrasted notably with the public repulsion toward these acts that permeated the press. This disparity flows in part from the distinctive functions of courts and the media. Appellate courts safeguarded the rights of defendants, while journalists sought newsworthy items that would appeal to readers and sell papers. In the sensationalist reporting style of the era, the sexually violated girl served as a powerful symbol of lost innocence in need of protection. By the 1880s, however, the long-standing suspicions about girls who falsely claimed rape began to collide with emerging concerns about child welfare. Enabled by the growing political skills of organized middle-class women, a campaign to redefine statutory rape targeted the sexual and legal privileges of white men.

THE CALL TO RAISE the statutory age of consent occurred within the context of the new meaning of childhood in industrial America. In the past, youths had begun their working lives on family farms, but increasing numbers now attended public schools, delayed their entrance into the workforce, and experienced a longer period of dependency in families. One measure of this extension of childhood was the trend toward increasing the legal age of marriage. Previously around twelve years for girls and fourteen years for boys, by the early twentieth century state legislatures were raising the threshold to around sixteen years for girls and eighteen years for boys.[18] The mission of the New York Society for the Prevention of Cruelty to Children (NYSPCC), founded in 1875, provides another indicator, for the agency served boys or girls who were under the age of sixteen. Similar child-saving organizations soon appeared throughout the country, typically run by native-born, middle-class men and women. They reached out to working-class and immigrant youths, many of them toiling in industrial jobs and living in urban tenements, whom they considered to be in need of Americanization and moral uplift.

By focusing on youth at risk, child-savers sometimes called attention to sexual assault. The NYSPCC, which initially targeted child neglect, added physical abuse and, later, sexual relations, including incest, to its concerns. The Pennsylvania SPCC alluded to incest in a report that explained that because of their "terrible nature" certain family practices "must forever remain—from the very foulness of the crimes—a part of the unwritten history" of the Society. Though discreet in print, the agents of the Pennsylvania SPCC did help daughters report sexual abuse by their fathers and stepfathers to the police.[19] More frequently these agencies reported sexual risks outside the family and attributable to city life.

One of these risks, and a major trigger for the age-of-consent movement, was the specter of prostitution and venereal disease that loomed large in nineteenth-century cities. As public health surveys exposed the extent of sexual commerce, medical authorities sought ways to control the spread of gonorrhea and syphilis. Britain and France experimented with state regulation of prostitution through licensing laws that required periodic medical tests, a policy advocated in a few U.S. cities. Activists in the American social purity movement, who supported chastity for women and men, vigorously opposed these measures as immoral and ineffective. They tried to shift the blame from women to men, elaborating upon the image of young working girls lured or forced into brothels by deceptive male procurers. Raising the age of consent, they believed, would make it easier to prosecute men who recruited young women, to protect girls from sexual ruin, and to deter the spread of disease.[20]

The antiprostitution movement in England provided the immediate impetus for American efforts to revise statutory rape laws. In 1861 the British Parliament increased the age of consent from ten to thirteen years, a change welcomed by purity reformers. Over the next decades fears about the "white slave traffic" proliferated. Anti-vice narratives sensationalized the sale of young women into brothels by procurers who had abducted and sometimes drugged their victims, often achieving their "ruin" through seduction or rape before the sale. The reference to racial slavery in the term was telling. It played upon lingering abolitionist sentiments but applied these sympathies largely to the sexual enslavement of white, not black, women. By blaming prostitution on abduction and rape, middle-class reformers rejected earlier presumptions of working-class female depravity. Now they refused to believe that girls of any class would choose to enter the trade. In 1885 British journalist William Stead greatly intensified popular outrage over the sexual exploitation of young women when he exposed the sale of girls into prostitution by purchasing a thirteen-year-old virgin (a valuable commodity on the sex market) through a procurer. Stead went to prison for the ruse and then wrote a widely read fictionalized account of the episode in his newspaper. The same year, after mass protests, the British Parliament increased the age of consent to sixteen years.[21]

In response to the British campaign, the U.S. Woman's Christian Temperance Union escalated its efforts to achieve a single standard of chastity for men and women. Founded in Ohio in 1874, the WCTU's membership quickly spread throughout the country. By 1900 nearly two hundred thousand women had joined. Despite the focus on temperance, it was not a single-issue organization. The WCTU identified the welfare of women, children, and the home as a suitable political project that required the expansion of female public authority and ultimately woman suffrage. Under the banner "Home Protection" the organization identified drunkenness as a major cause of violence and condemned men of any race who assaulted women and children.[22]

The WCTU built a social purity coalition that included male clergy of all denominations, members of the Knights of Labor and the Populist Party, and male and female suffragists who supported their goal of increasing the legal age of consent. To sway public opinion, temperance advocates published pamphlets, articles, and novels that decried not only drinking but also the ruin of young girls and the failure of contemporary rape laws to deter their fates. Utilizing the indirect political means available to women, WCTU members circulated petitions in every state and territory complaining that current laws failed to protect "womanhood and girlhood" from the "increasing and alarming frequency of assaults upon women, and the frightful indignities to which even little girls are subject." Signers appealed to legislators to revise the age of consent to at least eighteen years, which, they argued, paralleled legal and social standards for reaching majority.[23]

The statutory rape campaign testified to women's growing politicization. In the 1880s and 1890s, the WCTU gathered tens of thousands of signatures in the states: fifty thousand in Texas in 1891, fifteen thousand in Florida in 1901, and thousands more presented to the U.S. Congress to raise the age in the District of Columbia. Thanks in part to the efforts of the Knights of Labor, whose members were concerned about the vulnerability of young working women, these petitions included the signatures of men as well as women. In addition, women relentlessly lobbied male state legislators. The prolific writer and later suffrage activist Helen H. Gardener, who publicized the campaign in her popular novels and magazine articles, tried to shame these officials by creating "The Black List of States." This chart illustrated where "a little girl may consent to her ruin" in a visual hierarchy of statutes, moving downward from states that set the age as low as under ten to those that had raised it to seventeen. Southern states topped the list with the lowest standards, suggesting how the racially specific panic about sexual threats left intact the sexual privileges of white men.[24]

When WCTU members persuaded elected officials to adopt their views, these male allies in turn helped convince their colleagues of the justness of the cause. In language combining the moral outrage of temperance activists with a dose of paternalism, these men publicly advocated statutory reform. State senator G. W. Granberry of Arkansas called on legislators to "throw every safeguard" around working girls who were vulnerable to men who were "watching for victims to indulge their brutal lusts." An Oregon representative alerted his colleagues that "little girls just over fourteen years old had been ruined and enticed to lead a life of shame in brothels." Rather than blame these prostitutes for their fate, these legislators believed, the state should step in to control men. A state senator in Iowa wrote that it was the duty of government to protect the helpless and immature against the "scoundrel" who wished "to destroy female morality."[25]

By 1900 legislatures in thirty-two states—primarily in the North and Midwest—agreed to increase the age of consent to between fourteen and eighteen years. Eleven states and territories set the age at eighteen, including California, where the legislature gradually increased it between 1887 and 1897. Reformers could not control precisely how statutes would emerge from the legislative process, however. Statutory revisions often reduced penalties, required corroborating witnesses for conviction, and occasionally required proof of prior chastity. Some states made underage sex a misdemeanor rather than a felony, particularly if the male was also under the age of consent.[26]

Although proponents used the term "age of protection" to refer to these statutes, a strong equal rights strain ran through their rhetoric, especially among suffragists who supported the cause. Well before the British reforms triggered the WCTU campaign, the short-lived suffrage paper, the *Revolution,* addressed the problem. An 1869 article by "P.P." (the male feminist Parker Pillsbury) condemned New York law for abandoning girls over age ten "to the lust of such human fiends" as a man who claimed that an eleven-year-old girl had consented to have sex with him. Adding the case to the suffrage arsenal, Pillsbury editorialized further: "Who can ever expect any extermination of such indescribable horrors, until woman herself, the mother of these babes, has a voice in both the making and executing of the laws?"[27] Augusta Howard declared in 1892 that as long as the age of consent remained ten years, "there will be thousands of woman suffragists" who would "do their utmost to arouse the public conscience to such iniquity." Pro-suffrage men continued to invoke the language of equality to support protection. One man wrote to the *Woman's Journal* in 1886 that laws presuming that a ten-year-old girl could consent to sex constituted "discriminating against female children in favor of those who wish to outrage and ruin them." Henry Blackwell warned purity activists that it was "almost hopeless" to reform the laws "by the votes of men alone."[28] For him, enfranchisement and protection went hand in hand.

Some suffragists realized that calling for state protection could contradict their goal of female independence, but they justified statutory rape reform as an expedient strategy, necessary only until women achieved full citizenship. "As long as the laws are not wholly just to women—i.e. as long as women have no voice in them," one writer explained, "it will be necessary to keep the age of protection at a high figure." Others acknowledged that the laws could be discriminatory toward young men, who might be imprisoned for having consensual sex with their peers. They reasoned, however, that given the privileges allowed to males, women needed protection to achieve a semblance of equality. Once women could vote, they would be able to advance "the cause of every girl and woman before a court," just as the vote "now aids every boy and man." Until that time they had to accept the reality that "no law can be made so perfect as not to be capable of being sometimes so construed as to work injustice."[29] In short, in a world that was unfair to women, men would have to put up with some inequalities.

Another way that suffrage advocates justified the imbalance in the laws was to cite the unequal losses experienced by men convicted of rape and the young women they had "ruined." They embraced rather than questioned the nineteenth-century purity ideal, citing practical as well as abstract moral reasons for doing so. Suffragists believed that the loss of virginity left a young woman vulnerable to becoming a prostitute, because she could no longer aspire to marry or find respectable labor. A rapist might be fined or serve a short prison term, but the "nonlegal, irreversible life sentence of the female" could include selling herself "into the slavery of shame." Punishing men would supposedly encourage a single standard of morality rather than allow the burden of ruin to fall entirely on women.[30] For suffragists, judicial leniency denied protection to girls and privileged the men who assaulted them.

In a twist on the theme of just punishments, Helen H. Gardener wrote approvingly about a statute proposed in Illinois that would add disfranchisement and withdrawal of the power to hold public office or serve on a jury as an addition to imprisonment for having sex with a girl under age fourteen. "That is," Gardener explained, *"as a punishment for rape a man is made the legal and political equal of a woman."* Her language emphasized the political disabilities of women, but the proposed legislation reflected a broader trend toward disenfranchising convicted felons on the grounds that they lacked the moral standing to be voters.[31] Unlike these other limitations on suffrage, which often targeted African Americans and immigrants, Gardener wanted to reduce the political privileges of white men.

In convoluted ways, the principle of equality ran through the insistence that current laws treated the theft of a woman's purity more lightly than the theft of property. Echoing antiseduction rhetoric, reformers claimed that for the law to be just, it should accord equally harsh punishments for the gender-specific crime of loss of chastity. As a suffrage newspaper put it: "Is property of more value than virtue to the citizens of Iowa?" A woman's virtue was unlike property, though, for the question rested upon an implicit, and sometimes explicit, assumption that the loss of a woman's honor was a fate not only equal to theft but also worse than death—and therefore should be elevated from a minor to a serious crime, even, in the view of some writers, a capital offense. In a variation on the theme, the WCTU frequently argued that the age at which a woman could consent to sexual relations should be the same as the age at which she could own property, which was typically over eighteen. "Make the age of majority twenty-one for girls as for boys, and protect the person of the minor as surely as her property," proclaimed a suffragist writer.[32] In these arguments, women should have the same right to ownership of their sexuality that men and women had to their property.

Questions of equal rights also informed debates over the propriety of women's participation in the age-of-consent campaign, given the public discussions of sexuality involved in promoting it. The belief that female delicacy required reticence about sex served to reinforce women's secondary political status. Judges sometimes justified the exclusion of women from criminal trials on the grounds that they should not be exposed to testimony about sexual assault. Conservative newspapers chastised WCTU members for the unwomanly behavior of discussing rape. In an article headlined "The Least Talked About the Better," the *Atlanta Constitution* condemned women's efforts as a "public indecency." In response, the local WCTU situated their work within the broader discourse on race and rape. If the *Constitution* could run "startling headlines" about sexual assaults by black men, they argued, women should have the right to discuss rape in public. Their comment echoed the advice of WCTU president Frances Willard, who had warned temperance women not to be "too prudish" to allude to or "take up arms against these awful crimes."[33] In doing so they claimed a right to sexual speech in the name of protecting girls.

A related struggle ensued when politicians questioned whether women could be present during legislative debates on age-of-consent laws. When men claimed that it was "not womanly to speak of these things," reformers asked them to consider "the harm that has been done because we have been silent on these vital questions." They counted as a measure of success being able to observe these debates from seats in the galleries. As Helen H. Gardener explained in 1895, noting a shift in the Texas legislature, "Four years ago it was considered a really disgraceful thing that a blessed white-haired mother should have heard the discussion." Now she reported a lawmaker's remark that "if there is a woman in Texas who would *not* be present at such a discussion, I never want to meet her, for I want always to respect women." During debate in the Tennessee state legislature, a confident opponent of raising the age of consent turned to the galleries and stated that he "hoped this incident would teach the women not to be pe-titioning the legislature concerning things they knew nothing about." But Tennessee did increase the age of consent to sixteen, and the women in the galleries helped demolish one obstacle to political participation.[34]

Enfranchisement facilitated the process of revising statutory rape laws. As social purity advocate and physician Emily Blackwell pointed out in 1895, the first states to increase the age of consent to eighteen were the ones in which women "had a direct voice in politics—Wyoming and Kan-sas." Events in Colorado offered further proof of the efficacy of suffrage. As soon as women gained the right to vote there in 1893, one of the three women elected to the state legislature, Carrie Clyde Holly, introduced a bill to raise the age of consent to twenty-one, the age of majority for property rights. In 1895 the Colorado legislature approved a compromise bill that delineated eighteen as the age of consent. As more women achieved state suffrage, statutory rape reform gained momentum. In 1910, the year in which women gained the vote in Washington State, the state legisla-ture abolished the law requiring corroborative evidence in rape and se-duction cases. Enfranchised in 1911, women reformers in California esca-lated their political entreaties to extend the age of consent, adding the threat of electoral retaliation. Within two years California enacted a stat-ute setting the age at eighteen and lawmakers increased prison terms for rape, setting a minimum of one year and a maximum of fifty years.[35]

Conversely, southern states lagged in both statutory rape reform and woman suffrage. Although some southern legislatures acted before women became voters, most did not do so, and legislators who did support the reform often paid the price of defeat at the next election. By 1913, two of the three states that retained the common-law age of ten were in the South (Georgia and Mississippi), as were seven of the eight states that set the age at fourteen. This disparity inspired some southern women—such as Mary Latimer McLendon, who led the Georgia Woman Suffrage Asso-ciation—to argue for enfranchisement in order to enact a reform agenda that included raising the age of consent. By 1908 even McLendon's sister, the vocal white supremacist Rebecca Latimer Felton, campaigned for woman suffrage, in part for its instrumental value in protecting white women from violence from either black or white men.[36]

THE ACHIEVEMENTS of the age-of-consent movement are particularly impressive given the range of criticisms raised by opponents. Those who fought against revised statutory rape laws occupied a complicated political landscape. Some who tried to defeat, water down, or repeal the acts articulated patriarchal and white supremacist views. They feared that both white and black women would use the laws against white men, eroding the sexual privileges they enjoyed. But African Americans also expressed skepticism on grounds that the laws would be applied to protect only white women, and libertarian free-love advocates objected to expanding the protective arm of the state.

One set of opponents simply held that the statutes were unnecessary, either because girls could take care of themselves or because existing laws and practices already protected them. According to Representative A. C. Tompkins of Kentucky, "When backed by good moral training I regard the twelve-year-old girl as being as capable of resisting the wiles of the seducer as any older woman." Implicit in his statement was the racially specific definition of the "seducer" that contrasted with the image of the black rapist, from whom white women presumably required protection. Tompkins may have been influenced by a fellow Kentuckian, Dr. C. C. Mapes, who wrote that young women rarely needed legal protection. "Under ordinary circumstances," Mapes confidently stated, "no female who has arrived at the age of understanding, be she never so weak, so long as consciousness remains, can be forced against her will to participate in the act of copulation by a male be he ever so strong." A proponent of both criminalizing abortion and more open discussions of sexuality, Mapes far preferred that mothers teach morality to their children than that politicians change the laws. Indeed, he blamed the failure of mothers to do so for the seduction of their daughters. Other critics insisted that existing laws already protected chaste girls from "lecherous scoundrels," referring to forcible rape or seduction statutes that treated certain consensual relations as a kind of second-degree rape. Apart from the law, one Tennessee legislator contended, "the shot-gun remedy was the best that had ever been invented for the protection of virtue."[37] Given the racial context of this debate, he referred to shotgun marriage, not to lynching.

A second set of arguments concerned the rights of boys and men. The laws criminalized consensual relations with underage girls but blamed the male partner alone. Connecticut senator Joseph Hawley made this point during the debate over the bill to raise the age of consent to sixteen years for the District of Columbia. Although the girl "may be the blameworthy person," he explained, only the boy would be punished. Congressional committee members feared that the accused man or boy might have "been 'more sinned against than sinning.'" Even some advocates found the gender imbalance problematic. Helen H. Gardener expressed concern about the inequity in the male and female age of consent and recommended discretion in sentencing boys under age eighteen. A coalition that included judges, prosecutors, WCTU members, and child protection advocates helped revise the Colorado statute to set the age of consent for both sexes at eighteen. Other states created an age of consent for males and lesser penalties for underage boys convicted of statutory rape.[38]

The courts soon raised questions of equity for boys and men, portending later concerns about protecting the rights of defendants. In 1890 the Kansas Supreme Court criticized the statutory rape law that had been enacted three years earlier. In appealing the conviction of a nineteen-year-old male for statutory rape after he had impregnated his sixteen-year-old girlfriend, the defense lawyer neatly summarized the opposition case. In *State v. White* he complained that the legislature "cannot convert pure and simple fornication into rape." The court overturned the conviction on a technicality and let the new law stand, but commented that the effort to protect girls "wholly overlooks the protection of boys." Claiming that in Kansas women were considered to be "nearly equal with males" in property rights, vocations, and even partial franchise (after 1885 women could vote in municipal elections), the opinion characterized the statutory rape law as "a theory of vast inequality" that presumed "a greater superiority on the part of the males over the females than has ever before been promulgated or admitted or believed." For all of its egalitarian trappings, however, a very traditional fear of the female seductress informed this recommendation. As the Kansas ruling put it, the law "overlooks the fact that some girls under the age of eighteen years are incorrigibly wicked and depraved, even common prostitutes."[39]

Reversing the reform discourse on men who ruined young women, opponents dwelled on these depraved girls, who, they feared, would undermine the liberty of innocent men. Legislators in Arkansas raised the specter of "designing and unprincipled females" who tried either to "entrap unwary and unsuspecting youths and blackmail them into marriage" or simply to extort money from them to avoid charges. An Iowa official questioned the assumption that an eighteen-year-old was chaste, writing (with emphasis) that *"the majority of inmates of houses of ill-fame have fallen long before they have arrived at that age."* Thus, men could be liable to life in prison "for yielding to the solicitation of a prostitute who had long before been despoiled of her virginity." White southerners had a particular concern that raising the age of consent would, as a Tennessee writer put it, "enable loose young women, both white and black, to wreak a fearful vengeance on unsuspecting young men." In a reversal of narratives in which employers seduced working-class women, parents were encouraged to ask, "Who of us that has a boy sixteen years old would be willing to see him sent to the penitentiary on the accusation of a servant girl?"[40] In the South, that servant was likely to be black.

As this warning suggests, the statutory rape campaign not only targeted men's sexual privileges but also had the potential to challenge white supremacy. In the fears of one Mississippian, "This would enable negro girls to sue white men." Similarly, Representative Tompkins of Kentucky objected because the laws put the "negro female on the same plane as the white female." His critique exemplified the racial and sexual ideology that had long denied sexual protection to black women. In his view, black women differed "psychologically and functionally." Raising the age of consent, Tompkins wrote, would provide "a terrible weapon for evil . . . when placed in the hands of a lecherous, sensual negro woman, who for the sake of blackmail or revenge would not hesitate to bring criminal action even though she had been a prostitute since her eleventh year!" In 1904 state senators in Mississippi blocked an effort to change the age of consent from ten to fourteen, lest African American girls be able to sue white men. In some southern states, statutory rape laws applied only to white women. Similar arguments appeared when opponents to a bill introduced in the Texas legislature claimed that Mexican girls matured sooner than white girls and therefore had the ability to consent to sex at an earlier age. These fears were addressed by requirements of a girl's prior chastity, which were written into many statutes, because jurors were likely to presume the chastity of white, but not of black or Mexican, young women.[41]

Age-of-consent laws did offer a legal tool that could potentially undermine white men's access to women of color, and some southern white women welcomed this possibility. The Georgia WCTU considered it "an added reason for the bill's passage" that it would offer protection to "colored girls." Long dissatisfied with white men's access to black women, and often humiliated by the evidence of mixed-race children attributable to their male kin, white women had a strong interest in deterring this behavior. In that project they shared common ground with white supremacists. Speaking to the Texas state legislative committee considering an age-of-consent bill, WCTU state president Helen Stoddard referred to the "mulatto children" she observed on the streets as a reason to include protection of young black women. "I think the colored girl needs protection," she explained, "and more than that, the Anglo-Saxon man needs the restraints of this law to help him realize the dignity and sacred heritage he possesses by being born into the dominant race of the world."[42]

Given such rhetoric, it may not be surprising that African American women had ambivalent feelings toward efforts to raise the age of consent. Middle-class black women who engaged in racial uplift denounced all men who exploited young women. Some of them specifically decried sexual immorality among poor blacks. But they remained wary of the laws, even when some black clergy supported them. Perhaps the women's groups feared that the laws could be used to prosecute men of their race without necessarily protecting black women. Leaders of the National Colored Woman's Congress proposed "the same standard of morality for men as for women" and urged that "mothers teach their sons social purity as well as their daughters," but they stopped short of endorsing criminal penalties through age-of-consent laws. Both white and black members of the WCTU favored age-of-consent laws in order to protect young women of any race. But their explanations for the vulnerability of black girls differed. African American women blamed white men for assaults, whereas white women often accused the girls of having a "low standard of morals."[43]

Aside from these ideological tensions, the WCTU's short-lived interracial coalition to protect young women from assault did not survive the realignment of southern politics at the end of the nineteenth century. As long as black men could vote in the South, the WCTU tried to draw African Americans into the temperance camp in the hope of outlawing alcohol. By the 1890s white supremacists were successfully invoking the specter of interracial rape to disqualify African American men from voting. In the process they helped undermine the Populist and labor coalitions that had supported temperance. Once black men could no longer vote, white WCTU chapters in the South lost most of their interest in reaching across race lines. They increasingly focused social purity efforts on young white women and narrowed their concerns to white slavery. African American temperance and social purity workers continued their protective work into the twentieth century. They condemned the rape, seduction, and the impregnation of young black women, especially domestic workers in the South, but they did not endorse statutory rape reform.[44]

Another set of critics, anarchist free lovers, found the laws problematic because they represented unwanted state intervention into private life and denied young women the choice of sexual partners. Lillian Harman took the lead in questioning the wisdom of raising the age of consent. At age sixteen she had "wed" Edwin C. Walker without benefit of state or church, choosing to cohabit illegally. Harman opposed the laws in large part because they constituted the "surrender of self-hood of the young women of America." Rather than seeking protection by the state, she invoked her right "to profit by my mistakes." In the journal *Liberty,* she offered rebuttals to every argument presented by the "impertinent and prudish women" who advocated raising the age of consent. Harman also criticized Knights of Labor leaders for "pandering to popular prejudices" when they supported the cause and for posing as "champions of outraged virtue" when they accused her of condoning the ruin of little girls because she opposed the laws.[45]

Harman shared with social purists and suffragists a belief in a single standard of morality for men and women. Like them she rejected sexual violence. To achieve equality, however, Harman wanted to extend to women the sexual freedom enjoyed by men, "not by making man a slave with woman, but by making woman free with man,—not by leveling down, but by leveling up." She considered "authoritarian" solutions of government intervention both ineffective and unjust. For one, they did not address the underlying sources of the problem of women's sexual vulnerability. If not for "state-enforced ignorance of sexual matters and the anti-natural teachings of a reactionary church," she argued, women would not need government protection because they would have the knowledge with which to protect themselves from unwanted sex.[46]

Like those conservative critics who blamed mothers for the ruin of their daughters, Harman argued that girls trained by "intelligent mothers" would be able to make wise choices. Unlike the conservatives, who expected maternal training to produce chaste daughters, Harman expected that with sexual wisdom girls could be both sexually proactive and better able to defend themselves. Sexually educated daughters would benefit more than be harmed "by relations that they desire." In her ideal, "the more liberty coupled with responsibility that we have the less there will be of sexual relations that are not desired." And if a girl did make a "mistake in judgment," her life would not be ruined if the family and society would not place so much weight on her sexual honor.[47]

Given the present "dense misinformation of the masses," however, Harman accepted the need to set some age at which girls required protection. For her, puberty represented the point at which a girl should be able to engage in consensual sexual relations. Once she was "already several years past the age of womanhood, equipped by nature with the capacity of maternity, and even acknowledged by the law to be competent to marry," the state should not revoke what Harman considered to be her sexual rights. Nor should the law provide grounds for imprisoning a man for up to life for participating in consensual sex. Harman considered the penalty rather than the sexual act to be the greater "outrage." To free-love advocates, mothers who accepted this remedy inculcated "imbecility" in their daughters and were guilty of a "callous disregard of human rights."[48]

Harman's emphasis on human, rather than women's, rights tipped the balance between protection and equal rights in the opposite direction of suffragists. The latter group recognized the need to compromise in an unjust world, but they wanted men to relinquish their rights. Like some critics and some proponents of the laws, Harman identified their contradictory goals but came down on the side of liberty for women as well as men. Harman took the principle of woman's ownership of her body further than suffragists as well, rejecting the protection of either men or the state. In the nineteenth century, however, Lillian Harman's was a rare female voice critical of both the age-of-consent laws and the underlying ideology of female purity that made seduction or rape so frightening to women who aspired to respectability. Neither her solution, nor the doubts raised by southern white men and African American women, discredited statutory rape reform at the time, but all of these dissident voices foreshadowed later problems in the enforcement of the revised laws.

AT THE END of the nineteenth century, statutory rape reform provided a major victory for social purity, temperance, and suffrage advocates in their quest to diminish white men's sexual and political privileges. For some it promised to serve as a legal wedge that could apply more broadly to all rape cases. As their president emphatically told the WCTU in 1900, "There is growing sentiment in favor of legally protecting womanhood *at any age* as well as girlhood in her minority."[49] In this vision, the consent defense and the requirement of proof of resistance might cease to undermine prosecution of sexual assault. In practice, though, statutory rape reform could further narrow the definition of rape. By identifying children as the primary victims of assault, it deflected attention from the rape of adult women and reinforced the expectation of female chastity to prove rape. Even the mandate to protect children and adolescent girls could be narrowly applied. As one legal scholar has argued, after 1900 the age-of-consent movement "lost its feminist bite" and became more conservative, more nativist, and more racist. While southern temperance groups lost interest in African American girls, in the rest of the country the laws targeted immigrant and working-class men.[50] Despite these limitations, temperance and suffrage advocates could take credit for calling national attention to the sexual vulnerability of girls, for redefining statutory rape in most states to include adolescent girls, and for expanding women's political participation, one step toward the achievement of suffrage. They left unanswered, however, the questions of how to balance special protection with equal rights for women and how to balance the rights of defendants with those of their accusers.

8

From Protection to Sexualization

In 1897 the California Supreme Court heard the appeal of a man named Lee who had been convicted of raping a thirteen-year-old girl. Lee's attorney argued that the jury in his trial should have been instructed that the girl had "made no outcry and no immediate disclosure, and that there was but little indication of violence to her person." This evidence could be interpreted to show that the girl had consented. A decade earlier, when the age of consent in California and most states was ten years, Lee might have been successful in challenging his conviction. But by the time of Lee's appeal, the legislature had revised the statutory rape standard to age sixteen. As the opinion that affirmed the conviction explained, in this case the "consent of the girl is immaterial." In subsequent opinions the California court made clear that, if she was under the age of consent, an adolescent girl who claimed that she had been sexually assaulted did not have to prove that she had cried out or resisted. As the justices repeatedly insisted, "the law resists for her."[1]

By removing questions of consent and resistance, the new statutory rape laws had the potential to strengthen the prosecution of men who took sexual advantage of adolescent girls. In the first decades after their enactment the revised statutes seemed poised to fulfill the goal of reformers: to give young women greater leverage in court and thus discourage underage sex. By the 1920s, however, the deep-seated beliefs about female culpability held by opponents of the laws, combined with a sea change in sexual values and behaviors, helped dilute this legal mechanism. Medical writers and judges remained fearful of false accusations against men. Some suggested that even young children could be considered "willing" victims who should be held responsible for their complicity in having sex with older men. Judges began to punish underage girls for their sexual behavior. Equally important, some young women openly

147

balked at the restrictions imposed by age-of-consent laws. Their views, along with court decisions, press coverage, and medical writing about statutory rape in the early twentieth century, all contributed to a process in which the sexualization of both girls and women superseded the era of protection envisioned by reformers.

AT FIRST STATUTORY RAPE REFORM did draw attention to the sexual vulnerability of girls, as evidenced by greater activity in the courts. Fewer than one-third of the rape convictions reviewed by the California Supreme Court in the 1870s and 1880s involved adolescent girls. In the two decades following the initiation of reform, two-thirds of the appellate rape cases involved girls between the ages of eleven and eighteen.[2] A study of one Michigan county court showed a surge in statutory rape charges after the state legislature made the legal age of consent fourteen in 1887 and then increased it to sixteen in 1895. In the 1880s the Ingham County court heard one underage sex case; from 1890 to 1910 the court ruled on twenty-six cases. Conviction patterns also changed in this jurisdiction, and not only for charges that involved young girls. In the two decades before statutory rape reform, just below 20 percent of all sexual assault cases ended in conviction. In the two decades after revision, almost half did. After the 1890s, conviction rates for the rape of adult women in this county began to surpass those for nonsexual assaults.[3]

Although incest was never the focus of statutory rape reform, the discourse on underage sex may have influenced the prosecution of this crime as well. Nationally, the bulk of appellate incest rulings in the nineteenth century appeared during the height of the age-of-consent campaign. In Ingham County, Michigan, only after 1900 did the court records include incest prosecutions, which tripled from 1900 to 1930.[4] The handful of cases concerning incestuous sexual relations that reached New York State appellate courts clustered in the twenty years after the legislature set eighteen as the age of consent. Before 1890 two incest cases reached California's appellate courts, which affirmed one and reversed the other conviction. In the four decades after California began to revise the age of consent, the appellate courts heard twenty incest cases and affirmed convictions in eighteen of them. In contrast, the Georgia Supreme Court reversed convictions in almost half of the sixteen incest appeals it heard between 1893 and 1918, when the legislature belatedly increased the age of consent to fourteen.[5]

While the new laws may have intensified prosecution, the fruits of reform proved to be quite uneven, depending largely on the compromises
embodied in various state laws. To protect men from unfair accusations,
some legislatures allowed a girl's reputation for chastity to be admissible
as evidence or mandated corroborative testimony for conviction. New
York law both required corroboration and allowed evidence about prior
sexual relations. In contrast, in the state of Washington courts could convict a man who had sex with an underage girl "even if her own conduct
and admissions" and the "testimony of other witnesses" raised doubts
about her chastity. Similarly, under the District of Columbia statute evidence of "immoral and unchaste character" was not admissible if the
prosecuting witness in a rape trial was under the age of consent.[6]

California provides an example of the fairly strict application of statutory rape law. The legislature gave the state strong responsibility for protecting underage girls from either unwanted or consensual sex, and the
courts seemed committed to implementing both the letter and the spirit
of law. As one justice explained, the "obvious purpose" of the legislation
was "the protection of society by protecting from violation the virtue of
young and unsophisticated girls."[7] At least in the first decade after the
revised statutes went into effect, these goals seemed paramount. Attempts
to portray girls as sexually experienced did not make a difference in court.
In Sacramento, an agent of the SPCC witnessed candy store operator An-
tonio Kuches, age twenty-eight, take fourteen-year-old Emma Metz into
his back room. He held her down and exposed himself before the agent
intervened. To support his claim that the girl had invited his actions, in
court Kuches attempted to disparage her character. He claimed that she
"commonly indulged in indecency of speech" and implied that her failure
to cry out for help indicated consent. At the time of the incident Metz was
between fourteen and fifteen years old, technically just over the age of
consent set by the 1889 law. Yet protective sentiments may have influenced
the California State Supreme Court, which affirmed Kuches's conviction
for attempted rape, suggesting a willingness to eliminate as a defense inti-
mations about the purity of a girl's character.[8]

Abundant appellate opinions in California in the early twentieth
century confirmed lower-court convictions of men from a variety of
backgrounds—a watchman, a dentist, a boardinghouse owner, to name
a few. In a classic application of statutory rape law to consensual relations,
defendant John Williams was convicted because he had sex with a girl
under age sixteen after he walked her back from a New Year's Eve ball in

the first hours of 1914. The girl did not cry out, nor did she report the incident for some time, but she testified that Williams "overcame her by having first aroused her passions which deprived her of the power of resistance." The court sentenced him to five years in prison. A case that closely followed the antiprostitution narratives led to even harsher punishment. Fourteen-year-old Gertrude Genant admitted that she had relations with several men after W. J. Parrish, her employer at a Chico boardinghouse, decided that she was "old enough to learn" about intercourse and proceeded to "use" her. Parrish was sentenced to fifteen years in prison. In other convictions the sentences ranged from five to thirty years, the latter term for a father who had assaulted his daughter. In contrast to prison terms of fifteen years for forcible rape, the Alameda County court sentenced men found guilty of statutory rape to terms of approximately ten years.[9]

New York State also differentiated between forcible and statutory rape, the latter presumed to be consensual. In 1887 the legislature set the age of consent at sixteen, and in 1892, with support from reformers who wanted wider prosecution, New York created two degrees of rape. The first applied to violence and carried a prison term of five to twenty years; the second applied to intercourse with an underage woman that did not involve violence, punishable by up to ten years in prison. In 1895 New York increased the age of consent to eighteen. As in California, the new laws precipitated a rise in the number of appeals. Before 1887 the New York Supreme Court heard only a handful of rape cases, but between 1890 and 1910 it ruled on thirty rape cases, two-thirds of them with complainants under age eighteen.[10] The greater ease of prosecuting statutory rape at the local level no doubt contributed to the busier appellate agenda. As reformers intended, statutory rape reform enabled girls and prosecutors to bring rape charges to trial by mediating the requirements of chastity and resistance.

To appreciate this influence, consider the obstacles facing a young woman who charged rape when the age of consent in New York was still ten years old. In the early 1870s a fourteen-year-old servant girl, Frederica Brussow, accused an older man, Charles Dohring, of assaulting her in a barn where she was working. Brussow testified that she had struggled and tried to cry out, that she had rejected his offer of a new dress if she would consent, and that he "held her down and threw her clothes up over her head." Reversing Dohring's conviction for rape, the appeals court stated that the jury should have been instructed that Brussow had to have offered the utmost resistance. "If a female, apprehending the purpose of a man to be that of having carnal knowledge of her person, and remaining conscious, does not use all her own powers of resistance and defence, and all her powers of calling others to her aid, and does yield before being overcome by greater force," the court explained, "a jury may infer that, at some time in the course of the act, it was not against her will."[11]

Two decades later a different climate prevailed, enabling New York prosecutors to win convictions when men forcibly assaulted young women. Even though the revised rape statute did not technically apply to Minnie Heath, who at age sixteen was just over the threshold for protection under the 1887 statute, her case benefited from the change. A rural migrant to New York City, Heath testified that Patrick Connor, the fifty-year-old office manager for whom she worked, had locked her in the office after the other workers had gone home. There he succeeded in raping her, despite her resistance. Connor claimed that she had consented, because there was insufficient evidence that she had resisted "to the utmost of her ability." In contrast to the Dohring case, the appeals court affirmed Connor's conviction, ruling that the "brutality and violence exhibited in this case were quite sufficient to engender that degree of fear requisite to confuse the mind and paralyze the efforts of his victim to free herself from the grasp of her assailant." That Heath was "a young, virtuous and, apparently, truthful girl," that she reported the assault immediately to a relative, and that she sought medical treatment confirming her account all may have impressed the court. That the crime fit the narrative circulated by the age-of-consent movement, involving a vulnerable working girl pinned down by an exploitative employer, may also have influenced the ruling.[12]

Statutory cases seemed to dominate the response to rape at the turn of the century. To some extent, the new laws redefined the crime of sexual assault as one committed against adolescent girls, continuing the trend in late nineteenth-century press coverage that featured ever younger victims. The laws achieved several of the proponents' goals by highlighting underage sex and giving prosecutors and families more leverage in forcible as well as consensual cases. But long-standing doubts about the morality of young women and even of young girls resurfaced quickly, as did persistent concerns about the rights and privileges of white men accused of sexual assault. In light of the diminishing importance of female purity in modern America, these critiques increasingly shaped the enforcement of statutory rape law.

SOON AFTER THE INITIAL WAVE of legislative successes, the protective impulse that led states like California and New York to revise the age of consent upward to eighteen came into conflict with the historical experiences of adolescents and changing understandings of female sexuality. The innocence that reformers associated with an idealized Victorian girl contrasted with the model of the "new woman" that gained popular appeal in the early twentieth century. Just when psychologists were proposing that adolescence was a unique life stage preceding full adulthood, older girls were seeking greater autonomy and adventure. In urban economies, more young working women, many of them under age eighteen, lived apart from their families as boarders or lodgers. In contrast to an earlier era of courtship within or nearby the home, the burgeoning commercial worlds of urban amusement parks, theaters, movie houses, and dance halls provided ample opportunities for young working-class men and women to mingle and engage in flirtations and unsupervised "dating." In this system, young men paid for meals and amusements while young women provided companionship that could include sexual contact, blurring the line between commercialized sex and consensual relations. It soon became apparent that many of the girls covered by statutory rape laws seemed uninterested in being protected by them.[13]

At issue, in part, were the nagging questions of when a girl could consent to sexual relations. The declining age of menarche in the early twentieth century (due in part to enhanced nutrition) created a longer gap between the age at which a girl matured sexually and the age at which she matured emotionally.[14] It was largely this cohort of adolescent girls that the age-of-consent laws protected. But as more girls sought sexual adventures, the older reform narratives of female vulnerability lost some of their power. New standards of girls' behavior, along with older suspicions about children's rape claims, helped redefine the meaning of statutory rape after 1900.

Above all, the consenting young woman complicated the call for protection that had driven statutory rape reform. As anarchist free lovers such as Lillian Harman had predicted, the broad application of the new laws meant that some women who were willing sexual partners could not legally consent. When fourteen-year-old Drusilla Low disappeared from her family's ranch in California, she had chosen to live with her "paramour," another rancher who wished to marry her. Only because of her age did the state charge him with rape. Especially after 1897, when California increased the age of consent to sixteen, questions of when a young woman had the capacity to consent recurred. Sometimes the court continued to extend protection to young women, as was the case in the Sacramento River town of Colusa for a young woman who was just short of her sixteenth birthday. She voluntarily went into a man's room at the Farmer's Hotel and then made no resistance to his sexual advances. The state prosecuted him, and in affirming his conviction for rape, the California Supreme Court ruled in 1900 that "the law, in such case, conclusively implies incapacity of the girl to give consent; and the law resists for her, regardless of her actual state of mind at the time."[15]

Although California courts usually upheld convictions for sex with an underage girl, a 1903 case reveals the continuing controversy over when a girl was mature enough to consent. A twelve-year-old girl married an older man and retrospectively accused him of statutory rape during their initial, and consensual, sexual intercourse. The technical grounds for reversal concerned improper questioning during the trial; the fact that the lower court had imposed a harsh sentence of thirty years in prison may have also affected the decision. But the California Supreme Court opinion that reversed the judgment opened by citing testimony that the girl appeared to be mature—"large, thoroughly developed in her sexual organs, and as mature as the ordinary woman in the prime of life." The implication was that age alone did not determine the need for protection. In 1904 the *Los Angeles Times* reported that a local court had been lenient in sentencing an African American man convicted of the rape of a black girl because she "was maturely formed, though under the statutory age."[16] Racial views had long influenced assumptions about female maturity, but the question of when a girl might become sexually active by choice could apply to both black and white young women.

Patterns in the procedural grounds that led appellate judges to reverse convictions, along with the language of their opinions, suggest how courts balanced the protection of girls and of accused men. Lack of sufficient evidence to prove that a girl was underage gave the benefit of the doubt to some appellants.[17] Failure to report promptly also raised questions about the motives of the accuser. One fourteen-year-old girl waited more than six weeks—until she was arrested on another matter—to accuse a night watchman in San Pedro, California, of raping her while they had walked on the beach one evening. The California Supreme Court reversed the man's conviction in part because the lower court had not allowed questions about why she had delayed reporting. The decision incorporated long-standing concerns about false charges, quoting an earlier case that echoed Lord Hale's words when it cautioned that "so heinous" a charge against a child of fourteen could excite sympathy for her yet "place the defendant, however innocent, at the mercy of her evidence."[18] In this view, the statutory rape laws could extend too much leverage to children.

The opinion of a juror in an Iowa statutory rape trial in 1891 suggested the results of this line of thinking. Three working-class girls between the ages of ten and thirteen, all under the age of consent, ran off for several days with some adult "sporting" men. Prosecutors portrayed the girls as prostitutes who came from immoral families. Explaining why they acquitted one of the defendants, even though they did not think he was innocent, the juror stated that "the character of the witnesses made the jurors feel like letting him go." His further logic realized the fears of reformers that male jurors could be too sympathetic with their peers. "Some of the jurors have been a little wild themselves," the man acknowledged, "and they were not anxious to convict him."[19]

The tone of press coverage of rape further illustrates how public attitudes shifted from a protective to a skeptical approach to sexually active girls. The *Los Angeles Times* generally applauded statutory rape laws, commenting regretfully in 1892 that "the Riverside rape fiend" had escaped conviction because the girl he assaulted had already turned fourteen, the age of consent at the time. But the *Times* also began to express concerns about the behavior of underage girls. In reporting statutory rape charges against a twenty-year-old shoe salesman in 1900, the paper noted that the thirteen-year-old girl, Matilda Ditner, ran around town "at all hours of the night with companions who took her to saloons." At the request of her widowed German immigrant mother, the story noted, the court sent Ditner to the Whittier reform school.[20]

The press had to acknowledge that underage girls brought to court by social welfare workers or the police sometimes had become involved with older men by their own volitions. In 1897 Blanche Cunningham, age thirteen, was found near Los Angeles living "in squalor in a tent" with an eighteen-year-old young man and another couple. A judge reluctantly dismissed the statutory rape charges after Cunningham acknowledged in court her willing relationship. After reporters learned that she had "consorted with" other men, "including two or three negroes," and had stolen several hats from a woman's house, the *Los Angeles Times* referred to her as "one of the most depraved girls of her age in this or any other city." In a tell-all interview, Cunningham acknowledged her guilt on all charges and implicated other young women. "I don't deny it," she confessed. "But I want you to understand that I'm not the only plum with a speck on it. There are fifteen girls I can name in this town, none of them older than fifteen years, who are as bad or worse than I am."[21]

Concern about the depravity of girls could even extend legal protections to some men who were not white. Fong Chung had been convicted of rape for having intercourse with Lillie Ida Davis, age thirteen. Along with her fifteen-year-old sister, Davis had been having sex with a number of Chinese and white men in exchange for gifts and money, with their parents' knowledge. Justice P. J. Cooper clearly stated in his 1907 opinion that the offense was statutory, so that "no matter how depraved was the girl," it constituted rape. Yet Cooper also articulated his concern that the charge itself "creates a feeling of prejudice and hostility in the minds of the jury, particularly in the case of a Chinaman." He held that the district attorney "in his zeal" had tried to construct a case of "the defendant's outrage upon an innocent girl of tender years." By asking "insulting and immaterial questions" about Chinatown vices, the prosecution had denied the defendant "the right to be protected" from such improper interrogation. That right, Cooper insisted, applied to all, "whether the witness be a Chinaman, a negro, one in the most humble walks of life or one in high position."[22] On these grounds the court reversed the conviction.

The racially egalitarian stance in the Fong Chung case was quite rare. Typically ideas about race reinforced the sexualization of nonwhite girls, who had never been presumed to be innocent. In parts of the South where legislators resisted reform because they did not want to extend protection to African American girls, the age of consent remained between ten and twelve. Race affected the implementation of statutory rape laws, as well. In 1907 a Florida court sentenced a forty-five-year-old white laborer to ten years in prison for having carnal intercourse with a nine-year-old African American girl while he was drunk. Within a year of his imprisonment, however, supporters called for clemency for this "hard working and ignorant white man," insisting that he had already reformed and had "suffered enough punishment." He received a conditional pardon from the governor. Few nonwhite girls appeared in northern statutory rape cases. In one intraracial rape trial, a "colored girl twelve years old" reported that two men had abducted and raped her. Although her stepfather testified that two neighbors had confessed to the crime, his corroboration did not suffice for the New York Supreme Court, which overturned the men's convictions.[23]

Class as well as race influenced which girls were most vulnerable to unwanted sex. Adventurous young working women sometimes engaged in consensual relations, but they could also be coerced or forced into having unwanted sex. Child welfare advocates, anti-vice crusaders, and the press all pointed out this risk. The 1910 grand jury investigation into the "white slave trade" in New York listed rape as a factor in twenty-two of the fifty-four indictments issued for trafficking in girls. Anti-vice reformers often blamed the urban dance-hall subculture for providing opportunities for what one investigator referred to as "forcible seduction." Two young women in San Francisco encountered this risk in 1920 when a man they met at a dance hall took them to a house where a dozen drunken men subjected them to "insults and brutalities." Vice investigators in New York City observed, but they did not intervene in, cases when a girl was "induced to go in the back of a poolroom, down a cellar, up on a roof, or into an empty apartment" where "the young men violate her one after another until she can't stand any more." Several men bragged to investigators about their techniques for manipulating the young women they dated into areas where they could have sex without anyone hearing the protests.[24]

Some young women learned to avoid these settings; others simply turned down dates with men who did not appeal to them or did not seem trustworthy. But other women who partook of urban nightlife wound up having unwanted sex, and because they had taken risks, the outcome was not necessarily defined as sexual assault. In contrast to the protective stance of many nineteenth-century reformers, the fears about prostitution and juvenile delinquency that escalated during the early twentieth century helped construct what scholars later termed "the crime of precocious sexuality." Especially if a girl came from a working-class or immigrant family, being sexually active entailed the risk of being labeled a delinquent. Some underage girls, like Matilda Ditner of Los Angeles, found themselves sentenced to reform school because of their sexual activities. When a North Carolina mother reported to the police that her daughter had been pressured into having sex with two older friends of the family, the court not only sentenced the men to five years in prison but also sent the girl to reform school because the men had given her money. Aside from ordering incarceration, criminal courts could treat girls punitively. In Alameda County, California, officials interrogated young women about their sexual experiences and conducted compulsory pelvic exams.[25]

In the new century, the conjunction of sexually active adolescent girls and the extension of statutory protection up to age eighteen produced a very different climate than nineteenth-century reformers described in their campaigns to increase the age of consent. Juries, judges, and social workers took a less protective and at times more punitive stance toward young women who had consensual relations. The risks of unwanted sex may have persisted, but adolescents, rather than the state, were increasingly expected to take responsibility and then faulted for failing to protect themselves.

THE OPINIONS OF MEDICAL and psychiatric experts contributed to the blaming of girls in age-of-consent cases. Like their predecessors in the nineteenth century, Progressive-era physicians often contested the image of female innocence that lay at the heart of statutory rape reform. Doctors who worked with police departments and courts frequently questioned the veracity of children, and those who published in medical and legal journals echoed the views of legislators who had opposed the new statutes. Along with these earlier doubts, new psychological interpretations began to infuse the literature.

In contrast to the white slave narratives that peaked around 1910, the psychiatric theories adopted by some physicians and social workers in the decades after World War I considered the "hypersexual female," rather than the prostitute, as a key source of urban vice. Skeptical medical authorities warned that most women who reported rape were hysterical and had actually been engaging in consensual sex, or "innocent playfulness." Exciting men beyond their ability to exercise control, one physician claimed, "converts spooning into the criminal act [of rape]." Young women could internalize this view of female complicity, as did one who told a psychiatrist that she felt responsible for allowing a man to escort her home, thus leading him on in a way that resulted in her rape.[26]

Psychologists applied another new diagnostic category, the psychopath, to sexually active young women as well as to prostitutes. In doing so they assumed that these young women must be mentally ill to engage in sexual relations outside of marriage, especially because working women could now earn wages without resorting to prostitution. These psychiatric views, which reversed Victorian ideas about female innocence, tended to depict men as the sexual victims of women. The diagnosis of psychopathic personality could be racially specific as well, for white girls were deemed abnormal if they were sexually active whereas black girls were seen as innately immoral.[27] For all adolescent girls, new social freedoms carried risks of unwanted sex and of being labeled delinquent.

Even before Sigmund Freud's ideas about infantile sexuality became popularly known in the United States in the 1930s, children began to appear in this literature as desiring partners, rather than as victims of rape. In 1896 Freud proposed that childhood sexual trauma underlay the hysterical physiological symptoms he observed in many of his adult female patients. The following year, however, he rejected this interpretation and instead attributed accounts of seduction by fathers to fantasies that emanated from a child's sexual desire for the parent of the opposite sex. Legal writers began incorporating these views, as did John Henry Wigmore in his influential treatises on evidence. In 1915 Wigmore cited criminal psychologists to warn judges that some women habitually lied about rape; in 1934 he invoked "modern psychiatrists" who studied the "psychic complexes" of "errant young girls and women" to call attention to their "false charges."[28]

The belief that children desired sex with adults and fabricated rape and incest charges recurred in medical literature published in the early twentieth century. Travis Gibb, who worked with the NYSPCC, blamed children for sex crimes and questioned whether underage sex should be considered rape at all. He used the term *willing victim* to refer to girls between the ages of twelve and sixteen who, because of the low moral standards of their environments, became sexually active. When they had relations with older men, Gibb believed, it was willingly and "usually for pay." Only because of the age-of-consent laws, he complained, could the state prosecute these men. Sociologist William I. Thomas, author of *The Unadjusted Girl* (1923), cited Gibb approvingly and added his own view that girls often manufactured tales of seduction and betrayal to explain their fall from virtue, when in fact they used sex "as a coin would be used, to secure adventure and pleasure."[29]

Dr. Gurney Williams, who described himself as the "Sometime District Police Surgeon of Philadelphia," agreed that most underage sex cases should not be considered rape. "Many of these girls lie as easily as a morphine fiend," he wrote. Underpaid working girls, Williams acknowledged, were "constantly fighting to protect their virtue," but he lamented that many of them succumbed to the temptation to buy comforts by selling their bodies. He claimed to have conducted fourteen thousand vaginal examinations and investigated hundreds of rape cases. "The more patients I see," he wrote in 1913, "the more I am impressed with the fact that *we seldom find cases of rape in healthy, robust girls in possession of their faculties and who are above the age of fourteen, provided they were not a willing party to the assault*" (his emphasis). Invoking his medical authority, Williams tried to shift responsibility for underage sex from men to girls. He claimed that because "the mere crossing of the knees absolutely prevents penetration . . . a man must struggle desperately to penetrate the vagina of a vigorous, virtue-protecting girl." Saying that the statements of girls "often amount to nothing," Dr. Williams advised mothers not to bring charges to court unless they had overwhelming physical evidence to corroborate their daughters' stories.[30]

Not all forensic physicians shared these views. Dr. Frank Draper, a medical examiner in Massachusetts and a professor of legal medicine at Harvard University, generally supported the new statutory rape laws and credited women social reformers for helping enact them. Draper seemed relieved, however, that in Massachusetts they had failed to increase the age of consent to eighteen, which for him represented the "danger of overdoing the protective principle." In contrast to Gibb and Williams, Draper did not blame children and young girls. In an acknowledgment of the abuse of power, that was rare for its time, he suggested that girls were more vulnerable to rape because adults had both ease of access to children and authority over them. Like his colleagues, Draper warned doctors to be on guard against fraudulent accusations of rape that could involve extortion, but he also instructed them to examine the child repeatedly, lest they overlook signs of trauma.[31]

More typically, physicians worried about false charges. In a revealing symposium published in the *American Journal of Urology and Sexology* in 1918 and 1919, the editors hoped to alert lawyers to "the great danger that men are often in from false accusations by female children and women." The editorial recirculated earlier claims "that *a number of men have been hung*" because of fabricated charges. Although capital punishment remained rare for white men, the journal used the quote to reiterate the fears that men's sexual privileges, if not their lives, were in danger. At present, the editorial continued, "not in one out of ten cases are the charges of rape found to be true," pointing the blame particularly at young girls who were "sometimes remarkable liars and *devilishly cunning* inventors." One issue in this series included more than a dozen short articles culled from French, British, and American medical texts from the past few decades with titles such as "Lying Child Found Out by Trick," "Characteristic Example of Female Revenge," and "Father Falsely Accused by Bragging Daughter."[32]

As the last title suggests, enduring skepticism about incest claims contributed to the disbelief of children. Many doctors simply denied the possibility that fathers sexually abused their daughters. Even Progressive-era social hygiene advocates, such as pioneering public health physician Alice

Hamilton, accepted the dominant wisdom that venereal disease in girls resulted from unsanitary households rather than from unwanted sex within the family. Many physicians continued to attribute incest almost exclusively to lower-class, immigrant, and black families. Although Travis Gibb acknowledged that these crimes undoubtedly occurred "among the well-to-do," who avoided "the unpleasant notoriety" that came with prosecution, he still believed that most incest cases occurred among the poorer classes. Along with environmental influences such as crowded living conditions, he noted the folk belief among some immigrants that having sex with a virgin could cure venereal disease.[33]

The recurrent doubts about girls who accused their fathers of rape may be indicative of the distress felt by these doctors about the decline of patriarchal authority within the family. One writer in the symposium on false accusations expressed relief that an "unhappy father was acquitted" after a thirteen-year-old girl claimed that he had violated her two years earlier. Reporting that a fourteen-year-old girl, whose father had been having sex with her, exposed him for assaulting an eleven-year-old girl, a medical writer condemned the child's betrayal, not her father's. Labeling the daughter "one of the most virulent little minxes he'd ever seen," the doctor attributed her revelation of the rape to jealousy of the other child.[34] Children can, of course, be untruthful. Whatever the merits of individual cases, however, the accumulation of these stories in a medical journal left the distinct impression that most children lied about rape and that men had become victims of their wiles.

By the 1920s, physicians and jurists were reinforcing their respective beliefs that girls were prone to lie about rape and incest. The leading child guidance scholar, Dr. William Healy, who directed the Judge Baker Clinic in Boston, published accounts of girls who had been willing victims of incest. Legal texts, such as revisions of Wigmore's treatise on evidence, then incorporated Healy to support the view that girls made false accusations of rape. Whether intentionally or unintentionally, medical texts explained, girls were known to "accuse an innocent person." Fathers increasingly defended themselves from incest charges by attacking the character of their daughters. At the same time incest began to disappear from public view, as evidenced by sparser reporting in newspapers and the closing of courtrooms during incest hearings.[35]

Despite, or perhaps because of, the skepticism about children's accounts, most assaults on adolescent girls continued to go unreported. Clinical records and social surveys, many of them written by women professionals who worked with delinquent girls, hint at the broader problem. In 1912 gynecologist Clara Seippel wrote that over a six-month period, fifty-three of the children treated for venereal disease in Chicago had been victims of sexual assault. She suggested that hundreds of other cases went unprosecuted, including those in which fathers were never suspected of having infected their daughters. Some social workers also noted the frequency of incest in the histories of girls sentenced to reformatories. In 1910 Jane Addams told professional colleagues that almost 10 percent of the girls committed to an Illinois industrial school for sexual immorality had "become involved with members of their own families." Two years later Dr. Edith Spaulding wrote that 30 percent of the venereally infected female delinquents she studied had been sexually involved with relatives. Among delinquent girls treated by therapists at the Judge Baker Clinic in 1920, almost half reported incestuous sexual relations and one out of five reported nonincestuous rape. A study of girls on city streets during the 1930s found that 20 percent had been raped within their families.[36] All of these reports linked sexual assault with some form of juvenile delinquency, a formulation that in turn influenced the definition of rape in the early twentieth century.

Most of the girls studied by social workers and scholars did not refer to their experiences as rape. Some interpreted coercive and even violent acts as a kind of sexual initiation. Like courts and welfare agencies that defined rape as the act of a stranger rather than of a family member, young women did not necessarily consider incestuous relations to be a crime. Records of one agency reveal that almost half of the "strangers" who had sex with girls were in fact family friends who had long abused children with impunity before being reported. Rather than interpret these acts as rape, many young women internalized the view of themselves as delinquents, an identity suggested by professional social workers who sometimes referred to "forced sex delinquency" rather than sexual assault.[37] Once raped, some girls did in fact accept money for sex, whether to escape from abusive homes or because they had assumed the legitimacy of this practice. Just a generation after statutory rape reform promised to extend protection to them, adolescent girls who had consensual or coercive sex were being redefined as prostitutes, the discourse on rape supplanted by one on delinquency.

IN LEGAL, psychological, and medical literature, the flip side of the complicitous, sexualized woman was the victimized man. The image had precedents in the debate on the criminalization of seduction, epitomized by an anonymous writer who warned in 1888 that some "evil disposed women victimize young men and boys and lead them into vicious pathways." Opponents of statutory rape reform had predicted widespread injustice to men if the laws passed. By the 1920s, though, a broader range of commentators elaborated on particular dangers posed by sexually active women. Unlike the social purity advocates who had blamed men for woman's fall, antiprostitution campaigns during and after World War I targeted women themselves for engaging in commercialized sex and for spreading venereal disease, at the expense of men. Simultaneously, American popular culture more frequently portrayed white women not as sexually naive but rather as erotically curious and alluring. In contrast to nineteenth-century reformers who insisted that girls under age eighteen did not have the capacity to consent to sex, by 1924 more experts agreed with a lawyer who wrote that "in this day of wide-spread sexual instruction," a sixteen-year-old girl "should be well able to protect herself."[38]

In this climate it is not surprising that some courts began to treat men more leniently in statutory rape cases, especially if both parties were young. Critics had long complained about the injustice of young men serving long prison terms for engaging in consensual relations with young women, who typically went unpunished. In 1890 the Kansas Supreme Court had rejected the argument that the age-of-consent statute inflicted cruel and unusual punishment in the case of a sixteen-year-old boy sentenced to five years in prison for having sex with a sixteen-year-old girl. In 1903, however, the California Supreme Court reversed a conviction by calling for stricter procedural scrutiny in statutory rape cases, because the girl might be "the older and more aggressive of the two." The court pointed out that while she might "be a common prostitute and seduce a boy of fifteen," only he was "guilty of a felony, while to her the law awards no punishment." The opinion suggested that unequal protection disadvantaged young men.[39] Doubts about the fairness of the law may have influenced judges who rejected imprisonment in some cases. Between 1910 and 1920, two-thirds of the men convicted of statutory rape in Alameda County, California, received probation, an alternative offered to under one-fifth for those convicted of forcible rape. New York courts initially sent men to prison for one to ten years, depending on whether underage girls had consented or were coerced. After 1916, however, suspended sentences or short prison terms prevailed.[40]

Significantly, black and immigrant men continued to be imprisoned. In Alameda County, African American men received the harshest sentences for sex with underage girls. One black man, who was willing to marry his fifteen-year-old consensual partner (who was also black), was sent to San Quentin prison for ten years. There were notable exceptions. Generally a nonwhite man in California fared better in court if he represented himself as "a good American," a family man, and an industrious worker, especially if white witnesses testified to his decency. In 1933 a married black man, Harold Garrison, stood trial in Los Angeles for statutory rape after he ran off with a fifteen-year-old black co-worker. His white employer told the court that Garrison had previously "lived up to his responsibilities as a man and provided for his family." When the judge pronounced a sentence of probation rather than jail, he cited this testimony as evidence that Garrison had "conducted himself as a good negro in the past."[41]

Trying to become a family man did not benefit Ricardo Alva, age twenty-five, a Mexican migrant who was imprisoned for statutory rape after he tried to elope with a twelve-year-old girl, also from Mexico.[42] In some cases, though, citizenship could convey advantages. In overturning a conviction for the rape of a twelve-year-old, an appellate justice in Texas considered it "too serious a matter" to deprive "the liberty of a citizen, even though he be an ignorant and unknown Mexican," by sending him to prison on the testimony of a child. Asian immigrants, unable to make citizenship claims, could be at a disadvantage in court. An assessment that one migrant from Japan charged with statutory rape had a "lower than normal sex drive typical of Oriental men" did help keep him out of jail. But economic competition could reinforce sexual fears about Asian immigrants. In 1930 California Judge D. W. Rohrback wrote that the Filipino male was "mixing with young white girls from thirteen to seventeen. He gives them silk underwear and makes them pregnant and crowds whites out of jobs in the the bargain."[43] Hard times and residual fears about the sexual vulnerability of white girls could skew the application of statutory rape laws.

European immigrants, particularly those considered too dark-complexioned to qualify as white, could also pay a high price for statutory rape convictions. At a time when courts sentenced white men to probation for having sex with underage girls, a California judge sentenced Frank Silva, a twenty-three-year-old immigrant worker, to seven years in prison for this crime. Even some jurors in the case felt that the sentence was "entirely out of proportion to the offense charged." The judge, however, invested the case with the fate of a moral society. He told Silva, "By your assaulting the virtue of girls . . . you were assaulting the very foundation of the cornerstone of the government." For some immigrants the consequences of statutory rape included deportation. The Immigration Act of 1917 allowed the exclusion of anyone who had been convicted of a crime "involving moral turpitude," including "carnal knowledge," within five years of entry into the country. Under this provision a resident alien named Bendel was deported in 1927. He had been living in the United States since 1908 and had served a two-year jail term for having sex with a fifteen-year-old girl. Six years later, when he tried to reenter the country from Canada, this criminal record provided grounds to deport him.[44]

For native-born white men, extending the age of consent to eighteen may have evoked more sympathetic treatment—the older the girl, the more likely the presumption that she had been sexually active. After the New York legislature set the age threshold at eighteen, the number of appellate rape cases increased dramatically, but the court reversed most of the convictions involving girls between the ages of sixteen and eighteen.[45] Pauline Jenner had charged a twenty-one-year-old cloakmaker with raping her at his workplace. In 1902 the court overturned his conviction, in part because it believed that "[her testimony about] screaming and resisting to the extent of her ability, is certainly very improbable." Florence Killeen could not convince the court that John Swasey had abducted her into his rooms for the purpose of sexual intercourse—the kind of case that antiprostitution reformers envisioned would keep girls from a life of vice—because none of the required corroborating witnesses persuaded the court. The fact that Killeen admitted her prior sexual experience no doubt counted against her.[46]

In the next decades the zeal for protecting adolescent girls clearly abated. After peaking in the first decade of the century, appellate rape cases declined in New York State, as did the proportion of cases involving complainants under age eighteen. In New York City the courts continued to punish assaults on very young children with prison terms, but by the 1930s, 80 percent of the city's statutory rapes cases had been converted from felonies to misdemeanors. Age-of-consent prosecutions soon became rare in New York. The pejorative term *jail bait*, used to refer to underage sexual partners, implied that girls who had sex with older men were both willing and devious. In other locales the once-popular statutory rape charge lost its allure as young women once considered innocents became redefined as sexual delinquents. Between 1920 and 1930, underage sex declined from three-fourths to one-fourth of the rape cases considered by California appeals courts.[47] The view of girls as aggressors and boys as victims spread throughout the criminal justice system. As the mother of a young man imprisoned for statutory rape wrote angrily in the 1930s, girls "can get boys or men in trouble this way [and] then they laugh about it."[48]

Like this mother, liberal reformers questioned the fairness of incarcerating young men who had consensual relationships with their peers. Judge Ben Lindsey, who generally favored probation over prison when he sentenced youths in his Denver juvenile court, believed that girls "often have as much to do with it as the boys." An influential author who helped shape modern American views on marriage and sexuality, Lindsey preferred to call it "a 50–50 case," presuming that underage sex involved the mutual participation of the sexual partners. He wanted to distinguish between violent rape, which he considered a rare occurrence, and the more frequent "indiscretions" of youth that others were "*calling* rape." Better to rehabilitate "youthful rapers" through social work methods, he believed, than to send them to prison and further disadvantage their struggling families.[49] Lindsey's perspective could not have been further from that of the protectionists, who had tried to expand the definition of rape and give the benefit of the doubt to adolescent girls. As Americans placed less value on female chastity, however, courts became more comfortable with Lindsey's move to decriminalize consensual sex, or at least to minimize the penalties.

These reactions to age-of-consent laws had implications for the redefinition of rape for adult women as well as for adolescent girls, and for forcible as well as statutory rape. The very focus on youth may have deflected attention from the classic cases of violent assault against women.[50] At the same time the growing skepticism about girls could make older women seem even less believable in rape cases, especially if they could not prove that they were chaste. For decades courts had struggled with the question of whether to admit evidence of a woman's past sexual experience, and not only her general reputation. Numerous appeals hinged on whether the accuser had been chaste. In 1911, for example, an Iowa court overturned a conviction for rape on the grounds that the jury should have been able to consider prior "voluntary sexual relations with the defendant" to show "the consent of the prosecutrix." At a time when women were more likely to have some sexual experience, legal writers argued that admitting this evidence provided men with necessary protections in rape cases. A woman "already guilty of indulgence in illicit sexual intercourse," a law review article argued in 1916, would be more likely to consent again. Thus the "previous unchastity of the prosecutrix" should weigh heavily in determining consent in all rape cases.[51]

Concerns about threats to men's lives, similar to those expressed in debates over incest accusations, recurred in discussions of the forcible rape of adult women. In states that retained the death penalty for rape, courts were advised to balance "the interests of a prisoner" more "than those of the prosecutrix" because her "life and liberty are not in jeopardy."[52] The logic of weighing a man's life against a woman's reputation could seem compelling. By the 1920s, however, the majority of states had abolished capital punishment for rape, as for most other crimes. Most of the eighteen states that retained this penalty were in the South, where the punishment was disproportionately applied to African American men. White men might well be deprived of their liberty through imprisonment, but they rarely faced execution. Summoning the specter of unjust execution—for white men, not for black men subject to lynching—reframed an older hyperbolic claim. In the past, rape was often considered a fate worse than death for women. Now, however, rape accusations against men seemed the greater threat.

For two generations a coalition of reformers had attempted to broaden the definition of rape by limiting the consent defense and the resistance requirement. During the Progressive era medical and legal authorities sought to reverse this trend and narrow the grounds for conviction. At times their views echoed pre-Victorian endorsements of aggressive male sexuality and a concomitant distrust of designing women. This libertine tradition had never disappeared, but it had been on the defensive during the period in which Americans were formulating an ideal of middle-class morality centered on the reproductive family. In the early twentieth century, gender lines blurred as women sought professional opportunities and began to achieve suffrage. At the same time a constellation of ideas affirmed the value of sexual pleasure in its own right and loosened the bonds between sexuality and reproduction.[53] In the context of this sexual liberalism, women who complained of sexual assault seemed at best outdated and at worst psychologically damaged and criminally deceptive.

The work of Dr. William J. Robinson illustrates the connection between liberal sexual values and the demonization of adult women who charged rape. The editor of the *Journal of Urology and Sexology*, Robinson in many ways represented a break with Victorian-era medical views of sex. He was an influential public advocate of birth control, published the work of sex radicals, championed sex education, and questioned the criminalization of abortion. But he shared with his medical predecessors a deep fear that women could infringe on men's sexual liberties. In the nineteenth century Robinson had blamed men's impotence on "frigidity" in women. In the early twentieth century he railed against women who falsely accused men of rape. His journal published the 1918 symposium on the subject in which doctors blamed girls and women for allowing men to engage in "the amorous sport" of lovemaking and then refusing intercourse when it was too late for the men to stop. In his 1928 popular guide to sex and marriage Robinson argued that a "distinct type of woman" enjoyed "a peculiar sadistic pleasure from accusing men, and seeing them suffer." Only 10 percent of all rape charges, he insisted, were true.[54] The misogynistic tone of Robinson's views of rape suggested that the greater autonomy of modern girls and women may have challenged the sense of entitlement that physicians shared with other white men.

TRACKING THE AGE-OF-CONSENT LAWS from enactment to enforcement demonstrates the extent to which American sexual values were in flux in the early twentieth century. Initially the laws called attention to the sexual vulnerability of adolescent girls. By negating the consent defense, they granted leverage in the courtroom for many young women. But the protective framework that inspired the laws eroded as modern theories of female sexuality, along with the behaviors of adolescent girls themselves, displaced the Victorian protective impulse. Building on earlier representations of desiring and duplicitous girls and women, new psychiatric views of the hypersexual female exacerbated the obstacles to implementing the laws. Although the press remained more sympathetic to young victims, physicians and psychologists often portrayed children as "willing victims" and castigated adult women as deceitful and vengeful. Appellate courts properly guarded the rights of defendants, but they increasingly did so in terms that overrode the intent of the new laws. By the 1920s and 1930s the application of statutory rape law was contributing to, as much as limiting, white men's sexual privileges. The language of protection that had characterized reform in the nineteenth century now appeared in defense of those men who could invoke their status as citizens to avoid, or to overturn, convictions for having sex with underage girls. This convergence of the older distrust of female deceit with the sexualization of girls helped shape the discourse on rape for all women, whatever their age and whether they brought forcible or statutory rape charges.

9

The Sexual Vulnerability of Boys

In 1914 police in Long Beach, California, uncovered a local "society of queers" when they arrested fifty formerly respectable men for the crime of "social vagrancy." In addition to frequenting certain clubs, members of this social group held risqué parties at which both men and women cross-dressed. Most alarming to the newspaper editor who publicized the scandal was the accusation that older men had recruited younger men, known as "chickens," into their world. The reporter sent to investigate this Long Beach subculture voiced the fear that youths exposed to "this immoral purpose" might "like the sensation" and be converted to a life of homosexuality. His reaction echoed anxieties that had surfaced a few years earlier during a sex scandal in Portland, Oregon. The dozens of predominantly white, middle-class men arrested there in 1912 for socializing at drag parties had been consenting adults. The youngest attendee was nineteen years old. Yet the press and the court highlighted the danger posed to youths. A prosecutor claimed that older men went after "young fellows that looked good to them; these young chickens, were just dragged and thrown from one to the other, and when they got to one man they had to go to them all."[1]

Such local episodes signaled a growing anxiety in Progressive-era America that homosexuality could spread like a contagious disease from adult men to youths and boys. Like the adolescent girls targeted by age-of-consent laws, young men seemed to be at risk of either seduction or assault by older men. The recent statutory rape reforms may have prompted recognition of the sexual vulnerability of boys by drawing attention to adolescents. The breakdown of Victorian sexual ideals, which made female sexual agency more imaginable, also generated unease that men could be victims and not only aggressors. A growing recognition of same-sex relationships compounded the problem. In the first decades of

168

the twentieth century, concerns about children merged with discomfort about both gender inversion and a homosexual peril to redefine the victims of sexual assault as either male or female youths.

By the 1930s an earlier cultural silence about sexual relationships between men and boys had been replaced by vocal public concern about sex crimes against boys. As in the past, certain groups of men represented particular sexual threats. While African American men were overrepresented in interracial rape cases, they were rarely charged with sodomy, perhaps because of the cultural associations of black men with hypermasculinity rather than with effeminacy. Certain foreign-born men came to be associated with perversion, reflecting in part the nativist sentiments that contributed to the enactment of immigration restriction in the 1920s. By then the popularization of Freudian ideas was accelerating public awareness of both childhood sexuality and same-sex relations. Soon the newly emerging figure of the homosexual supplanted the immigrant as the primary sexual peril for boys. By recognizing boys as objects of sexual seduction or victims of assault, doctors, jurists, and social reformers contested the long-standing Anglo-American definition of rape as a heterosexual act. In the process the sexual vulnerability of children began to displace the protection of adult women in the discourse on sexual assault.

DURING THE INITIAL debates over raising the age of consent, boys had appeared only fleetingly as victims, and then in purely heterosexual terms. At the time critics complained that the proposed laws could lead to the unjust imprisonment of boys and young men who had been seduced by girls or women. In 1886 the WCTU had professed a willingness to extend protection to boys, but not quite yet, for girls remained their priority. Imagining a gender reversal to make her point, a WCTU member explained, "When old women of eighty, and married and unmarried women of middle age, *in good society and of fine social standing,* go about ruining boys of ten and twelve and sixteen it will be time to sound the alarm for boys as we are now sounding it for girls." State Representative Carrie Clyde Holly of Colorado, who introduced age-of-consent legislation soon after her election to office, questioned the logic of the critics who worried about boys as victims of seduction. Was it really "necessary to protect the world against the allurement of the lamb?" she asked. Holly challenged opponents of statutory rape reform to offer proof that "boys can be assaulted in the same way."[2]

Other women reformers, however, admitted that the laws they supported were indeed biased because they safeguarded only one sex. Boys and girls could "tempt each other," suffragist Anna Garlin Spencer admitted, noting that the statutory rape crusade overlooked "the need of protecting little boys and half-grown boys against debauchment" by women. Even so central a figure in the movement as Helen H. Gardener wrote in 1895 that she would have preferred that "age-of-protection bills" shield "youth rather than sex."[3] Like most of her colleagues, however, Gardner agreed to table the larger goal of gender equality in favor of the short-term gain of protecting girls. Even if the nineteenth-century age-of-consent campaign had sought to include boys, however, the laws would have defended them only from seduction or coercion by women. The debate never moved beyond the framework of heterosexual relations to ask whether boys could be the victims of men. This limitation is not surprising, given the legal definition of rape at the time as a crime committed by a man against a woman.

When child-savers first raised the question of sexual coercion and assaults upon boys by adult men, sodomy laws provided the legal framework for doing so. For the most part, nineteenth-century sodomy laws criminalized penetrative anal intercourse, an act that was associated with sexual relations between men. Almost every state and territory outlawed sodomy, buggery, bestiality, or "the infamous crime against nature." This crime was considered to be so unspeakable that many laws failed to mention the precise act. As a 1919 California court explained, "every person of ordinary intelligence [understood] what the crime against nature with a human being [was]." Nineteenth-century court decisions presumed that anal intercourse was always forcible.[4] Unlike rape prosecutions, however, both partners in a sodomy case could be guilty of the crime.

Abundant historical evidence reveals that same-sex activity, or sodomitical acts, whether consensual or coercive, regularly occurred in the nineteenth century. All-male environments such as ships, the military, prisons, mining camps, and boarding schools or colleges provided one kind of setting conducive to sodomy. Although moralists occasionally issued jeremiads against the sinfulness of this behavior, during most of the century Americans seemed to ignore sodomy. The theories of French historian Michel Foucault notwithstanding—he argued that the Victorian era witnessed an expanding discourse on sexual deviance and its regulation—public reticence about male-male sexuality prevailed in the United States until the very late nineteenth century. In the 1870s, for

example, when a student at Princeton University infected with rectal gonorrhea the male friend whose bed he shared, a physician wrote that the
cause of transmission must have been a cloth that slipped between them
in the night. In a rare nineteenth-century sodomy trial, in which a man
was accused of having sex with a thirteen-year-old boy, a Missouri court
noted that "this is a case which, however frequently committed, is rarely
brought to the knowledge of the police." Even in the early twentieth century, some courts chose to hear sodomy cases in private rather than
openly publicize the act.[5]

Arrest and prosecution for sodomy remained unusual through much of
the nineteenth century. New York City records reveal only twenty-two
indictments for sodomy between 1796 and 1873. According to the *National Police Gazette,* during one six-month period in 1846 officers made
only three arrests for sodomy, compared to eighteen for attempted rape,
eight for murders, and over three hundred for prostitution. In cities such
as San Francisco and Boston, as well, arrests for rape and prostitution far
exceeded those for the "crime against nature."[6] Between 1800 and 1880,
appeals courts throughout the country heard only twenty cases concerning this crime. Nor did many men serve prison terms for sodomy in the
nineteenth century. And at a time when daily newspapers routinely reported crime stories culled from police registers, they rarely published accounts of sodomy. In the 1840s the short-lived "flash press" of New York
City—weekly papers that promoted heterosexual libertinism—launched a
campaign against men who engaged in sodomy and masturbation, targeting immigrants in particular. But the mainstream press did not feature
these acts. In contrast to regular coverage of rape cases, American newspapers rarely discussed sodomy before the 1870s.[7] Despite the criminalization of sodomy, same-sex relations remained largely invisible.

Though seldom used to punish consensual relations, sodomy laws did
serve another function. Rape statutes did not apply to same-sex relations,
but prosecutors could apply sodomy laws to prosecute nonconsensual sexual acts between men, particularly if they involved the use of force. Most
historians agree that the nineteenth-century statutes served "primarily as
instruments to regulate sexual assault," rather than to prosecute homosexual conduct. In the early twentieth century, military trials for sodomy reflected this understanding. Soldiers testified, "They ravished me like they
would a woman" or "I was raped like a bad woman."[8]

Prosecution for sodomy frequently involved not only the use of force
but also a relationship between a man and a boy. This pattern can be

found as early as the colonial era, when sodomy cases typically involved an older man who had sex with a social subordinate, such as a young servant or a boy. One of the first relevant appellate court decisions, an 1810 Maryland case, involved a conviction for the use of force against a youth while "attempting to commit *Sodomy*." The few New York City prosecutions in the nineteenth century included the case of George Mason, who in 1857 had sex with several boys aged eleven to fourteen. When prosecution expanded after 1890, children predominated in New York City sodomy cases. Newspaper reports of arrests typically included boys or youths. A few exposés of sodomites in mid-nineteenth-century New York City referred to boys and youths as the "prey" of older men, as did an early complaint about sex in prisons that "boys are prostituted to the lust of old convicts."[9] Around half of a sample of national newspaper reports of these cases involved sex between adult males and boys.[10]

In a sense, sodomy law served as a kind of unofficial age-of-consent mechanism for male-male sexual relations. Although the laws usually applied to both partners who engaged in anal sex, considering one of them the "accomplice," their wording often exempted youths from being considered accomplices or from having to prove that they had not consented. Like some statutory rape laws, many sodomy statutes suspended the requirement of corroborating evidence if the "partner" in the crime had been either unwilling or was a minor who was "incapable of granting consent." An 1891 Connecticut court ruling illustrates this principle. Two boys, aged twelve and fifteen, had "consented to the act" of buggery. Even though the younger child had "submitted without resistance," the court held that "still the act was done by force."[11]

This legal precedent was already in place when, at the end of the nineteenth century, several historical factors converged to draw attention to sexual relations between men and boys. In the growing commercial and industrial cities, wage-earning men more frequently lived apart from families and enjoyed much greater personal autonomy, and anonymity, than in the past. Freed from community controls over their sexual lives, those who were so inclined could seek out other men as sexual partners. Alongside the urban sexual subculture surrounding the brothel, cities offered new opportunities for same-sex relations. By the early twentieth century, certain locations—parks, docks, bathhouses, public restrooms, and red-light districts—became magnets for men who sought male sexual partners. In New York City, both the bohemian neighborhood of Greenwich Village and the increasingly African American neighborhood of

Harlem nurtured areas of tolerance for men and women whose gender identity or sexual desires set them apart from the norms of the reproductive family.[12]

In addition to these new social spaces, the intellectual framework for understanding same-sex relationships was shifting. Together with an earlier religious language of sin, a medical language of disease emerged within the new specializations of sexology and psychiatry. In the past an act of sodomy did not necessarily mark a man (or a woman) as a lifelong practitioner. By the 1890s, however, innovative sexual theories originating in Europe were circulating in the United States. Writers such as Richard von Krafft-Ebing referred to "sexual inversion" as a medical condition. Press accounts of the 1895 British trial of Oscar Wilde for "gross indecency" heightened public awareness of same-sex relationships. Medical references to the sex pervert as a degenerate type proliferated, as did the category of the "homosexual" who neither desired nor (like the invert) identified with the opposite sex. By the era of World War I, a concern about perverts, fairies, inverts, and homosexuals had become more visible in America. In 1917, for example, Dr. Charles Burr warned the American Academy of Medicine that American boys were becoming effeminate rather than masculine, raising the problem of what the *Los Angeles Times* labeled "Homosexuality: A New Menace."[13]

Even though sodomy had been condemned throughout the nineteenth century, it was only after the emergence of both urban subcultures and medical theories of sexual perversion that same-sex male relations attracted serious notice among American reformers. Along with their attacks on the brothel and the saloon, those who wanted to suppress urban vice began to take an interest in enforcing sodomy laws. Never as influential as the related antiprostitution and social hygiene campaigns, antisodomy efforts remained mired in the legacy of reticence. Yet the broader attacks on prostitution, and especially the vice investigations conducted in most major American cities during the Progressive era, revealed to the public glimpses of a subterranean homosexual culture. Social reformers identified young working men who, like young working women, sometimes traded sexual favors for money, meals, or movies. Vice reports mentioned the overlapping worlds of the prostitute and the sodomite in brothels and saloons, including accounts of young boys who sold oral or anal sex. In 1911 the Chicago Vice Commission called homosexuality one of the worst vices in the city, while some cities, such as New York, assigned police officers to patrol "male prostitutes." Although he never

acted on the promise, one Oregon congressman reacted to the 1912 homosexual scandal in Portland by calling for a federal commission to help
"stamp out infamous crimes."[14]

Despite this recognition of sodomy, and in contrast to abundant media
coverage of prostitution, even in the early twentieth century newspaper
reports of same-sex relations remained rare.[15] In 1909 the Washington
State legislature made it a misdemeanor to publish detailed accounts of
sodomy or of trials for other sex offenses.[16] During the 1912 Portland sex
scandal, one newspaper declined to detail the case and condemned another paper of "aiding the spread of degeneracy among youth" for doing
so. According to the *Oregon Journal,* "every child and boy in Portland
will sooner or later learn the facts, and thereby will be laid the foundation for infection and contamination." Even the Portland Vice Commission chose to suppress information. In a two-hundred-page report that
concentrated on prostitution, the Commission acknowledged that dozens of young boys "had been seduced by male inverts" in the year preceding the 1912 scandal. Yet the report devoted only one paragraph to the
subject because the Commission felt that sharing its knowledge "could
do no possible good . . . and might do irremediable injury."[17] Silence
seemed preferable to exposing the extent, and the possibility, of same-sex
relations.

One of the few detailed accounts about sodomy, published in the *National Police Gazette* in 1895, is worth noting for its overlapping concerns
about age, race, and urban opportunities for sexual contagion. The article's title, "Nameless Crimes Out West," promised discretion, but the
story dwelled on sordid details and named the crime of sodomy in particular. It claimed that in Indianapolis the police had discovered that several
boys had been "lured to their ruin" by two "colored men." In a tale described as "so horrible, so disgusting and so beastly, that it is almost beyond belief" (yet, the paper insisted, was truthful and "vouched for"), the
older black men had invited the white boys to their rooms. There they
incited the passions of the youths by showing them vulgar pictures, which
induced the boys to commit "the nameless crime." The "intimacy" with
the colored men continued, but other local men also came to these rooms.
These white men, the paper reported, would pay the boys one or two dollars to "commit the act." To this disturbing combination of older black
men recruiting younger white boys who sold sex to older white men, the
Gazette added a caveat about the transmission of a permanent sexual
identity: "When once a man or boy falls victim to this beastly habit, it is

no easy matter to break away," the paper warned, "and unless he has a very strong will power, he will find himself visiting men of this class on every occasion."[18] Whether an imaginary or factual account, the article marked an association of sodomy with threats to youth.

A range of evidence points to greater regulation of male-male sexual relations by the early twentieth century. In New York City, annual average arrests for sodomy increased from 21 in 1896–1900, to 69 in 1906–1910, to 101 in 1916–1920.[19] Appellate courts throughout the country heard fewer than ten cases related to sodomy per decade between 1850 and 1880; during the 1880s they ruled in fifteen such cases and during the 1890s over sixty. New laws and new terminology helped expand the grounds for prosecution. In the past, sodomy laws criminalized only anal sex; increasingly states added oral-genital contact and the broader category of "unnatural and lascivious acts" to the list of crimes. The Oregon sodomy law expanded after the 1912 Portland scandal to include "any act or practice of sexual perversity." Three years later the California legislature first criminalized fellatio and cunnilingus. Applicable to heterosexual as well as homosexual acts, these statutory revisions point to a discomfort with the growing acceptance among Americans of the legitimacy of nonreproductive sexual relations. As sexual liberalism began to infiltrate mainstream culture, moral authorities drew a stronger boundary between normal and abnormal practices. Even after World War I, when the sexualized urban youth culture and prostitution elicited less public concern, sodomy and other perversions loomed large as challenges to the primacy of the reproductive family.[20]

Proposals to sterilize sexual perverts provide another measure of the alarm over the spread of homosexuality. In the 1880s and 1890s, a few doctors had begun to perform surgical castrations or vasectomies, claiming they could eliminate sex perversion. Most of these procedures took place in state institutions, such as prisons and homes for the "feeble-minded," a term then applied to those considered mentally subnormal. Indiana passed the first state eugenic law in 1907, and over the next decade fifteen more states followed suit. Along with the goal of preventing the reproduction of the insane, feebleminded, and mentally defective population, these laws sanctioned the sterilization of sexual perverts both as a means to diminish sexual activity (which it would not achieve) and as a punishment. In the wake of the Portland sex scandal, for example, an Oregon newspaper editor called for the extension of the existing state eugenic sterilization law to include "perverts" in order to keep them from infecting others "with the venom of their disease." Oregon governor Oswald West also favored the "emasculation" of "degenerates who slink, in all their infamy, through every city, contaminating the young, debauching the innocent, cursing the State." California's statutes, which allowed for "asexualization" of recidivists who had been imprisoned at least two times for rape, assault with intent to rape, or seduction, also included the imprecise category of "a moral or sexual degenerate or pervert." We do not have an account of how many inmates were sterilized for sex crimes, but the impulse to sterilize parallels the practice of castrating black men for rape, whether by law or by lynch mobs.[21]

Evidence on convictions and sentencing is also scarce, but suggestive. The 1880 census showed only 64 men serving prison terms for sodomy in the United States, but in 1890 that number had increased to 244 prisoners. These figures included men such as Frank Pierce of Alameda County, California, who pled guilty to sodomy with a ten-year-old boy and was sentenced to fourteen years in prison. The data from Oregon, which in 1913 increased the maximum penalty for sodomy to fifteen years in prison, shows that average terms lengthened over time. Men convicted between 1886 and 1906 served just over eighteen months; those convicted in the next decade served just over twenty-one months, while those convicted between 1917 and 1926 served almost thirty-three months.[22]

A major function of these expanded statutes and the increased prosecution and punishment for sodomy was to include boys as well as girls in the protective regulation that had been initiated by revised statutory rape laws. In New York City, the NYSPCC played a leading role in accelerating the prosecution of sodomy. In its early years the Society was more attentive to sexual assaults on girls, largely because they believed that these crimes could lead to social ruin and a life of prostitution. But the NYSPCC also helped redefine sodomy. The Society supported the 1892 amendments to New York laws that criminalized oral as well as anal sex committed on "any male or female person." By the early twentieth century the NYSPCC initiated most of the complaints against men suspected of having sex with boys.[23]

The broader child-saving movement influenced the shift from protecting girls to protecting children of both sexes. In the early twentieth century, states passed "age-sensitive" laws that applied to all children and to a wider range of sexual acts than rape or sodomy. These statutes punished adults who committed "any lewd or lascivious act" or took "indecent and improper liberties" with a child under fourteen to sixteen years old, depending on the state and the statute. Unlike age-of-consent legislation, these laws criminalized acts of fondling that did not include penetration. Unlike earlier rape statutes, they were not limited to female victims. In Illinois the category of "crimes against children" included "any immoral, improper or indecent liberties with any child of either sex under the age of 15 years with the intent of arousing, appealing to or gratifying the lust or passions or sexual desires of either such person or child."[24] In a number of states the crime of "contributing to the delinquency of a minor," which initially aimed at those who enticed young women into prostitution, began to include boys.

Like girls, boys were now being treated as victims of sexual assault. Like girls, boys who showed resistance were more believable victims. And like girls, even boys who had consented might be considered victims, rather than accomplices, by virtue of their age.[25] As in rape cases, men charged with crimes related to sodomy tried to defend themselves through a range of familiar arguments. Appellate courts reversed convictions, for example, for lack of proof of "actual penetration." In New York State, even though the law did not require corroboration of a victim's testimony, an appellate court ruled in 1902 that the testimony of a youth "of limited intellect" was not enough to justify a sodomy conviction. In contrast, in a case in which a man was sentenced to life imprisonment for committing sodomy with a seven-year-old boy, the appellate court in Georgia ruled that no corroboration was needed if a child was too young to be an "accomplice."[26]

The unsuccessful appeal of a sodomy conviction by R. B. Harrison of Los Angeles in 1910 reveals other similarities between rape, age-of-consent, and sodomy cases. For one, Harrison's attorney tried to invoke the authority of Lord Hale by pointing out to the court that the charges against him "were easy to make and hard to disprove." Harrison and William Strandberg, age thirteen, had been seen naked together through the opening of some boards in a bathhouse dressing room. The youth testified that they had "engaged in similar acts" before. Because he was under age fourteen, however, Strandberg could not be an adult accomplice, even if he had consented. The court's view in this case emphasized that the older man had excited the boy's passion: "The defendant had first done lascivious things to and with the private members of witness' person, which aroused his sexual passion, and that sodomy was the resulting act." As in other sodomy opinions, the justices expressed their moral outrage. "His whole story," wrote Justice Allen of the California appeals court, "was one shocking in its fullness of description of repeated unnatural and disgusting acts committed between himself and the defendant."[27] By 1912 the California Supreme Court extended the statutory rape principle to boys in a sodomy ruling, using language that echoed the age-of-consent movement: a "child of tender years . . . might be easily overawed into submitting without actually consenting." In 1923 the same court held that under age fourteen a child "is presumed incapable of committing a crime and cannot therefore be deemed an accomplice."[28]

Prosecutors clearly began to use sodomy laws to punish men who had sex with children. Between 1800 and 1895, 27 percent of all reported sodomy cases in the nation involved adults who had sex with minors (all boys). Between 1896 and 1910 that proportion had increased to 45 percent (again, all boys). Between 1911 and 1925, 43 percent of sodomy cases involved minors (twice as many of them boys than girls).[29] Measured by convictions, courts took charges of sodomy with boys at least as seriously as rape charges. Between 1906 and 1926, New York City's conviction rates for cases of sodomy with young boys were similar to those for the rape of young girls. When victims were in their teen years, however, men charged with sodomy with boys were 50 percent more likely to be convicted than men charged with the rape of girls. Those convicted of sodomy in New York City were also more likely to serve prison terms, typically at least five years, whereas those convicted of forcible or statutory rape were more likely to have their sentences suspended or serve under a year in prison.[30]

It is possible that the stigma associated with sodomy suggested to prosecutors that boys who came forward must have had even stronger cases than girls who accused men of rape. Or judges and juries may have believed that boys suffered more harm from the experience of "abnormal" sex with men than girls suffered by having normal, even if nonconsensual, heterosexual relations. In the case of heterosexual rape, mature girls may have seemed more like willing participants than victims, while boys seemed unlikely to consent to sodomy. Jurors and judges may also have assumed that girls, but not boys, engaged in sex for money, because prostitution was so deeply associated with women at the time.[31]

The emergence of modern ideas about gender and sexuality also heightened interest in boys as victims of sexual crimes. As women gained access to public life—participating in higher education, wage labor, politics, and both consumer and popular culture—they encroached on previously male terrain. Though still economically dependent on men's greater earning power, young working women were no longer merely the objects of men's attentions but became active participants in heterosocial life. Medical, legal, and cultural authorities increasingly acknowledged female sexual desire. Historically, whenever women gain access to male privilege, some critics see portents of a masculinity crisis. Opponents of suffrage, for example, frequently depicted the specter of feminized men displaced by masculinized women. One cartoonist imagined enfranchised women behaving like the conquerors of Rome in a drawing titled "The Rape of the Sabine Men."[32] In the early twentieth century, coincident with suffrage victories, a new emphasis on rugged masculinity percolated throughout the culture. The narrowing of opportunities for middle-class men to be "self-made," along with the encroachment of the women's movement, encouraged the quest for new expressions of manliness, ranging from the camping trips of the Boy Scouts to the "strenuous life" and hunting expeditions of former president Theodore Roosevelt. Increasingly, disdain for the "sissy" and the idealization of male physical prowess merged with the discourse of civilized society that differentiated white men from both other races and women.[33]

The fears that men might become like women could spill over into the fear that boys could be feminized through sexual relations with older men. Just as men and boys seemed to be losing their masculine authority, the category of homosexuality as a permanent identity began to supplant the idea of sodomy as an occasional act. Already challenged by women's growing independence, now men also faced sexual jeopardy within their own gender—being seduced and converted to homosexuality. As a result, the demand to monitor the boundaries of both masculinity and heterosexuality intensified.

LIKE THE RACIALIZATION of the rapist in the nineteenth century, which functioned to exclude African Americans from the rights of citizens, the identification of certain male immigrants as threats to boys reinforced the racial ideologies forming in the early twentieth century. The "new immigrants," though valuable members of the growing industrial labor force, encountered deep antipathy to their claims of inclusion in the American polity. A nation long dominated by an Anglo-American Protestant elite worried about the incorporation of millions of Italian, Polish, or Mexican Catholics, as well as Eastern European Jews, within their midst. Chinese, Japanese, South Asian, and Filipino immigrants represented even greater cultural challenges. Americans of British and northern European heritage—the "old immigrants"—considered themselves superior to all of these groups in an imaginary racial hierarchy. Invoking the newly popular theories of eugenics, they referred to the new immigrants as "inferior stock." One respectable writer, popular novelist Honoré Willsie, reported approvingly in the suffrage press about the eugenicist view that "this overwhelming influx from south Europe" would not only make Americans become smaller, darker, and "more mercurial," but would also "change our type of crime—murder, rape and sex immorality will become more common than the Anglo-American crimes of burglary, drunkenness and vagrancy." Around the country, nativist groups called for restrictions on immigration and tighter limits, such as literacy tests, on access to citizenship.[34]

As with the sexual demonization of southern black men, accusations of sexual immorality fueled the hostility to incorporating new immigrants into American culture. At first the demonization of immigrants as sexually immoral focused on prostitution. One of the earliest immigration restriction laws, the Page Act of 1875, attempted to limit the importation of women for "the purposes of prostitution." Particularly directed at Chinese women, it paved the way for the 1882 Chinese Exclusion Act. Charges of immorality extended to Chinese men as well, inciting panic about the seduction and ruin of white women. Because Americans stereotyped Asian immigrant men as effeminate, however, they tended to view them as seducers rather than as violent rapists. New York journalist Jacob Riis popularized images of Chinese men luring white women into their laundries, where they introduced them to opium and a consequent life of moral and sexual dissipation. In 1910, Massachusetts legislators even considered introducing a bill restricting women under age twenty-one from entering a hotel or restaurant run by someone who was Chinese.[35] In the 1920s male Filipino laborers became associated with endangering white women, particularly when these groups interacted at dance halls or formed interracial unions, and in 1930 police in San Francisco were authorized to arrest Filipinos seen with white girls.[36]

Eastern European immigrants were also implicated in the moral ruin of women. The vice investigations conducted in most major cities in the early twentieth century included exposés of swarthy southern European men depicted as procurers or pimps and of young female Jewish "sex delinquents" arrested for prostitution. In 1910 Commissioner General of Immigration Daniel J. Keefe reported on the "enormous business" of "trafficking foreign women for purposes of prostitution," which included "the seduction and distribution" of some American, as well as alien, women and girls. Antiprostitution crusader Clifford Roe singled out Jewish "cadets" (procurers) and "French, Jewish, and Italian" brothel owners. He listed "outrages" as a means of forcing women into prostitution, as in the case of "Mabel," who "at last was the victim of a slave trader by force and the use of chloroform."[37]

While concerns about the immorality of immigrants typically identified the risks to young women, they also alluded to same-sex relations. A California physician who treated several teenage boys for rectal gonorrhea blamed the condition on "sodomistic practices" and claimed that though once rare, "since the influx of foreigners from those countries where unnatural practices are common, more cases are now seen." Attributing to immigrants a penchant for sexual perversion drew upon the ideas of early sexologists such as Krafft-Ebing, who devised a theory of "racial degeneracy" that associated perversion with "primitive" races, the lower classes, and poor immigrants. On the West Coast, nativists warned that the Chinese would bring "paganism, incest, sodomy," as well as miscegenation, to America. Similarly, the Asiatic Exclusion League held that Asian Indians were "effeminate . . . and degraded."[38] More precise concerns about boys appeared in the work of child protection agencies. Just as physicians writing about incest had targeted working-class families, groups such as the SPCC frequently pointed to the poor, to immigrants, and particularly to the urban tenements in which they lived as the culprits in sodomy cases concerning boys. The assumption that the poor had a more primitive, uncontrolled sexuality, encouraged by the social Darwinist ideas of the time, informed these interpretations.

The association of foreigners with sodomy extended beyond depictions of the working class, as illustrated during the 1914 trial of Jewish factory manager Leo Frank in Atlanta. He was not an immigrant himself, but in the context of southern Populist antipathy to Jews, Frank's ethnicity helped mark him as sexually depraved. Charged with the murder of a thirteen-year-old female employee, Frank was also depicted as a pervert. Like European writers who portrayed Jews as effeminate, perverse, and degenerate, southern accusers claimed that Frank had desired oral sex with young girls and they spread rumors that he had a relationship with an office boy. Populist politician Tom Watson labeled Frank a "rich depraved Sodomite" and warned that sexual perverts craved "boys, men, even animals."[39]

Several other new immigrant groups faced prosecution for sexual crimes with boys, with an intriguing focus on men from Greece and Italy. This association may have formed because Mediterranean cultures allowed physical contact among men, or because they tended to overlook same-sex relations as long as men retained their masculine identities as active, rather than passive, partners. The phrase "the Italian vice," a reference to homosexuality in use since the Renaissance, appeared in the anti-obscenity crusade of Anthony Comstock when he described a teacher who had sex with his male pupils.[40] Mediterranean immigrants appeared in sodomy cases throughout the country. In 1889 a court in Florida convicted an Italian-born sailor of attempting sodomy upon a twelve-year-old boy; in 1907 another Florida court sentenced a Greek immigrant to eight years in prison for committing a "crime against nature" with a seventeen-year-old German-born male. Fears of homosexual contagion from Mediterranean immigrants echoed in the comments of the judge considering a parole request from an Italian laborer convicted of sodomy: "Keep in mind that [in] turning him loose upon the community other persons maybe [*sic*] corrupted into the practice of this unnatural crime." Although Greek immigrants represented less than 1 percent of the male population of Portland, Oregon, at the turn of the twentieth century, they appeared in over 11 percent of the arrests during the sex scandal in 1912. Authorities became particularly alarmed about "immoral boys who pander to the passions of vicious Greeks." Some of these "boys" were really youths, such as the nineteen-year-old American-born laborer found with a thirty-five-year-old Greek immigrant, whom detectives arrested.[41]

In addition to perceptions that men from the Mediterranean were prone to sodomy, immigrant social life in the United States may have played a role in linking sexuality and ethnicity. The skewed sex ratio of primarily male immigrants from Greece and Italy, like those from China, could encourage same-sex relations. Sex between older and younger men or boys took place in the mining, logging, and hobo camps of the Northwest, where male immigrants regularly served as itinerant laborers. This subculture had terms for the older "wolves" and the younger "jockers" or "lambs" whose respective sexual roles were either penetrative or receptive. These relationships could be consensual, convenient, or coercive. Younger men might be seduced on the road, or they might offer themselves "for the price of a meal" and some entertainment, as did some young urban working women. The predominantly working-class and immigrant men who served time in jails and prisons also referred to inter-

generational relationships between older "wolves" and younger "punks."
As long as they remained the active partners, however, working-class and
immigrant men in cities like New York who occasionally had sexual relations with other men did not consider themselves to be homosexual.[42]

Whatever the source of the belief that immigrants indulged in "perverse," nonreproductive sexual practices, the insinuation had practical
implications for the eligibility for entry into the United States and ultimately the possibility of citizenship. In the early twentieth century, sexual
perversion itself was not an explicit basis for excluding immigrants, but
officials found other reasons to deny entry to those they suspected. If
they detected what they considered signs of "arrested sexual development" or "defective genitalia," immigration officials might exclude individuals on the grounds that they were "likely to become a public charge,"
regardless of their actual wage-earning potential. Put more directly, one
Public Health Service board rejected an otherwise healthy Irish farm laborer because "effeminately developed" individuals like him were "unde-
sirable in any community." A doctor examining a young Greek man in
1912 warned against admitting those with deformed genitals because
they "may be sexual perverts." In 1911, when the U.S. Immigration
Commission reported on the traffic in women for immoral purposes, the
authors also expressed concern about the "traffic in boys and men for
immoral purposes." The report called for even stronger restrictions "applied with even greater rigidity . . . in the case of men." Immigration
officials lamented the fact that "moral perverts" were not specifically excluded by law.[43]

Even if admitted, new immigrants could face barriers to inclusion when
they deviated from sexual norms. Men who admitted having sex with
other men might be deported. Those who did not engage in illegal acts still
bore the weight of racialized sexual stereotypes. Asian male immigrants in
particular represented a feminized masculinity that could threaten to corrupt young men. A study of British Columbia sodomy cases in the early
twentieth century found that a disproportionate number of prosecutions
named South Asian immigrants. Over half of the consensual homosexuality trials during this period involved Sikhs, referred to as "Hindoos."
Even though the Sikh population was not large, they were more likely to
face sexual surveillance and regulation as a means of discouraging further
immigration.[44]

Officials in the United States also associated homosexuality and sodomy with Asian immigrants. A 1926 California court decision referred

to sodomy as a "disgusting Oriental depravity." Just as proximity between a Chinese man and a young white woman raised fears about seduction, the sight of Chinese men and white boys together signaled
sexual danger. In one California sodomy case, Chinese immigrant Dong
Pok Yip had put his arm around Albert Hondeville, age nine, while they
were fishing. A suspicious observer follow them and witnessed the older
man partially undressed in the company of the boy. Dong was prosecuted for "trying to use the boy as a female." In another California case,
a Sacramento railway worker saw Ah Soon conversing with a group of
young boys and followed the Chinese man, making a citizen's arrest
when he observed him touching a boy "on his privates." Ah Soon claimed
to be helping the boy get undressed, but the court sentenced him to
three years at San Quentin prison for "lewd and lascivious conduct with
a minor child."[45]

Either of these interventions could have been justifiable protections of
boys, but just as the demonization of the black rapist eclipsed sexual assaults by white men, the identification of immigrants as seducers of the
young could mask relationships that elite men had with boys. At least
one letter to the editor of a Portland, Oregon, newspaper suggested that
authorities were lenient with the predominantly white, middle-class men
involved in the homosexual scandal of 1912. "If these degenerating
practices were committed by Greeks or Hindus," the writer charged,
"these lily whites . . . would be in favor of drowning them [in the local
river]."[46]

A 1913 California Supreme Court ruling that reversed the conviction
of a white man, Samuel Robbins, provides a stark contrast with the cases
of the Chinese men observed with white boys. Robbins's housekeeper
testified that she had observed him in a bathroom with a sixteen-year-old
boy whom he had befriended, and the youth testified that Robbins had
attempted to penetrate him. The court, however, refused to uphold a conviction for such "degrading crimes" based on "mere suspicion plus the
story of an accomplice." In some close relationships, the justices reasoned,
"the influence of mature thought and association with men may aid in the
development of the best qualities of the children."[47] Clearly, race and class
helped determine the reputation of the adult, which influenced the court's
judgment. More elite men like Robbins typically had same-sex relationships with boys in their homes or at private parties, and thus avoided de-
tection. Working-class men such as Dong Pok and Ah Soon were more
likely to be observed on city streets or in other public areas.

At the opening of the twentieth century, reformers, police, and courts had begun to take greater notice of the sexual vulnerability of boys. While they largely situated the problem within working-class and immigrant neighborhoods, officials did expose the private worlds of some elite white men. Even so, their fears about the corruption of youths, combined with scandals that exposed middle-class and elite homosexual worlds, did not yet constitute a full-fledged moral panic. For most Americans who even took note of these phenomena, the category of the invert remained tied to notions of the effeminate fairy, rather than conjuring the aggressive homosexual. Yet this incipient discourse about the risks of sexual contagion through intergenerational same-sex relationships paved the way for stronger reactions in the decades after 1920.[48]

The redefinition of boys and young men as rape victims intensified during and after World War I. Wartime tends to accelerate social change on the home front and, in modern eras, to expand governmental authority. World War I had this effect on the regulation of sexuality, setting the stage for postwar realignments in ideas about sexual assault. Just as the campaign against venereal disease among soldiers invigorated the anti-prostitution and social hygiene efforts of Progressive-era reformers, the process of screening young men for military service drew the government into the effort to categorize sexual perverts. Though the military did not yet exclude men from service based on their sexual desires, officials did employ new categories, such as the "degenerate" and the "psychopath," that would soon come to stand for a more treacherous homosexual type. For these reasons, World War I represented a pivotal moment in the longer transformation of the cultural meanings of sexuality, as would World War II.[49]

In mutually reinforcing ways, the realignments of both female and male sexuality had important implications for the response to sexual assault. The nineteenth-century image of the young woman as an innocent victim in need of state protection did not long survive the new representations of female sexuality that proliferated in the early twentieth century. Depictions of young women who infected soldiers and sailors with venereal disease echoed older concerns about the dangerous seductress, while an increasingly sexualized postwar popular culture portrayed young flappers seeking the thrill of sexual play. Against the backdrop of women gaining national suffrage, some writers simplistically portrayed sexual emancipation as a consequence of political rights. In this climate protective responses to young women diminished, as is evident from the history of statutory rape reform.

Meanwhile, inchoate fears about the homosexual threat to boys and young men coalesced and soon extended far beyond the scattered prewar expressions of concern. Both the proliferation of urban meeting places for public sex—in parks, lavatories, and bathhouses—and the increased surveillance of youth through juvenile protective agencies brought the presence of young male hustlers to the attention of police. In Chicago, the Juvenile Protective Agency discovered that newsboys on city streets sometimes sold sex as well as papers. Even as the postwar era witnessed an easing of restrictions on heterosexual behavior such as divorce, adultery, and youthful sexual expression, boundaries around nonreproductive relations tightened. Along with the prostitute, the male sexual pervert came to be seen as a serious challenge to social order. The charge of perversion could still be attached to men who attacked women—for example, when a newspaper labeled a naked man who attacked two young girls in Los Angeles in 1920 a "moral pervert"—but increasingly the term became a code word for homosexuality.[50]

Heightened surveillance of homosexuality after World War I is evident in the passage or revision of state laws related to sodomy. Most states had already criminalized sodomy, and several had expanded that term to include oral as well as anal sex. But a range of new statutes either targeted sexual perversion or extended protection to male as well as female children. Among them were laws against "indecent, lewd, or lascivious" conduct with a child of either sex. When in 1925 the U.S. Children's Bureau surveyed laws related to sex offenses against children, it found that thirteen states included boys in the statutes they enacted. Ten of these states protected boys up to age sixteen and another three up to age twenty-one. Laws prohibiting "indecent liberties with minors" passed in North Dakota in 1923 and in Minnesota and New York in 1927. In 1929 Minnesota enacted a statute against schoolyard loitering; in the same year California passed a child molestation statute. In contrast to classic rape laws that defined sexual assault as a heterosexual act, the language of the new legislation was intentionally gender-neutral. Rather than naming boys or girls, they referred to acts such as oral and anal sex and to suspicious activities, such as fondling children.[51] At a time when the links between sexuality and reproduction loosened in American culture, rape was being redefined far beyond its historical moorings in the theft of a woman's honor and the insurance of a husband's paternity. Beyond the risk of pregnancy or a woman's "ruin," sexual acts with minors increasingly were portrayed as a threat to normal heterosexual development.

The expanding definition of unacceptable sexual behaviors coincided with broader prosecution, typically initiated by the state or by welfare agencies. Arrests for sodomy escalated in cities such as Boston and New York. At the beginning of the century, New York police arrested around fifty men annually for this crime; in 1917 alone that number rose to over one hundred. Before World War I the Los Angeles police had arrested only a handful of men for sodomy; in 1923 they arrested over one hundred. The focus on children contributed to this increase. The proportion of sodomy arrests that involved sex with children in large cities rose from under one-fourth during the nineteenth century to 44 percent between 1896 and 1925. Throughout the United States between 1926 and 1940, 48 percent of sodomy cases prosecuted forcible sex with boys.[52]

A number of trends during the interwar decades pointed toward the greater public outcry about the sexual dangers faced by boys. Most significantly, the popularization of Freudian ideas introduced the concept of childhood psychosexual development. In this schema, sexual trauma in childhood might thwart, or "pervert," development toward normal heterosexual desire. Several highly publicized criminal cases that employed psychiatric terms to explain homosexuality as a perversion articulated the link between "abnormal" or "arrested" development and homosexuality. In defending two Chicago teenagers who murdered a younger boy in 1924, Clarence Darrow claimed that Richard Loeb and Nathan Leopold, though not insane, were psychopaths. Although never formally accused of homosexuality, the two killers exhibited what psychologists considered to be "mutual sex perversions." In the 1930s a more widespread social phenomenon triggered fears of perversion. During the Great Depression masses of unattached, unemployed men wandered the country, signaling social disorder generally but also viewed as a threat to boys and young men. In 1932, for example, the U.S. Children's Bureau issued a memo on the "transient boy" that identified the risk of sexual initiation by degenerates and perverts. In theater and film, the more benign image of the effeminate fairy was rapidly being replaced by that of the aggressive homosexual predator.[53]

The term *psychopath*, which derived from an earlier concept of "moral insanity," had been applied initially in the early twentieth century to describe female prostitutes or men who were socially adrift, such as the unemployed. Once considered a biological, or constitutional, condition, during the 1920s the term increasingly referred to a psychological state. By the 1930s, the variant *sexual psychopath* applied to men who acted on their uncontrollable sexual impulses, often by assaulting children rather than adult women. In the mid-1930s these psychopaths came to be seen as a major peril to both male and female children. After a series of highly publicized child murders, newspapers around the country magnified their coverage of sex crimes. Citizens' groups demanded that the police and politicians respond to the problems of rape and child sexual murder. The mayor of New York City commissioned a report on sex offenses, which declared in 1937 that "boys as well as girls may be the victims of sex crime." The same year, Federal Bureau of Investigation director J. Edgar Hoover called for a "War on the Sex Criminal" and charged that "the sex fiend, most loathsome of all the vast army of crime, has become a sinister threat to the safety of American childhood and womanhood." In New York City, arrests for sex offenses doubled from 1936 to 1937.[54]

In the late 1930s five states enacted new psychopath laws; another twenty-one states passed laws between 1947 and 1955. These statutes targeted men convicted of exhibitionism, sodomy, child molestation, or rape. If diagnosed as sexual psychopaths, these men could be transferred to state mental hospitals or psychiatric wards of prisons for an indefinite period, until the institutional psychiatrists declared them cured. Almost all of the men declared psychopaths were white. Significantly, black men convicted of rape continued to be sentenced to prison or executed, giving the impression that white men who committed sexual crimes had to be mentally ill, while black men committed willful violence.[55] The moral panic over sexual psychopaths spread nationally after World War II, but it originated in the interwar decades with the identification of boys as potential victims of sexual assault and of homosexuality as a dangerous condition.

Psychopaths could attack women as well, but for the most part the focus on children displaced earlier attention to women's sexual vulnerability. In 1939 an account titled "The Sex Offender," published in a professional journal, made no mention of the forcible rape of women. In New York the Mayor's Committee on Sex Crimes, echoing earlier medical views of girls as "willing victims," claimed, "In most sex crimes, the fact that a particular girl is a victim of a sex assault is no accident. Generally there is to be found something in the personality, the environmental background, or the family situation of the victim . . . which predisposes her to participation in sex delinquency."[56] Authorities seemed to believe that boys were less willing than girls to have sex with men, even though sodomy laws had criminalized same-sex acts for either male partner. Data from New York City during the 1930s is suggestive: only 20 percent of men indicted for statutory rape were convicted, compared to 51 percent of men who were indicted for sodomy. Judges in New York sentenced men convicted of sex with teenage boys more harshly than those who had sex with teenage girls.[57] These disparities in the punishments for sex crimes against boys and girls would later erode in New York, but the initial vigilance about boys provides a measure of change from the initial wave of legislation to protect the purity of girls.

IN THE FIRST DECADES of the twentieth century, boys emerged as potential victims of sexual assault against the backdrop of multiple historical transitions. These included the shift from sodomy as an act to a concept of homosexual identity; nativist reactions to the new immigration; and shifting gender relations as more women entered public life and expressed their sexual agency. In contrast to nineteenth-century constructions of rape, which defined the crime as an assault by a man against a woman, medical and legal authorities increasingly presumed that women could be sexually proactive and men could be sexually assaulted. Child-saving impulses, along with fears about the possibility of homosexual contagion, helped transform the target of rape concerns. If adult women now seemed less "rapable," as statutory rape reformers found, children of both sexes were redefined as the assault victims in need of protection. Older constructions of female vulnerability did persist, especially in southern and rural areas, as did older views of same-sex relationships as being the product of all-male work settings rather than as a lifetime identity formed either congenitally or through contagion. But the meaning of rape had begun to expand beyond a narrow heterosexual act. Many states now enacted sex crime laws that were gender-neutral.

While ostensibly about preventing sexual violence against boys or male youths, the moral panic that culminated in the sexual psychopath laws was as concerned with protecting boys from acquiring homosexual identity as it was about protecting them from assault. Sodomy laws permitted the prosecution of rapists, but they also functioned to enforce a moral antipathy to certain nonreproductive sexual acts lest they lose their stigmatized status. Similarly, the age-of-consent movement had sought to protect adolescent girls as much from adopting the identity of the casual prostitute, who engaged in sex for favors without shame, as from forcible rape. That is not to say that reformers and prosecutors did not sincerely care about sexual assault. Rather, the process of identifying boys as victims also served to rein in an expanding sexual category—the homosexual—by conflating it with predatory and abusive practices toward children. Like the demonization of African American men as rapists, the association of immigrants and homosexuals with child sexual abuse masked other forms of assault committed by native-born white men, including heterosexual rape and incest.

In the 1890s southern black journalist Ida B. Wells documented how few lynchings of African American men involved accusations of sexual assault against white women. Wells had to leave the South, under threat of death, for suggesting that consensual interracial relationships triggered some rape charges. She continued to inspire the northern-based anti-lynching movement and lectured in England to gather support for the cause. (Manuscripts, Archives and Rare Books Division, Schomburg Center for Research in Black Culture, the New York Public Library, Astor, Lenox and Tilden Foundations)

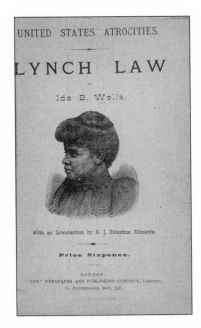

Elisabeth Freeman, a white suffragist, investigated the lynching of seventeen-year-old Jesse Washington in Waco, Texas, for the alleged rape and murder of a white woman. W. E. B. Du Bois published the report as "The Waco Horror" in the NAACP journal, *The Crisis,* in July 1916, including shocking pictures of smiling white onlookers watching Washington's burned body. (Elisabeth Freeman Collection of Margaret Johnston)

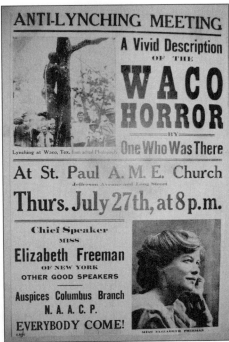

"A MILLION WOMEN UNITED FOR THE SUPPRESSION OF LYNCHING

ANTI-LYNCHING CRUSADERS

OF BROOKLYN

WILL HOLD A

MONSTER MASS MEETING

AT THE ACADEMY OF MUSIC

Lafayette Avenue and St. Felix Street, Brooklyn, N. Y.

Thursday Eve., November 9, 1922, at 8 o'clock

IN BEHALF OF THE BROOKLYN QUOTA

SPEAKERS:

Mrs. MARY B. TALBERT, of Buffalo, National Director

Hon. JAMES WELDON JOHNSON

Mrs. ALICE DUNBAR NELSON, State Chairman of Delaware

MELVILLE CHARLTON, A.A.G.O., at the Organ
Teacher of Piano Organ Theory. 465 Cumberland St.

HARRY T. BURLEIGH, Composer-Baritone

All of our Ministers are in sympathy with this Crusade and are invited to the platform.

Master of Ceremonies: Dr. HENRY HUGH PROCTOR

COME EARLY   SEATS FREE

This movement is endorsed and supported by the Republican Party

Brooklyn Anti-Lynching Crusaders, Headquarters 385 Cumberland Street, Phone 1905, President.

The Anti-Lynching Crusaders formed within the NAACP in 1922. Led by Mary B. Talbert, president of the National Association of Colored Women, the group raised money for the cause and supported a federal anti-lynching bill.

In 1930 Texas suffragist Jessie Daniel Ames helped found the Association of Southern Women for the Prevention of Lynching. Members rejected the claim that lynching protected white women from rape by black men, and they called on southern sheriffs and citizens to protect accused men from mobs. (AR.E.004-D[009], Jane McCallum Papers, Austin History Center, Austin Public Library)

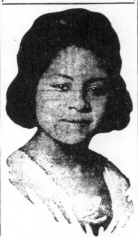

ACCUSER

MRS. MAURICE INGRAM

Acting upon instructions from Mrs. Maurice Ingram, apartment 427, 2728 Wabash Ave., Attorney Henry Hammond secured a warrant for the arrest of P. J. O'Brien (white), 7610 Champlain Ave., connected with the city health department, on a charge of attempted rape.

Mrs. Ingram claims that when O'Brien came to her apartment on the afternoon of Jan. 16 to make a report regarding the heat he forced her to the floor and attempted to assault her. She states that the timely entrance of Miss Clara Davis, a roomer in her home, prevented him from accomplishing his purpose.

She charges that O'Brien left her place and went across the hall to the home of Mrs. Angie Clift, who noticed that he acted in a queer manner. She asserts that Mrs. Clift succeeded in having him tell her his name and address.

Mrs. Ingram has been confined to her bed under the doctor's care since the alleged occurrence and promises some sensational testimony when the case is called before Judge John A. Bugee Feb. 24.

During the Great Migration, African American newspapers regularly reported stories about white men accused or convicted of assaulting black women, such as this 1924 account in the *Chicago Defender*. The reports were intended to help discredit the popular belief that most rapists were black men and to emphasize the respectability of African American women. (ProQuest LLC, used with the permission of the *Chicago Defender*)

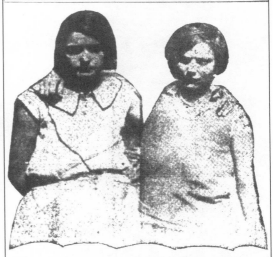

"DIDN'T TOUCH ME!"

Ruby Bates (right), on whose testimony eight boys were sentenced to die in the electric chair in Alabama, has written a letter in which she denied that the boys attacked her near Scottsboro in 1931. Her letter has been made public by the International Labor Defense. Victoria Price (left) is the other woman who charged the boys with rape.

Publicity about the trials of nine black youths accused of the rape of two white women near Scottsboro, Alabama, in 1931 called international attention to interracial rape charges and southern courtroom bias. One of the accusers, Ruby Bates *(left)*, recanted her testimony in the Scottsboro case and joined the defense effort. Victoria Price *(right)* stood by her account despite contradictory evidence. (ProQuest LLC, used with the permission of the *Chicago Defender*)

The American Magazine · March, 1955

SUCCESSFUL LIVING FOR THE FAMILY

How Safe Is Your Youngster?

By J. Edgar Hoover

DIRECTOR, FEDERAL BUREAU OF INVESTIGATION

From the 1930s through the 1950s the national press and public authorities emphasized the threat posed to both boys and girls by male strangers, who were often labeled "sexual psychopaths." At the same time, the media paid little attention to children who were abused in families, schools, and religious settings.

During the southern civil rights movement, activists protested the legal impunity enjoyed by white men who assaulted black women. In 1959, after four white men in Tallahassee, Florida, kidnapped and repeatedly raped Florida A&M University student Betty Jean Owens, other students held a "passive resistance" strike to protest the assault and to demand the prosecution of the assailants. An all-white male jury found the men guilty and sentenced them to life in prison. (ProQuest LLC, used with the permission of the *Chicago Defender*)

In the late 1970s, college students and grassroots feminist groups launched Take Back the Night marches across the country to raise awareness of how the threat of sexual assault limited women's mobility and their economic opportunities. (Photo courtesy of the University of Wisconsin–Madison Archives)

With the emergence of women's liberation in the 1960s, a radical feminist movement reframed rape as a political issue, renamed victims as survivors, condemned marital rape, urged self-defense training, and organized to provide services and prevent violence. In 1972 members of the Chicago women's liberation movement imagined the effects that a war on rape might have in the near future. (Copyright 1972 by the Chicago Women's Graphics Collective)

Enacted in 1994 with bipartisan support, the Violence Against Women Act (VAWA) declared that all people in the United States "shall have the right to be free from crimes of violence motivated by gender." When political opponents tried to block reauthorization of the act in 2012, feminist, social work, and labor organizations rallied in support. (Copyrighted material reprinted with permission from the National Association of Social Workers, Inc.)

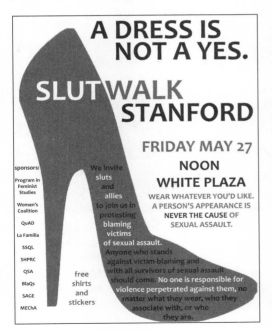

In 2011 a Toronto police official advised that if women wanted to avoid being raped, they should not dress like sluts. In response, young women took to the streets in "SlutWalks" to insist that their clothing did not justify rape. (Image courtesy Jon Derman Harris)

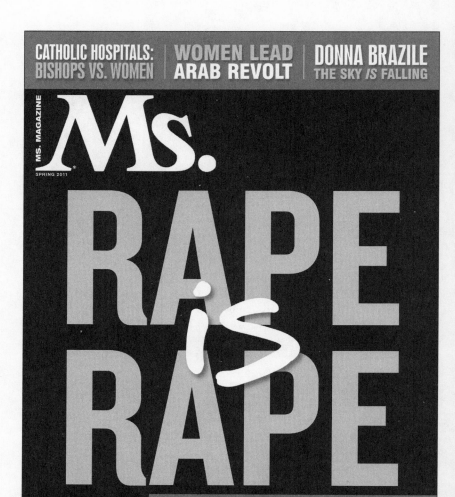

Ms.

MS. MAGAZINE

SPRING 2011

RAPE
is
RAPE

And not just when it's "forcible"

The modern feminist movement expanded the definition of rape to include all nonconsensual sexual acts, whether against a woman or a man, violent or nonviolent, by an acquaintance or by a stranger. When some politicians sought to tighten the definition by limiting an exemption in laws restricting abortions to apply only to forcible rape, feminists insisted that "rape is rape." (Reprinted by permission of *Ms.* magazine, copyright 2011)

10

"Smashing the Masher"

In the summer of 1910 suffragists in Washington, D.C., declared that the "masher" must go. For decades these "male flirts" had been trying to force their attentions on women on city streets, sometimes merely calling out sexual insults, sometimes physically harassing them. Periodically urban police chiefs in cities ranging from Chicago to San Francisco had declared war upon these white men they called "obnoxious oglers." Now, as the national suffrage movement entered its successful final decade, intolerance for these "male pests" led to calls for an official role for women in solving the problem. In Washington, the Women's Equal Suffrage Association offered to appoint special agents who could serve as "female policemen." Just as women could be truant officers or agents of the Humane Society, Mrs. R. B. Ezekiel explained, they could be commissioned to patrol the streets and investigate mashers. Expanding women's police powers, she told the press, "would do much to remedy the evil."[1]

Although Ezekiel's plan for suffragist street monitors did not materialize, over the following decade American women did expand their public authority in response to mashers. Both white and black women in northern cities fought back, went to court, and arrested men. The revolt against the masher signaled an important transition in American women's public lives as they navigated urban space as workers and consumers. Parallel to the quest for full citizenship as voters, the call for safety to travel alone meant greater access to both labor and leisure. Women recognized that street harassment impeded their mobility and marked them as intruders on historically male space.

The "insults" and "annoyances" of the masher did not necessarily constitute a form of sexual assault, although newspapers sometimes applied the term to describe physical and well as verbal acts. On a spectrum of sexual offenses, mashing occupied the least violent end, followed by consensual

191

underage sex and coercive seduction, in contrast to the more physically assaultive acts of attempted rape, rape, and rape murder. Although the masher posed a more benign threat, the drive to redefine street harassment as a crime, along with the language of women's rights that pervaded the discourse, paralleled other efforts to draw boundaries around the sexual privileges enjoyed by white men. For a short period women assertively protested unwanted sexual attentions and insisted that any sexual offense warranted police action.

Reactions to the masher provide a clue to the changing contours of women's public lives in the early twentieth century. Early commentary called for chivalrous male protection, but over time both white and northern black women rejected dependence. They physically resisted these annoyers themselves and pressed charges, usually for the misdemeanor of disorderly conduct. The outcry against the masher—like legal reforms aimed at seduction, statutory rape, and urban vice—diminished after World War I. Just as sexual liberalism granted women greater sexual agency, humorous representations of mashers supplanted feminist aspirations for public authority. Yet the image of female independence on the streets resonated long after the masher panic had subsided.

White men predominated as mashers, as they did in the narratives produced by antiseduction and age-of-consent campaigns. Given the racialized image of the rapist, an African American man who merely looked a white woman directly in the eye on a southern street could be construed as a sexual assailant, not merely a flirt. On the West Coast an Asian man who approached a white woman could inspire mob action as well.[2] In this way the coding of nonviolent mashers as white reinforced earlier racial contrasts with black men's presumably violent sexual assaults across race lines and the sodomitical acts ascribed to new immigrants. Generally missing from these scenarios were sexual crimes directed at black women. When African Americans created a new political base during the northern migration, however, they identified and condemned the interracial dynamics of harassment.

POPULAR INTEREST in the masher emerged just as urban growth provided new opportunities for gender and class mixing in public space. The term first appeared in the marginal world of the theater. In nineteenth-century slang, *mash* referred to a sweetheart or a "crush," implying an infatuation (a "mash" note was a kind of love letter). Initially it applied in particular to relationships between actresses and men in their audiences. An 1882 guide to theatrical and circus life described mashers as "masculine theatre-goers" whose "wild ambition [is] to attract and hold feminine attention."[3] But the word applied more broadly to the man "who imagines himself a 'lady-killer,'" whether the lesser type who lurked around burlesque house stage doors or the more elite category of the foppish gentlemen.[4]

Several European sources prefigured the American masher and contributed to his identity. The fictional character Don Juan, a libertine seducer who sought female conquests, appeared in early definitions of mashers. A caricature on a 1905 American postcard contrasted a flashily dressed masher, who believed that his dashing charms would attract women, with a more sinister and presumably more forceful Don Juan. The *flâneur*, a detached male spectator of the urban crowd, strolled the streets of Paris and London in the nineteenth century. While he did not insult women, feminist scholars have pointed to his privileged male gaze as a form of sexual objectification. In contrast, women on the streets could not safely stare at members of the crowd lest they invite unwanted attention or be taken for prostitutes. Like the masher, the elite dandy made a public spectacle of his fashionable clothing. Middle-class men in England who adopted these styles in the late nineteenth century might be called *mashers* or *cads*, insinuating a threat to women's honor.[5]

Despite his excessive attention to fashion, the masher remained a heterosexual figure. In contrast to the furtive eye contact characteristic of homosexual urban haunts, the masher openly approached his targets.[6] Early depictions of mashers in the United States included men who tried to seduce married women, sometimes placing them in the vicinity of the brothel, a locus associated with seductions and assignations.[7] Increasingly, however, the masher appeared in mainstream social spaces and not only in the marginal worlds of the brothel and the theater. Rather than objects of passionate attachment, his targets were female strangers who traveled without male protectors; his goals were to force his attentions on them in hopes of symbolic or actual sexual conquest.

Men had bothered or insulted women in public in the past, but the growth of commercial cities after the late eighteenth century provided new opportunities. As early as the 1770s some American women expressed concerns about urban sexual dangers and complained that they should be able to have the liberty to travel freely without risking their reputations. At the turn of the nineteenth century, young Quaker women in Philadelphia accused "young gentleman gapers" of behaving "not only irreverently, but shamefully indecent" when they stared, pointed, or rudely commented en route to their house of worship. One young woman explicitly referred to men's "intruding so much on our rights." In response, men accused the women of being "flirts" who invited their attentions by their very presence on the streets.[8]

In nineteenth-century New York City, single male wage earners sometimes formed rowdy public subcultures, and groups of working women sometimes attracted attention as they strolled boldly down the streets. But at a time when the phrase "public woman" remained synonymous with prostitute, the unescorted woman could be considered fair game for men's attentions, wanted or unwanted. Rape by gangs of young men appeared in the courts, reported by young working women. For the protection of women of all classes, by midcentury several cities had enacted ordinances against "insulting females in the street."[9] Travelling on new forms of transportation within or between cities also posed risks. As journalist E. L. Godkin noted in 1882, women could now be seen "in the streets, in horse-cars, omnibuses, excursion boats, railroad trains, and hotel corridors." When women reported that men disturbed them when they traveled unescorted, transportation companies created separate waiting and seating areas for "ladies," understood as white women, in order to protect them from the unwanted attentions of fellow passengers.[10]

By the late nineteenth century more women defied the boundary between public and private by entering urban commercial spaces. Respectable middle-class matrons ventured into public unescorted when they frequented downtown department stores. Working-class women, who had to traverse the streets to get to their jobs, also strolled out to shop, show off their clothing, and banter with their peers. Working girls attended the theater (previously patronized largely by men and prostitutes) and enjoyed other forms of urban leisure, from dance halls to public beaches. An 1882 cartoon depicting the popular Coney Island beach in New York suggests the fears evoked by these unescorted women, as well as the belief that men needed to protect them: a sinister-looking masher appears like a creature from the sea and ominously ogles two women until a gentleman comes along to rescue them from the annoyance. Similarly, early silent films featured male protectors who rescued young women and often thrashed or humiliated the offender.[11]

En route to downtown, either shoppers or shopgirls might encounter the masher. Ellen Henrotin of Chicago—a former national president of the General Federation of Women's Clubs, state suffrage advocate, and

president of the cross-class National Women's Trade Union League—
made this point when she explained that "the working girl is just as often
the object of the ogling as the society girl."[12] Ladies' magazines and etiquette books cautioned women to take responsibility for avoiding contact
with men on streets, refuse to speak to them if approached, and avoid
calling attention to themselves by talking or laughing loudly. Rather,
they should look serious and maintain a "mantle of reserve" in public. In
1909 "A Working Girl from Detroit" wrote to the *New York Times* about
learning this lesson. After a few weeks in the city she had come to understand the blank looks on women's faces on the subway as their "armor
against the offensive stares of the New York 'masher.' "[13]

By the early 1900s a more critical tone began to characterize popular
representations of men identified as mashers. They included a range of
characters, from the "matinee masher" who touched women in movie theaters to the more violent ruffian on the streets. The latter appeared in a
newspaper report that applied the term *masher* to a man who grabbed a
woman, told her "I want you, my honey," and tried to put a "love powder"
in her mouth to knock her out. Some of the mashers reported in the press
simply tried to insult women, calling out to them with foul language.
Other men tried to convince women to make their acquaintance and go
off with them ("Want to take a ride, little girl?" was one masher's modus
operandi). Other men took pains to ingratiate themselves over time.[14]

Theodore Dreiser incorporated the latter tactic in his 1900 novel *Sister
Carrie,* in which he defined the masher as "one whose dress or manners
are calculated to elicit the admiration of susceptible young women." In
the opening scene of the book, traveling salesman Charles Drouet attempts to pick up eighteen-year-old Carrie Meeber on the train as she
travels from the countryside to live with her sister in Chicago. His fashionable clothing and knowledge of department stores draw Carrie into
conversation, the first step in her gradual fall from virtue. Along with the
display of "good clothes," which was essential to Drouet's method, his
character had a repertoire for persuading women to accompany him: "Let
him meet with a young woman once and he would approach her with an
air of kindly familiarity, not unmixed with pleading, which would result
in most cases in a tolerant acceptance. . . . If he visited a department store
it was to lounge familiarly over the counter and ask some leading questions. In more exclusive circles, on the train or in waiting stations, he
went slower." First he walked her to the parlor car, then he carried her
bag, then he lowered the shade.[15]

Like most mashers, Drouet was a white, middle-class man, although his employment set him apart from men categorized as urban loafers. In contrast to the racialized representations of rapists and sodomites, only rarely did the white press refer to the masher as an immigrant or an African American man. In the 1880s the term occasionally applied to a black man who married a white woman, but references to black street flirts were very rare. One female journalist argued that foreign-born men living in New York City actually had more respect for women than did the native-born men who called out to them.[16] For the most part, these native-born white men claimed the streets as their territory and put women on notice that they might have to run a gauntlet of insults if they wished to appear in public unescorted.

Women, however, were beginning to question this assumption. Their discontent with annoyances by men on city streets escalated during the Progressive era. As more women worked for wages and sought professional careers, they encroached on male preserves, economically and spatially. At the same time, concerns about "women adrift" in the city, which fueled both the white slave scare and urban anti-vice crusades, contributed to greater national publicity about street harassment. Newspapers and popular magazines began to take the masher more seriously than in the past in a discourse that included political critiques of male sexual privilege.

At one level, fears that young women could be lured into prostitution by mashers paralleled the concerns that drove revised statutory rape laws. In 1900, for instance, Justice J. Lovely of the Minnesota Supreme Court referred to the masher when he defended that state's law criminalizing sex with girls under age sixteen. The statute, he ruled, did not target the young men who had consensual relationships with peers but rather intended to prevent "a more mature specimen of masculinity familiarly known as the 'masher,'—a parasite upon woman" from leading unsuspecting girls into "that social abyss from which return is very difficult."[17] The masher, however, differed from the classic procurer depicted in anti-vice literature. He did not engage in commercialized vice and, in addition to seducing young working women, he also openly insulted older, respectable, and middle-class women.

As critics of statutory rape reform pointed out, not all women wanted protection. Some enjoyed innocent flirting in public. According to Chicago's police chief, "The street 'masher' would not long exist if it were not that there are women who are not averse to a street flirtation or acquaintanceship." In the past a white woman making eye contact with a man on the street could signal a willingness to sell sex. Now, however, it might mean a willingness to take a stroll or to be taken out for a meal. The trend toward "treating" and "dating" among urban youth helped blur the line between romantic flirtation and commercial prostitution.[18]

Representations of women in the press coverage of mashers reveal a gender system in transition from female dependence on men to aspirations for independence. When reporters first identified the masher phenomenon, they emphasized men's duty to protect women or made fun of women's fears and their efforts to defend themselves. In 1901, when the Chicago chief of police waged a crusade against mashers, he asked men to demonstrate their "chivalry as a protector of defenseless women," while he blamed women for encouraging the problem. Several Chicago club women also called on men to protect them, as did Dr. Julia Holmes Smith, who stated that the best remedy would be for men to "thrash the street masher." Women who fought back remained comic characters.[19]

Over the next decade, however, this tone changed as club women, suffragists, and some working women spoke out against mashers and argued for their rights to move freely in public. Women's rights supporter Eleanor Gates publicized this new stance in a series of magazine articles. Only "ultraconservative people" believed that women should not travel alone, she explained. Gates insisted that "*every* girl has a legal right to travel about alone without having to endure annoyance." Nor should women have to rely on men to protect them when they had the capacity to resist insults on their own. "Personally," she wrote in 1906, "I admire the woman who visits swift and thorough punishment where punishment is due. *She* leaves no doubt in anyone's mind. She knows her rights, and she claims them. She it is who will bring about a prevailing right attitude toward women." Her insistence on the right to travel was not simply a matter of convenience but also one of physical safety. In an allusion to more violent crimes, Gates hinted that "the annoying of women" was "only one phase of the subject," which included other stories that "would not bear publication."[20]

Even among those who granted women the right to travel alone, the question of what constituted an inappropriate interaction remained unsettled. An anonymous writer in the *Medical Times* took pains to rebut most of Gates's assertions, attributing the problem to women's misunderstandings. The "worst masher," he explained, was merely a man who was trying to find a prostitute. A truly decent woman was safe from him because "her obvious purity" would not attract his attentions. In other instances "the 'masher' . . . is simply lonesome and yearns for woman's society, without ulterior motives." Again, it was up to women to steer clear if they were not interested.[21] The contrast between Gates and her critic highlighted the blurred boundaries of acceptable speech among strangers in this transitional period, when women increasingly moved into public spaces.

Despite his defensiveness about men's public behavior, the *Medical Times* writer did give young working-class women credit for being able to rebuff the unwanted attentions of strangers without feeling victimized. In an egalitarian move of sorts he argued that because talking to a man on the street no longer marked a woman as a streetwalker, then by implication, talking to a woman on the street should not mark a man as a masher. Working-class women themselves made similar distinctions, as one reminded readers of the *New York Times* in 1907. Not all men who spoke to women on the street were mashers, she pointed out, and she appreciated the courtesy shown by "men of all classes" when she was "obliged to go around alone" in the city. Other working women simply enjoyed flirting after hours.[22] Despite these distinctive interpretations of street interactions, at the heart of the masher debates lay a common theme: women's growing independence.

THE FLURRY OF ATTENTION to the masher in Chicago after 1905 illustrates the shift from a protective to a self-reliant ideal for women. Although the major newspaper in that city, the *Chicago Daily Tribune*, rarely covered rape accusations or trials, it provided the densest national reporting on the masher. The impetus for this coverage was in large part a crime wave that began in 1905, when the murders of around two dozen Chicago women created a panic over female safety. In particular, the sexual assault and strangling of Mrs. Bessie Hollister in January 1906 provoked an anticrime campaign and the hiring of hundreds of additional police officers.[23]

In their reactions, the police, citizens' groups, and the press tended to conflate the masher problem with these murders, raising the stakes for minor offenses and imputing sexual motives to the killers. "The masher and the murderer of Mrs. Hollister belong to the same species," one prominent club woman told the press. In a feature article about women's fears after the killings, authorities promised that the police would arrest mashers and loiterers, as if the former group had incited the killings. The tenuous link between the murders and mashing is clear from a compilation of the crimes. Of twenty-four murders identified by the *Chicago*

Tribune, other than Mrs. Hollister only one involved "criminal assault," a legal term for rape. One woman had been killed by a man "who was said to have forced his attentions upon her." The paper speculated that other women may have committed suicide during the year "because of the attentions" that men had thrust upon them.[24]

Linking the murders of women to street harassment meshed with desires for law and order and for urban economic growth. By cracking down on men who loitered in downtown streets and around hotels, such as the fashionable Palmer House, the police provided a service to the owners of factories and department stores by making the streets safer for women to go to work or to go shopping. These businessmen in turn supported the *Chicago Tribune,* which escalated coverage of the masher. "What Can Be Done to Rid the Palmer House Block of Mashers?," a *Tribune* banner asked in 1906. The article called the men who lingered near the women's entrance to the hotel "degenerates" and compared them to "the cutthroat and hold-up man."[25] In short, the masher could serve conservative ends in the name of protecting women, a recurrent theme in sex panics historically.

Chicago women may have felt threatened by both murderers and mashers, but they were not silently afraid. In 1906 lawyer and ardent suffragist Catharine Waugh McCulloch, who had been active in the drive to raise the age of consent in Illinois, reflected on the recent murders and the subsequent public indignation. She pointed out that the problem was not merely a recent one. The criminal justice system, she argued, had been ineffective in punishing men who attacked women, as evidenced by the fact that over the past decade the Illinois State Supreme Court had reversed three-quarters of the rape convictions it heard on appeal. More important than punishment, McCulloch continued, was the prevention of crimes against women. Along with well-lit streets and better policing, McCulloch called for a political form of "self defense." She rejected the chivalry of men, noting that the time when "knights defended the women of their households" was long gone. For her, the best way to enforce the law was "by the ballot." Only when women sought to "raise themselves up to the full stature of citizens," as voters, would they be able to safeguard themselves.[26]

Illinois women would gain partial suffrage in 1913, but short of exercising full political rights they increasingly turned to physical self-defense, a frequent motif in press coverage of the masher. Initial reports of women who used force to repel mashers reflected a trend in newspapers such as the *National Police Gazette* and in early silent films to titillate and amuse readers with images of women engaging in "physical culture."

But a different tone began to characterize *Chicago Tribune* reports featuring women around the country who successfully fought back against harassers. In contrast to earlier portrayals, these women were presented as more heroic than comic, subjects rather than objects. Typical stories included a Philadelphia stenographer who took boxing lessons from her brother and then knocked out the man who was forcing his attentions upon her; the married woman who struck a New York railway conductor in the face; and a Japanese visitor to New York who used jiujitsu against an electrician who tried to speak to her on the street. In Cleveland, Mrs. Frank Gilbert's boxing lessons paid off when she punched a masher on the streetcar. Gilbert told the press that she hoped to form a "society for the suppression and annihilation of mashers" that would admit only women and offer "talks on exercise and self-defense."[27]

Reports of local Chicago women also began to emphasize female independence rather than reliance on men to prevent unwanted sexual attentions ranging from mere annoyance to physical assault. A letter to the *Worker's Magazine* praised a young female millinery store employee's method for successfully dispensing with a masher who ogled the exiting workers each day. Pretending not to see him, she "opened her umbrella full in his face," knocking his high silk hat into the gutter. The press ran flattering portraits of two seemingly demure young women who had vanquished a masher on a streetcar, one of them a fourteen-year-old who used a hatpin and the other a sixteen-year-old who was "now carrying a pocket revolver."[28] Female athleticism may well have sold papers, but the nature of the images also signified greater admiration for women's independence.

Perhaps the most enthusiastic coverage of local efforts, headlined "Chicago Women Train for Defense," reported on the large numbers of "business women" who now "claimed their rights to open air exercise" in the parks. These women, the reporter insisted, gathered not to improve their health or looks but rather as the result of their "terrorized winter" when the murders began. Female coaches trained the participants in hockey, rowing, and tennis. Reflecting the craze for exercise among the "New Women" of the early twentieth century, the article struck a feminist note. As the instructors explained, sports did not necessarily provide the brute strength to fend off assailants, but they did cultivate the self-reliance, self-esteem, and confidence that provided a woman with a "ten-fold keener intuition of what her assailant is going to do," thus enabling her to avoid attack.[29]

Chicago had a well-developed network of women's clubs, and their members spoke out about the "growing evil" of mashers. Some comments echoed the law-and-order theme, calling for vigorous prosecution and blaming the police for not doing their job well enough. A few club women even called for the whipping post for mashers. But a common complaint was more political: women's reluctance to appear in court to prosecute men because of their fear of notoriety. When accosted, Mrs. Frederick K. Tracy advised, it was a woman's duty to call the police, go to court, and prosecute. "It is not disgraceful, it is only being a woman, to go into court on such an errand."[30] Like suffragists who were calling for jury service for women, club women attempted to contest the association of the court as an all-male space and inspire women who took risks on the streets to step into the public realm of the courthouse to ensure their safety. Some male officials reluctantly accepted this advice, such as Chicago school superintendent W. L. Bodine, who urged women to throw aside false modesty and testify in court. An insulted woman, he advised, should "help your sex by prosecuting the masher," or at least "slap him in the face, even spit in his face . . . [to] brand him publicly as a masher."[31]

Nowhere in the response to the masher did Chicagoans publicly suggest that women should not be able to move freely at night, even at the height of the murder scare. According to Mrs. W. C. H. Keough, women had the right to safe travel and should be able to go out unaccompanied. Thousands of Chicago women, she reminded readers, did not have the luxury of remaining in their homes. Those who worked in shops, factories, and offices could not necessarily reach home before nightfall. Similarly, suffragists rejected the advice of the chair of the Chicago Vice Commission, Reverend Walter T. Sumner, who warned working women to wear more modest and less suggestive clothing to avoid unwanted attention from mashers. Lena M. Roche wrote that insults resulted not from what women wore but from "the vileness of the 'masher' mind." Like other suffragists, Roche called for greater female authority. Appointing "a few public-spirited women on the police force for a month or two" would put an end to mashers, she claimed.[32]

The panic over the masher subsided in Chicago as civic leaders shifted their attention to an anti-vice campaign against prostitution, but around the country women continued to resist and report men who approached, harassed, or tried to assault them on city streets.[33] Advice literature supported their right to protect themselves. If a man did not treat a woman with respect in public, one manual advised in 1913, "a young girl who was a victim of persistent and unwanted attentions must be excused for defending herself even roughly." New York City probation officer Alice

Smith, of the Woman's Night Court, told the press that "the thing to do is to haul the masher into court." That was the approach of Mrs. George Howe, a self-described "ardent suffragist," who took the lead in driving away "Broadway flirts" in New York. Fed up by the constant approaches of men who tried to follow her, in 1914 she vowed to prosecute the next man who "flirted" with her. As a result, a judge sentenced Dr. Ernest White to ten days in the workhouse for physically accosting Howe while she walked down Broadway. Howe also had a larger vision: as a club woman, she told the press, she wanted to create "a crusade" of respectable women against "these Broadway 'mashers.' "[34]

Some American women fulfilled the suffragist vision of arresting mashers themselves. In the past only a few women had provided private protective services, such as female matrons paid by women's clubs to patrol train stations and shopping districts. Now cities began to appoint women police officers, beginning with Mrs. Alice Stebbins Wells, who joined the Los Angeles force in 1910. In the same year suffrage supporter Alice Clement became one of ten women appointed as police officers in Chicago, charged specifically with protecting young women from vice. In 1916 the *Atlanta Constitution* proclaimed that policewomen around the country were the "biggest factor in putting the fear of the law into annoyers of girls." By the 1920s more than two hundred U.S. cities had almost three hundred women on police forces. Many of these policewomen functioned as quasi social workers charged with protecting women and children. They arrested men for mashing, typically charging them with disorderly conduct, although a few cities passed specific antimashing ordinances. They also arrested men for attempted rape and sexual assault. One New York City detective posed as a stenographer and then arrested the manufacturer who hired her when he tried to assault her in his office at night.[35] These female police officers represented the hopes of the women's movement for economic independence and full citizenship.

Most of these officers were white, but by the 1920s black policewomen served in Los Angeles, New York, and the District of Columbia. The crusading *Chicago Defender* campaigned for the appointment of "race policewomen" to protect black women from men "who go beyond 'mashing'" by insulting black girls and women. With the support of the black alderman elected by Chicago's growing migrant population, in 1918 Grace Wilson became the first African American policewoman in that city. In addition to nabbing robbers and a murderer, Wilson arrested several men accused of rape, including a twenty-eight-year-old man accused of assaulting an eleven-year-old girl. In Washington, D.C., policewoman H. O. Burwell arrested a white man who was molesting a black woman on a streetcar. Because the masher resisted arrest, the local judge fined him ten dollars, explaining that "it makes no difference whether an officer is white or black."[36] Though an exceptional incident, the case signaled new expectations among African Americans that sexual protection could provide an entry point for expanding public authority.

For over a decade, between the Chicago murders and World War I, press coverage of the masher emphasized women resisting or arresting men. Images of self-defense, boxing lessons, and quick responses to mashers held up an ideal of female self-reliance as a better form of sexual protection than men's chivalry. A cartoon published during World War I directed readers to draw the connection between women's economic independence and their freedom from unwanted sexual attentions. "It used to be reasonably safe for a masher to insult a defenseless girl," read the caption under an image of loafers harassing a fearful young woman. But now that "so many girls have been working in munitions factories," the strip continued, "the masher is taking a hazardous chance," evidenced by a bold woman smashing a masher over the head with her closed umbrella.[37]

ALTHOUGH THE URBAN PRESS periodically reported stories about mashers and women's triumph over them, representations of female public authority seemed to have peaked during World War I. The image of the harmless street flirt began to supplant that of the dangerous male pest, while policewomen came under greater scrutiny. Benign representations of mashers had never entirely disappeared. Coincident with efforts to suppress public flirtation, popular songs such as "The Flirt" and "Wouldn't You Like to Flirt with Me?" depicted men tempted by female beauty as well as young women willing to go off with them. In his 1914 silent film *The Rival Mashers,* Charlie Chaplin triumphed as the sympathetic underdog who won the attentions of women on the street at the expense of a seemingly more powerful male flirt.[38] By the 1920s women's magazines popularized the "It" girl, epitomized in film by Clara Bow playing a working girl who knew how to flirt, get the right man's attention, and retain her virtue. For white middle-class youth, not only flirting but even premarital intercourse became more common, though still taboo to admit. Middle-class men, once advised to exercise sexual self-control or channel their desires to the underworld of prostitution, now expected access to women from their own social worlds. As modern men openly sought sexual conquests, efforts to contain their expressions of interest seemed as outdated as expectations that women did not want to flirt.[39] The white masher transformed into the male flirt, his attentions to women less ominous and his behavior more in tune with new masculine ideals.

With movies, music, and magazines popularizing an image of the adventurous flapper and the benign male flirt, and with courtship and dating in flux, guardians of street morality seemed outdated. "How's a man going to tell the difference between a decent woman and an indecent one," a police chief despaired in 1920. Given women's dyed hair and "flimsy frocks," columnist Winifred Black commiserated with him, "Who can blame the mashers . . . for trying to mash women and girls like this?" A news account of a New York man who was fined ten dollars for wishing Happy New Year on the street to a woman he did not know clearly implied that authorities had gone too far. A letter to the *Chicago Tribune* making light of the "vulgar tricks" of mashers advised that women simply ignore them: "Why should a girl notice a so-called 'insult' any more than she would notice a few raindrops, except to hurry out of reach?" In this view, decent women could take care of themselves without help from the authorities. Similarly, the joke in a 1924 episode of a comic strip about a working woman, "Winnie Winkle: The Breadwinner," though largely at the expense of a man with roving hands, also contrasted a resilient young woman who evaded his unwanted advances with an hysterical old-fashioned prude who comically threatened to arrest the man when he mistakenly put his arm around her in a movie theater.[40]

The behaviors associated with the masher did not disappear, although the scene of the crime began to move from downtown shopping districts and movie theaters to cars.[41] Many young white women willingly entered the vehicles of men they knew, sometimes along with groups of friends and sometimes alone. The backseat became known as a locus of consensual sexual encounters, but the line between consent and coercion could be unclear in the enclosed space of the automobile. Some women learned that one form of "joy riding" took them to remote spots where they might be abandoned if they did not agree to at least a petting session. A 1923 study of gangs in Chicago noted that privileged young men as well as gang members regularly picked up girls who were "utter strangers, on the street" and then drove them to the countryside, where they left them if they refused to have sex. Two years later, after several instances of kidnapping and physical attacks in cars, Chicago's police chief issued a warning to young women not to accept rides from strange men. In Los Angeles a revived "campaign against the masher" targeted "pests who attempt to lure women into automobiles."[42]

Despite these caveats, both an earlier sense of urgency and the valorization of female self-defense diminished. Some critics balked as soon as women began to fulfill suffragist aspirations for police powers. In 1911, the year California enacted woman suffrage, the press labeled detective Fay Evans "the flirt cop" after she arrested a string of mashers over a few days; the Los Angeles police chief commented when he fired her that Evans's unflattering clothing "would make most any man stare." A few years later the *Chicago Tribune* referred disparagingly to Alice Clement when she arrested a real estate dealer who made advances to her in a movie theater, calling the charge a "flirt case." When New York City established a "subway squad" in 1924, with plainclothes policemen arresting "subway pests" who approached plainclothes policewomen, complaints about innocent men being victimized by "hysterical or notoriety-seeking women" followed the crackdown.[43] Like the move from protecting girls through statutory rape laws to blaming girls for entrapping men, the discourse on the masher could serve to shift public sympathies from women toward men, especially those arrested by women.

A woman arresting a man who had made advances toward her upended gender conventions to an alarming degree. Some reactions were joking. "Chicago Is No Longer the Happy Hunting Ground for the Masher" was the headline in a national humor magazine after a "supposedly helpless girl," actually a policewoman, arrested a man who tried to flirt with her. In one of the rare intraracial masher references in the black press, the *Chicago Defender* published a light verse in 1920 describing the plight of a man who followed a woman down the street, whispered an invitation into her ear, and found out that "this maid petite was the copper on the beat," so he wound up "in a cell that's not so neat."[44] In real life, though, arrest might lead to a lenient response. In 1926 a man who had pestered a woman to go for a boat ride with him in the park defended himself in court on the grounds that he "really didn't know it was a policewoman" he had approached. The judge dismissed the charges, implying that women were fair game, whether or not they had police authority.[45]

DURING THE PEAK of white press attention to mashers, African American writers rarely addressed the subject. Aside from humor, black mashers were as anomalous in the African American press as in white newspapers. Surely there were black dandies who flirted with women of their race in public, but they did not provoke a moral panic. Never confined to a domestic sphere, most black women had experience in navigating public space, where white men posed the greater threat. In the South they had long endured sexual insults from white men as they traveled, but they had little recourse for complaints. The northern migration and the mounting political consciousness of the New Negro, though, raised expectations that African American women could move more safely in integrated thoroughfares. The *Chicago Defender* noted in 1914, "It is next to impossible for a woman of good appearance to walk in the street unescorted after 7 o'clock without being repeatedly subjected to the insults and indecent assaults of white men."[46] Soon the black press began to highlight the racial dynamics of street harassment.

After World War I, just as the white press lost interest, northern black papers began to target white men who sexually insulted or approached African American women. Published since 1893, the *Baltimore Afro-American* turned attention to mashers only after 1920. Writers often applied a derogatory slang term for whites, referring to them as "Ofay mashers." The coverage provided a platform for protesting a range of sexual affronts to black women, from attempted pickups to physical assaults. Like the white press, stories of resourceful women emphasized female self-sufficiency, but male protection remained an important theme. Throughout the coverage the black male journalists insisted on the sexual respectability of black women who moved in public space, continuing earlier efforts to redefine sexual assault—or insult—as unacceptable for women of their race.

Many of the masher accounts in the black press highlighted women who triumphed when white men approached them at work or on the streets. One story applauded a "plucky" Miss Boyer who fought off a "white masher" when he tried to embrace her in the hotel elevator car she operated. Boyer managed to reverse the car, exposing him to public view on the first floor. The *Afro-American* concluded that with this kind of treatment, "it will not take long to make work in hotels safe for colored girls." Similarly, when a "masher of the Caucasian race" tried to purchase the favors of Mildred Washington, the "only colored performer" at a Los Angeles theater, she loudly exposed him to a crowd while visibly returning the check he had offered her.[47] Resisting white mashers contributed to African American women's quest for sexual respectability and economic opportunity.

Along with resilient black women who could defend themselves, police and courts began to restrict white men's sexual access. In 1924 New York City police arrested a southern man who tried to flirt on the subway with Estelle Richardson, described by the press as a young black "woman of culture." When she refused his attentions, the man told her that if they had been in Georgia, "I would have you strung up." Undeterred by the threat, Richardson and a white woman who had witnessed the scene detained the southerner until the police arrived. In Kansas City, Missouri, a white man paid a fine of one hundred dollars for "making suggestive remarks" and "jingling his money" as he followed two black women down the street, treating them as if they were prostitutes. Though rare, these minor triumphs suggested the importance of sexual safety as an element of racial dignity after World War I.[48]

While highlighting women's capacity for self-defense and insisting that police respond, the black press also exhorted male protection. At a time when African American men aspired to the familial and political authority that had long been denied them, reports of resistance to mashers included men who came to the rescue. A story about several young women who were giving "their tormentors a sound thrashing" emphasized that a male friend "finished off what the girls had begun." Whether it was safe to act as a protector, however, depended on the context. Some men who intervened were themselves physically attacked by white mashers, a reminder of the limitations on black male authority. "Why don't our men ever resent insults to us from the other men?" asked an African American woman who recounted an incident at a train station, where some drunken white men yelled "Hello, baby!" and began to annoy her. When she requested that they move on, one of the harassers turned to a "colored man" and asked if anyone had been bothered. No doubt concerned for his own safety, the man replied that he "couldn't say."[49]

When white men intruded into black neighborhoods, the dynamics of confrontation reversed. After the 1920s the African American press increasingly targeted white men in cars who attempted "to make dates" with young black women, assuming that they would trade sex for money. Some women did work the streets selling sex, but these men also insulted respectable women. A columnist for the Baltimore paper repeatedly complained that local police did nothing to rid their community "of ofay auto mashers, who often insult some decent and hard-working women." More than insult, some incidents resembled sexual assault, as when an "Ofay flirt" tried to force a young black woman into his car. In 1933 black men in Baltimore responded to the screams of a woman who was resisting a white man by beating the "auto masher." Just a few days later two white men flirting from their cars wound up in the hospital after being attacked by black men.[50]

In contrast to these critiques of white mashers, reports of black men who harassed women of their own race remained rare. The *Afro-American* did hold black men accountable for treating women with respect within the context of white men's improprieties. After a group of black men made "vulgar insinuations" toward a passing black girl, a white man who had observed the incident followed her and made "indecent proposals." "Naturally," the paper editorialized, "when he saw the men of her own race insulted her, he felt that he too could do so with impunity." For the most part, though, only humorous depictions alluded to intraracial harassment. On a few occasions the editorial cartoon "People We Can Get Along Without," which emphasized racial uplift, censured "The rats who contaminate our busy street corners and pose for the sole purpose of flirting with every woman who passes" and the "sheiks" who tried to charm girls they did not know.[51]

The absence of black mashers makes sense, given the efforts of the anti-lynching movement to refute white stereotypes of uncontrollable black male sexuality. Yet these papers did include intraracial black rape cases, especially in the 1920s when African American women in the North turned to police and courts to report attacks. Perhaps black women did not complain to authorities about mashers. They may not have considered the "sheiks" to be as threatening as white women did or as problematic as interracial harassment. Navigating public space was not as new for them as for most white women. Unless a physical attack gave reason to charge rape, some black women may have felt constrained from reporting insults lest they fail to express solidarity with men of their race.[52] The critique of interracial mashing, though, protested white men's intrusions into African American neighborhoods. It also reflected a broader press strategy of exposing white men's sexual crimes as part of the anti-lynching effort to deconflate rape and race.

IN THE EARLY TWENTIETH CENTURY, the effort to identify unwelcome sexual comments and to seek legal redress emerged within the contexts of both women's growing public presence as wage earners and a racial justice movement. Even without the explicit threat of violence, mashing served to defend the boundaries of historically male space—the streets, the workplace. Fighting back, physically and legally, was a form of resistance to sexual threats at a time when working and middle-class women of any race sought greater public safety.

The revolt against the masher clearly had limits. Although the racial coding of mashers exposed white male offenders, it also deflected attention from more violent sexual assaults by white men, leaving intact the image of the black man as rapist. Even calls for policewomen could play into conservative law-and-order campaigns, and they did not succeed in expanding female public authority in the way suffragists envisioned. The implicit bargain that granted the "New Women" greater sexual agency, while revitalizing an aggressive masculine ideal, made protection of, and by, white women a less pressing public concern. Reactions to suffrage and to women's public authority may have contributed to the stall in the policewomen's movement after the 1920s. In reporting the elimination of policewomen in one city, the *Chicago Defender* editorialized that "the more extreme feminists may see in these decisions a blow to the equal rights theory, but it is to be doubted whether the great mass of the fair sex will worry" if men monopolized the "drudgery" of police work.[53]

The masher threat peaked as greater numbers of white women sought access to public space. In the growing climate of sexual liberalism, however, fear about sexual insults gave way to a greater acceptance of flirtation, just as concerns about statutory rape gave way to an acceptance of youthful sexual adventure. Perhaps white women, like many black women before them, learned how to take care of themselves on city streets by avoiding or refusing unwanted invitations from strangers. Yet women of any race remained vulnerable to unwanted sexual attentions, while their repertoire for acceptable responses seemed to narrow. After the 1920s the negotiation of urban space for the purposes of wage earning, shopping, or flirtation increasingly took the form of individual resistance rather than a social movement. For a short period, however, the revolt against the masher provided a political response to sexual vulnerability. Tributes to self-defense, suffragist visions of police authority, the willingness of black women to report white men to authorities, and the reactions of black men all contested white men's sexual entitlements.

11

After Suffrage

In the nineteenth century, women's rights advocates such as Elizabeth Cady Stanton, Lucy Stone, and Henry Blackwell envisioned the vote as key to undermining women's sexual vulnerability. By 1915 women had gained the franchise in most western states, and the ratification of the Nineteenth Amendment in 1920 extended woman suffrage nationally. In the postsuffrage era, however, the prosecution of sexual violence did not change markedly. In 1931 the first policewoman appointed in New York City, Mary Hamilton, expressed her dismay in an exaggerated claim that in her city, "there hasn't been a conviction of a man for rape in twenty years." Her larger point was that without women's full participation in the justice system as jurors and as judges, sexual assault would continue to go unpunished.[1]

The diverse postsuffrage arguments for women's influence on sexual violence reflected a growing schism within the women's movement. In the past a strategy based on protecting female purity had succeeded in the campaigns to criminalize seduction and increase the age of consent in most states. By the 1920s the case for enforcing female purity was losing much of its salience. More American women earned wages and sought education, and the younger generation embraced sexual liberalism. The response to the masher illustrates women's rejection of male protection and the reluctance of courts to prosecute unwanted sexual attentions. Reactions to statutory rape laws similarly downplayed the importance of female chastity. Within the women's movement, too, equal rights rhetoric challenged the older protective approach as activists who considered themselves "feminists" called for gender-neutral laws and a reliance on individual sexual choice.

Neither strategy proved to be very effective in achieving the lofty expectations of women's rights advocates that suffrage would transform legal responses to rape. Among the external obstacles were deep-seated biases against women's formal authority that suffragist predictions had underestimated. Resistance to women's jury service incorporated the specter that female jurors would be harsh on rapists, while Lord Hale's warning about the risk to men of false rape accusations continued to influence most judges. Internal to the women's movement, postsuffrage conflicts over the proposed Equal Rights Amendment (ERA), which sought to eliminate gender distinctions in the law, fractured the response to rape. In the process of rejecting sexual difference, some ERA proponents sounded strikingly like earlier opponents of rape reform when they accused women of being the seducers of men. Equally problematic was the sheer inattention to the problem of rape in the postsuffrage women's movement, including continuing silence about the marital exemption. With no single pressing goal, such as increasing the age of consent or winning the vote, the question of sexual violence moved to the margins of the feminist political agenda, where it would remain until the 1960s.

SUFFRAGE MADE A DIFFERENCE during the early twentieth century, for newly enfranchised women in several states were able to extend statutory rape reform. In the West new women voters succeeded in increasing the age of consent from sixteen to eighteen, as they did in California in 1913. Soon after the ratification of the Nineteenth Amendment, former suffrage leaders began to pressure southern state legislatures to revise their statutory rape laws. By 1923 these efforts were paying off. North Carolina and South Carolina set the age of consent at sixteen years. Fear of women voters swayed legislators in Arkansas and Kentucky to pass statutory rape reforms.[2]

Much of the postsuffrage discussion of rape took place in the context of educating women about their new legal rights. Within the compendiums of laws that former suffragists circulated, the topics of seduction, statutory rape, and judicial leniency were presented as inequalities that still needed to be addressed. In her list of over a dozen laws that discriminated against women in Illinois, Marian Walters included "low punishments for rape" and the fact that seduction was only a misdemeanor rather than a more serious crime.[3] The League of Women Voters, which evolved from the National American Woman Suffrage Association (NAWSA), produced a voter education guide in 1921 that pointed out legal disparities in property rights, marriage, labor, and education. Several items related to sexual protection: Did women know the "age of consent" in their states? Did they know the minimum punishment for rape (as well as for bastardy, seduction, or pandering)? Was there "any adequate law against taking indecent liberties with young girls"? Other materials reiterated the theme that rape laws constituted a double standard of justice. According to *The Woman Citizen's Library* (billed as "a systematic course of reading in preparation for the larger citizenship"), "Criminal assaults upon little girls are generally dismissed with a trifling fine for 'disorderly conduct,' while larceny sends a man to the penitentiary." Even when laws mandated strong penalties for rape, the literature pointed out, trial procedures, such as the corroboration requirement, continued to make convictions difficult.[4]

Especially problematic to new women voters were all-male juries, another obstacle to women's full inclusion as citizens. Jury duty is an obligation of citizenship from which women were either excluded or exempted, largely because of beliefs about the primacy of their domestic identities and their more delicate sensibilities. By serving on juries, opponents feared, wives and mothers would neglect their families and be exposed to sordid issues, including sexual crimes. The latter argument echoed the rationale for excluding women from practicing law—they might, as a Wisconsin court explained in 1875, have to face "unclean" questions about crimes including "sodomy, incest, rape, seduction." Others worried that women jurors would be too sympathetic to female defendants and too hard on men. Despite these long-standing biases, the enactment of woman suffrage unleashed a desire to extend the rights and the obligations of citizenship to both sexes, including jury service. Some states quickly permitted new women voters to serve on juries, as did the state of Washington in 1911. In 1920 the Nineteenth Amendment triggered jury duty for women in other states. Elsewhere, however, the effort to add women to juries stalled. Eleven years after the introduction of a women's jury duty bill in New York, politically active women continued to press for mandatory jury service as "the right, duty and privilege of a citizen, hence the obligation of women as citizens." They finally achieved their goal in 1937.[5]

To overcome concerns about female jurors, women's rights supporters offered a range of arguments. On the one hand, they made equal rights claims: Because women paid taxes and obeyed laws, they should also be able to serve on juries; women defendants deserved to be tried by a jury of their peers; and female jurors would contribute to more just treatment for men who stood trial.[6] On the other hand, they suggested that women had unique capacities to understand female defendants and crimes against women. In this view, women would empathize particularly with the plight of the rape victim. The question of how women might affect sexual assault cases ran through the arguments over jury service.

An evaluation of the performance of female jurors in the state of Washington in 1913 illustrates the egalitarian arguments for women's right to serve and their capacity for fairness in sexual assault trials. After twenty months of inclusive juries, G. M. Farley surveyed the resulting judgments and insisted that men had not been punished too harshly nor women treated lightly. He praised women jurors for refusing large monetary awards in breach of promise suits and found that in cases of "social crimes," a code for sexual assault, women had not been biased. While Farley seemed eager to assuage the concerns that women would be prejudiced in rape cases, he made a telling distinction when he wrote that "the sympathy of the women jurors has been largely with the accused man, where the woman complainant has been of a vicious or depraved character." In contrast, he noted, when the "victim has been young and innocent," women jurors were ready to treat "the accused with great unanimity." As with male jurors in the past, he seemed to reassure readers, with mixed juries a woman's sexual history still mattered.[7]

The argument that women jurors would arbitrarily rule against men in rape trials figured in a case decided by the California Supreme Court in 1918. Evan Mana appealed his conviction for rape on the grounds that the lawmakers had acted unconstitutionally in allowing women to sit as jurors. "May it not be possible," Mana's counsel argued, "that women, sitting in such a case, would be bound to return a verdict of guilty on the slightest pretext," such as "to avoid reflections upon her own chastity." Adding a rhetorical flourish, he suggested that a man charged with rape had as much chance for acquittal "at the hands of a woman jury" as an icicle had in surviving "the domains of his Satanic Majesty."[8]

In response to this challenge to women's jury service, Gail Laughlin submitted an amicus brief on behalf of "various organizations for women." Originally from Maine, Laughlin was practicing law in San Francisco during the state suffrage campaign, in which she played an active role. She would later help draft the federal Equal Rights Amendment. Soon after California women won the vote in 1911, Laughlin drafted a bill to enable women's jury service and then lobbied for its passage. After initial legislative defeats and a six-year public education campaign waged by women's groups, the state legislature finally passed the law in 1917.[9] That law triggered Mana's appeal.

In her brief Laughlin insisted on women's equal capacity for fairness. Unless the counsel for the defendant "denies to women the intelligence to discriminate between guilt and innocence," she wrote, "it would be only the guilty who would suffer." Moreover, Laughlin argued, excluding women from juries denied their rights and tacitly approved of their "inferiority in civil society." In *Mana* the California Supreme Court ruled to uphold the constitutionality of the woman jury law, even though the decision granted that states had the right to limit jury service. An article in the California state constitution, the justices explained, prohibited disqualification from the pursuit of vocations or professions "on account of sex" (a landmark nondiscrimination provision drafted by women lawyers in 1879). Their central rationale was that by granting women suffrage in 1911, California had settled the question of women's qualifications, so the legislature was "amply justified" in extending jury service.[10] Mana's conviction for rape stood.

Those who emphasized not only abstract rights but also the unique status of women jurors also cited rape cases to support their cause. According to Catharine Waugh McCulloch, the Illinois lawyer and suffragist, the goal of equal justice applied not only when women were defendants and required a jury of their peers but also when women brought rape charges to court. Even when male jurors convicted the accused, McCulloch complained, they "generally fix inadequate penalties for wrongs done women and girls." In her view, "when either a wronged woman or an accused woman stands before a jury of men it is not an impartial jury. It is a jury of her political superiors." In a similar vein, advocates invoked maternal experience to justify jury service. In Oregon they argued that adolescent sex cases in particular required "the sympathetic consideration which only women can give."[11]

Complaints about the absence of female jurors in rape cases recurred in the international suffrage press that American activists read in the early twentieth century. The *International Women's News* bemoaned the exclusion of women from the jury in the 1913 trial of more than two dozen German men who had been accused of the "criminal misuse of little girls under 14." The court convicted the majority of the men but cited "extenuating circumstances" to explain the light sentence of less than three years' imprisonment. According to the suffragists, "the Court declared that as the children had been previously seduced" the real victims were the men "who had not moral strength enough to resist temptation!" To the reporter who detailed the case, the ruling epitomized the injustice of women's political powerlessness: "No woman's voice from the judge's bench or jury box could make itself heard on behalf of outraged childhood."[12] Female jurors would presumably impose harsher sentences for childhood sexual abuse to mark the seriousness of the crime and to deter it.

The belief that women jurors could overcome judicial lenience toward rapists influenced some southern white women to revise their views about male protection. In the 1890s Rebecca Latimer Felton's rhetoric seemed to sanction lynching as a means of preventing rape. By 1908 she was placing more emphasis on woman suffrage than on the mob. Her sister, Mary Latimer McLendon, advised white men to "stop all this foolish talk about disfranchising the negro" and favored women's political power as a form of self-protection. When women gained the vote in Georgia through national enfranchisement, Felton turned her attention to the jury system. All-white male juries, she now argued, were too lenient toward white men, including those who assaulted black women or lynched black men. She noted that a white male jury had sentenced a white man to only one year on the chain gang after he raped a black woman in front of her children. Felton sounded like a racial liberal when she pointed out that, had the races had been reversed, a black assailant would have faced lynching. Recalling her earlier pro-lynching sentiments, she painfully admitted that southern courts did not "deal out justice" to rapists or lynchers. Women jurors, Felton and other southern women now believed, could undermine both kinds of crimes.[13]

New laws enacted in the wake of women's enfranchisement occasionally incorporated this gendered understanding of juror qualifications in rape cases. In 1921 Oregon's amended jury duty law not only included women but also accepted a requirement proposed by women's groups that if a trial involved a minor under the age of eighteen (whether male or female), at least half of the jurors should be women. That meant that the law applied to all statutory rape trials. Soon after its passage, a man convicted of the rape of a nine-year-old girl appealed the verdict on the grounds that certain male jurors had been disqualified. In contrast to the Mana decision in California, which emphasized women's full citizenship as the basis for jury service, the Oregon Supreme Court accepted the difference rationale. "Anyone who has occupied the circuit bench and seen a poor, frightened girl, a stranger to a courtroom, forced to detail the facts in regard to her injury or shame to a jury composed of strange men," the opinion read, "has felt that the presence of a few of the mothers of children in the jury-box would be more in accordance with humanity and justice."[14]

Whether female jurors had any impact on the prosecution of rape cannot really be tested. Even after state legislatures revised statutes to eliminate references to male jurors, many courts continued to permit the exclusion or exemption of women from juries. In 1923, when women could serve on juries in eighteen states (and the territory of Alaska), more than half of these states allowed exemptions to potential jurors solely for being female. One of the first women to serve as a state supreme court and federal judge, Florence Allen of Ohio, continued to promote inclusive juries, but her language hinted at the persistence of opposition. In trials ranging from robbery to rape to murder, Allen insisted, "we have had success with women jurors." When she reiterated her view in 1930, Allen maintained that cases related to family law, seduction, and rape showed that the first decade of woman suffrage had lifted "the handicap under which women rested." Yet she gave no specific examples to support her view that women jurors made a difference, and she remained an exceptional figure as a female judge.[15]

The road to full access to jury duty, as to the appointment or election of women as judges, would be long and tortuous. In 1931 twenty-six states still excluded women from juries. Only decades later, and after concerted effort by groups such as the League of Women Voters and the National Woman's Party, would all states add women to jury rolls. As the pool of women practicing law slowly increased over the first half of the twentieth century, women remained underrepresented as state trial and appellate judges.[16] The question of how female jurors and judges might influence the outcome of rape trials remained moot, for so few had the opportunity to do so.

SHORT OF ATTAINING jury duty and judicial authority of their own, enfranchised women continued to criticize the response to rape in the criminal justice system. On rare occasions they mobilized politically when they felt that judges or police forces failed to take sexual assault seriously. One episode in California, the recall of police court judge Charles Weller, resonated with the suffrage-era quest for women's public authority. In 1911, the year in which California passed the state woman suffrage amendment, voters also adopted a measure allowing the recall of judges as part of the Progressive-era experiment in fostering more direct government. Two years later, women's clubs in San Francisco employed the mechanism to oust Judge Weller because they believed that he was lenient toward men accused of sexual assault.

Charles L. Weller, the son of an early California governor and senator, had a long career as an attorney before his appointment to the San Francisco police court bench in 1906, a position to which he was elected the following year and reelected in 1911. As a judge he ruled on infractions of city laws, dismissing some cases and setting bail for others. Some of Weller's rulings hint at his treatment of women in court, which on the surface did not seem especially problematic. In 1910 he sentenced the first man arrested in a crackdown on mashers to ninety days in jail, suggesting sympathies with efforts to make the streets safe for women. Other rulings implied egalitarianism. In 1911 Weller injected a political note when he fined a woman for speeding by announcing that women's "new status" as voters meant there would no longer be any chivalry in his court. Perhaps an equal rights impulse animated his opposition to the creation of a special women's court, which the Women's Auxiliary to the Juvenile Court had recommended in order to protect female defendants and plaintiffs from "morbidly curious crowds." Whatever his motive, Weller's position could have marked him as unfriendly to reform.[17]

Like other police court judges, Charles Weller heard sexual assault cases and typically set bail at five hundred dollars or less. Several men had forfeited that sum and avoided trial. For defendants who went to trial, Weller sometimes granted a series of continuances and then dismissed the case if the woman who had complained did not appear at one of the rescheduled court hearings. In 1910 he repeatedly postponed the trial of two Mexican men who had assaulted and impregnated a fifteen-year-old Mexican girl, Berta Rocha. Weller also required the pregnant Rocha to testify repeatedly, did not allow women into the courtroom, and dismissed the case for lack of evidence because Rocha missed court when she was giving birth. In January 1912, after three underage girls accused John Woolsey of rape, Weller refused a request from the district attorney's office to raise the bond above one thousand dollars. Woolsey left town.[18]

The Woolsey incident might have passed unnoticed, but it became pertinent later in the year when the Hendricks case became a cause célèbre in San Francisco. In December 1912, two seventeen-year-olds, Esther Minter and Marie Bruhn, accused Albert Hendricks, a married automobile dealer, of trying to assault them in his car in San Francisco's Golden Gate Park. A married couple driving nearby heard the young women's cries and helped rescue them, thus corroborating the girls' testimony. After police arrested Hendricks, Judge Edward Shortall set bail at three thousand dollars cash. Shortall refused a request to lower the amount, but while he was out of town, attorney William Hagerty, a former police commissioner, appealed to Judge Weller to reduce it to one thousand dollars. Hagerty argued that Hendricks had a family, his wife was expecting another child, and as a substantial businessman and owner of four automobiles he was unlikely to jump bail. After Weller complied with the request, however, Hendricks skipped town. It was not the first time a man accused of assault had forfeited his bond in Weller's court, but it would be the last time.[19]

The Hendricks case galvanized San Francisco's women's clubs and the public. It took place soon after woman suffrage passed in California and during a period of heightened sensitivity to women's safety. In addition to the revolt against the masher, a flourishing discourse on white slavery attributed prostitution to the abduction and rape of young women. Antivice crusaders channeled concerns about female vulnerability into their efforts to restrict commercial sex districts in major American cities, including San Francisco's Tenderloin district. Local reformers successfully lobbied for the 1913 state law that restricted sex establishments.[20] In the same year women's clubs succeeded in extending the age of consent in California to eighteen years. As in other cities, such as Chicago, antiprostitution soon dominated the reform agenda, but the Hendricks case briefly made sexual assault trials a focus for women's complaints about the criminal justice system.

For years club women in San Francisco had been frustrated by the police court's unwillingness to take seriously their concerns about the sexual vulnerability of girls. As part of their civic reform efforts club members observed the police courts, followed rape trials, and befriended rape victims. They did not like what they saw. "The women of this city are getting tired of the lackadaisical manner in which seducers are punished," the president of the Women's Political League announced soon after Hendricks left town.[21] In other cities women reformers could only try to influence the judicial and political process, but in California they could now exercise their rights as voters.

Members of the Oceanside Women's Club spearheaded the public response to the Hendricks case. After trying to rid their beach neighborhood of disreputable men, they viewed Weller and the police court as obstacles to their efforts to discourage immorality in public places. As club president Mrs. Otto Fullmore told the press, "Too many outrages of this kind have been perpetrated on the beach to allow any such criminal as Hendricks to go unpunished." She complained about lax police courts and expressed the demands of "the mothers of the community" for better protection of their daughters. Pent-up complaints about Weller now emerged from local women. The judge had issued only a reprimand to a man who had been arrested for subjecting two sisters to "insults of a felony status," and the low level of bail he set showed how little he valued women's protection. In contrast, Judge Shortall came across as a protector of "womanly virtue."[22]

Even as club members spoke out against the judge, they insisted that they were "not after Judge Weller's scalp" but only wanted justice. They granted Weller's request for a chance to explain himself to the club women and their supporters, who now included local clergymen, the Woman's Civic Club, the Women's Political League, and a representative of the Juvenile Protective Association. The event proved disastrous for the judge. At a meeting called at a local church, Weller tried to defend himself by explaining that he had acted out of sympathy for the plight of a responsible business and family man, and that he had only followed the custom of the court. The *San Francisco Chronicle* described the response to his remarks as a "bitterly hostile mass meeting" at which women hissed, booed, and shouted for Weller to be thrown out of office. At the end of the gathering, women circulated a petition for his recall. The petition charged Weller with neglect of duties, negligence in court, and the abuse of his judicial power "by extending undue and unreasonable leniency to persons charged with the commission of heinous and vicious offenses."[23]

Judge Weller had clearly been caught up in a larger historical current. Anti-vice forces battled with established politicians and police departments nationally. San Francisco had a well-earned reputation for graft-ridden municipal government, and suffragists had supported the trials of corrupt city officials just a few years earlier. Now the club women found themselves involved in these municipal politics. Although they won the support of clergy and progressives, they faced opposition from the Bar Association and "organized vice" and even encountered political sabotage. Soon after their Recall League began circulating petitions, they realized that one of their male campaign managers had created a bogus front organization that was withholding or destroying petitions. The League recovered, ultimately submitting ten thousand signatures, well over the seventy-five hundred required to put the recall on the next election ballot.[24]

In the process, these new women voters learned a great deal about running a political campaign. Some of them had already been engaged in the suffrage movement, and they knew the importance of abundant press coverage. They organized mass meetings that attracted over a thousand San Franciscans. They employed witty public images, such as the banner announcing their campaign slogan, "All's Well that Ends Weller." In this labor-friendly town, they knew to court the workers' vote, holding a rally at lunch hour outside an ironwork plant and gaining the endorsement of the bakers' union. They learned how to appoint district captains to coordinate petition gathering and how to follow the legal guidelines for doing so. A visiting British suffragist invited to speak at one of the League's rallies explicitly linked their cause to women's responsibility to become involved in politics. For weeks they insisted they would not support any candidate to replace Weller, because they represented a moral and not a political campaign. Then the Recall League endorsed attorney Wiley F. Crist for the office. In a move that revealed the underlying concerns motivating community support, Crist campaigned on the issue of white slavery. As his flyer explained, "I fully believe that by laxity in the enforcement of the law, the police courts aid and abet the nefarious white slave traffic." He promised, if elected, to work for "the suppression of this vicious and rapidly growing menace to womanhood," reinforcing the focus on prostitution rather than sexual assault.[25]

On April 22, 1913, the Recall League won a narrow victory when voters ejected Weller from office by a margin of around eight hundred votes out of a total of almost sixty thousand ballots cast. Women claimed a political triumph. The *Los Angeles Times* predicted that city police courts in San Francisco would now mandate tighter bail requirements. The national reform magazine *The Independent* considered the recall evidence that "woman suffrage worked well." Others disagreed. Elections registrar Harry Zemansky argued that the low turnout of women in the election (a third of registered female voters, compared to just over half of male voters) showed that they had lost interest in voting "now that the novelty of exercising their suffrage right has worn off." Although the narrow margin made it unlikely that they had swayed the outcome, it had been women and not men, the Recall League pointed out, who initiated the recall, walked the streets, gathered petitions, and canvassed neighborhoods. The Civic League report concluded, that "It would seem that woman's influence, rather than woman's vote, had decided this election and accomplished the success of their measure."[26] Whether by their votes or their influence on male voters, San Francisco women had capitalized on discontent over judicial leniency in rape cases to flex their new political authority.

Immediately after the ouster of Weller, San Francisco club women tried to extend their momentum. At first the Recall League transformed itself into the Women's Committee of Justice to work in particular for the welfare of both boys and girls who found themselves at the mercy of the police court. They nominated candidates for police judge at the next election and campaigned for the creation of a night court. Within a few months the Oceanside Women's Club, which had initiated the recall of Weller, called for the removal of the police chief, a campaign that never materialized. Before merging back into the network of San Francisco women's clubs and municipal reform groups, the Women's Committee of Justice asked the judges of the superior court to consider including women as grand jurors. It was four years after the recall election that California women gained access to jury duty.[27]

At the height of the recall campaign, San Francisco women's club members articulated their understanding of gender and politics in the dual terms of upholding morality and making women full citizens. They had "inherited from the fathers in our city" a system of "injustice and immorality," they complained. But the mothers of the city could uproot this vice, "supplanted by courts of justice . . . where a girl's virtue may be considered the foundation of good citizenship." In the words of an officer of the Susan B. Anthony Club: "We want some woman-made laws so we can protect our girls." In San Francisco that protection increasingly focused on preventing girls from becoming prostitutes, as women's clubs turned their attention to monitoring dance halls, trying to restrict the red-light district, and protecting prostitutes brought before the police courts.[28] Perhaps anti-vice efforts fit better with downtown interests in law and order; perhaps local justices learned to avoid the pitfalls that felled Judge Weller. Whatever the reasons, judicial leniency in rape trials disappeared from the women's club agenda.

The short-lived San Francisco protest prefigured the broader political landscape after women gained suffrage nationally. Despite some achievements in jury service and some exceptional legal challenges, national suffrage failed to usher in a new era of women's authority to redefine rape. Whether or not new sexual values, including the presumptions of female consent, made it harder to mobilize to protect female purity, suffrage itself could not carry the weight of changing criminal justice procedures. For one thing, new women voters were not necessarily political activists. Although membership in the WCTU and NAWSA swelled during the quest for suffrage, after 1920 only a hard core of activists carried the woman's movement. When NAWSA transformed into the League of Women Voters, its membership declined.

Despite postsuffrage efforts to educate women as citizens, it would take another generation before American women began to vote in equal proportion to men. It would take yet another generation, and the massive entry of women into the paid labor force, for the revival of the women's movement to coalesce. When it did in the 1960s, second-wave feminists successfully organized to achieve full citizenship through jury service. By 1968 all fifty states included women jurors, and in 1975 the U.S. Supreme Court rejected voluntary rather than automatic inclusion of women in jury pools. Not until 1994, however, did that Court rule that preemptory challenges on the basis of sex were unconstitutional. By then American women had launched a widespread legal and cultural critique of sexual assault.

ASIDE FROM THE SLOW PACE of all social change, serious political fault lines weakened the organized women's movement after 1920 in ways that affected its response to rape. In the immediate aftermath of the ratification of national suffrage, conflicting strategies that had once coexisted began to diverge. An equal rights approach sought to eliminate a range of discriminatory laws throughout the states in order to place women on an equal economic and political footing with men. A gender difference approach favored the expansion of women's influence as women, with the goal of achieving a more just society. The latter agenda included improving working conditions for both women and men and providing public health services to mothers and children. For black and some liberal white women, it also meant rejecting the second-class citizenship imposed on African Americans by Jim Crow segregation and reinforced by the threat of lynching.

These distinctive worldviews came into direct conflict in the early 1920s. The younger, more militant branch of the suffrage movement, epitomized by the Congressional Union, which had been co-founded by Alice Paul, took the form of the National Woman's Party (NWP). Members believed that ending all forms of legal distinctions between men and women would best achieve the goal of equal rights. To that end the NWP members proposed the ERA, which was introduced into the U.S. Congress in 1923. In one expansive act they hoped to end gender discrimination, including women's lower wages and salaries and their limited job opportunities. Many former suffrage allies opposed the ERA, fearing that it would undermine labor legislation that allowed states to regulate working women's hours or wages. Alice Paul and the NWP dismissed the broader social reform agenda. Instead they single-mindedly pursued the ERA. For decades the term *feminist* signified their quest for equal rights. It became an anathema to the labor, settlement, and public health activists who wanted to retain gender-specific legal categories that protected women and children.[29] Inevitably the political analysis of rape reflected these fault lines.

When equal rights feminists revisited the legal reform of rape, they sometimes agreed with strategies based on gender difference, even as they elaborated their egalitarian perspectives. Earlier in her career, Alice Paul had been sympathetic to statutory rape reform, expressing concern in 1911 that so many states retained a low age of consent. She also pointed out lingering gender inequalities, such as the chastity requirement incorporated into some statutory rape laws and the remnant of patriarchal authority in seduction laws that still allowed only a father to bring suit for the loss of a daughter's services. In the early 1920s feminists like Paul combined the framework of sexual protection and equal rights when they lobbied to give mothers "a joint right with the father to collect damages when action is brought on account of the seduction of their child" and complained about corroboration requirements because they applied to women's testimony in seduction cases "though the defendant is allowed to testify in his own behalf without restriction!"[30] Though calling for equality, they did not necessarily reject the protective approaches that had been put in place in the previous century.

Opponents of the ERA, both social reformers and former suffragists, raised alarms about the ways the proposed constitutional amendment could contradict protective measures. Blanket equal rights legislation, they claimed, might eliminate laws against sexual crimes. Although the amendment would not necessarily do so, raising the specter of sexual anarchy played to protective instincts. Progressive journalist Norman Hapgood exaggerated that if the ERA passed, "of course all penalties for rape, and for the seduction of minors will be wiped out." When the League of Women Voters (LWV) and other national women's groups rejected the ERA in 1923, they included an objection that it would endanger "penalties for rape." A pamphlet about the ERA published in 1922 by the National Consumers League and recommended for study by the American Association of University of Women also raised questions about the consequences for laws that attempted to protect women from sexual coercion and assault. It asked women to consider what would become of the penalties for seduction, for violating the federal Mann Act, which intended to undermine the white slave traffic, and for rape if the ERA should become law. In a study somewhat misleadingly titled *Toward Equal Rights for Men and Women,* published by the League of Women Voters in 1929, Ethel M. Smith maintained that greater male physical strength justified rape laws that applied "unequally to the sexes." She referred to laws that punished adolescent boys more strictly than adolescent girls who engaged in underage sex. "But if this is inequality and injustice," Smith asked, presuming that her readers would agree, "what would justice be?"[31]

The NWP defended the ERA in terms that tried to balance protection and equality. Members argued that the amendment "would not endanger penalties for rape, but would merely establish the principle that such penalties should apply to the person committing the offense." "The person," not the male person, for in this view either a man or a woman could be guilty. To support this point, NWP members cited the precedent of the Colorado rape law that provided equal penalties for men or women. Washington State lawyer Lady Willie Forbus reiterated the position that women, too, could commit sex crimes. She called for white slave laws that protected minors of both sexes against the "viles of vamps (and worse) of the other sex," alluding to both seductive women and prostitutes. Her position recalled the concerns of nineteenth-century free lovers that seduction laws denied women's sexual agency. It resonated as well with more recent efforts to protect boys and men from female sexual coercion. "The designing woman who ruins boys," Forbus wrote, "is an equal sinner with the designing adult who ruins girls."[32] In the quest to achieve equality, Woman's Party members embraced parity with men in the capacity for sexual crime.

In taking issue with the protective approach to seduction during the 1920s, equal rights advocates could also resemble the antifeminists who railed against gold diggers and complained about rape laws that were unfair to men. Journalist Dorothy Dunbar Bromley, who considered herself a "new style" feminist, wrote critically about seduction laws and breach of promise suits. Both of these options, she wrote in the LWV journal, encouraged women to exploit and "profit materially from their relationship with men," inside or outside of marriage. Bromley clearly preferred more equal relationships that did not presume women's dependence. Similarly, the British feminist Catherine Gasquoine Hartley raised egalitarian concerns when she urged a careful examination of the principle that seduction caused prostitution. "We women have got to remember," Hartley wrote, "that if many of our fallen sisters have been seduced by men, at least an equal number of men have received their sexual initiation at the hands of our sex." In her book *Women's Wild Oats*, published in the United States in 1920, Hartley acknowledged that she once believed that seduction led to the downfall of innocent young women. Now, however, she had "been compelled to give up" this view in light of evidence that irresponsible girls had sex without concern about the reproductive consequences.[33]

The equal rights advocates contributed to a broader effort to reverse special protective legal treatment of women in the interest of promoting individual liberty. For some time sympathies for young men who might be victimized by age of consent laws helped slow the momentum of that protective movement, especially once the age of consent reached sixteen. The criminalization of seduction came under attack as well. A 1921 legal survey of state seduction laws emphasized their function in enforcing marriage through the threat of imprisonment, the classic complaint shared by free lovers and antifeminists. Popular culture increasingly portrayed women who filed seduction or breach of promise suits as gold diggers who extorted settlements from consensual sexual partners. During the 1930s a dozen states abolished their seduction and breach of promise statutes. Newly elected women officials sponsored several of these bills. In Indiana, for example, Roberta West Nicholson (the sole woman in the state legislature) referred to "blackmail suits . . . in which principals attempt to capitalize on some one's indiscretion." She introduced the bill to abolish breach of promise suits.[34]

The transformation of marriage, increasingly understood as a companionate rather than an authoritarian institution, also helped to undermine protective laws. In this framework, antiseduction laws gave the state authority to enforce marriage merely because a couple had engaged in premarital relations. Given the growing belief that sexual experimentation en route to marriage was no sin, the idea of sexual ruin carried much less weight than in the past.[35] This approach reflected the new system of courtship, but it could overlook the continuing risk of unwanted premarital sex and premarital pregnancy, which disproportionately affected women. Seduction law also provided a legal mechanism by which women could complain when male acquaintances coerced them sexually without the physical force courts required for rape convictions. In the era of sexual liberalism, women no longer needed to sue men for damages to their reputations, but in the process they lost one means of enforcing the right to refuse consent.

WHILE POSTSUFFRAGE feminists dissociated themselves from earlier protective approaches, they did not provide an alternative agenda for addressing women's sexual vulnerabilities. When they questioned inequalities in rape laws, they did so largely in the service of promoting equal rights agendas. Like suffrage for an earlier generation, the ERA now promised to eliminate the problem, presumably by fostering economic independence. With a focus on laws and formal rights, equal rights advocates never provided a structural analysis of the class or race dynamics that contributed to seduction, rape, or courtroom bias. Moreover, both protective and equal rights approaches focused on the public arena but ignored the private realm of the family. When they listed problematic and discriminatory laws, for example, neither suffragists nor postsuffrage feminists targeted the marital exemption in the legal definition of rape (nor did they explicitly address incest). Even as they questioned the principle of marital unity in the quest for equity in property laws and suffrage, sexual rights within marriage remained unexplored.[36]

Suffragists and feminists were not alone in making this omission. Earlier women's rights advocates had also been wary of questioning a husband's entitlement to sexual relations with his wife. In the late nineteenth century, only free lovers had provided a radical critique of marriage that defined a husband's conjugal imperative as a form of sexual slavery. Since then, however, the prosecution of anarchist free lovers under federal obscenity laws had effectively silenced most of these critics. In 1905 the *International Socialist Review* included an article entitled "Sexual Slavery" that provided an economic analysis of marriage as a form of prostitution. The publisher had to explain to readers that the missing pages in the printed volume had been removed because the government found the article "in violation of postal laws."[37] In Europe several writers had begun to question the principle of conjugal rights. Swedish feminist Ellen Key considered them "a gross violation of love's freedom," and British sexologist Havelock Ellis raised the question of whether the marriage contract sanctioned rape. But very few American feminists in the early twentieth century broached the question of the marital exemption.[38]

The notable exceptions incorporated anarchist and socialist critiques of sex and marriage. The preeminent American anarchist, Emma Goldman, who lectured widely on issues related to marriage and sexuality, provided an economic analysis of marital sex in her 1910 essay "The Traffic in Women." A Russian Jewish immigrant who carried on the free-love tradition, Goldman depicted marriage as a form of dependence that required women to exchange sexual service for men's support. A woman had to "pay for her right to exist, to keep a position in whatever line, with sex favors," she wrote. It was "merely a question of degree whether she sells herself to one man, in or out of marriage, or to many men."[39] In this formulation, conjugal rights had to be purchased—not simply seized—and women implicitly consented to the bargain, albeit under pressure to survive. Women were victims of systematic enforced sex, rather than victims of individual male lust. A popular lecturer before World War I, Goldman influenced a generation of radicals and bohemians, but she lost her American audience after being deported in 1919 during the postwar Red Scare.

Socialist feminist Charlotte Perkins Gilman more explicitly identified marital rape as a crime. In her 1915 utopian novel, *Herland*, three American male explorers stumble upon a community of self-sufficient women who have never known male domination. Each of the men marries one of the local women, and some of them find sexual harmony. But the aggressive male character, Terry, insists on his conjugal rights even though his wife, Alima, has made it clear she does not want to be alone with him. Terry believes that "a woman loves to be mastered" and so he hides in his wife's bedroom one night. Alima struggles against him and calls out to a small group of "strong grave women" who help her subdue her husband. "In a court in our country," one of other men explains, "he would have been held quite 'within his right,' of course." In contrast, the court in *Herland* banishes the men and sends them back home.[40]

The treatment of marital rape in Gilman's novel incorporated a range of modern ideas about sexuality. Terry's defense of his behavior revolved around his understanding that "a man's needs, a man's desires" entitled him to "master" his wife. The view that men had stronger sexual drives than women recurred in the literature on marriage in the early twentieth century, whether writers supported or questioned men's conjugal rights. As the ideal of companionate marriage infiltrated advice books after the 1920s, critics of men's "marital rights" urged husbands to be considerate lest they undermine the possibilities for intimacy and "sexual harmony."

Unwanted sex, the experts warned, might produce frigidity or even lesbianism in their wives and increase the risk of divorce.[41] Only rare marriage advice authors called compulsion "a species of rape as revolting within the marriage bond as it is without" or named the principle of "conjugal duties" as a form of "legal rape."[42]

The grounds for divorce did expand in the first decades of the twentieth century, but the law did not redefine rape to include marital relations. A wife could divorce her husband if he had raped another woman but not because he assaulted her.[43] The success of individual women who complained of unwanted marital sex in their petitions for divorce, using the grounds of cruelty, depended entirely on the sympathies of judges. Women had a better chance of gaining a divorce if they argued that marital sex had been not only forced but also frequent, had taken "unnatural" forms, and had posed a risk to their health.[44] In practice, then, asserting a right to refuse a husband's desires did not in itself suffice, and in law the marital exemption remained intact until the late twentieth century.

CLEARLY, THE SUFFRAGE VICTORY did not transform the definition or prosecution of rape. Nor did it sustain a broad mobilization to protect or empower women in response to the threat of sexual violence. Not only modern sexual values but also the internal political fault lines within the women's movement helped to preclude the possibilities for a feminist redefinition of rape. Postsuffrage feminists' conflicting approaches to laws concerning seduction and rape reflected the paradox that characterized the women's movement at this transitional moment. Though a belief in the distinctive characteristics shared by women had once held the suffrage coalition together, the quest for equal rights threatened to undermine a solidarity rooted in gender difference.[45] An older generation of social reformers had generally retained gender-specific arguments, but younger "New Women" who came of age in the 1910s and 1920s increasingly rejected the difference framework.

Whether influenced by the promises of female sexual agency or by equal rights political ideology, younger feminists questioned the protective impulse that had motivated earlier anti-rape efforts. Their views resonated with other trends in American law and culture. By the 1930s the term *seduction* no longer signified woman's sexual ruin, the adolescent victim had ceased to catalyze anti-vice campaigns, and the figure of the masher had become more humorous and less threatening. Along with new sexual agency for white women, however, came a renewed emphasis on liberated women as seducers themselves. As African American women knew from long experience, sexualization could entail a loss of protection. It could also reinforce stereotypes of female duplicity and deny women standing as believable victims of rape.

12

The Anti-Lynching Movement

In the first decades of the twentieth century, the African American quest for citizenship faced formidable obstacles. Pseudoscientific authorities insisted that the white race was unquestionably superior to all others, an ideology that found popular expression in the revival of the Ku Klux Klan after World War I. Politicians in the South argued that the disfranchisement of black men through poll taxes and literacy tests paralleled national electoral reforms intended to achieve good government. Empowered by the U.S. Supreme Court ruling in *Plessy v. Ferguson* (1896), which sanctioned "separate but equal" public facilities, legislatures in most southern states enacted laws to segregate transportation, amusements, and residential neighborhoods.[1]

This white supremacist infrastructure continued to rest upon the manipulation of sexual fears and the practice of lynching. When South Carolina senator Benjamin Tillman proudly told the U.S. Senate in 1900 that his state had disenfranchised blacks, he linked their exclusion from citizenship to the protection of white women: "We of the South have never recognized the right of the negro to govern white men, and we never will. We have never believed him to be equal to the white man, and we will not submit to his gratifying his lust on our wives and daughters without lynching him." Another South Carolina politician, Governor Cole Blease, invoked sexual threats to deny civil rights to African Americans: "Whenever the constitution of my state steps between me and the defense of the virtue of white womanhood," Blease proclaimed in 1912, "then I say to hell with the Constitution."[2]

These views echoed throughout national politics. In his State of the Union address in 1906, President Theodore Roosevelt opposed lynching but still attributed the practice to "the perpetuation, especially by black men, of the hideous crime of rape." Cultural representations of African

American men as sexual threats to white women reached mass audiences. In 1900 a best-selling book titled *The Negro a Beast* depicted apelike black men ravishing virginal white women. Viewing the 1915 silent film *The Birth of a Nation*, based on Thomas Dixon's novel and play, *The Clansman*, audiences cheered the white mob that lynched a black man depicted as a monstrous would-be attacker of a young white girl. President Woodrow Wilson, who presided over the racial segregation of the nation's capital, screened *The Birth of a Nation* at the White House and attested to the accuracy of its historical content.[3]

Even as the annual number of lynchings declined in the early decades of the twentieth century, mob violence became more vicious. At the peak of the lynching epidemic in the early 1890s, on average over one hundred blacks were murdered annually. That figure fell to sixty-five for the years between 1909 and 1913. Yet in 1916 a mob in Waco, Texas, tortured, mutilated, and burned alive seventeen-year-old Jesse Washington, accused of the rape and murder of a white woman. In 1906 the Atlanta press reported rumors that black men were raping white women, triggering riots in which white mobs killed thirty African Americans and injured hundreds more. Those who migrated to the North did not necessarily find a safe haven. After a false interracial rape accusation in 1908, white mobs in Springfield, Illinois, burned the black business district and lynched two black men. After World War I, the number of lynchings rose and deadly race riots erupted in northern cities when black veterans returned home expecting a due measure of respect. By 1924 lynchings declined to fewer than twenty per year, but a higher proportion of these resulted from allegations of sexual offenses.[4]

In response to the entrenchment of white supremacist politics, a national movement for racial justice took root. The Great Migration of African Americans out of the South and into northern cities ushered in the era of the "New Negro." A defiance of racial discrimination began to supplant the deference required for survival in the South. Northern urban enclaves enabled a bolder response to racial violence, expressed through a flourishing black press that condemned lynching. Soon after the Springfield riot an interracial group founded the National Association for the Advancement of Colored People (NAACP). Black artists and writers addressed the racial dynamics of sexual violence. In 1919, pioneering northern black filmmaker Oscar Micheaux provided a counternarrative to *Birth of a Nation*'s demonization of black men in his film *Within Our Gates*, which depicted a southern white man attempting to rape a black woman as she resisted his violent advances.[5]

"Every Negro question at times becomes a matter of sex," the leading black intellectual W. E. B. Du Bois explained in 1925. "Voting? They want social equality. Schools? They are after our daughters. Land? They'll rape our wives."[6] To achieve the elusive goal of full citizenship, from 1900 through the 1930s African Americans worked to reject the myth of the black rapist, particularly through the campaign to eliminate lynching. Black journalists and reformers, liberal white allies, and interracial organizations took incremental steps toward redefining rape as a crime committed by white as well as black men, against black as well as white women. By 1940 lynching had declined markedly, in part because segregation had been firmly institutionalized in the South, and in part because southern economic interests favored the rule of law.[7] But the remnants of mob violence against African Americans forced some white liberals throughout the country to question the southern justification for lynching. Disentangling the association of rape and race lay at the heart of the early racial justice movement and provided the groundwork for later civil rights critiques of racial discrimination.

IN THE 1890S the potential costs of protest had silenced many southern black critics. Alexander Manly barely escaped North Carolina alive after questioning the rape justification for lynching. Ida B. Wells lived in exile in Chicago. Only after black migration out of the South expanded from a trickle to a steady stream did the anti-lynching campaign take off. Compelled by economic hardship and political disfranchisement, a million and a half African Americans migrated north in the first quarter of the twentieth century. In Chicago, New York, and other cities they found new platforms from which to question racial injustice. Especially within a growing middle class, black men sought to establish the familial and political authority that had been denied them in the South. Increasingly these men took leadership of the anti-lynching movement, in which they often assumed the role of protectors of black women.

African American newspapers in the North provided a critical forum for redefining rape. In 1905 Robert Abbott began publishing the *Chicago Defender*, which soon became the leading national medium for opposing racial prejudice. Read widely in the South, the *Defender* played an important role in encouraging the migration. As a story about the "brutal burning" of a black man accused of rape in Tennessee in 1917 concluded emphatically, "Do You Wonder at the Thousands Leaving the Land Where Every Foot of Ground Marks a Tragedy . . . to Seek Their Fortunes in the North?" Those who attributed the exodus to a quest for better wages, the report insisted, were "Insulting Truth." Abbot was comfortable with sensationalist journalism, and he could exaggerate stories about crimes against African Americans. Still, his approach epitomized the political lens through which other black papers, such as the *Baltimore Afro-American* and the *Pittsburgh Courier,* understood rape.[8]

One significant target of the new political discourse was the criminalization of consensual interracial sex. White southerners portrayed all interracial unions as inherently illicit, and they passed antimiscegenation statutes to prevent the "unnatural" practice of black men marrying white women. African American writers raised two concerns that linked the ban on interracial marriage to the racialization of rape. Legitimizing mixed-race unions, they held, would help refute the premise that no white woman would agree to have sex with a black man, the basis for many rape charges. Making marriage legal would also undermine the practice of concubinage, which allowed white men to have black mistresses who raised their children without the possibility of marriage. The *Chicago Defender* referred to concubinage as a form of "passive seduction or actual rape of our girls and women." Race leaders from the moderate Booker T. Washington to the radical W. E. B. Du Bois favored "lawful marriages" because the "wicked devices" of antimiscegenation laws made "the seduction of women easy and without penalty" for white men. Du Bois offered reassurance that his opposition to the ban was "not because we are anxious to marry white men's sisters, but because we are determined that white men shall let our sisters alone."[9]

At a time when southern states tightened restrictions on interracial marriage, the nascent civil rights movement rallied to prevent the extension of antimiscegenation laws to the North. Support for interracial marriage had been inexpressible a few decades earlier, and it remained so for southern blacks. By the late 1920s, however, the *Chicago Defender* clearly announced itself "for miscegenation." In an editorial the paper drew out a distinction between rape and miscegenation: "the first is a crime—the latter is a custom—an American custom, with millions of American citizens as living examples thereof." For years white men had exploited black women, whether in consensual or nonconsensual unions. Now, the paper reasoned, interracial marriage might give the black woman some leverage

when a white man "defiles her."[10] This logic resembled the goal of antiseduction laws, which pressured white men to marry the women they
impregnated.

An even stronger motif was the exposure of sexual assaults committed
by white men against black women. As in the late nineteenth century,
between 1910 and 1940 rape reports in the New York, Atlanta, and Los
Angeles daily press almost always involved white female victims, and a
majority of the assailants identified were black men. Only the Los Angeles
press reported significantly on black, as well as Hispanic, victims. The
black press complained about this silence. The *Baltimore Afro-American*
noted in boldface that "Not a Single Daily Paper Has Mentioned" the
rape of a twelve-year-old "colored girl" by a white man, while "Every
Daily Paper in the City Carried Black Headlined News Articles" about
the rape of a sixteen-year-old white girl by a "colored man."[11]

The African American press self-consciously attempted to compensate
for this bias. Although each black paper reported some intraracial rape
cases, especially if they involved prominent men or very young girls, the
dominant theme was that ignoring white rapists perpetuated racial discrimination.[12] At the beginning of the century the southern black press
began to emphasize that white men in a given location, such as Chicago,
committed more rapes than did black men throughout the South. This
comparison later became a mainstay of anti-lynching rhetoric. Exposing
white men as sexual threats to black women vied with anti-lynching stories in the northern black press to make the same point. A 1911 *Chicago
Defender* article about a Portland, Oregon, assault was headlined "White
Gentleman Commits Rape," with the subhead "That's All Right—It Was
on a Colored Girl—Permitted by the United States Government and the
Confederacy." Underlying these reports was black men's unspoken griev-
ance that they could not fully attain the status of manhood because they
could not defend their own women from assault. No "real man," explained one article about insults to black women, "would stand for such
treatment to any woman."[13] As in coverage of white mashers, the black
press encouraged male protection of black women.

Reports of white men's attacks upon black women pointed to both
southern and northern assailants. The *Chicago Defender* minced no
words in a 1911 report that "the majority of the male whites of the south
revel in the intimacy of our women and think, like the small, narrow
minded dogs that they are, that all our women are susceptible to the al-
lurements of their arts and persuasions." When reporting the Tuskegee

Institute data on lynchings for 1918, the *Defender* noted that the numbers did not include "women who were murdered because they refused to
bow to the beastly desire of southern white men." But national stories
reported assaults in Chicago, Philadelphia, and other migrant communities as well. The headlines inverted the racial tropes that pervaded the
white press. In place of the term "Negro Rapist," they used the phrase
"White Man" followed by verbs such as "Charged," "Rapes," "Held,"
"Attempts," or "Assaults." The lead to one report epitomized the message
that "the ability to rape, and the desire to commit such an act, is not . . .
copyrighted by any particular race."[14]

As in the white press, black journalists constructed the ideal female
victim as young and innocent, but they redefined rape to include black
women in this category. When the *Chicago Defender* covered the Mattie
McFarland case in 1912, it reported that a "little innocent Negro child
was violated" by a white attendant at the Cook County Hospital. Also
referred to as "Little Mater McFerrin," the seventeen-year-old girl had
been impregnated by Frank Chaplin, whom the paper described as a
"white monster." Other reports concerned young black girls around the
country who had been assaulted by older white men, including a ten-year-
old approached by a railroad guard in Washington, D.C., and an eight-year-
old "criminally assaulted" in Kansas by a sixty-two-year-old white "huck-
ster." When a school janitor raped an eight-year-old Chicago girl, the
Defender editorialized, "We do not believe in lynching, but when the law
won't convict a huge scoundrel who will stoop that low then a rope and a
tree are the right things." The writer preferred, however, to use the law.[15]

Adult black women also appeared in these press accounts, particularly
when they accused white men in positions of authority. The *Chicago Defender* targeted several doctors who assaulted black women in hospitals or
private offices. After an employee of the health department attempted to
rape Mrs. Maurice Ingram when he entered her apartment, the paper ran
a flattering picture of her above the notice that she was prosecuting the
man, clearly noting that he was white. A major line of complaint was directed at law enforcement officials. An unusual migration story with rape
at the center featured Mrs. Olivia Law, a widowed black woman who left
Mississippi after Deputy Sheriff William Pears attempted to rape her.
Pears followed Law when she moved to Chicago with her children and
threatened the family with an ax if she would not "become his paramour." Both the *Defender* and black women's clubs raised money to help
her prosecute Pears.[16]

Along with airing white men's crimes against black women, the African American press monitored police and court procedures and drew out racial disparities. In this way they paved the way for later legal challenges to practices that discriminated against black defendants, an important plank in the civil rights movement from the 1930s onward. News stories editorialized about "the machinery of justice working poorly" when white men were arrested for "assaulting colored girls," and they praised a "prominent colored citizen" who pressured local police to follow up on accusations. The press editorialized about the unequal application of capital punishment for rape, pointing out "Cases in Contrast" in sentencing. The *Baltimore Afro-American* noted that prison sentences for blacks were more than three times longer than those for whites. When a Chicago court sentenced a white man to only one year in prison for the rape of a sixteen-year-old black girl, the paper protested that her race "does not change the complexion of the crime. A Colored girl has the same right to protection that a white girl has."[17] Triumphant headlines noted when white men did pay for their sexual crimes against black women: "Southern 'Gentleman' Is Sentenced to Die for Rape" read one of them. Reporters and editors celebrated anything that unsettled the association of black men as rapists. "It Wasn't Our Race This Time in Beastly Role," the *Chicago Defender* boasted in 1922 when two white men were jailed for the rape of a twelve-year-old "Negro girl" in North Carolina, adding that in this case the "usual mob is missing."[18]

The reference to the "usual mob" reflected a major feature of the African American press during the first three decades of the twentieth century—an escalating critique of lynching. The call for the rule of law permeated the anti-lynching campaign. Black papers in the North and the South exposed the horrors of mob violence through graphic descriptions and illustrations of the hanging, burning, and mutilation of black bodies. A common theme in their coverage was to reject white rationales "that this crime was necessary to stop the raping of white women by black men." Lynching had little or nothing to do with rape, the black press continued to insist. The papers published semiannual or annual statistical reports reinforcing Ida B. Wells's earlier conclusion that only a small proportion of lynchings involved accusations of sexual assault.[19]

One way black journalists attempted to deepen the wedge between rape and lynching was to question white women's accounts of sexual assault. From the relative safety of northern enclaves, black writers sought to extend to men of their race a defense that white men accused of rape had been making successfully for centuries: courts should distrust women because they tended to fabricate rape charges. This critique of duplicitous white women was not unique to the black press, as the changing discourse on statutory rape reveals. In contrast to nineteenth-century reform narratives that emphasized the protection of white women's innocence, twentieth-century American fiction and film frequently portrayed young working-class white women as temptresses and gold diggers. The black press also increasingly pointed to white women's culpability, a theme that had been too dangerous to pursue in the South.

These allegations escalated during and after World War I. In 1918 the *Chicago Defender* blamed southern white soldiers for inciting white women to make false accusations that black soldiers had assaulted them. More direct indictments of white women appeared during the next decade. The *Defender* claimed that a prominent southern white woman had invited a black railway waiter into her compartment and then "trumped-up charges" of rape. In San Francisco, the paper reported in 1923, a "new type of woman bandit" approached "race men and women on the streets," threatening to scream and charge them with rape if they did not give her money. When three young white women in Tennessee admitted that they had lied about a black man's assault on their grandmother, the headline in the *Baltimore Afro-American* emphasized the women's perjury, rather than the ten-year sentence that the jury nonetheless imposed on the black defendant.[20] These stories foreshadowed the national attention paid to false accusations of interracial rape during the 1930s. By then the campaign to undermine the association of rape and lynching had spread to white liberals in an interracial anti-lynching movement.

THE SEEDS OF A CROSS-RACIAL CRITIQUE of lynching can be found at the turn of the century, when a few progressive whites in the North questioned the legitimacy of the mob and southerners concerned about the economic effects of the region's tarnished reputation sought to control lynching. Some of these critics adopted Ida B. Wells's analysis that lynching had little to do with rape, while others equivocated. In 1900 a white southern scholar long concerned about the "Negro Problem" tried to undermine the association of black men with sexual violence. Writing in *Popular Science Monthly*, Nathaniel Southgate Shaler pointed out that "probably not one in ten thousand" of the five million black men in the United States had been convicted of rape. Taking social class into account,

Shaler suggested, white men were probably just as likely as black men, if not more likely, to commit rape. Others simply considered lynching an illegitimate or ineffective response to rape. "Granted that usually lynchings have been for diabolical outrages," a clergyman wrote in 1894, "it still remains that lynching is itself a crime." Northern social reformer Jane Addams rejected the chivalry that lay at the heart of the lynching-for-rape formula, but she too reinforced the demonization of black men by arguing that "the suppression of the bestial" could not be achieved by the brutality of lynching.[21]

Other early white critics, such as journalist Walter Page, opposed lynching not to achieve justice for African Americans but in the self-interest of southern whites. Page warned that the barbaric practices of the mob could incite revenge from blacks, while a reputation for lawlessness could stunt commercial investment in the South. Over the next decades other proponents of modernizing the southern economy echoed the concern expressed in the *Montgomery Journal* that lynching "does us incalculable harm on the economic side" and implied "a low state of civilization" in the region.[22]

Those concerned primarily with the rule of law also worried about the spread of mob violence. At a public debate on the utility of lynching to prevent rape, the chief justices of the supreme courts of New York and of Delaware insisted that only fair trials could ensure that an innocent man would not be convicted of rape. In the 1890s, Georgia supreme court chief justice L. E. Bleckley equated those who lynched to those who raped, both of whom "put themselves outside of the law." Georgia governor William Atkinson agreed that lynching multiplied the number of criminals. Even the argument that it spared rape victims from the ordeal of courtroom testimony, he wrote, did not excuse the murder of the defendant. According to former Mississippi governor Andrew Longino, southern tolerance for lynching had originated with "a sublime respect for the virtue and honor of our white women," but, he continued, the disregard for law that it fostered had the brutalizing effect of encouraging further acts of lawlessness for far lesser offenses. Some southern critics recommended speedier trials and the elimination of appeals in the hope that swift legal action would deter mobs.[23]

White women reformers in the South also began to reevaluate the efficacy of lynching as a form of sexual protection. Temperance advocate Vara A. Marjette pointed out that no matter "how horrible the punishment," lynching did not stop assaults. She also accused some white women of "hysterically crying rape" when simply approached by black men. In 1920 Rebecca Latimer Felton decried the lynching of an older African American man who tried to protect several black girls from the drunken white men who assaulted them. The mob, Felton concluded, served to "shelter the white rapists," and justice would not prevail as long as "our judges pussyfoot around these lynching atrocities."[24] Another southern white woman, Juliette V. Harring, recounted the gruesome burning alive of a black man, rumored to have committed rape and murder, "while women with babies in their arms made themselves comfortable and looked on without shame." Writing in 1922, when postwar ethnic conflicts attracted international humanitarian attention, Harring asked why there was no "cry for relief" for those subject to lynchings akin to the "righteous indignation" over "atrocities practiced upon the Armenians by the Turks, and on the Jews by the Russians."[25] Like other southern liberals, Harring recognized that America had a race problem and she wanted southerners to address it.

One step in that direction was to dismantle the rape rationale for lynching. In 1916 the University Commission on Southern Race Questions, formed four years earlier by a group of professors, issued a pamphlet to male college students reiterating the argument that most lynchings responded to crimes much less serious than rape or murder. A few years later a group of white community leaders in Nashville, Tennessee, gathered at the YMCA at the request of the chancellor of Vanderbilt University. Decrying the long "silence of the best people," which had allowed lawlessness to flourish, these business and professional men agreed that lynching had little to do with rape and was in any case never justified. One speaker, theologian W. F. Tillett, charged that the vigilantes who claimed "to revenge the rape of women" were in fact the kind of men "guilty of the same crime themselves," not only against "colored women" but also "with regard to their own white women."[26] These southern white critics broke gender as well as race ranks when they dissociated themselves from the mob.

Even more frequently than in the South, northern white liberals were now rejecting the association of race and rape. Magazines read by middle-class reformers—such as the *Independent, Outlook,* and the *Chautauquan*—reported the data compiled by *Chicago Tribune* associate editor George P. Upton and by the Tuskegee Institute to show that "criminal assault is not the 'usual cause'" of lynchings. Many writers pointed out that those accused of minor crimes, along with men falsely accused of rape, suffered. That lynch mobs also killed black women, the *Nation* and other periodicals argued, belied the "motive of chivalry." In the radical journal *The Masses,* the white socialist and NAACP cofounder Mary White Ovington used fiction to undermine the southern rape narrative. The title of her short story "The White Brute" reversed the press shorthand for rapist ("The Negro Brute") to describe several southern white men at a railroad station. They threaten a newlywed black man that they would hang him "to the nearest pole" if he did not let them take his bride away with them. Although the bridegroom pleads with them not to touch his wife, the white men strike him down, assault her, and then send the couple off in the Jim Crow car to return home. The story showed how the fear of lynching reinforced the rape of black women while it also exposed the powerlessness of the local white bystanders, who sympathized with the couple but did not intervene.[27]

The 1915 lynching of Leo Frank in Atlanta helped catalyze northern opinion. Many southerners presumed that thirteen-year-old Mary Phagan had died defending her honor from the advances of her employer. In a break with southern patterns, the black janitor who testified against Frank in court was not himself the defendant, in part because the charge was murder, not rape. Around the country, belief in Frank's innocence prompted massive appeals to Georgia governor John Slaton, who commuted Frank's death sentence to life imprisonment. In response, men calling themselves the Knights of Mary Phagan removed Frank from prison and hanged him. The mob helped give rise to the second Ku Klux Klan, which spread from the South into the Midwest during the 1920s.[28] White men had been lynched before, and at the time Jews could not necessarily claim white privilege. Still, the death of this northern migrant to the South after a national campaign to save his life raised widespread ire. Comparing Frank's fate to that of southern blacks, the *Milwaukee Free Press* editorialized that Georgians were "unfit for citizenship . . . something worse than barbarians." The *New York Times* described the "arch-savagery" of the lynch mob as symbolic of "the madness that has obsessed Georgia." National leaders commented on the lynching and called for punishment of the murderers.[29]

Despite heightened national consciousness about lynching, the belief that black men lusted after white women remained powerful. After World War I a German propaganda campaign that accused French African soldiers of raping German women fueled the definition of rape as a racial crime. Even some progressive women's organizations called for the removal of these black troops, although national suffrage leader Carrie

Chapman Catt convinced them that the rape charges were false.[30] In the South, supporters of lynching continued to complain that the wheels of justice moved too slowly to avenge the honor of white women and that the crime deserved a fate worse than death. Those who questioned this formula risked being labeled incendiaries. As one conservative women's paper claimed during the post–World War I Red Scare, "The Northern Bolshevist tells the Negro that he must kill, rape and riot to 'take over' the land from the whites."[31] Many southerners who condemned lynching still skirted the issue of rape, leaving open the one justification that could excuse the mob. Only organized political efforts could begin to change these attitudes.

THE PERSISTENT SUPPORT for lynching threatened the quest for racial progress, for without the rule of law and equal protection, African Americans could not enjoy the full rights of citizens. Preventing mob violence and securing the rights of defendants required new forms of intervention. One key approach was to hold public officials responsible for the actions of lynch mobs; another was to bring northern resources to bear on local rape accusations or lynchings. Gradually the NAACP took leadership on both fronts. The organization initiated a national network to investigate lynching, spearheaded an interracial movement that questioned the racialized definition of rape, and lobbied for federal intervention to deter lynching.

For decades local sheriffs had either colluded with lynch mobs or refused to prosecute vigilantes for murder. Many southern law enforcement officers shared the beliefs that motivated mob members, assuming the guilt of black men accused of rape. They also believed that swift punishment would spare white women the ordeal of a courtroom spectacle and would eliminate the possibility that a convicted defendant might appeal the verdict. African Americans had long complained of the laxity of law enforcement, but only occasionally did states address the problem. An 1893 Georgia law penalized sheriffs who did not protect prisoners from mobs. In 1896 the Ohio state legislature passed an anti-lynching statute that held the county liable for mob violence, allowing up to five thousand dollars in damages to the legal representative of the victim. An Illinois law enacted in 1905 allowed the removal from office of a sheriff or deputy who failed to protect a prisoner from a lynch mob. After a white mob in Cairo, Illinois, lynched, mutilated, and burned a black man accused of raping and killing a white girl, Ida B. Wells-Barnett (she had married in

1895) persuaded the governor to apply this anti-lynching law to remove the sheriff from office. In 1911 black leaders such as Booker T. Washington praised Alabama governor Emmet O'Neal when he instigated the removal from office of a county sheriff who had allowed a lynching.[32]

Since the end of Reconstruction, the federal government had offered little recourse when state officials failed to protect black men. By pressing for prosecution of lynch mobs, the nascent civil rights movement provided the first opportunity for federal reengagement in protecting African American citizens. In a case that involved interracial rape, lynching, and a showdown between local and federal authorities, the U.S. Supreme Court ruled in *U.S. v. Shipp* (1909) that sheriffs and vigilantes could be liable to punishment. The case emerged from a rape accusation in Chattanooga, Tennessee, by a white woman who testified that she thought that Ed Johnson was the black man who had assaulted her, although she was not sure of her identification. Johnson, who insisted on his innocence, was convicted and sentenced to death. A federal district court agreed to postpone the execution until Johnson's lawyer could argue before the U.S. Supreme Court that the state had denied the defendant a fair trial, in part because all blacks had been excluded from the jury. Justice John Marshall Harlan—who earlier in his career had issued an opinion against racially exclusive juries and who had dissented in the *Plessy* decision—persuaded the high court to grant the appeal and stay the execution.[33]

Before the Supreme Court could hear the case, however, a white mob angered by the delay broke into the jail and killed Johnson. The lynching triggered a protest by Chattanooga's black community as well as a response from the justices who had accepted the appeal. Justice Harlan pronounced the lynching an open defiance of the U.S. Supreme Court's mandate. In March 1909 the Court ruled that local sheriff Joseph Shipp and several members of the lynch mob had acted in contempt of the Court for allowing the murder of Johnson while his case was still being decided. In principle, *U.S. v. Shipp* was a victory for federal protection over local tolerance for lynching. It proved to be a mixed one, however. As soon as Sheriff Shipp had served his three-month jail term, the white residents of Chattanooga welcomed him home as a hero. Nonetheless, for the first time the federal government had taken a stand on lynching.[34]

It would take much more external pressure to force states to protect the right to a fair trial for African Americans accused of crime. One major step in this direction took place in 1909, the year of the Shipp decision, when an interracial group of reformers in the North, disturbed by the violence committed during the race riot in Springfield, Illinois, the previous summer, created the National Negro Committee, the forerunner of the NAACP. The group's initial sponsors included the white social reformers Mary White Ovington and Jane Addams, the wealthy white newspaper editor Oswald Garrison Villard, anti-lynching crusader Ida B. Wells-Barnett, and leading African American scholar W. E. B. Du Bois. At the inaugural meeting, Wells-Barnett denounced lynching and called for federal intervention to stop it. Although she did not remain active in the NAACP (other founders excluded her from leadership, and she deemed the organization too conservative), Wells-Barnett continued to investigate lynchings and riots. Eventually the NAACP would lobby Congress to pass legislation to prevent lynching and to protect the rights of African Americans accused of crime. The organization would also provide legal aid for black defendants and monitor their court proceedings. Like African American newspapers, the NAACP journal, the *Crisis,* exposed racial disparities in sentencing for rape, the lynching of innocent black men for this crime, the myth that lynching prevented rape, and the failure of the white media to report white men's assaults on black women.[35]

Ovington recalled that when the NAACP first addressed lynching in 1911, the initial strategy was to publicize mob violence in order to "show the criminality of the white." They found, however, that the belief that rape justified lynching made their cause so unpopular that it was "difficult to get prominent speakers to appear on a platform and denounce the burning of human beings at the stake."[36] Although the organization initially shied away from anti-lynching activism, W. E. B. Du Bois sustained the critique in print. In 1910 Du Bois became the NAACP's director of research and the editor of the *Crisis*. Within a decade that publication's circulation reached one hundred thousand, primarily NAACP members. Du Bois exposed the horrors of lynching. He took issue with what he called Booker T. Washington's "professional optimism" about the declining number of lynchings, suggesting that the practice was more widespread than the Tuskegee data revealed. Du Bois and the NAACP took a more political approach, monitoring the voting records of candidates for Congress and asking them, for example, if lynching could ever be justified. When Washington died in 1915, Du Bois and the NAACP were poised to assume the leadership of the anti-lynching movement.[37]

The killing of Leo Frank in 1915 and the horrors of the burning of Jesse Washington in Waco, Texas, in 1916 helped push the NAACP toward a national campaign against lynching. An internal memorandum titled

"Practicality of a Successful Attack" pointed out that "the tortures are becoming more frightful year by year," while the crimes for which blacks were lynched became "more trivial," ranging from gambling to "writing [a] letter to a white woman." In 1916 the NAACP finally established a Committee on Anti-Lynching. The national office began to hire field secretaries who infiltrated communities where lynchings or race riots took place. Their reports exposed weak evidence for accusations of rape, the identity of members of lynch mobs, and the collusion of jailers who aided them.[38]

One of the earliest NAACP field-workers, the young white suffragist Elisabeth Freeman, was organizing women in Texas in 1916 when NAACP secretary Roy Nash asked her to investigate the recent lynching in Waco. Previously impressed by Du Bois's support for woman suffrage, Freeman took the job. Operating under cover of her suffrage activity, she was able to extract copies of court documents, talk to officials, and learn about members of the lynch mob. She also gained the trust of local African Americans. Freeman believed that Washington had been guilty of murder but not necessarily of rape. Appalled by the tolerance for the lynch mob and the collusion of local authorities, she wanted them to be prosecuted. Du Bois published an article in the *Crisis* based on her report to the NAACP, accompanied by shocking photographs of the large mob and Washington's burned corpse. To raise funds for the NAACP, Freeman undertook a national speaking tour. Along the way she attempted to create alliances between the anti-lynching and the woman suffrage movements, which was not an easy task. She encountered resistance from single-issue white suffragists and from black women in the NAACP who feared that white female voters would do little to fight racial injustice.[39]

In the meantime the NAACP anti-lynching campaign provided new avenues for confronting the rape myths at the heart of mob violence. When Walter White joined the staff in 1918, he realized that the "overwhelming majority of Americans, including Negroes" believed that most lynchings responded to the rape of white women by black men. In response, the NAACP organized a two-day Anti-Lynching Conference in New York City in 1919. At a meeting at Carnegie Hall an audience of twenty-five hundred heard speakers who included suffrage leader Anna Howard Shaw and recent presidential candidate and former U.S. Supreme Court associate justice Charles Evans Hughes. Hughes invoked the rule of law. Shaw condemned "any man, white or black" who perpetuated a "criminal offense against womanhood" and called lynching a crime against every race. The meeting raised substantial funds, most of them pledged by cosmetics entrepreneur Madam C. J. Walker. It led to a resolution to work for the "awakening the national conscience" and to support the federal bill introduced in 1918 by a white congressman from Missouri, Leonidas Dyer, that would make lynching a felony under federal law.[40]

NAACP officials subsequently reiterated the point made at the New York conference that most sexual assaults were committed by white, not by black, men. James Weldon Johnson, soon to become the group's executive secretary, told a Chicago audience that lynching data refuted the widespread idea "that rape and the lynching of members of the Race in the South bear the relation of cause and effect." In an anti-lynching pamphlet published in 1921 by the recently established American Civil Liberties Union (ACLU), NAACP field secretary William Pickens referred to the myth of the black rapist as "one of the successful illusions" in history. Only 19 percent of the black men lynched over the past thirty years, he wrote, had even been charged with rape. Pickens contested claims in the white press that black assaults on white women led to the race riots in northern cities such as East St. Louis and Chicago, insisting that neither these events nor recent lynchings in the South had anything to do with rape.[41] Lynching, Pickens explained, helped suppress protest against the unjust agricultural practices that kept southern black families in "debt-slavery," while the race riots after World War I reacted to "the new spirit, claims and self-respect of the colored ex-service men." His interpretations foreshadowed those of radicals and trade unionists, influenced by the Communist Party in the 1930s, who blamed lynching on capitalists' need to ensure a docile black labor force.[42]

As publicity about lynchings expanded, so did the response from the NAACP. In 1917 Johnson, then a field secretary, investigated the burning and dismemberment of Ell Persons in Memphis for allegedly raping a white girl. He found little evidence that Persons had committed the crime. The more blatantly southerners defied the law, the more support the NAACP gained. In 1919 a Jackson, Mississippi, newspaper felt so confident that officials would not intervene to prevent violence that it ran a headline announcing that a mob would lynch a black man accused of assaulting a white woman at five o'clock that day. White supremacist governor Theodore Bilbo told the press that he was "powerless to prevent it." The *Nation* published an image of the headline under the title "The Shame of America."[43] By 1920, ninety thousand Americans had joined the NAACP.

The organization increasingly focused on passing the Dyer Bill, which created fines and imprisonment for any sheriff or other state official who failed to make a reasonable effort to prevent a lynching by, or to prosecute members of, a mob of three or more people. As Representative Leonidas Dyer explained, when states failed to protect the lives of citizens, Congress had to act. Liberal southerners had mixed responses to the bill. In 1918 the Tennessee Conference of Charities and Corrections asked President Wilson to issue a special proclamation on lynching and called for a federal law to prevent it. But other southerners who opposed lynching rejected the Dyer Bill on the grounds of states' rights, asserting that they did not want the federal government to intervene in southern affairs. That was the position of the fairly liberal Commission on Interracial Cooperation. The specter of federal legislation, along with concerns about enforcing the rule of law to attract economic investment, may have inspired some of the relatively weak anti-lynching statutes enacted in Kentucky, Georgia, Virginia, and several other southern states during the 1920s.[44]

Most southerners, however, continued to invoke the threat of rape. As one Mississippi congressman insisted, the anti-lynching legislation was in fact "a bill to encourage rape." During the filibuster, Senator Thaddeus Caraway of Arkansas charged that the real intent of the NAACP in sponsoring the anti-lynching bill was "to make rape permissible, and to allow the guilty to go unpunished if that rape should be committed by a negro on a white woman in the South." Alabama senator James Thomas Heflin claimed that the anti-lynching bill "was putting a premium on the crime of rape and sowing dragon's teeth in the paths of white women in the South and in other sections of the country." Such rhetoric helped defeat the legislation in 1922 and whenever it was reintroduced for more than a decade. As then-senator Theodore Bilbo of Mississippi declared during a filibuster of a revised anti-lynching law in 1938, passage of the act would "open the floodgates of hell in the South" and increase rape, lynching, and riots "a thousandfold." The "blood of the raped and outraged daughters of Dixie," he warned, would be upon the garments of those "responsible for the passage" of the measure. As long as southerners defended lynching in the name of protecting white women from rape, little progress could be made in imposing federal oversight of southern justice.[45]

Meanwhile, the NAACP sought every opportunity to undermine the association of rape and lynching. In 1919 an official of the organization wrote to secretaries of state, legislative bureaus, and county court clerks around the country requesting the number of indictments for first-degree rape over the past decade and asking whether the data had been classified by race. During the 1920s the NAACP began to intervene in local cases to defend black men accused of rape. The national office located attorneys, who typically worked pro bono, and helped raise money for court costs, often with support from local black churches. Some accusations, the organization learned, were made to protect white men who had been the actual assailants.[46] In other instances white women had engaged in consensual relationships with black men and then charged rape. Such was the case for Ben Bess, convicted for the rape of Maud Collins in South Carolina. As William Pickens explained, the relationship between Bess and Collins had been consensual and long-lasting, but she charged rape "to save her own reputation." When Collins recanted her accusation after Bess had served thirteen years in prison, the organization helped him gain a pardon.[47]

In the process of defending black men accused of interracial rape, the NAACP looked closely for evidence of female duplicity. In 1920, accusations that black circus workers had assaulted a white woman in Duluth, Minnesota, resulted in the lynching of three black men and the arrest of over a dozen others. In response, a local branch of the NAACP formed in Duluth to defend the other black men who had been indicted. "What I want particularly," the pro bono attorney explained, "is anything that shows that the story given by the girl is untrue." Charges were eventually dropped against all but two of the men; one of them went to prison.[48] Allegations of white women's complicity, which had once endangered the lives of black editors in the South, increasingly served to raise doubts about rape accusations. In 1924 the NAACP came to the aid of Oswald Durant, a black Word War I veteran who was attending medical school in Tennessee when a white telephone operator accused him of assaulting her. The local chapter president told the press that "some good white people say it is a put up job" to protect a white man who had been involved with the operator. The trial court sentenced Durant to life in prison, but the NAACP retained a local white criminal lawyer who successfully argued before the Tennessee Supreme Court to reverse the conviction on procedural grounds. The state never retried the case.[49]

By the 1920s the NAACP waged a multipronged campaign to redefine rape and undermine lynching. Field secretaries investigated rape and lynching cases around the country; the national organization supported federal legislation to punish lynch mobs and their enablers; and local chapters raised funds for lawyers to represent black men accused of rape. They defended them in part by raising the problem of false rape accusations by white women, a defense long available to white men. It was in this context that Walter White, who would soon become the long-term director of the NAACP, wrote in a 1929 study of lynching that corroboration requirements for rape testimony were needed so that "the unsupported word of a woman" would not suffice in court. In language that reflected contemporary psychological theories White noted that revelations that "hysterical" women had made interracial rape charges had produced "a growing skepticism" about these claims. He also attributed this change to a greater willingness among southern white women to reject the necessity of lynching for their protection.[50]

IN THE 1920S, after more than a decade of black male leadership in the anti-lynching movement, new activism emerged among women. Now enfranchised, northern black women had some political leverage compared to their southern counterparts, and they actively engaged as citizens.[51] The spate of deadly race riots after World War I, including one in Chicago, brought the issue of violence even closer home in the North. Immediately after the war the Northeastern Federation of Colored Women, along with other black women's clubs and the Baptist Women's Convention, passed anti-lynching resolutions. The National Association of Colored Women (NACW) created an Anti-Lynching Department, led by educator Nannie Burroughs, which successfully worked for the passage of an anti-lynching bill in Pennsylvania. In 1922 delegates from the NACW lobbied congressmen, as well as President Warren Harding, in support of the Dyer Bill.[52]

Perhaps the clearest expression of black women's intersecting gender and race consciousness in this period, the Anti-Lynching Crusaders formed in 1922 within the NAACP. The group's ambitions were encapsulated in the slogan "A Million Women United to Stop Lynching," a goal they hoped to achieve within a year. Wells-Barnett considered their efforts far too limited and conservative for her taste, but the Crusaders represented the flowering of her campaigns to end both lynching and the rape of black women. Led by Mary B. Talbert, president of the NACW, the Crusaders hoped to involve white as well as black women in their fundraising campaign. Initially they called attention to the fact that women, as well as men, were victims of lynching, reiterating the central theme of the movement that rape had nothing to do with most lynchings. Targeting women's clubs and church youth groups, they requested both prayers and financial donations. The Crusaders suggested that if women sacrificed "everything that is considered a non-essential such as candy, chewing gum, perfumes, powder, rouge," for a week, they could contribute the dollar these items would cost to help support the NAACP.[53]

Although they fell far short of achieving their financial goals, the Crusaders successfully initiated pockets of interracial cooperation to defeat lynching. In 1922 the suffragist newspaper *The Woman Citizen* praised the Crusaders for "'making terrible facts known" about both lynching and the rape myths that supported it. "Introduced and managed by colored women," the paper proclaimed, the Dyer Bill "has won also the enthusiastic support of white women, as well as of men of both races." Major white women's organizations, including the National Consumers League and the National Council of Women, endorsed the anti-lynching legislation. In contrast, the single-issue National Woman's Party, which championed the Equal Rights Amendment, refused to endorse the anti-lynching bill on the grounds that it did not centrally concern women.[54]

As in the past, African American women combined their anti-lynching activism with efforts to gain the sexual respectability that might protect them from assault. In the late nineteenth century, black club women had found few sympathetic white female allies, but in the intervening decades some Baptist and Methodist women began to cooperate across the race line, building on their shared commitment to proselytizing middle-class morality. During the Progressive era black club women continued to seek white support. In 1920, when several hundred white women observers attended the NACW conference, African American women called on them to learn about the treatment of southern black women. That same year Charlotte Hawkins Brown, a founder of the National Council of Negro Women, told the Woman's Interracial Conference in Memphis about the insults she endured from white men and the failure of white women to come to her support. "When you read in the paper where a colored man has insulted a white woman," she told the gathering, "just multiply that by one thousand and you have some idea of the number of colored women insulted by white men." Moved by her account, the group promised to assume "responsibility for the protection of the Negro women and girls in our homes and on the streets" and to insist that public officials prevent lynchings.[55]

Gradually more white women in the South began to respond to the call to engage in interracial dialogue. The Southeastern Federation of Colored Women's Clubs issued a detailed position paper calling southern white women's attention to lynching, to the working conditions of domestic servants, and to the abuses African Americans suffered on streetcars and railway cars. In 1922, when the white Georgia State Federation of Women's clubs expressed its opposition to lynching, Margaret Murray Washington predicted that only when federations in other southern states "take a stand against this evil" would male authorities "see that lynching is put down. . . . It is women's work now as always."[56]

In 1931 Texas suffragist Jessie Daniel Ames founded the major expression of white women's resistance to lynching, the Association of Southern Women for the Prevention of Lynching (ASWPL). Ames's evolving consciousness of racial injustice derived from her exposure to racial inequality within schools and prisons and from her distaste for the revived Ku Klux Klan. In the 1920s she worked with the League of Women Voters to organize "citizenship schools," although at the time she did not challenge the disfranchisement of black men and women. In 1922 Ames joined the liberal white Commission on Interracial Cooperation (CIC), attempting to convince Texans to improve the educational and economic opportunities for African Americans in their state. She became director of women's work for the CIC in 1929.[57]

Lynching had been declining for years, but when the incidence began to rise at the beginning of the Great Depression, Ames felt compelled to address the problem. In 1930 she called a meeting of a dozen southern women, many of them involved in church and missionary groups. Her purpose was to discuss how to "stop or abate this particularly revolting crime." Invoking the data that dispelled the rape justification, and recognizing that women as well as men participated in the mobs, the group resolved "to repudiate lynching in unmistakable language as a protection to Southern women." As Ames explained, "Unless this idea of chivalry could be destroyed, lynchers would continue to use the name of women as an excuse for their crimes and a protection for themselves."[58] Already enfranchised, the southern white women who joined the ASWPL were prepared to break with the remaining system of dependencies and claim the full rights of citizens, speaking up for their own defense and rejecting false protectors. Ames recognized that black and white women shared a common political ground. "White men hold that white women are their property," she wrote, and "so are Negro women."[59] White women had a unique standing from which to question gender and race hierarchies and a unique obligation to take responsibility for their role in perpetuating them. Echoing the views that had once provoked death threats to Ida B. Wells, ASWPL members admitted that consensual interracial relations often led to the execution of black men for rape.

With approximately thirty thousand members by 1936, the ASWPL represented an impressive vanguard among southern white women. To influence other southerners, these activists not only spoke out against lynching but also took concrete action to prevent it. Their public education campaign alerted club and church women, college students, and public officials to the injustice of lynching. With missionary zeal they garnered more than forty thousand women's signatures to the pledge to resist lynching. They also targeted local sheriffs, convincing over a thousand of them to sign a pledge that they would act to prevent lynching. ASWPL members investigated local lynchings and publicized their findings in the press, attempting to expose false claims that the practice concerned the "safety of white women." By alerting authorities to potential lynchings and refusing the chivalrous protection of white men, they earned the label of "lady insurrectionists" from the antiracist southern writer Lillian Smith. At least one journalist credited the ASWPL for a further decline in lynchings, which reached a low of six in 1938.[60] Ames did not, however, support the Costigan-Wagner Act, the revised anti-lynching bill introduced in Congress in 1934. She preferred that southerners resolve the problem through intervention, education, and improving the condition of blacks rather than through federal intervention.

Significantly, these southern women acknowledged white men's complicity both for lynching and for the rape of black women. As Ames explained in 1936, "White men have said over and over—and we have believed it because it was repeated so often—that not only was there no such thing as a chaste Negro woman—but that a Negro woman could not be assaulted, that it was never against her will." Now, however, these liberal white women could empathize with black women's plight. They called for a single standard of respect for women of all races and an end to the double standard that ignored or forgave white men while holding that "an assault by a Negro against a white woman is a hideous crime punishable with death by law or lynching."[61] Whatever their influence on southern justice, the very fact of southern white women breaking racial ranks with white men to claim a common vulnerability with black women signaled a major historical shift that prefigured the interracial civil rights movement of the next generation.

DURING THE 1890S BLACK WOMEN, particularly in their northern clubs, had been central to opposing lynching. At that time black men in the

South could not risk speaking out against racial injustice, and white women rarely responded to requests for support. In the first decades of the twentieth century, however, the confluence of the migration of African Americans to northern cities and the expansion of alliances among reformers broadened opposition to lynching and placed it on the progressive agenda. Northern black newspapers publicized the horrors of lynching and the myth that rape justified the practice. Even liberal white southerners, for a variety of reasons, now wanted to rid the region and the nation of the practice that had come to symbolize backwardness and barbarism. A vanguard of black and white women reformers articulated a political critique that combined opposition to racial discrimination with the empowerment of women as citizens who were no longer the dependents of men. Confronting unfounded accusations of interracial rape played a critical role in these efforts.

Even with the growth of interracial alliances, however, the movement had clear limits. Despite heavy lobbying by the NAACP and the private support of First Lady Eleanor Roosevelt during the 1930s, Congress never enacted an anti-lynching bill. Southern politicians valued states' rights and rejected federal intervention, especially if it threatened white supremacy, so they continued to invoke the threat of rape by black men to oppose the legislation. So critical were southern Democrats to the success of the New Deal that President Franklin Roosevelt refused to risk any political capital by alienating this important segment of his party base. These political considerations outweighed growing liberal intolerance for lynching.[62]

While lynching declined to a handful of murders each year, images of promiscuous, impulsive African Americans remained powerful. As in the past, rumors about black-on-white rape could trigger race riots, leaving a trail of death and destruction in African American neighborhoods. Police sometimes invoked the threat of the mob to extract confessions from black men accused of rape. Over time southern whites came to prefer the courts to vigilantes, knowing that white elites controlled the legal process and that swift trials, inadequate counsel, and flimsy evidence resulted in "legal lynchings." A skeptical black attorney later characterized their perspective this way: "We don't need to lynch the niggers. We can try them and then hang them."[63] During the 1930s, however, an interracial rape case in Alabama exposed the injustice of this process and galvanized a national civil rights movement.

13

Scottsboro and Its Legacies

In March 1931 deputy sheriffs in rural Alabama arrested nine black youths who had been riding the rails in search of work. A group of young white men, forced off the train after a racially charged fight, had alerted the authorities. Also aboard that day were two young white women, former textile mill workers Victoria Price and Ruby Bates. As the deputies prepared to take the black youths to jail in the nearby county seat of Scottsboro, the women claimed that the prisoners had sexually assaulted them. Within sixteen days of their arrest, the so-called Scottsboro Boys had been convicted of rape, eight of them sentenced to be executed.[1] Unlike hundreds of other incidents of interracial rape accusations in the South, the Scottsboro case came to national and international attention, in large part due to the intervention of the Communist Party (CP). As part of an effort to expand the appeal of communism to southern blacks, in 1932 the CP's International Labor Defense committee (ILD) wrested control of the case from the NAACP and took credit for saving the lives of the defendants.[2]

For more than a decade the local trials, state and federal appeals, retrials, and parole and pardon applications in the Scottsboro case produced a national conversation about race and rape. This discourse built upon the earlier efforts of black journalists, the NAACP, and liberal whites to undermine the southern belief that black men posed a constant sexual threat to white women. Since the 1930s, however, Scottsboro has overshadowed these precedents in historical memory. Considered "the most famous rape case of the century," Scottsboro became synonymous with racial injustice. The subject of extensive political commentary at the time, it also inspired creative reinterpretations, including a one-act play by Langston Hughes in 1931, a television play in 1977, and a Broadway musical in 2010.[3]

The Scottsboro case had lasting legal effects. The appeals in the convictions of defendants Ozie Powell and Clarence Norris led to landmark rulings by the U.S. Supreme Court based on procedural inadequacies during the trials. In 1932 the court ruled in *Powell v. Alabama* that the lack of the right to counsel in a state court constituted a denial of the due process guaranteed by the Fourteenth Amendment. Based on the same principle, the decision in *Norris v. Alabama* (1935) held that jury rolls could not exclude blacks. In both cases the Supreme Court shored up the constitutional rights of citizenship for African Americans, after over a half century of neglect by federal authorities.[4] The defendants themselves, who spent years in prison under harsh conditions, benefited only belatedly from the circuitous legal battles.

The public conversations about race and sexuality that were also a legacy of Scottsboro can be seen as a watershed in the changing meaning of rape. The case challenged both the deep association of black men with sexual threat and the expectation that they would be killed when charged with rape. At the same time it built upon the historic belief that women, especially those with reputations for immorality, lied about rape. Scottsboro and its aftermath provided rich historical markers for the redefinition of rape for black men, white women, and black women. The case exemplified a central dilemma within the modern politics of rape: how to extend the legal protections enjoyed by white male citizens to African American men without undermining women's rights to legal protection.

AT THE OUTSET, long-standing stereotypes about African American men pervaded the Scottsboro case. As defendant Clarence Norris recalled when he learned about the charges made by Bates and Price, "I knew if a white woman accused a black man of rape, he was as good as dead." Perhaps it was this knowledge that led several of the young men to claim, at first, that their comrades had indeed committed the rapes but they themselves had not been involved. Even after the defendants denied the charges, most white southerners presumed that all nine of the young men were guilty. This conclusion rested largely on beliefs about race. Newspapers in the South recirculated stereotypes of brutal black beasts and compared the alleged crime to "the way back dark ages of meanest African corruption." In a letter to the editor, a reader of the *Birmingham News* claimed, "The Negro is a great, big manchild . . . sex is the dominating quality of his makeup and he can no more help it than can a monkey or an African Gorilla."[5]

Given these attitudes, it is not surprising that white male jurors repeatedly found the defendants guilty, even as the evidence wore thin. In a surprise appearance at the second trial, Ruby Bates testified for the defense that she and Victoria Price had lied about the rapes because they feared being arrested for vagrancy. Bates later apologized publicly to the defendants for putting them through their ordeal. Price stuck to her story, but medical evidence introduced in court contradicted her claims of brutal assault, and testimony from Lester Carter, who had been her sexual partner the night before the arrests, provided an alternative explanation for the physical evidence of sperm. Nonetheless, jurors continued to convict. One southern newspaper stated explicitly what others may have suspected was the real presumption: even without evidence of the rape, the Scottsboro defendants deserved to be punished for stepping out of their place in the racial hierarchy by throwing those white youths off the train.[6]

For all of these remnants of southern injustice, the Scottsboro case also marked a new direction in the response to interracial rape charges. Most obvious is the fact that no lynchings occurred. A mob had initially formed outside the Scottsboro jail, but local officials did not acquiesce, as so many had done in the past. Rather, the sheriff called the governor, who sent national guardsmen to protect the prisoners. Other lynchings did take place in the South during the 1930s, but none of the Scottsboro defendants died at the hands of a mob. Southern liberals in organizations such as the Commission on Interracial Cooperation (CIC) and the Association of Southern Women for the Prevention of Lynching (ASWPL) could take pride in this outcome. But they also had to acknowledge that avoiding lynching did not necessarily achieve the end of justice. Scottsboro helped turn the attention of liberals from the mob to the courtroom, to the procedural reforms that could undercut "legal lynching," and to the deeper underpinnings of white supremacy. At their 1934 meeting, for example, the ASWPL not only reaffirmed its opposition to lynching but also framed the mob as a "logical result" of denying "a voice in the control of government to any fit and proper citizen because of race."[7] In this way the case contributed to the growing momentum of the broader racial justice movement.

The mobilization of national support for the defendants undoubtedly accounts for the fact that the men escaped execution by the state despite their repeated convictions and death sentences. The ILD hired investigators who unearthed new witnesses and evidence, as did the ACLU and the CIC. The ILD also hired the skilled New York criminal lawyer Samuel Leibowitz. Despite the serious disadvantages Leibowitz brought to a southern courtroom setting (for instance, he was Jewish and anti-Semitic outbursts were directed at him), he carefully set up the grounds for the successful appeals that resulted in the U.S. Supreme Court decisions establishing the rights to counsel and to jury service regardless of race.

At the second trial, Leibowitz introduced evidence of the absence of blacks from the jury rolls. White southerners readily acknowledged this practice. The arguments they invoked to justify the exclusion of blacks from juries—"want of intelligence, experience or moral integrity"—paralleled stereotypes about black men's proclivity to sexual violence. One editor explained in court that Negroes, like women, lacked the sound judgment to serve on juries. The trial thus exposed the link between the prosecution and definition of rape and the limited citizenship accorded to African Americans, who celebrated this opportunity to challenge the "lily-white jury system." Critics did not, however, extend this critique to women, who rarely served on juries. Notably, however, soon after the *Norris* decision a group of black women in Alabama marched to a county courthouse and asked to be added to jury rolls.[8]

Despite the procedural victories, Alabama jurors continued to convict the defendants. But as the trials and retrials dragged on, public opinion became more skeptical of the verdicts, even in the South. The evidence Leibowitz accumulated, the costs of repeated prosecution, the long appellate process, and the negative publicity about southern justice eventually began to wear down Alabama's resources. By the later trials, instead of the death penalty the courts imposed life or long terms in prison. Alabama dropped the charges against four of the defendants in 1937 and during the 1940s granted parole to four of the convicted men. Several of them moved to northern cities, where they struggled to adjust after years of unjust imprisonment, as did Haywood Patterson, who had escaped from an Alabama prison.[9]

The response to Scottsboro represented a flowering of the liberal and interracial coalitions that had begun to form in opposition to lynching. Communists initially monopolized the defense, but in 1935 the NAACP and four other liberal organizations joined with the ILD to form the Scottsboro Defense Committee. For decades the black press had taken the lead in exposing false rape accusations and championing defendants in interracial rape cases. Scottsboro provided further fuel for this publicity. African American newspapers followed the trials, appeals, and retrials far more than did the white press.[10] But without the support of white editors, clergy, and organizers, along with the legal team, the death sentences might well have been carried out.

In the wake of Scottsboro, mobilization against interracial rape accusations became a staple among leftists and liberals. On the legal front the NAACP moved beyond its earlier focus on lynching by expanding support for black men charged with rape. During the 1930s the NAACP raised funds for Jess Hollins, sentenced to death in Oklahoma for the rape of a white woman with whom he claimed to have had a consensual relationship. On appeal the U.S. Supreme Court overturned the conviction based on the ruling in *Norris* because no blacks had been on the jury panel.[11] In subsequent years the black press referred to a series of "New Scottsboro" cases in New Jersey, Arkansas, and the army. In San Francisco both the NAACP and the ILD tried to defend Festus Coleman, accused of the rape of a white woman in 1941, in what they labeled "California's Scottsboro." After Coleman's conviction by an all-white jury, a coalition of liberal and radical groups in the San Francisco Bay area raised funds, held rallies, and agitated for pardon until his eventual parole in 1951.[12]

The issues raised by the Scottsboro case spurred further civil rights activism after World War II. In 1946 the ILD joined with other groups to form the Civil Rights Congress (CRC), which publicized and provided attorneys for cases of southern black men accused of rape. Even when the appeals did not succeed, they could mobilize local African American communities to work for their rights as jurors and as voters. In the wake of wartime courts-martial of black soldiers, the national office of the NAACP increasingly agreed to aid black defendants in rape cases. In 1949 the association coordinated the defense of several black men accused and convicted of sexually assaulting a white woman in Groveland, Florida. The NAACP appealed to the U.S. Supreme Court, which overruled the convictions based on pretrial publicity and local prejudice. Although the retrial also resulted in a conviction, the NAACP persuaded a newly elected governor to commute the death sentence to life imprisonment. More successful was the 1953 case of Ruffin Junior Selby of Virginia. Despite an alibi and the lack of evidence linking him to the crime, Selby had been charged with a brutal rape and murder. The NAACP raised money to pay for a defense lawyer, and a jury that included one African American member quickly acquitted him.[13]

As in the Groveland case, civil rights groups built upon the constitutional challenges that emerged from Scottsboro to address broader disparities in the criminal justice system. In 1949 a Virginia court sentenced to death seven African American men who had confessed to the gang rape of a white woman. The national NAACP and local branches in Virginia organized a letter-writing campaign to save the "Martinsville Seven" from execution. In an appeal to the U.S. Supreme Court, NAACP lawyers pointed out that only black men convicted of raping white women had been sentenced to death in Virginia, whereas "white men had always been immune from such a penalty." The court declined to hear the Martinsville case, the governor refused to commute the sentences, and in 1951 the men were executed. In subsequent years, however, executions of African American men for rape declined in Virginia. In the long run the Martinsville case laid the groundwork for later rulings by the U.S. Supreme Court, which held in *Furman v. Georgia* (1972) that the death penalty was unconstitutional, in part because of its unequal application to blacks. In *Coker v. Georgia* (1977) the court eliminated capital punishment for rape.[14]

For black men, the legacy of Scottsboro was mixed. The lives of most of the defendants in the case were ruined. Even sympathetic observers at times distanced themselves from the prisoners. The director of the Tuskegee Institute, F. D. Patterson, insisted at a 1940 parole hearing that self-respecting Negroes detested the "heinous crime of rape" and referred to the convicted men as the "lowest class of human beings."[15] But Scottsboro's lasting impact included a rethinking of standard southern practices, including lynching and legal lynching. Race continued to structure the prosecution of rape. At times, however, black men now had legal resources and public support; far fewer faced lynching; and in much of the nation a rape accusation no longer meant an automatic death sentence.

IN CALLING NATIONAL ATTENTION to the plight of black men falsely accused of rape, the Scottsboro case helped to destabilize the southern defense of white women's honor. The trial evidence that most effectively evoked sympathy for the accused concerned working-class women's sexuality: Ruby Bates's recantation of her rape charges; Lester Carter's testimony that he had been sexually intimate with Victoria Price the night before the arrests; and investigative reports that Price and Bates had prior sexual relationships, sometimes for pay, with white and black men. The evidence played into a range of stereotypes about duplicitous and immoral women who cried rape to protect themselves.

Coverage of Scottsboro captured cultural shifts that had been brewing for at least two decades. Just as the protective strategies that propelled antiseduction and statutory rape reform had fallen out of favor, so too the chivalrous protection that helped enforce white supremacy could not survive white women's acknowledgment of their own sexual agency. Jurists had asked before whether sexually active women, and even prostitutes, could be raped, but Scottsboro raised that question more publicly and in relation to interracial sex. Some critics simply dismissed Price and Bates because of their sexual histories; others applied an analysis of class that stressed the role of poverty in determining women's sexual options and their testimonies.

Class and the assumptions of morality it carried had never entirely disappeared from the prosecution of rape in the South. During much of the nineteenth century a black man accused or convicted of assaulting a white woman might invoke her reputation for immorality to defend himself, to appeal for lenience, or to request a pardon. With the rise of Jim Crow segregation and lynching, southerners extended chivalrous protection to poor white women even if they had tainted reputations. Still, some elite whites continued to support clemency or pardons for black men convicted of rape on the grounds that the white accuser had not been sexually pure. In short, failing to live up to the standards of white propriety could deny a woman the racial privilege of refusing consent. In parts of the South, if a rape case went to trial and the accuser had a reputation for swearing or sleeping around, or even if she lived near African Americans, a jury might acquit the defendant or recommend a lesser sentence.[16]

The deportment and sexual pasts of the accusers in the Scottsboro case played a central role in the debates over the fate of the defendants. Ruby Bates and Victoria Price came from the lowest status of southern whites. Sometime mill workers in Huntsville, Alabama, they were riding the rails in search of work during the Depression. But that work included hustling, or trading sex for money. In Huntsville they had lived around African Americans and they had slept with black as well as white men. Price was married, but she had spent time in the workhouse for adultery. She had also been arrested for vagrancy, a charge often applied to prostitutes. When Price saw the deputy sheriffs during the train stop in 1931, she feared being arrested again. By charging rape she was claiming the status of a southern white woman worthy of protection from black men.[17]

The strategy proved to be highly effective. As a reader explained in the Winston-Salem, North Carolina, *Journal* in 1932, "In the South it has been traditional . . . that its white womanhood shall be held inviolate by an 'inferior race' whether the woman was a spotless virgin or a 'nymph de pavé.'" The president of the Woman's Missionary Society in Birmingham summarized the views of "Christian leaders" in Alabama: "Regardless of the status of the girls justice must be meted out and quickly, since they were white girls." Northerners bemoaned the challenge these views presented for the defense. According to ACLU founder Roger Baldwin, "whatever the evidence, no Negro can be acquitted when a white woman, even of the lowest character, accuses him." This prejudice ran so deep in the South, he realized, that defendants could not challenge the word of any white woman.[18]

As Baldwin understood, doubts about the veracity and the honor of white women escalated during the Scottsboro trials, especially after Ruby Bates retracted her original testimony and claimed that Price had put her up to charging rape. The ACLU investigation of Bates and Price revealed the women's "promiscuity" with both black and white men, while the CIC concluded in its report that "these girls were prostitutes." Drawing on these investigations, Samuel Leibowitz employed the time-honored technique of undermining the character of the accuser. He called Victoria Price a "brazen" woman and during his cross-examination highlighted her conviction for adultery and her liaisons with black men. Applying a northern standard, Leibowitz presumed that a jury would not convict on the uncorroborated word of an immoral woman. Even some southerners began to lean toward his view. In the 1933 retrial of Haywood Patterson, Judge James E. Horton Jr. instructed the jury that it could take into account that Price and Bates were "women of the underworld" and "of easy virtue."[19]

Horton's doubts about the women's testimony appeared as well in his comments on Price during a motion for retrial: "The proof tends strongly to show that she knowingly testified falsely in many aspects of the case." The clearest expression of this view appeared when Horton overturned the initial convictions during the second trial. "History . . . and the common experience of mankind," he wrote, "teach us that women of the character shown in this case are prone for selfish reasons to make false accusations both of rape and of insult upon the slightest provocation or even without provocation for ulterior purposes." The judge recognized from earlier precedents that juries often convicted based on a woman's "uncorroborated testimony," even though the witness was "wanting in chastity." He also cited the many reiterations in case law of Lord Hale's warning that rape was a charge easily made but hard for an innocent man to refute.[20]

Doubts about the word of women were not new, but a southern white judge extending Hale's protective principle to African American men was unusual. It did not sit well with most southerners. Critics vilified Judge Horton, who lost his bid for reelection. A more conservative judge, William Callahan, presided at the next round of trials. His instructions to the jury echoed dominant southern legal precedents: "Where the woman charged to have been raped . . . is a white woman, there is a very strong presumption under the law that she will not and did not yield voluntarily to intercourse with the defendant, a Negro." It did not matter, in his opinion, "whether she be the most despised, ignorant and abandoned woman of the community, or the spotless virgin and daughter of a prominent home of luxury and learning."[21] In short, the word of a white woman should be adequate proof of interracial rape.

National press coverage of the trial mirrored the fault lines in Alabama. The *Los Angeles Times* portrayed Victoria Price in a positive light and avoided any mention of her sexual past, but when Ruby Bates testified for the defense at the second trial, the paper cast doubt on her morality, highlighting the prosecution line that northerners had provided her with a "new dress and a new story." Other papers, however, took a different stance. The courtroom correspondent for the *New York Times* raised doubts about Price's veracity and shifted to a positive tone toward Bates after she recanted her rape charge. Even some southern journalists questioned the rape account. A North Carolina paper warned against the tendency in the region to lynch or legally execute men "when some psychopathic woman has a day dream and sticks to it on the witness stand."[22] Throughout the country uncertainty about rape accusations increasingly crossed racial lines.

Stereotypes about promiscuous women recurred among leftist writers, though they were often mediated by sensitivity to class. In a short commentary on the case written in 1931, the black author Langston Hughes called on "the mill-owners of Huntsville" to pay decent wages so that "their women . . . won't need to be prostitutes." While blaming capitalists for driving working women to desperation, Hughes nonetheless excluded these women from legal protection in his closing question: "And who ever heard of raping a prostitute?" Covering the trials for the Associated Negro Press, radical journalist John L. Spivak similarly described the

262 | Redefining Rape

background that produced Victoria Price. "When you have no money to buy pleasures nor have been given other interests," he wrote, "the only thrill left is sex." The "shanty and the mill" had killed all feeling in her, he wrote, so that she was willing to sacrifice the lives of the defendants in order to feel like "a somebody." Yet Spivak, too, generalized that past promiscuity negated the possibility of rape: "Being raped does not trouble her. She rapes easily and apparently likes it."[23] Along with his use of rape as an active verb that made women complicitous, Spivak revived the libertine defense that women enjoyed being forced to have sex.

Other writers who wanted to exonerate the Scottsboro youths tried to avoid demonizing Bates and Price by citing the effects of poverty. In her report for the ACLU, Hollace Ransdell wrote that Victoria Price had "been in direct contact from the cradle with the institution of prostitution as a side-line necessary to make the meager wages of a mill worker pay the rent and buy the groceries." After describing conditions in Huntsville, Ransdell concluded, "Promiscuity means little where economic oppression is great." Journalist Mary Heaton Vorse explained Price's "callousness" toward the defendants by invoking the low wages and long hours she had experienced in the mills, as well as her time in the workhouse. Harsh lives, Vorse wrote, filled with "hunger, dirt, [and] sordidness" had turned Price and Bates not only into "hobo children" but also into "semi-prostitutes." What, she asked, "had Ruby ever seen in life that rewarded virtue with anything but work and insecurity?" Southern white liberals also recognized the circumstances that produced the women's behaviors. The CIC called them "scared little mice, caught in a trap." ASWPL founder Jessie Daniel Ames, puzzling to understand why some white women imagined rape when no danger existed, expressed wonder about "whether the fears have been put in their minds by men's fears." In any case, she continued, "some women appear to live in a state of constant terror of being criminally assaulted."[24] This vulnerability could trigger rape accusations.

The publicity about the sexual lives of Victoria Price and Ruby Bates influenced the ways many Americans understood rape. After Scottsboro, accusations by southern white women did not necessarily mean that an interracial assault had taken place. The case also served as a reminder that white women sometimes consented to have sex with black men. True, old-school southerners continued to demand the protection of the honor of all white women. Judge Callahan and all of the jury members suspended disbelief about the women's claims, even after Bates changed her account. But for many liberal southerners, and in much of the national media, the image of poor white women falsely accusing black men of rape called into question not only southern justice but also the salience of women's honor. Liberal members of the ASWPL such as Jessie Daniel Ames had to come to terms with "certain groups of white women who, by their conduct, invite approaches from negroes and then take action against them." One ASWPL member suggested in a letter to Ames that "the law should differentiate between the respectable women and the immoral women in defining the meaning of assault and fixing a proportionate penalty."[25] Her proposal echoed the informal standard applied in the South before the rise of Jim Crow and the epidemic of lynching.

That these questions about a woman's sexual past could influence the legal response to rape is suggested by the outcome of a 1939 Virginia case. A seventeen-year-old white woman, Ruby Hogan, accused three black men of raping her while she had been out drinking with them and her white male escort. The black men admitted having sex with Hogan but claimed that she had consented in exchange for liquor. The judge's ruling is remarkable for its lenience toward the black, rather than the white, participants in the incident. He held Hogan on a delinquency charge, fined and sent her white escort to prison for eighteen months for contributing to the moral delinquency of a minor, and merely required a bond from the black men.[26] The decision drew on southern traditions by holding the white man responsible for protecting his date, but absent in this case was the traditional white supremacist script that defined all interracial sex as rape.

In the political climate of the 1930s, an analysis of class could mediate attacks on poor women's immorality. Over the next decades, however, those sympathies diminished, especially within the anticommunist and generally antifeminist climate of the Cold War era. In place of class, psychological interpretations of rape charges intensified. Reactions to the Scottsboro trials may have sowed the seeds of later theories popularized by writers such as sociologist Wilbur Cash and psychoanalyst Helene Deutsch. In an influential study published in 1941, Cash attributed the southern "rape complex" to "neurotic old maids and wives, and hysterical girls," who made false accusations. Several years later Deutsch echoed earlier medical arguments when she proposed that "rape fantasies" had led to the conviction of many innocent men accused by "hysterical women." Professional publications increasingly expressed these views as well. Echoing a suggestion in the 1934 edition of Wigmore's treatise on evidence, an article in the *Yale Law Journal* in 1952 called for psychiatric exams for women who charged rape, because their unconscious sexual desires could lead to false accusations. In popular culture, Harper Lee's 1960 novel *To Kill a Mockingbird,* set in a southern town in the 1930s and the basis for a widely acclaimed film, incorporated the image of the poor white woman whose desires for a black man led to false rape charges and unjust conviction.[27]

In her 1975 book *Against Our Will,* feminist journalist Susan Brownmiller blamed the communist propaganda during the Scottsboro trials for encouraging this line of argument. While she credited both the anti-lynching movement and the communists for undermining the myth of the black rapist, Brownmiller pointed to another harmful myth that characterized the case. By emphasizing "the rape lie," she held, communist propaganda reinforced the distrust of white women who reported rape: "If one case convinced the American public—and international opinion—that lying, scheming white women who cried rape were directly responsible for the terrible penalties inflicted on black men, the name of that case was Scottsboro." The history, of course, was more complex. Distrust of poor white women who accused black men of rape long predated Scottsboro. It had survived among whites even during the Jim Crow era. African Americans journalists had made the point for decades. The psychological interpretation of hysterical women who falsely accused men had an even longer history, as evidenced by the concept of the "willing victim" in statutory rape and incest cases over the previous decades. Of particular significance, though, was the intent of liberal and leftist commentators on the Scottsboro case to extend to black men the kinds of defense strategies long employed by white men accused of rape.[28]

The limitations of the "rape lie" strategy are also important, for it by no means served to exonerate most black men accused of interracial rape. Two notorious Mississippi cases reveal the enduring power of rape charges to enforce white supremacy. In appealing the conviction of Willie McGee, a black man convicted of the rape of a married white woman, CRC attorney Bella Abzug introduced the evidence that the two had engaged in a consensual relationship. Neither this revelation nor a communist-inspired "Save Willie McGee" campaign could prevent his execution in 1951. In the second case, the white men who in 1955 brutally murdered young Emmett Till because he had whistled at a white woman continued the long tradition of vigilantes policing the boundaries of interracial relations.[29] As in the past, white women's honor could still provide an excuse for racial terror.

Indeed, as the civil rights movement began to chip away at the foundation of segregation and as more African Americans demanded equal rights, the specter of the black rapist recurred. After the Supreme Court mandated school desegregation in *Brown v. Board of Education* (1954), white resistance drew upon the threat of interracial sexual assault. One Citizen's Council speaker rallied whites to boycott integrated schools in New Orleans with the warning, "Don't let your daughter be raped by those Congolese. Don't wait until the burr-heads are forced into your schools."[30] Each drive toward full citizenship for African Americans, from Reconstruction through the modern civil rights movement, has faced the manipulation of these sexual fears, and each movement has struggled to undermine the racialized definition of rape.

FROM ITS ORIGINS in the work of Ida B. Wells-Barnett, the anti-lynching movement included a dual defense—of black women's honor and of black men accused of rape. Scottsboro, however, seemed to narrow the focus. When African American women figured in the case at all, it was largely as the loyal mothers of the accused who stood by their sons and helped raise money for their defense. Courtroom and appellate strategies highlighted the importance of extending civil rights to black men. The rights to counsel and access to jury service applied to black women, but much of the commentary focused on an implicitly male "citizen." White writers concerned about the inclusion of African Americans on juries after the *Norris* decision did not point out or protest the fact that women could not sit on southern juries.[31] In the late 1940s, when she represented Willie McGee, Bella Abzug never questioned the exclusion of women, whether white or black, from juries. "In those days we were never consciously raising that issue," she later recalled. Moreover, attention to the black woman as a victim of rape diminished within the dominant discourse on Scottsboro. Jessie Daniel Ames considered an awareness of "the sexual abuse of black women" to be a logical extension of the anti-lynching movement. Yet two years after proclaiming 1940 a lynchless year, the ASWPL disbanded, affirming that their priority was the protection of black men.[32]

A little-known political effort to suppress an intraracial rape charge, while exceptional, is suggestive of the dilemma that civil rights activists faced in a movement focused on the defense of black men. In the summer of 1940 one the Scottsboro defendants, Olen Montgomery, was living in Detroit. Ever since all charges had been dropped against him three years earlier, he had been struggling in the North to find work and stability. In late July, Detroit police arrested Montgomery for "criminal assault" against a married black woman, Pauline Faulkner. Montgomery contacted the NAACP, where Roy Wilkins and Thurgood Marshall quickly made inquiries and provided a lawyer. Concerned about the effect of the incident on the remaining Scottsboro appeals, Wilkins and Marshall were determined to keep it out of the press.[33]

In fact, the *New York Times* and the *Chicago Defender* did publish short accounts, reporting that an unnamed "Negro woman" ran screaming to the police saying that Montgomery had attacked her at knifepoint. The stories also claimed that the police had found him in bed with the knife by his side. According to the NAACP investigation, a landlady called the police when she found Montgomery and Faulkner passed out together on a bed. Faulkner, said the NAACP, was too drunk to remember what happened, and the day after the incident she declined to make a formal complaint. The police dropped all charges.[34] Whatever transpired between Montgomery and Faulkner, the NAACP's reluctance to call attention to an intraracial black rape complaint points to the delicacy of the issue for civil rights activists at the time.

For decades African American women had complained about intraracial rape. Beginning in Reconstruction they turned to the state to prosecute rape charges against men of their own race. The rise of Jim Crow in the South restricted their opportunities to do so, but during the northern migration these accusations resurfaced. Black women reported intraracial rape to the police, and the northern black press named men who assaulted both strangers and acquaintances. In the 1920s, rape reports in the *Chicago Defender* were as likely to cover black-on-black assaults as black-on-white rapes. In the 1930s, however, the Scottsboro case directed press attention to the defense of black men accused of assaulting white women. As critical coverage of interracial cases expanded, the proportion of black-on-black rape stories declined. From 1935 to 1945, the *Defender* ran twice as many stories on black-on-white rape as on intraracial black rape.[35]

While black-on-black rape reports diminished, the black press offered more coverage of white men who assaulted black women. White papers such as the *Chicago Tribune* rarely reported these crimes, but the black press continued to do so. Reports of white-on-black assaults, which increased in the *Chicago Defender* between the 1920s and the 1940s, often emphasized black women's forceful resistance. They also named elite white men who attacked or molested black women, under headlines such as "Dixie Cop, Ousted in Rape Scandal, Arrested Again" and "Carolina Cop Held in Rape of Girl, 15." As in the past, the majority of articles called attention to attacks on girls and young women under the age of twenty, but they also identified the particular vulnerability of black domestic workers, women such as Bessie Creech. When Creech, an unemployed migrant to Washington, D.C., from North Carolina, answered an ad for a job as a maid and waitress, several white men assaulted her. The government prosecuted the men, but the *Baltimore Afro-American* reported that "an all-white, all-male jury" failed to reach a verdict.[36]

The fact that the state prosecuted these white men for interracial rape points toward an important shift in criminal justice practices, even in parts of the South. In the decades after Scottsboro, more white men began to lose their centuries-long immunity from prosecution and faced juries when accused of assaulting black women. In Virginia, courts had rarely tried white-on-black rape cases. In the 1940s, however, black communities pushed to get police to arrest, and courts to punish, white men who raped black women. In some of the cases lenience prevailed; others evidenced a declining tolerance for the abuse of authority. In 1946 a Richmond court convicted two white police officers who offered a ride to an African American woman and then raped her. One of the officers appealed on the grounds that the woman had not resisted sufficiently ("Protesting, she consented," the lawyer proposed). The appellate court upheld the sentence of imprisonment for seven years, a term that the black press considered to be far too lenient. Pressure from the African American community helped dissuade the governor from pardoning the men after they had served two years of their sentences. Even failed prosecution could mark new attitudes. In North Carolina a white judge who presided over the 1951 trial of a white man charged with assaulting a fifteen-year-old black girl declared that the acquittal made him "ashamed of my state" because "the evidence was overwhelmingly in favor of the girl."[37]

Elsewhere in the South, African American lawyers and community activists organized to support black women who reported assaults by white men. In early 1945 a local NAACP branch in Alabama began to investigate a series of gang rapes of black women by white men. "These men," the branch president wrote, were "taking advantage of the war hysteria to force their beastly desires upon innocent women." The NAACP intervened in Virginia in 1950 to secure the indictment of a white man who had assaulted a black girl (an all-white jury acquitted the defendant). Black men and women also fought back against mashers in Virginia during the 1950s. A black husband claimed self-defense when he stabbed and killed the white man who had tried to persuade his wife to have sex with him. The judge suspended his sentence for manslaughter. Similarly, after a black teenager killed the man who assaulted her in his car, a grand jury did not indict her for murder.[38]

After World War II, white-on-black rape cases helped fuel the campaign to undermine white supremacy. Rosa Parks, who had helped raise money for the Scottsboro defense in the 1930s, drew on the networks from that case, as well as her connections within the NAACP in 1944, when she formed the Alabama Committee for Equal Justice for Mrs. Recy Taylor. Taylor had been assaulted by seven white men who claimed that she was a prostitute and had consented to have sex for pay. An all-white male grand jury failed to indict the assailants. Protests from the black press, women's groups, and trade unions, as well as petitions from around the country, resulted in a second hearing. Once again, however, the men remained free.[39]

Like other unsuccessful campaigns, the Taylor case had broader ramifications for the civil rights movement. Thanks in part to the evidence that Parks collected about sexual assaults against black women, the African American community in Montgomery escalated pressure on authorities to prosecute white assailants. In 1949 local clergy and the NAACP exposed the rape of Gertrude Perkins by two police officers. Their newspaper publicity campaign helped force a grand jury to consider the charges, but the jurors did not indict the men. In the 1950s, black women in Montgomery began to protest the sexual insults they encountered from city bus drivers. The Committee for Equal Justice for Mrs. Recy Taylor eventually flowed into the Montgomery Improvement Association, which waged the successful antisegregation bus boycott of 1955 and helped launch the political career of Martin Luther King Jr.[40]

In subsequent cases southern courts did hold white men accountable for the rape of black women. In 1959 four white men in Tallahassee, Florida, assaulted college student Betty Jean Owens. Despite the typical defense strategy of impugning her character ("Are you going to believe this nigger wench over these four boys?" their attorney asked), this time the jury found the defendants guilty. In 1965, at the height of the civil rights movement, white prosecutors in Hattiesburg, Mississippi, filed rape charges against Norman Cannon, a young white man named as the assailant of a black teenager, Rosa Lee Coates. Cannon claimed that Coates had agreed to have sex for pay, but Coates testified persuasively that he had abducted and then "ravished" her. The jury convicted Cannon of rape, a capital offense, then recommended a life sentence as an act of

ercy. The *New York Times* heralded the outcome of the case as "a major
reakthrough."[41] Although white defendants would continue to claim
hat the black women who accused them of rape were prostitutes who
onsented to sex, that defense no longer guaranteed acquittal.

HE RESPONSE to the Scottsboro case sustained and expanded previous
fforts to redefine rape in American culture. White leftists and liberals
ow joined with African Americans who had been agitating for decades
o extend legal protections to black men accused of rape. Yet the case also
narked a turning point. After Scottsboro, African American men accused
f assaulting white women no longer faced automatic death sentences,
whether implemented by the mob or by the state. They continued to be
rosecuted, convicted, and executed at a higher rate than white men, but
he dynamics were changing.[42] The publicity campaigns and the U.S.
upreme Court rulings in the Scottsboro case meant that the press was
nore likely to acknowledge the possibility that black defendants were in-
ocent, and the state increasingly had to respect black defendants' rights
o counsel and to a jury of their peers. In the South particularly, the defi-
ition of rape no longer encompassed all sexual relations between black
nen and white women, given the greater recognition of consensual inter-
acial sex. It would take decades for southern legal practices to respond to
hese redefinitions and for African Americans to gain access to juries.
till, one legacy of Scottsboro was to deepen the wedge that black activ-
sts had long tried to interject between rape and race.

Scottsboro also built upon and contributed to the rethinking of white
women's sexuality. Many medical and legal professionals had bristled at
ntiseduction and revised statutory rape laws for threatening white men
with a kind of sexual blackmail. In the postsuffrage era, more women had
egun to question the protective strategies that had driven these reforms.
Given the greater sexualization of white women in American popular and
ommercial culture, including depictions of flirts and teases, the time
nay have been ripe for a legal defense of black men that revived the histori-
al distrust of poor women's rape accusations and employed the strategy of
mpugning the moral character of accusers. Scottsboro illustrates how, without the gendered purity divide that had characterized nineteenth-century
American culture, a class divide could reemerge as the measure of which
women could refuse to consent to sex. At the same time, the case signaled
 diminution of a century-long effort to resist the narrowing definition of

rape for women of all classes and races, for it revived limitations on which women could be believed in court.

The aftermath of Scottsboro provides another indicator of how the experiences of black women and white women increasingly converged in post–World War II America. Just as patterns of paid labor and sexual behavior became more similar for black and white women, the treatment of rape became less clearly defined by race. African American women remained more sexually vulnerable than white women, but they began to gain a modicum of legal recourse against interracial rape. At the same time, the sexualization of white women removed some of the categorical protections they had once enjoyed in the name of preserving racial purity. Only after the revival of feminism in the 1960s, however—when both black and white women mobilized politically to attain their full rights as citizens—would an anti-rape movement begin to address the serious legal obstacles all women still faced when they charged men of any race with sexual assault.

14

The Enduring Politics of Rape

In the decades since Scottsboro, rape and its definition have continued to trouble Americans, spark debate, and shape social movements. The history of conflicts over who can be raped and who will be prosecuted for the crime reverberates in contemporary politics, illuminating the persistent tensions over how Americans understand both gender and race. In the past, rape often surfaced as a subsidiary concern to achieve instrumental goals, whether white supremacy, woman suffrage, or an end to lynching. By the late twentieth century, however, rape itself had become the explicit focus of political analysis.

The changing landscape of modern American political and social life helped to reshape the politics of rape. After World War II, a series of social upheavals transformed Americans' understandings of race, sexuality, and gender. The southern civil rights movement gathered momentum during the 1950s, reviving Reconstruction-era demands for full citizenship for African Americans. In the 1960s Congress enacted new civil rights guarantees and courts struck down discriminatory legislation, such as remaining state bans on interracial marriage. In the same decades, the sexualization of American commerce and popular culture, Alfred Kinsey's documentation of the diverse sexual practices of American men and women, and Supreme Court opinions curtailing the regulation of obscenity all contributed to the widespread embrace of sexual liberalism.

These social changes deeply affected the meaning of rape in two distinct stages. In the immediate postwar period, calls for racial justice and a growing emphasis on sexual privacy focused attention on the rights of accused men. At this time the legal reforms initiated by social purity advocates and suffragists over the previous century largely fell out of favor. As women's labor force participation increased, and as a younger generation encountered the contradictions of the "sexual revolution," a mass revival of feminism challenged patriarchal privilege in the private as well as the public spheres. After 1970, feminists expanded the definition of sexual assault far beyond earlier legal strategies. By the end of the century, a self-identified anti-rape movement exerted extensive influence on local, national, and international law. Throughout this recent history, many of the political strategies advocated in the past resurfaced, as did both the arguments against them and the internal conflicts over race and rights that had characterized earlier campaigns.

IN POST–WORLD WAR II AMERICA, efforts to reform the prosecution of sexual assault shifted significantly away from the suffrage-era focus on empowering women. The protection of accused men dominated legal discourse on rape in the 1950s and 1960s. Both the racial justice movement and the growing influence of sexual liberalism at midcentury contributed to this emphasis. In the South, NAACP local branches tried, often unsuccessfully, to defend black men accused, convicted, or sentenced to death for rape. The national office of the NAACP, which had once been more selective in supporting rape defendants, increasingly took on appellate cases concerning interracial assault. The continued migration of African Americans out of the South turned greater attention to the defense of accused black men in other parts of the country, as well. Throughout the United States, police were quick to identify black men as rape suspects. During the decade after World War II, for example, African American men in Chicago were over five times more likely than white men to be prosecuted for rape; when convicted, they received longer sentences. Local NAACP staff pointed out racial bias in police investigations and the identification of suspects. They helped publicize the disproportionate arrest and prosecution of black men and called on newspapers to cease identifying men accused of rape by race. During the 1960s the NAACP Legal Defense Fund launched a major campaign directed at racial disparities in the application of capital punishment for rape.[1]

As in the Scottsboro case, postwar support for African American men who stood trial for interracial rape could come into conflict with the project of enhancing women's legal standing. Attention to the rights of defendants, mandated by several Supreme Court rulings during the 1960s, encouraged stricter scrutiny of the testimony of accusers and led to calls for stronger corroboration requirements. The ACLU, which had once refused requests to support accused black men, now increasingly joined in their defense instead of referring them to the NAACP. The ACLU often adopted the strategy of discrediting white women's rape complaints by depicting them as sexually promiscuous.[2] Acknowledging that some white women made false accusations did help break down assumptions about black men as sexual threats. At the same time, it contributed to a larger cultural trend toward dismissing women's charges against either black or white men.

The strategy of discrediting accusers affected African American as well as white women. In intraracial rape cases in Chicago, for example, defense attorneys in the postwar decades increasingly tried to discredit black women's testimony. They cross-examined them about their sexual histories and implied that they had been sexually promiscuous. Any black woman who had been out on city streets at night, the questioning suggested, was likely to be a prostitute who had consented to sex. One black defense attorney who worked with the NAACP portrayed these accusers as promiscuous welfare mothers. Even when this strategy did not win acquittal, it might mediate sentencing. For convicted black men who invoked the consent defense, the average length of prison time was one-third that of cases that employed other defense strategies.[3]

Medical opinion continued to influence depictions of women in rape cases. In language echoing psychological theories that first proliferated in the 1920s, postwar legal scholarship emphasized the problem of the hysterical woman who falsely charged rape against any man. As the liberal jurist Morris Ploscowe concisely stated the prevailing view, "Ladies lie." Leading law journals included articles that claimed that because "stories of rape are frequently lies or fantasies" they should not suffice "to convict a man of crime." Critics called for tighter rules of evidence to protect men from unfair charges, repeating much earlier claims that a man could "lose his life or liberty" at the word of a woman. The belief that women commonly fantasized being raped, and that some of them believed their fantasies to be true, found its way into judicial opinions via later editions of Wigmore's treatise on evidence. Other writers reiterated earlier suggestions that psychiatrists should examine any woman who complained of sexual assault.[4]

In the era of the Kinsey reports, when periodicals such as *Playboy* and *Cosmopolitan* helped revise cultural norms, Americans increasingly claimed a right to sexual expression. By the 1960s both youths and adults were participating in a sexual revolution that embraced the erotic for its own sake, apart from romance or reproductive family life. In the process of questioning state regulation of morality, legal scholarship at times reiterated points previously made by the opponents of age-of-consent laws and physicians who questioned incest charges. Several writers blamed women for inviting sexual advances and then charging rape. In 1967 a major criminologist introduced the notion of rape being "victim-precipitated" for cases where "the behavior of the victim is interpreted by the offender either as a direct invitation for sexual relations or as a sign that she will be available for sexual contact if he will persist in demanding it." Similarly, an article in the *Stanford Law Review* restated nineteenth-century views that male sexual aggression was normal and that women were expected to say " 'no, no, no' (although meaning 'yes, yes, yes')" before they acquiesced to intercourse.[5]

These views proved influential, as evidenced by the widespread adoption of recommendations made by the American Law Institute in its Model Penal Code, published in 1962 as a guide to statutory revision in the states. The Code, which covered wide areas of the law, rejected state regulation of morality and called for tolerance in light of the climate created by revelations in the Kinsey reports of widespread sexual "derelictions" in the American population. Thus, it recommended an end to criminal penalties for fornication and adultery. Like other sexual liberals at the time, the drafters of the Model Penal Code differentiated between abnormal men who committed sex crimes—the mentally deranged psychopaths who came to epitomize the postwar white rapist—and normal men who engaged in noninjurious acts. The Code called for the decriminalization of consensual sodomy, making "deviate sexual intercourse" a crime only when it involved force.[6]

The rape section of the Code paid little attention to female complainants and concentrated on the protection of accused men. Drafted in part by Morris Ploscowe, it reflected the influence of modern psychological literature. The report on the Model Penal Code advised prosecutors to consider women's testimony carefully "in view of the emotional involvement of the witness and the difficulty of determining the truth with respect to alleged sexual activities carried out in private."[7] Along with incorporating the marital exemption, the Code called for corroborating witnesses in rape cases and a three-month statute of limitations on charges. A woman's past sexual history could be admissible evidence and could help determine the severity of the charges. Recommending distinctions between levels of rape, the Code considered felony rape a violent act (one that led to serious bodily injury) committed by a stranger. Without such injury, or simply if the victim had been "a voluntary social companion" of the accused or had "previously permitted him sexual liberties," the crime constituted second-degree rape. This provision incorporated a legacy of judicial opinion that presumed that an acquaintance or "an unchaste woman" was more likely "than a virtuous woman" to assent. Third-degree rape included underage sex, and the Code recommended that states adopt sixteen as the age of consent and require at least a four-year age difference between the parties. In line with this reform, legislators in several states introduced bills to lower the age of consent from eighteen to as low as fourteen.[8]

The rape provisions in the Model Penal Code contributed to the solidification of a concept that legal scholar Susan Estrich later termed "real rape," reinforcing the view that a violent act by a stranger constituted the legal standard.[9] This construction in turn could make it difficult for women to complain of other forms of sexual assault that seemed, in contrast, not to merit the same attention, including the coercive and forceful behaviors of acquaintances that had been targeted earlier by antiseduction and age-of-consent laws. Like post–World War II proponents of reform, some of the activists who had advocated statutory rape reform believed that distinguishing between levels of severity could result in stronger enforcement. By criminalizing seduction and underage sex, they hoped to encourage women to prosecute sexual assaults that did not necessarily meet the standards required to prove forcible rape. The wording of the Model Penal Code, however, risked reinforcing two key historical obstacles to conviction: disbelief in women's testimony and the implicit requirement of chastity.

Along with the legal attention to protecting male defendants and reducing penalties for lesser charges, media coverage of rape continued to highlight youths as victims. Beginning in the 1930s, children had become the focus of "sex crime" reporting, a process that heightened with the renewed sexual psychopath scare during the 1950s. Earlier fears about homosexual contagion through male child predators escalated during the Cold War, justifying arrests of gay men. Newspapers still reported other forms of sexual assaults, but adult women seemed to recede as subjects. In African American newspapers, for example, the outcry about the "white rapist" dissipated. Use of that term, one measure of attention to black women as victims, peaked between 1920 and 1950 and then declined precipitously in the postwar decades.[10]

A controversy about naming victims in the press signaled an intriguing ambiguity about publicizing rape. A reluctance to identify victims initially appeared during the Progressive era, when media critics sought to rein in sensationalistic crime reporting. In the 1920s some women's clubs called for the suppression of rape victims' names in the hope of encouraging girls and women to report assaults without having to fear damage to their reputations. A few states did pass laws prohibiting the naming of crime victims, but for the most part the reduction resulted from self-policing by journalists who aspired to a more professional code of ethics. For several years during the 1940s New York City police withheld the names of victims of sex crimes from newspapers, and in the postwar decades major white newspapers became more circumspect about naming women who reported sexual assault. Law-and-order proponents, such as FBI director J. Edgar Hoover, approved of withholding names in the hope that more women would report rape if they were not personally exposed.[11]

This move toward privacy could be viewed as a welcome relief for women who experienced rape, as well as an advance in journalistic standards. But the suppression of complainants' names could also send mixed messages about sexual violence by reinforcing the stigma attached to sexual assault and implying that women were ashamed of having been raped or of having reported it. Nameless stories also meant more impersonal press coverage. And because this protective practice originated in the juvenile courts, adding women to this category could be viewed as paternalistic rather than empowering. Some victims did bring suits against newspapers for invading their privacy by publishing their names, but in 1975 the U.S. Supreme Court rejected this argument in favor of freedom of the press. In the meantime, however, the press handled rape more discreetly than it had in the early twentieth century. Regarding one infamous criminal case—the 1964 murder of Catherine "Kitty" Genovese in Queens, New York—the *New York Times* elaborated on claims that witnesses failed to call the police far more than on the fact that the killer had attempted to sexually assault Genovese.[12] In short, the mainstream press's circumspection could underplay the reality of sexual assault.

THE REVIVAL OF THE FEMINIST MOVEMENT during the 1960s, and its growing influence over the following decades, practically reversed this course, moving from silence to public exposure and political activism. Second-wave feminists tried to put women's experience of sexual violence at the center of a new political analysis of rape. Although they built upon many of the historical precedents set in the suffrage era, including the demand for women's legal rights, the new generation of feminists in the later twentieth century launched a more radical critique that explicitly linked the problem of sexual violence to male privilege. As it evolved from the radical margins to the political mainstream, the movement proved far more effective than its predecessors in changing both laws and institutional practices. The rapidity of the shift, evidenced by an explosion in media coverage and legal reform, suggests that the spark of feminist politics ignited a backlog of fear and resentment among American women, many of whom had felt both physically at risk and politically disempowered by the threat of rape. Applying the radical feminist dictum "The personal is political," writers and organizers reframed sexual violence not merely as a private trauma but also as a nexus of power relations and a public policy concern.

Both the black freedom movement and the sexual revolution fueled this new analysis of rape. In the postwar decades black women in the South had begun to press rape charges against white men and to politicize interracial rape as a civil rights issue. Young white women who cut their political teeth in southern voter registration and community organizing campaigns in the 1960s brought the concept of personal empowerment they learned there into the revived women's movement. At the same time, the "sexual revolution" created both new opportunities and new dilemmas for white women. The decline of the purity ideal, the belief that sex was acceptable as an individual pleasure apart from any reproductive goals, and the availability of contraception all encouraged nonmarital sex. In the past, preserving chastity and preventing out-of-wedlock births had given them leverage in negotiating whether to consent to sex. In the new sexual order, the standard for consent had to be renegotiated. Why would a woman say no if sex presumably resulted in no harm? And who would believe that a woman had withheld consent, given new expectations of participation in the sexual revolution? Interracial relations created further dilemmas, as white women in the civil rights movement learned. While some chose to break the taboo on interracial sexual relations, others hesitated to acknowledge that they had unwanted sex with black men, knowing the consequences these men faced in the racist South.[13]

Aside from the blurred lines of sex among acquaintances, anxiety about personal safety made American women ripe for feminist analysis of sexual violence. In 1971 Susan Griffin published an essay in the radical press explaining that the fear of rape was a "daily part of every woman's consciousness." She exploded each of the myths about rape in American culture, addressed the legal obstacles to prosecuting sexual violence, named white male privilege as the heart of the problem, and recognized the particular vulnerability of women of color and the costs of the myth of the black rapist. Several years later journalist Susan Brownmiller elaborated many of these points in *Against Our Will: Men, Women, and Rape*. This best-selling book explored the power dynamics of rape in history, law, and culture; set an agenda for legal change; and alerted the public to the nascent feminist anti-rape movement.[14]

In the early 1970s this new political campaign coalesced rapidly. Along with reviving many past strategies, it broke through earlier silences and created innovative approaches that went beyond legal reforms. Reflecting the radical feminist emphasis on moving from personal experience to political action, the movement gestated in consciousness-raising groups in which women shared their experiences and then culminated in political demonstrations. A public "speak out" during a conference on rape held in New York City in 1971 jump-started the process. Rape, the women attending agreed, was a crime of violence, rather than a sexual act, and both law enforcement and women's groups needed to address the problem.[15]

Grassroots women's groups devoted to stopping rape sprang up across the country, from Washington, D.C., to Seattle. In many communities feminists created rape crisis hotlines that women could call to report assaults. On a far broader scale than their predecessors in the 1890s, they established rape crisis centers, which soon became a cornerstone of the movement. By 1976 over four hundred centers provided counseling, social services, and legal support for women who had experienced sexual violence. The anti-rape movement redefined women as "survivors" rather than "victims" and renamed behaviors once associated with the masher as "street harassment." While they often targeted men as the source of the problem of sexual assault, they also called on male allies to organize to help change gender conventions that contributed to sexual violence.[16]

Quite a few of the methods of the feminist anti-rape movement resembled earlier campaigns. Like newly enfranchised San Francisco women in 1911, Wisconsin feminists initiated the successful recall of a judge, Archie Simonson, in 1977. The judge had treated several young rapists leniently and blamed their crime on women's clothing. After the petition campaign, voters elected a female judge to replace the deposed Simonson. Like suffragists who championed female police authority, feminists questioned police responses to rape and called for the presence of female officers when women reported assaults. Groups such as Women Against Rape encouraged self-defense classes that incorporated the confidence-building goals first articulated during the response to the masher, when women trained athletically to claim their space on city streets. New strategies proliferated as well. During Take Back the Night marches, women walked en masse through dangerous urban districts to signal the strength of numbers and a refusal to limit their mobility. In response to both rapes and a series of murders of black women, more than five thousand joined the 1979 march in Boston. Earlier efforts relied on donations and volunteers, but in an era of government funding to address urban problems, local groups began to apply for federal and state grants to support their anti-rape programs.[17]

Along with radical local activism, on the national level liberal feminists who favored equal rights legislation turned their attention to rape statutes. In 1973 the National Organization for Women (NOW), founded in 1966, created a Rape Task Force to propose revisions to state laws. Women's groups challenged requirements of corroborative testimony and the use of "utmost force" to prove resistance. They called for revisions to police procedures and to the ways hospitals responded to assault. The concomitant push for full jury service for women, as well as the growing number of women lawyers and judges, seemed to fulfill suffragists' hopes for more equitable treatment in the courts.[18] As the momentum for legal reform spread, established institutions weighed in as well. In 1975 the American Bar Association (ABA) approved a resolution on rape laws that urged the revision of corroboration requirements and penalties, as well as the establishment of treatment centers "to aid both the victim and the offender." The ABA resolution further pointed to a trend toward gender-neutral rape law when it called for "a redefinition of rape and related crimes in terms of 'persons' instead of 'women.'" Gender-neutral statutes, once a radical proposition of supporters of the unpopular National Woman's Party, spread through the country after the 1980s.[19]

Though white women dominated both radical and liberal feminist organizations, women of color increasingly mobilized against rape, independently and in coalition with other groups. Following the tradition of Ida B. Wells and the black women's club movement at the turn of the twentieth century, influential African American writers such as Angela Davis and Alice Walker called attention to the intersections of gender, race, and sexual violence. Analyzing the trial of a southern black woman, Joann Little, for murdering the white jailer who raped her, Davis called on the antiviolence movement to be "explicitly antiracist." In the 1970s the National Black Feminist Organization co-sponsored events with New York Women Against Rape to create a more diverse movement than first-wave feminists had known. Boston feminists created the cross-race Coalition for Women's Safety, which recognized that "women of color are singled out as targets of violence both because of their race and their sex." Groups around the country addressed this problem. In East Los Angeles, Chicana activists established a bilingual rape hotline in 1976 to serve Spanish-speaking victims, while the Compton YWCA developed a rape crisis program to serve the black community just south of Los Angeles. Both black and Latina feminists helped to expand the services of the Washington, D.C., Rape Crisis Center and to diversify its staff. In 1980, under the leadership of black activist Loretta Ross, the Center organized a National Conference on Third World Women and Violence.[20]

Despite these alliances, feminists replayed many of the racial tensions that characterized earlier anti-rape movements, as the response to Brownmiller's book illustrated. *Against Our Will* exposed the injustices of lynching and the rape of black women, but her chapter on race raised hackles. Brownmiller questioned the continuing preoccupation of the American Left with the defense of accused black men. She also emphasized the rhetoric of radicals such as Eldridge Cleaver, who seemed to embrace rather than reject the myth of the black rapist. Most disturbing, perhaps, was her suggestion that Emmett Till had been trying to exercise male privilege when he whistled at a white woman, the act that led to his brutal murder by southern whites. Feminist scholars such as Angela Davis and Bettina Aptheker questioned "the racist dimensions" of Brownmiller's book and accused her of distorting the historical record. Women active in the civil rights movement condemned her for "fanning the fires of racism." The controversy highlighted a contradiction that Aptheker identified "between being able to resist the racist use of the rape charge against Black men, and at the same time counter the pervasive violence and rape that affects women of all races and classes."[21]

This conflict recurred as the anti-rape movement pressed for legal reforms, such as rape shield laws that would make a woman's past sexual history inadmissible as evidence. Resting on the chastity requirement, such testimony potentially deprived sexually active women of legal protection. To remedy this limitation, Michigan enacted a rape shield law in 1974, a reform soon adopted by other states. Feminists and civil libertarians who were concerned about the rights of defendants, many of them aware of the legacy of Scottsboro, expressed concern that these laws would eliminate a useful tool for countering false charges. The controversy flared up within the ACLU, where members debated the relative importance of protecting the sexual privacy of women and protecting the civil liberties of defendants, who remained disproportionately black men. The compromise that emerged in the ACLU called for closed judicial hearings to determine the relevance of a complainants' past sexual history. The ACLU opposed the federal rape shield law introduced in 1976 by Representative Elizabeth Holtzman, which became part of the Privacy Protection for Rape Victims Act that Congress passed in 1978. That statute compromised by allowing evidence only about a complainant's sexual history with the defendant, excluding any other past relations.[22]

Feminists and civil libertarians did agree on other reforms. Both groups questioned the usefulness of the death penalty for rape and believed that reducing prison sentences could encourage convictions. In an amicus brief filed on behalf of both NOW and the ACLU, feminist attorney Ruth Bader Ginsburg's arguments against capital punishment included the grounds that by treating women as the property of men, the death penalty for rape was a remnant of patriarchy. In 1977 the U.S. Supreme Court struck down the death penalty for rape. At other times feminists split between those who sought expanded state regulation and those who wanted to protect freedom of sexual expression. Such was the case in the controversy over pornography. Some radical feminists believed that pornographic depictions, particularly of violent sexual acts, incited rape. As Andrea Dworkin put it, "Pornography is the propaganda of sexual terrorism." When Dworkin and legal theorist Catharine MacKinnon introduced municipal statutes that would allow women to sue distributors of pornography for violating women's civil rights, many feminists joined with the ACLU to reject this strategy as a dangerous form of censorship.[23]

In perhaps the most striking divergence from earlier activists, feminists now confronted the marital exemption. Anarchist free lovers had long questioned the sexual rights of husbands, but suffragists had avoided a direct confrontation with the institution of marriage. Since the 1920s marital advice literature frowned upon the exercise of a husband's right to sexual services, yet the 1962 Model Penal Code left intact the marital exemption and extended it to common-law couples. Given the radical feminist analysis of power relations within the family and the emergence of a movement against domestic violence, the time seemed ripe for reevaluating this remnant of coverture.

Elaborating on arguments initially made by Elizabeth Cady Stanton and Emma Goldman, feminists called for sexual self-sovereignty within and outside of marriage. Influenced by writers such as Brownmiller, legal scholars gradually began to question the marital exemption, paving the way for legislative change. South Dakota first outlawed marital rape in 1975. The following year the ACLU approved a resolution calling for the redefinition of rape that addressed the exemption. In 1984 the New York State appellate court rejected the distinction between marital and nonmarital rape and declared the exemption unconstitutional. In language that incorporated the new feminist definition of rape, the judge explained that a "married woman has the same right to control her own body as does an unmarried woman." By the end of the century most states had modified their rape laws to include relations between spouses. The new laws often set a higher standard of force and lesser penalties for rape within marriage, but they signaled an important cultural as well as legal shift. Along with legal change, feminists tried to educate the public about the problem of marital rape, a major focus of the National Clearinghouse on Marital Rape, founded in 1978.[24]

Turning attention from stranger rape in the public sphere to unwanted sex in the private family helped expose the sexual abuse of children. For decades the media had represented the violent psychopathic stranger as the major sexual risk to children, an image closely linked to that of the homosexual predator. In the 1970s, opponents of the fledging gay rights movement successfully rallied under the cry "Save the Children" to repeal several of the first municipal statutes guaranteeing the civil rights of gay men and lesbians. At the same time, however, disbelief of children's accounts of unwanted sex within families sustained the historical silence about incest. Then a spate of feminist analysis and personal testimony began to challenge these patterns and uncover the extent of child sexual abuse.

The title of Florence Rush's book, *The Best Kept Secret,* epitomized the new approach. The molestation of children was far more widespread than previously thought, Rush explained, but it remained unreported in part because assailants often silenced children by threatening further harm if they revealed the abuse. Moreover, she argued, incest was not simply a private family affair but arose from broader cultural patterns that eroticized children and reinforced patriarchal authority. Unlike the child-blaming authorities of the past, feminist psychologists now questioned Freudian doctrine about childhood fantasies. Social scientists began to document the extent of the problem. One study suggested that as many as one-fourth of North American children had experienced some form of sexual abuse. Novelists such as Toni Morrison, Dorothy

Allison, and Jane Smiley portrayed the dynamics and the personal costs of incest for women from a range of race and class backgrounds.[25]

The vast majority of assaulted children were female, but by the end of the century more men were acknowledging their histories of having been sexually abused in families, schools, and religious institutions. The literature showed a pattern in which men who held positions of authority—including teachers, coaches, and clergy—took advantage of both girls and boys in their charge. Although women only rarely abused children, the recognition that some did so contributed to an analysis of power, and not only of gender, as the underlying context for child sexual assault. New understandings of male vulnerability encouraged a redefinition of rape though gender-neutral laws. The revelations of sexual assault against children, along with lawsuits that held individuals and institutions responsible, put pressure on schools and hospitals to identify signs of abuse and establish reporting guidelines. In the late twentieth century, speaking out and child assault prevention programs began to displace the silence of the past.

Like the attention to familial relations, the identification of "date rape," or "acquaintance rape," expanded the definition of assailants beyond the historical stereotypes of black, gay, or psychopathic men. In the nineteenth century, antiseduction and age-of-consent campaigns targeted white men who sexually coerced young female acquaintances. By persistently using the term *rape* to describe these behaviors, second-wave feminists took the redefinition process further. Like incest survivors, women who had unwanted sex with men they knew began to disclose their experiences. Social scientists documented the scope of unreported, unwanted, and often forceful sexual relations among the young. In one study, over a third of the women surveyed reported rape or attempted rape by an acquaintance, compared to just over 10 percent who identified strangers as their assailants. Yet, as the title of another exposé indicated, they "never called it rape." Neither did the men. In response to these studies and to complaints from students, their families, and lawmakers, schools and colleges began to articulate policies that would undermine tolerance for this conduct and undercut the "no means yes" construction of sex. At the same time, a men's antiviolence movement committed to ending coercive behaviors spread from campuses to communities. Men had been active in supporting earlier anti-rape movements, but now they organized as men who refused to objectify women sexually and who sought to undermine gender norms that privileged male aggression.[26]

By the 1990s the modern campaign against sexual violence had achieved an impressive agenda. Most states had revised their sexual assault statutes; nonconsensual sex within marriage and between acquaintances could now be defined as rape; educational and medical institutions began to take more responsibility for identifying assaults; and fiction, film, and personal memoirs addressed the power dynamics that feminists identified as central to both coercive and violent sexual encounters. Internal disagreements among feminists persisted, but their overall analysis moved beyond the earlier focus on protecting women's purity, beyond demands for formal political rights such as suffrage and jury service, and toward the assertion of women's right to sexual independence.

As in the past, however, legal reform did not necessarily transform individual behavior or criminal justice procedures. The enactment of the first rape shield laws led to increased reporting of rape but not to higher conviction rates. Defense attorneys continued to refer to women's past sexual behavior, and a majority of jurors expressed the belief that women's appearance and behavior provoked rape. Historical stereotypes about promiscuity continued to haunt women of color.[27] A range of earlier dilemmas persisted in late twentieth-century discussions of rape: between protecting and empowering women, between ensuring the rights of the accused and the rights of complainants, and in addressing both racial and gender stereotypes in the definition of assault. Even feminists, an increasingly diverse group, disagreed over just how far the redefinition of rape should go.

The risk of overdefining rape—of making the term too inclusive—troubled the movement. Like the response to statutory rape reform in the early twentieth century, the introduction of the term *date rape* triggered criticism that the antiviolence movement portrayed grown women as passive victims who lacked the capacity to refuse consent. Similar opposition greeted the emergence of the term *sexual harassment* to describe unwanted sexual attention short of assault, which undermined women's educational and employment opportunities. Some women and men disliked the idea of the state enacting laws to regulate such sexual behaviors. Critics cast doubt on the data showing the extent of acquaintance rape or questioned the blurring of the line that had defined "real rape" as physically violent and not merely a nonconsensual act.[28]

These arguments resembled those articulated by earlier medical and legal authorities who professed their revulsion toward violent rape but primarily feared that any standard short of physical injury opened possibilities for false accusations. Late twentieth-century libertarians echoed the earlier anarchists who opposed age-of-consent laws in the belief that young women should be able to take care of themselves and did not require state protection. Self-identified "individualist feminists" explicitly invoked Lillian Harman's statement, "I want the right to profit by my mistakes," to oppose expanding the legal definition of rape to include acquaintances.[29] Even feminists who supported broader definitions and stronger prosecution of sexual assault acknowledged the dangers of overdefining rape. When MacKinnon suggested that women found it "difficult to distinguish" between rape and intercourse because male dominance lay at the heart of heterosexuality, other feminist scholars balked. They warned that such conflations of sex and rape undermined women's agency and played into antisexual fears. They, too, echoed the views once expressed only by sex radicals such as Angela Heywood and Lillian Harman.[30]

The new frameworks for understanding child sexual abuse, which broke down the silence that had long protected offending adults from prosecution, also had the potential to trigger sex panics. Not long after most states rescinded their psychopath laws, and just as wage-earning mothers increasingly relied on child care, suspicions of child abuse began to focus on day care centers. In the 1980s claims of widespread sexual abuse and the use of children in "satanic rituals" sent innocent teachers to prison. These excesses in turn could contribute to a backlash against the testimony of children, reminiscent of nineteenth-century medical opinions and Freudian disbelief in incest accounts. Similar questions confronted adults who recalled childhood sexual trauma, with defense attorneys increasingly turning to expert witnesses who invoked the theory of "false memory syndrome" to discredit them. Which accounts to believe, and which acts constituted abuse, remained as controversial as they had been during earlier debates over the age-of-consent laws.[31]

A different kind of criticism faulted the anti-rape movement not for overextending its reach but rather for compromising its values to achieve institutional success. Originally nurtured by grassroots radical feminists, rape crisis centers began as alternative institutions run by volunteer collectives on shoestring budgets. To survive and to meet the expanding demand for services, many of them applied for grants from local, state, and national government agencies. With funding came professionalization, as paid social workers replaced political activists. The movement increasingly focused on support services for individuals, rather than on a political analysis of violence. At the same time, demands for stronger enforcement of rape laws could play into the law-and-order climate of the

Reagan era and beyond. Like suffragists who called for police authority for women, some feminists advocated the appointment of female police officers and female prosecutors to respond more sensitively to persons who had been raped. The anti-rape movement did benefit from the expansion of funding for police services, the use of rape kits, and the diversification of police forces. But as Angela Davis pointed out in 1985, police officers had historically assaulted rather than protected African American women. Asking which women would benefit from enforcement, and which men would be prosecuted, were legitimate questions, given the historical definition of rape.[32]

The response to a notorious crime committed in New York's Central Park in 1989 illustrated the persistent racial tensions in the antiviolence movement. Five African American and Latino youth who had been in the park at the time went to prison for a violent assault on a white female jogger. More than a decade later, DNA evidence showed that they had been innocent of the crime. After this revelation some feminist activists denied that race had anything to do with the rush to judgment. But as one local journalist noted, no defense akin to the Scottsboro case championed these falsely accused young men, who had been coerced into confessing to the crime. Legal scholar Kimberle Crenshaw pointed out that the extensive media attention to the victim of the Central Park assault contrasted with the lack of coverage of equally violent rapes of women of color in New York during the same week. The entire episode reverberated with the historical construction of rape, in which men of color were more likely to be convicted of rape and women of color less likely to be taken seriously as victims by police or jurors, whatever the race of the assailants.[33]

The capstone achievement of the late twentieth century anti-rape movement, the federal Violence against Women Act (VAWA), embodied many of the contradictions that accompanied mainstream success. An amendment to the Omnibus Crime Control and Safe Streets Act, VAWA passed in 1994 with bipartisan support after several years of congressional hearings. The law created an Office of Violence against Women in the Department of Justice. Because of the efforts of the National Coalition against Sexual Assault, it made rape as well as domestic violence programs eligible for over $1.5 billion in federal funding to improve both law enforcement responses to assault and services for victims.[34]

The VAWA incorporated the tensions between protection and rights that had characterized rape reform for over a century. Although the law employed gender-neutral terms, it concentrated on the particular disadvantages faced by women, not only because they more frequently experienced sexual assault but also because sex discrimination undermined the prosecution of rape. In shaping the bill, Congress took into consideration the particular impact of rape and domestic violence on women's economic and educational opportunities. Sexual violence, advocates argued, had an economic effect because it contributed to gender inequalities in wages and employment. Legislators noted as well the inconsistencies in state laws on marital rape, acquaintance rape, and rape shield laws, and the ways these could disadvantage female complainants. In addition to addressing the unique vulnerabilities of women, the law rested heavily upon the equal protection clause of the Fourteenth Amendment to justify federal action. All persons within the United States, the VAWA read, "shall have the right to be free from crimes of violence motivated by gender." A key element, the civil rights remedy, allowed plaintiffs to bring suit against anyone who committed such a crime in federal court, based on the federal government's power to regulate commerce.[35]

From the initial hearings on the bill, critics pointed to legal and practical flaws. Some suggested that the gender focus of the VAWA was too narrow. Members of the Women's Rights Project of the ACLU testified that although violence against women was a serious problem, the concept of a gender-motivated crime could limit the definition of rape. Elizabeth Symonds questioned why "a new Federal civil rights action should be provided for women, but not for individuals victimized because of their race, their ethnicity, their religion or their sexual orientation."[36] Civil libertarians also worried about potential infringements on the rights of those who were arrested for sexual assault and domestic violence.

From a different political perspective, constitutional conservatives challenged the civil rights remedy, which they found too expansive of federal authority, particularly in the application of the commerce clause. The latter argument narrowly prevailed when an appeal reached the Supreme Court. In *U.S. v. Morrison* (2000), a case involving a college student who brought a federal suit after the Virginia Military Academy only leniently penalized the two football players who had brutally raped her, the court struck down the civil rights remedy of the VAWA on the grounds that it exceeded congressional power to regulate commerce. The rest of the law remained constitutional but controversial. In the early twenty-first century, politicians fought over its reauthorization, with conservatives opposing features of its application to undocumented immigrants, same-sex couples, and Native American women.[37]

Since passage of the law, community activists have raised questions about its reliance on criminalization and policing, particularly the enactment of mandatory arrest policies for reported incidents of domestic violence. Historically, they have pointed out, low income and minority men have been disproportionately incarcerated without effectively curtailing rape and domestic violence. The expansive use of incarceration in the late twentieth century accelerated this pattern. In the tradition of radical grassroots activism, the group Incite! Women of Color Against Violence issued a statement in 2001 opposing incarceration and calling for economic justice as a more effective means of reducing violence. Placing the problem of sexual violence in broader structural contexts, they also challenged "men of color and all men in social justice movements" to take responsibility for achieving gender as well as racial justice.[38]

BY THE TWENTY-FIRST CENTURY, the process of redefining rape had expanded far beyond its original contours. For most of American history, rape had been defined either in law or through practice as a crime committed largely by African American men against chaste white women. The suspicions attached to all other scenarios protected the sexual privileges of white men in ways that reinforced their political dominance and limited the rights of other groups. In recent decades the term *rape* has come to encompass a range of coercive or violent behaviors, committed by men or women of any race, whether heterosexual or homosexual, in public or in private. The anti-rape movement continues to expand. Young women have intensified critiques of public threats by naming "street harassment" and by claiming women's right to dress as they please without being accused of inviting rape, the central message of contemporary "SlutWalks." Activists have targeted rape within the military, in prisons, and at Native American boarding schools and reservations. A global movement has convinced the International Criminal Court to prosecute sexual and gender violence as war crimes and has called attention to the role of rape in the trafficking of women as involuntary sex workers.[39]

The first anti-rape campaigns intensified during the era of the suffrage and anti-lynching movements, when white and black women and African American men fought for the formal rights of citizenship. In the wake of the modern civil rights and feminist revolutions, each group achieved greater political leverage. Those formerly excluded from full citizenship now serve as jurors, lawyers, and as judges in rape cases. For some critics, the vision of a "postfeminist" and "postracial" society suggests that these social categories should no longer matter in the response to rape. In practice, however, the data on assault, prosecution, and incarceration show that sexual violence is far from a gender- or race-neutral act. As legal scholars argued in their amicus brief in *Morrison,* "gender norms that have organized the criminal justice system for centuries cannot be eliminated by fiat or transformed overnight." The same can be said for racial norms.[40] Indeed, the contemporary response to sexual violence contains disheartening continuities with the past. These include the underreporting of rape, the racial profiling of perpetrators, the silencing of sexually abused children, and the victim blaming that attributes assaults to women's clothing or to their past sexual histories.

In the present, however, vocal critics continually expose each of these fault lines. Spurred by feminists and other advocates of women and children, journalists throughout the country investigate problems ranging from rape scandals in schools and colleges, to inept criminal justice procedures, to politicians who frame rape solely as the act of a violent stranger. The protests waged by those at the political margins a century ago have turned into mainstream policy debates. It is clear that the traditions of denying the rape of women of color and treating white men far more leniently than others have had enormous staying power. Equally persistent are the inevitable compromises and the unintended consequences that mark the limits of legal reform. But the history explored in this book suggests strongly that contestations over the meaning of sexual violence will continue as long as social inequalities, particularly those based on gender and race, characterize American life.

As in the past, *rape* remains a term in flux and the subject of political controversy. The moral reformers, suffragists, civil rights activists, and feminists who forced Americans to rethink the meaning of sexual violence helped reshape the contours of citizenship. Their goals of questioning white male sexual entitlements, challenging discriminatory criminal justice procedures, and undermining tolerance for sexual assault have been only partially realized. Yet their concerns, as well as the critiques and the dilemmas they faced, remain salient for those who continue to seek gender and racial justice. As the stories of the women and men who tried to redefine rape in American history reveal, even a construct that is as elusive as rape can be subject to political will as well as to political constraints.

Notes

Introduction

1. Arthur S. Brisbane, "Confusing Sex and Rape," *New York Times,* November 20, 2011, 12; Jason Linkins, "What's Behind the Drive to Redefine Rape in New and Insane Ways?," *Huffington Post,* February 1, 2011; David Nakamura, "Obama Denounces Rep. Todd Akin's Remarks on 'Legitimate Rape,'" *Washington Post,* August 20, 2012; Erica Goode, "Rape Definition Too Narrow in Federal Statistics, Critics Say," *New York Times,* September 29, 2011, 14; "Attorney General Eric Holder Announces Revisions to the Uniform Crime Report's Definition of Rape," FBI Press Release, January 6, 2012, accessed February 19, 2012, www.fbi.gov/news/pressrel/press-re leases/attorney-general-eric-holder-announces-revisions-to-the-uniform -crime-reports-definition-of-rape.
2. Margot Canaday, *The Straight State: Sexuality and Citizenship in Twentieth-Century America* (Princeton, NJ: Princeton University Press, 2009), 3, 27–29, 247. See also Barbara Young Welke, *Law and the Borders of Belonging in the Long Nineteenth Century United States* (New York: Cambridge University Press, 2010), esp. 3–6; Martha Gardner, *The Qualities of a Citizen: Women, Immigration, and Citizenship, 1870–1965* (Princeton, NJ: Princeton University Press, 2005); David K. Johnson, *The Lavender Scare: The Cold War Persecution of Gays and Lesbians in the Federal Government* (Chicago: University of Chicago Press, 2004); Marc Stein, *Sexual Injustice: Supreme Court Decisions from Griswold to Roe* (Chapel Hill: University of North Carolina Press, 2010); and Mae M. Ngai, *Impossible Subjects: Illegal Aliens and the Making of Modern America* (Princeton, NJ: Princeton University Press, 2004), esp. 110–114.
3. Jacquelyn Dowd Hall, "'The Mind That Burns in Each Body': Women, Rape and Racial Violence," in *Powers of Desire: The Politics of Sexuality,* ed. C. S. Ann Snitow and Sharon Thompson (New York: Monthly Review Press, 1983), 328–349; Jacquelyn Dowd Hall, *Revolt against Chivalry: Jessie Daniel Ames and the Women's Campaign against Lynching* (New York: Columbia University Press, 1979); Joel Williamson, *The Crucible of Race: Black/White*

Relations in the American South since Emancipation (New York: Oxford University Press, 1984); Dan Carter, *Scottsboro: A Tragedy of the American South* (Baton Rouge: Louisiana State University Press 1979); Susan Brownmiller, *Against Our Will: Men, Women, and Rape* (New York: Simon and Schuster, 1975).

4. For the sociobiological perspective, see Randy Thornhill, *A Natural History of Rape: Biological Bases of Sexual Coercion* (Cambridge, MA: MIT Press, 2000). On feminist interpretations, see Sharon Marcus, "Fighting Bodies, Fighting Words: A Theory and Politics of Rape Prevention," in *Feminists Theorize the Political,* ed. Judith Butler and Joan W. Scott (New York: Routledge, 1992), 385–403.

5. Richard A. Posner, *Sex and Reason* (Cambridge, MA: Harvard University Press, 1992), 395; Mary R. Block, "'An Accusation Easily to Be Made': A History of Rape Law in Nineteenth-Century State Appellate Courts, 1800–1870" (master's thesis, University of Louisville, 1992), chap. 2. On the shift in legal views on rape from being a crime against a father to being a crime against a woman, see Constance Backhouse, "Nineteenth-Century Canadian Rape Law, 1800–92," in *Essays in the History of Canadian Law,* ed. D. Flaherty (Toronto: University of Toronto Press, 1981), 208–210. Remnants of paternal representation persisted in seduction suits (see below, Chapter 2). Julia R. Schwendinger and Herman Schwendinger, "Rape, the Law, and Private Property," *Crime & Delinquency* 28, no. 2 (1982): 271–291.

6. Pamela Haag, *Consent: Sexual Rights and the Transformation of American Liberalism* (Ithaca, NY: Cornell University Press, 1999); Welke, *Law and the Borders of Belonging;* Susan Estrich, *Real Rape* (Cambridge, MA: Harvard University Press, 1987), esp. 29, 32, 37.

7. Lynn A. Higgins and Brenda R. Silver, eds., *Rape and Representation* (New York: Columbia University Press, 1991); Barbara J. Baines, "Effacing Rape in Early Modern Representation," *English Literary History* 65, no. 1 (1998): 69–98; Peggy Reeves Sanday, *A Woman Scorned: Acquaintance Rape on Trial* (New York: Doubleday, 1996), 59.

8. Simon Dickie, "Fielding's Rape Jokes," *Review of English Studies* 61, no. 251 (2010): 572–590.

9. Sharon Block, "Rape without Women: Print Culture and the Politicization of Rape, 1765–1815," *Journal of American History* 89, no. 3 (2002): 849–868; Sharon Block, *Rape and Sexual Power in Early America* (Chapel Hill: University of North Carolina Press, 2006), chap. 6, print 3; W. E. B. Du Bois, *Darkwater: Voices from within the Veil* (New York: Harcourt, Brace, 1920), 20.

10. Carole Pateman, *The Sexual Contract* (Stanford: Stanford University Press, 1988), 100–102. See also Susan Moller Okin, *Women in Western Political Thought* (Princeton, NJ: Princeton University Press, 1979); Haag, *Consent.*

11. Martha C. Nussbaum, *Sex and Social Justice* (New York: Oxford University Press, 1999); Robin West, "Sex, Law and Consent," in *The Ethics of Con-*

sent: Theory and Practice, ed. Alan Wertheimer and Franklin Miller (New York: Oxford University Press, 2009), 221–250. On the obligations as well as rights of women as citizens, see Linda K. Kerber, *No Constitutional Right to Be Ladies: Women and the Obligations of Citizenship* (New York: Hill and Wang, 1998). On the varied meanings of citizenship in the nineteenth century, see Nancy F. Cott, "Marriage and Women's Citizenship in the United States, 1830–1934," *American Historical Review* 103, no. 5 (1998): esp. 1444–48.

12. Linda K. Kerber, "The Meanings of Citizenship," *Journal of American History* 84, no. 3 (1997): 839; Nancy Isenberg, *Sex and Citizenship in Antebellum America* (Chapel Hill: University of North Carolina Press, 1998), 27. For purposes of immigration, a woman's citizenship was considered to be derivative of her husband's status. Gardner, *Qualities of a Citizen,* 123–124; Kerber, *No Constitutional Right,* chap. 1.

13. Amy Dru Stanley, *From Bondage to Contract: Wage Labor, Marriage, and the Market in the Age of Slave Emancipation* (New York: Cambridge University Press, 1998), 30; Cott, "Marriage and Women's Citizenship," 1444–50; Minor v. Happersett, 88 U.S. 162 (1875).

14. Margaret R. Somers, *Genealogies of Citizenship: Markets, Statelessness, and the Right to Have Rights* (Cambridge: Cambridge University Press, 2008), 46, 136, 103. On the importance of land and labor during Reconstruction, see, for example, Eric Foner, *Reconstruction: America's Unfinished Revolution, 1863–1877* (New York: Harper and Row, 1988), 109–110; Alice Kessler-Harris, *In Pursuit of Equity: Women, Men, and the Pursuit of Economic Citizenship in 20th-Century America* (New York: Oxford University Press, 2001).

15. Hall, " 'The Mind That Burns in Each Body.' "

16. The major legal sources for this study include all appellate court cases concerning rape, attempted rape, statutory rape, incest, sodomy, and related crimes for California, Georgia, and New York from 1870 to 1930; selected appellate cases from other states in prior and subsequent decades; and secondary studies of lower-court cases. Primary media sources include white and black newspapers; popular magazines; and medical and legal journals. The range of terms for sexual violence included variations on *rape, assault, outrage, ravish, insult,* and *seduce,* as well as terms for sodomy.

17. On prisons, see Estelle B. Freedman, *Their Sisters' Keepers: Women's Prison Reform in America, 1830–1930* (Ann Arbor: University of Michigan Press, 1981), 16; Regina Kunzel, *Criminal Intimacy: Prison and the Uneven History of Modern American Sexuality* (Chicago: University of Chicago Press, 2008), 153; Joanna Bourke, *Rape: A History from 1860 to the Present Day* (London: Virago Press, 2007), chap. 12. On rape charges during war, see Kristin Hoganson, *Fighting for American Manhood: How Gender Politics Provoked the Spanish American and Philippine American Wars* (New Haven, CT: Yale University Press, 1998), 49–51.

1. The Narrowing Meaning of Rape

1. Sharon Block, *Rape and Sexual Power in Early America* (Chapel Hill: University of North Carolina Press, 2006), 128–129, 78; Else L. Hambleton, "'Playing the Rogue': Rape and Issues of Consent in Seventeenth-Century Massachusetts," in *Sex without Consent: Rape and Sexual Coercion in America,* ed. M. D. Smith (New York: New York University Press, 2001), 30–31; Thomas A. Foster, *Sex and the Eighteenth-Century Man: Massachusetts and the History of Sexuality in America* (Boston: Beacon Press, 2006), 55.

2. Mary Beth Norton, *Founding Mothers and Fathers: Gendered Power and the Forming of American Society* (New York: Knopf, 1996), 347–348; Lawrence M. Friedman, *Crime and Punishment in American History* (New York: Basic Books, 1993), 41–42; Foster, *Sex and the Eighteenth-Century Man;* Cornelia Hughes Dayton, *Women before the Bar: Gender, Law, and Society in Connecticut, 1639–1789* (Chapel Hill: University of North Carolina Press, 1995), 54–55; Terri L. Snyder, "Sexual Consent and Sexual Coercion in Seventeenth-Century Virginia," in Smith, *Sex without Consent,* 49.

3. Dayton, *Women before the Bar,* 177, 232, 236–239, 237 (table 12); Block, *Rape and Sexual Power,* 142.

4. Block, *Rape and Sexual Power,* 8, 145–147, 191, 192n39. On views of rape in Puritan New England, see also Mary Beth Norton, *Founding Mothers and Fathers: Gendered Power and the Forming of American Society* (New York: Knopf, 1996), 351–353.

5. Block, *Rape and Sexual Power,* 173, 191–192, 192n39; Barbara S. Lindemann, "'To Ravish and Carnally Know': Rape in Eighteenth-Century Massachusetts," *Signs* 10, no. 1 (1984): 65; Hambleton, "'Playing the Rogue,'" 27; Kathleen M. Brown, *Good Wives, Nasty Wenches, and Anxious Patriarchs: Gender, Race, and Power in Colonial Virginia* (Chapel Hill: University of North Carolina Press, 1996), 208; R. Leon Higginbotham, *In the Matter of Color: Race and the American Legal Process,* vol. 1 (New York: Oxford University Press, 1978), 73, 281.

6. Richard Godbeer, *Sexual Revolution in Early America* (Baltimore: Johns Hopkins University Press, 2002), 103–104, 123–124; James Homer Williams, "Coerced Sex and Gendered Violence in New Netherland," in Smith, *Sex without Consent,* 73.

7. Block, *Rape and Sexual Power,* 21, 40, 50, 80, 92.

8. Lindemann, "'To Ravish and Carnally Know'"; Hambleton, "'Playing the Rogue,'" 35; Kirsten Fischer, *Suspect Relations: Sex, Race, and Resistance in Colonial North Carolina* (Ithaca, NY: Cornell University Press, 2002), 108, 182; Dayton, *Women before the Bar,* 250; Block, *Rape and Sexual Power,* 191; Clare A. Lyons, *Sex among the Rabble: An Intimate History of Gender and Power in the Age of Revolution, Philadelphia, 1730–1830* (Chapel Hill: University of North Carolina Press, 2006), 251n14; Brown, *Good Wives, Nasty Wenches,* 208–210.

9. Jennifer L. Morgan, *Laboring Women: Reproduction and Gender in New World Slavery* (Philadelphia: University of Pennsylvania Press, 2004), 84–87, 100; John Josselyn, *Two Voyages to New England* (1674), quoted in Wendy Anne Warren, " 'The Cause of Her Grief': The Rape of a Slave in Early New England," *Journal of American History* 93, no. 4 (2007): 1031.

10. Sharon Block, "Rape without Women: Print Culture and the Politicization of Rape, 1765–1815," *Journal of American History* 89, no. 3 (2002): 858–864.

11. Quoted in Lyons, *Sex among the Rabble*, 122. On contemporary British views, see Anna K. Clark, *Women's Silence, Men's Violence: Sexual Assault in England 1770–1845* (London: Pandora, 1987), 37; and Shani D'Cruze, "Approaching the History of Rape and Sexual Violence: Notes towards Research," *Women's History Review* 1, no. 3 (1992): 337–396.

12. Sir Matthew Hale, *Historia Placitorum Coronae: The History of the Pleas of the Crown,* ed. Sollom Emlyn, vol. 1 (London, 1736), 635; Block, *Rape and Sexual Power,* 128–130.

13. Dayton, *Women before the Bar,* 232–250; Block, *Rape and Sexual Power,* 20, 32, 37–50.

14. Foster, *Sex and the Eighteenth-Century Man,* 66–70; Godbeer, *Sexual Revolution in Early America,* 291–292, 307.

15. Marybeth Hamilton Arnold, " 'The Life of a Citizen in the Hands of a Woman': Sexual Assault in New York City, 1790 to 1820," in *Passion and Power: Sexuality in History,* ed. Kathy Peiss, Christina Simmons, and Robert A. Padgug (Philadelphia: Temple University Press, 1989); Christine Stansell, *City of Women: Sex and Class in New York, 1789–1860* (New York: Knopf, 1986), 23–26.

16. Thomas Jefferson to Samuel Kercheval, September 5, 1816, in *The Writings of Thomas Jefferson,* vol. 10, *1816–1826,* ed. Paul Leicester Ford (New York: G. P. Putnam's Sons, 1892–1899), 45–46. On Rousseau, see Carole Pateman, *The Sexual Contract* (Cambridge: Polity, 1988), 100–102. See also Martha C. Nussbaum, *Sex and Social Justice* (New York: Oxford University Press, 1999), 17.

17. On the elevation of respectable women to moral purity in the nineteenth century—one of the preconditions for the emergence of women's rights arguments—see Nancy F. Cott, "Passionlessness: An Interpretation of Victorian Sexual Ideology, 1790–1850," *Signs* 4, no. 2 (1978): 219–236.

18. On the rape of captive women, see Gerda Lerner, *The Creation of Patriarchy* (New York: Oxford University Press, 1986), esp. 80–89; on the integration of captive women where offspring did not necessarily inherit slave status, see Paul E. Lovejoy, *Transformations in Slavery: A History of Slavery in Africa* (Cambridge: Cambridge University Press, 1983), 7–8, 214; and James F. Brooks, *Captives and Cousins: Slavery, Kinship, and Community in the Southwest Borderlands* (Chapel Hill: University of North Carolina Press, 2002) 14–18, 34.

19. Pekka Hämäläinen, *The Comanche Empire* (New Haven, CT: Yale University Press, 2008), 45; Alice Nash, " 'None of the Women Were Abused': Indigenous

Contexts for the Treatment of Women Captives in the Northeast," in Smith, *Sex without Consent*, 17–18, 20; Godbeer, *Sexual Revolution in Early America*, 180; June Namias, *White Captives: Gender and Ethnicity on the American Frontier* (Chapel Hill: University of North Carolina Press, 1993), 89; Philip J. Deloria, *Playing Indian* (New Haven, CT: Yale University Press, 1998), 53.

20. Stephanie Wood, "Sexual Violation in the Conquest of the Americas," in *Sex and Sexuality in Early America*, ed. Merrill D. Smith (New York: New York University Press, 1998), 11–14; Virginia Marie Bouvier, *Women and the Conquest of California, 1542–1840: Codes of Silence* (Tucson: University of Arizona Press, 2001), 46–47; Antonia I. Castañeda, "Sexual Violence in the Politics and Policies of Conquest: Amerindian Women and the Spanish Conquest of Alta California," in *Building with Our Hands: New Directions in Chicana Studies*, ed. Adela de la Torre and Beatriz M. Pesquera (Berkeley: University of California Press, 1993), 15–33; Albert L. Hurtado, *Intimate Frontiers: Sex, Gender, and Culture in Old California* (Albuquerque: University of New Mexico, 1999), 13–14; Ramón A. Gutiérrez, *When Jesus Came, the Corn Mothers Went Away: Marriage, Sexuality, and Power in New Mexico, 1500–1846* (Stanford: Stanford University Press, 1991), 156. On the differential treatment of the rape of Mexican and Indian women in California under Mexican authority, see Miroslava Chávez-García, *Negotiating Conquest: Gender and Power in California, 1770s to 1880s* (Tucson: University of Arizona Press, 2004), 36–39.

21. Hurtado, *Intimate Frontiers*, 273–281; Castañeda, "Sexual Violence," 17–18; Clifford E. Trafzer and Joel R. Hyer, eds., *"Exterminate Them": Written Accounts of the Murder, Rape, and Slavery of Native Americans during the California Gold Rush, 1848–1868* (East Lansing: Michigan State University Press, 1999), 17; David Peterson Del Mar, *Beaten Down: A History of Interpersonal Violence in the West* (Seattle: University of Washington Press, 2002), 30, 37.

22. San Francisco *Picayune*, quoted in the *Frederick Douglass Papers*, October 16, 1851, reprinted in Thomas Foster, *Documenting Intimate Matters: Primary Sources for a History of Sexuality in America* (Chicago: University of Chicago Press, 2012), 55–56.

23. Edward E. Baptist, " 'Cuffy,' 'Fancy Maids,' and 'One-Eyed Men': Rape, Commodification, and the Domestic Slave Trade in the United States," *American Historical Review* 106, no. 5 (2001): 1619. The gradual emancipation of slaves in the North meant that black women could bring rape charges to court. For accusations against both white and black men in Massachusetts, see Catherine Adams and Elizabeth H. Pleck, *Love of Freedom: Black Women in Colonial and Revolutionary New England* (New York: Oxford University Press, 2010), 44–45.

24. Quoted in Joshua D. Rothman, *Notorious in the Neighborhood: Sex and Families across the Color Line in Virginia, 1787–1861* (Chapel Hill: University of North Carolina Press, 2003), 38; Block, *Rape and Sexual Power*, 183.

25. James R. Lewis, "Images of Captive Rape in the Nineteenth Century," *Journal of American Culture* 15, no. 2 (1992): 69–77; Namias, *White Captives;* Nash, "'None of the Women Were Abused'"; Wood, "Sexual Violation"; James F. Brooks, "'This Evil Extends Especially . . . to the Feminine Sex': Negotiating Captivity in the New Mexico Borderlands," *Feminist Studies* 22, no. 2 (1996): 279–309.

26. Block, *Rape and Sexual Power,* 207; see also Winthrop D. Jordan, *White over Black: American Attitudes toward the Negro, 1550–1812* (Chapel Hill: University of North Carolina Press, 1968), 155–157.

27. Daniel A. Cohen, "Social Injustice, Sexual Violence, Spiritual Transcendence: Constructions of Interracial Rape in Early American Crime Literature, 1767–1817," *William and Mary Quarterly* 56, no. 3 (1999): 481–526; Martha Hodes, *White Women, Black Men: Illicit Sex in the Nineteenth-Century South* (New Haven, CT: Yale University Press, 1997); Diane Miller Sommerville, *Rape and Race in the Nineteenth-Century South* (Chapel Hill: University of North Carolina Press, 2004); Block, *Rape and Sexual Power,* chap. 6. On rape by British soldiers, see also Mary Beth Norton, *Liberty's Daughters: The Revolutionary Experience of American Women, 1750–1800* (Boston: Little, Brown, 1980), 202–204.

28. Block, *Rape and Sexual Power,* 142–152, 163, 188–190, 195; Higginbotham, *In the Matter of Color,* 282; Dayton, *Women before the Bar,* 282. See also Fischer, *Suspect Relations,* 181–187. In mid-Atlantic and southern states, a secondary court system for slaves accused of crimes made convictions easier than in other courts. Block, *Rape and Sexual Power,* 168.

29. Edmund Morgan, *American Slavery, American Freedom: The Ordeal of Colonial Virginia* (New York: Norton, 1975). Also excluded as witnesses were children under the age of fourteen. Holly Brewer, *By Birth or Consent: Children, Law, and the Anglo-American Revolution in Authority* (Chapel Hill: University of North Carolina Press, 2005), 154, 159.

30. Nancy F. Cott, *The Bonds of Womanhood: "Woman's Sphere" in New England, 1780–1835,* 2nd ed. (New Haven, CT: Yale University Press, 1997); Linda Kerber, "The Republican Mother: Women and the Enlightenment—An American Perspective," *American Quarterly* 28, no. 2 (1976): 187–205; Jan Lewis, "The Republican Wife: Virtue and Seduction in the Early Republic," *William and Mary Quarterly* 44, no. 4 (1987): 689–721.

31. Carol A. Stabile, *White Victims, Black Villains: Gender, Race, and Crime News in US Culture* (New York: Routledge, 2006), 19.

32. Karen Halttunen, *Confidence Men and Painted Women: A Study of Middle-Class Culture in America, 1830–1870* (New Haven, CT: Yale University Press, 1986).

33. Dr. Michael Ryan, *A Manual of Medical Jurisprudence* (Philadelphia: Cary and Lea, 1832), 170; Bronson quoted in Mary R. Block, "'An Accusation Easily to Be Made': A History of Rape Law in Nineteenth-Century America" (PhD diss., University of Kentucky, 2001), 117.

34. Dr. Michael Ryan, *A Manual of Medical Jurisprudence,* 2nd ed. (London: Sherwood, Gilbert, and Piper, 1836), 319.
35. Michelle J. Anderson, "From Chastity Requirement to Sexuality License: Sexual Consent and a New Rape Shield Law," *George Washington Law Review* 70, no. 1 (2002): 54; People v. Abbott, 19 Wend. 192, 195 (N.Y. 1838).
36. Susan Gonda, "Strumpets and Angels: Rape, Seduction, and the Boundaries of Consensual Sex in the Northeast, 1789–1870" (PhD diss., University of California, Los Angeles, 1999), 170–171. See also Stephen Robertson, "Signs, Marks, and Private Parts: Doctors, Legal Discourses, and Evidence of Rape in the United States, 1823–1930," *Journal of the History of Sexuality* 8, no. 3 (1998): 345–388.
37. Charles P. Nemeth, "Character Evidence in Rape Trials in Nineteenth Century New York: Chastity and the Admissibility of Specific Acts," *Women's Rights Law Reporter* 6, no. 4 (1980): 219n21, quoting People v. Abbott, 19 Wend. 192 (N.Y. 1838).
38. Milo L. Bennett, *The Vermont Justice* (Burlington, VT, 1864), 575, quoted in Hal Goldman, "'A Most Detestable Crime': Character, Consent, and Corroboration in Vermont's Rape Law, 1850–1920," in Smith, *Sex without Consent,* 184.
39. Francis W. Anthony, "Rape [Part II]," *Boston Medical and Surgical Journal* 132 (January 17, 1895): 58; and People v. Hulse, 3 Hill 309 (N.Y. 1842), quoted in Block, "'An Accusation Easily to Be Made'" (PhD diss.), 6, 115–116.
40. People v. Dohring, 59 N.Y. 374 (N.Y. 1874); Ira M. Moore, *A Practical Treatise on Criminal Law and Procedure in Criminal Cases before Justices of the Peace and in Courts of Record in the State of Illinois* (Chicago: Callaghan, 1876), quoted in Lea VanderVelde, "The Legal Ways of Seduction," *Stanford Law Review* 48, no. 4 (1996): 856.
41. Robertson, "Signs, Marks, and Private Parts"; Gonda, "Strumpets and Angels," 141–142; Height v. People, 50 N.Y. 392 (N.Y. 1872).
42. James Mohr, *Doctors and the Law: Medical Jurisprudence in Nineteenth-Century America* (New York: Oxford University Press, 1993), 21, 31, 72; Edmund S. F. Arnold, MD, "Can Pregnancy Follow Defloration in Rape, When Force Simply Is Used?," *American Medical Times* 22 (November 29, 1862): 297–298.
43. Goldman, "'A Most Detestable Crime,'" 198–199 (table 8.1) for the period from the 1790s through the 1910s; Sean T. Moore, "'Justifiable Provocation': Violence against Women in Essex County, New York, 1799–1860," *Journal of Social History* 35, no. 4 (2002): 897, 902 (table 3), based on Essex County court records from 1799 to 1860. For a comparable rate in Canada see Karen Dubinsky, *Improper Advances: Rape and Heterosexual Conflict in Ontario, 1880–1929* (Chicago: University of Chicago Press, 1993), 24. In the United States, conviction rates for homicide, which varied widely by state, appear to be slightly higher than for rape. Randolph Roth, *American Homicide* (Cambridge, MA: Harvard University Press, 2009), 498n10.

44. Irene Q. Brown and Richard D. Brown, *The Hanging of Ephraim Wheeler: A Story of Rape, Incest, and Justice in Early America* (Cambridge, MA: Belknap Press of Harvard University Press, 2003), 112–113.

45. Brenda E. Stevenson, *Life in Black and White: Family and Community in the Slave South* (New York: Oxford University Press, 1996), 239; Thomas R. R. Cobb, *An Inquiry into the Law of Negro Slavery in the United States,* vol. 1 (Philadelphia and Savannah, 1858), 99. According to Cobb, "the penalties for rape would not and should not, by such implication, be made to extend to carnal forcible knowledge of a slave, the offence not affecting the existence of the slave" (86).

46. Mary R. Block, " 'An Accusation Easily to Be Made': A History of Rape Law in Nineteenth-Century State Appellate Courts, 1800–1870" (master's thesis, University of Louisville, 1992), 37; Sommerville, *Rape and Race,* 118.

47. Evelyn Brooks Higginbotham, "African-American Women's History and the Metalanguage of Race," *Signs* 17, no. 2 (1992): 257–258; Melton A. McLaurin, *Celia, a Slave* (Athens: University of Georgia Press, 1991), 88–93.

48. Block, " 'An Accusation Easily to Be Made' " (master's thesis), 37n47; Sommerville, *Rape and Race,* 66; Catherine Clinton, "Bloody Terrain: Freedwomen, Sexuality and Violence during Reconstruction," *Georgia Historical Quarterly* 76, no. 2 (1992): 315.

49. Dorothy E. Roberts, "Rape, Violence, and Women's Autonomy," *Chicago-Kent Law Review* 69, no. 2 (1993): 365; Deborah Gray White, *Ar'n't I a Woman: Female Slaves in the Plantation South,* rev. ed. (New York: Norton, 1999), chap. 1; Block, *Rape and Sexual Power,* 183; William Gilmore Simms, "Morals of Slavery," in *The Pro-Slavery Argument, as Maintained by the Most Distinguished Writers of the Southern States* (1852; repr., New York: Negro Universities Press, 1968), 230.

50. Lydia Maria Child, *An Appeal in Favor of That Class of Americans Called Africans* (Boston: Allen and Ticknor, 1833), 37. Child also hinted at the extent of coercive sex in a fictional depiction of the southern plantation as a harem that gave white men free sexual rein. Carolyn Karcher, "Rape, Murder and Revenge in 'Slavery's Pleasant Homes': Lydia Maria Child's Antislavery Fiction and the Limits of Genre," *Women's Studies International Forum* 9, no. 4 (1986): 323–332.

51. Chesnut quoted in White, *Ar'n't I a Woman,* 40–41; Thelma Jennings, " 'Us Colored Women Had to Go through a Plenty': Sexual Exploitation of African-American Slave Women," *Journal of Women's History* 1, no. 3 (1990): 45–74; Drew Gilpin Faust, *Mothers of Invention: Women of the Slaveholding South in the American Civil War* (Chapel Hill: University of North Carolina Press, 1996), 73; *The Secret Eye: The Journal of Ella Gertrude Clanton Thomas, 1848 to 1889,* ed. Virginia Ingraham Burr (Chapel Hill: University of North Carolina Press, 1990), 168–169. Estimates of the percentage of slave women who had sex with their masters range from 10 percent to 25 percent. Rothman, *Notorious in the Neighborhood,* 249n14.

52. Nell Irvin Painter, "Soul Murder and Slavery: Toward a Fully Loaded Cost Accounting," in Painter, *Southern History across the Color Line* (Chapel Hill: University of North Carolina Press, 2002), 15–39; Thelma Jennings, "'Us Colored Women Had to Go through a Plenty'"; Rothman, *Notorious in the Neighborhood*, 151, 160–163; Stevenson, *Life in Black and White*, 236–237.

53. Annette Gordon-Reed, *The Hemingses of Monticello: An American Family* (New York: Norton, 2008), esp. chap. 15; [Harriet Jacobs], *Incidents in the Life of a Slave Girl* (Boston, 1861), 84–85; Sarah M. Grimké, *Letters on the Equality of the Sexes and the Condition of Woman* (Boston: Isaac Knapp, 1838), 51–52, 128. See also P. Gabrielle Forman, "Manifest in Signs: The Politics of Sex and Representation in *Incidents in the Life of a Slave Girl*," in *Harriet Jacobs and* Incidents in the Life of a Slave Girl: *New Critical Essays*, ed. Deborah M. Garfield and Rafia Zafar (Cambridge: Cambridge University Press, 1996), 76–99.

54. Stowe quoted in Nancy F. Cott, *Public Vows: A History of Marriage and the Nation* (Cambridge, MA: Harvard University Press, 2000), 58; Child quoted in Sabine Sielke, *Reading Rape: The Rhetoric of Sexual Violence in American Literature and Culture, 1790–1990* (Princeton, NJ: Princeton University Press, 2002), 24; Wright quoted in Kristen Hoganson, "Garrisonian Abolitionists and the Rhetoric of Gender, 1850–1860," *American Quarterly* 45 (1993): 571.

55. Rothman, *Notorious in the Neighborhood*, 133; Stevenson, *Life in Black and White*, 240; Hodes, *White Women, Black Men*, 129–131; Thomas A. Foster, "The Sexual Abuse of Black Men under Slavery," *Journal of the History of Sexuality* 20, no. 3 (2011): 449, 453; Sommerville, *Rape and Race*, 157.

56. Fewer than 10 percent of the slaves executed in South Carolina between 1800 and 1855 had been convicted of rape; in Virginia only fifty-eight slaves were executed for the rape of white women between 1785 and 1865. Peter W. Bardaglio, "Rape and the Law in the Old South: 'Calculated to Excite Indignation in Every Heart,'" *Journal of Southern History* 60, no. 4 (1994): 769; Michael Hindus, "Black Justice under White Law: Criminal Prosecutions of Blacks in Antebellum South Carolina," *Journal of American History* 63, no. 3 (1976): 587, 595 (table 11); Philip J. Schwarz, *Twice Condemned: Slaves and the Criminal Laws of Virginia, 1705–1865* (Baton Rouge: Louisiana State University Press, 1988), 206, 209; Peter W. Bardaglio, *Reconstructing the Household: Families, Sex, and the Law in the Nineteenth-Century South* (Chapel Hill: University of North Carolina Press, 1995), 70, 74–75.

57. Bardaglio, "Rape and the Law in the Old South," 762; Bardaglio, *Reconstructing the Household*, 70, 74; Sommerville, *Rape and Race*, 88, 105–106, 179–182; Hodes, *White Women, Black Men*, 64, 138.

58. White, *Ar'n't I a Woman*, 164. The majority of soldiers who faced courts-martial for rape had assaulted black women. Crystal N. Feimster, *Southern Horrors: Women and the Politics of Rape and Lynching* (Cambridge, MA: Harvard University Press, 2009), 20. Feimster suggests that white women

typically did not report rape by Union soldiers. See also Faust, *Mothers of Invention,* 200.

59. Hodes, *White Women, Black Men,* 158; Faust, *Mothers of Invention,* 58–60; Sommerville, *Rape and Race,* 16; Feimster, *Southern Horrors,* 15. On similar responses to Mexican soldiers, see William D. Carrigan, *The Making of Lynching Culture: Violence and Vigilantism in Central Texas, 1836–1916* (Urbana: University of Illinois Press, 2004), 27.

60. Hannah Rosen, *Terror in the Heart of Freedom: Citizenship, Sexual Violence, and the Meaning of Race in the Postemancipation South* (Chapel Hill: University of North Carolina Press, 2009), 7–9, 195.

2. The Crime of Seduction

1. Mary Wollstonecraft, *A Vindication of the Rights of Woman and The Wrongs of Woman, or Maria,* ed. Anne Mellor and Noelle Chao (New York: Pearson Longman, 2007), 312–313, 274, 278, 280. At the end of the unfinished novel, Maria is convicted of adultery and commits suicide. The original title was *Maria: or, The Wrongs of Woman—A Posthumous Fragment* (Philadelphia, 1799).

2. John D'Emilio and Estelle B. Freedman, *Intimate Matters: A History of Sexuality in America,* 3rd ed. (Chicago: University of Chicago Press, 2012), chaps. 2, 3; Patricia Cline Cohen, "Safety and Danger: Women on American Public Transport, 1750–1850," in *Gendered Domains: Rethinking Public and Private in Women's History,* ed. Dorothy O. Helly and Susan M. Reverby (Ithaca, NY: Cornell University Press, 1987), 109–122.

3. Nancy F. Cott, "Passionlessness: An Interpretation of Victorian Sexual Ideology, 1790–1850," *Signs: Journal of Women in Culture and Society* 4, no. 2 (1978): 219–236; Nancy F. Cott, *The Bonds of Womanhood: "Woman's Sphere" in New England, 1780–1835* (New Haven, CT: Yale University Press, 1977); Linda Kerber, "The Republican Mother: Women and the Enlightenment—An American Perspective," *American Quarterly* 28, no. 2 (1976): 187–205; Ruth H. Bloch, "The Gendered Meanings of Virtue in Revolutionary America," *Signs: Journal of Women in Culture and Society* 13, no. 1 (1987): 37–58.

4. Wollstonecraft, *Rights of Woman,* 119–120.

5. Susan Gonda, "Strumpets and Angels: Rape, Seduction, and the Boundaries of Consensual Sex in the Northeast, 1789–1870" (PhD diss., University of California, Los Angeles, 1999), 30–31, 223; Rodney Hessinger, " 'Insidious Murderers of Female Innocence': Representations of Masculinity in the Seduction Tales of the Late Eighteenth Century," in *Sex and Sexuality in Early America,* ed. Merrill D. Smith (New York: New York University Press, 1998), 262–282; Daniel A. Cohen, *Pillars of Salt, Monuments of Grace: New England Crime Literature and the Origins of American Popular Culture, 1674–1860* (New York: Oxford University Press, 1993), 167–168; Claire Lyons, *Sex*

among the Rabble: An Intimate History of Gender and Power in the Age of Revolution, Philadelphia, 1730–1830 (Chapel Hill: University of North Carolina Press, 2006), 314–317. See also Carroll Smith-Rosenberg, *This Violent Empire: The Birth of an American National Identity* (Chapel Hill: University of North Carolina Press, 2010), 172–184.

6. *Friend of Virtue* (1852) quoted in Mary P. Ryan, *Cradle of the Middle Class: The Family in Oneida County, New York, 1790–1865* (New York: Cambridge, 1981), 119–120; Pamela Haag, *Consent: Sexual Rights and the Transformation of American Liberalism* (Ithaca, NY: Cornell University Press, 1999), 11.

7. *Advocate of Moral Reform* quoted in Barbara Berg, *The Remembered Gate: Origins of American Feminism: The Woman and the City, 1800–1860* (New York: Oxford University Press, 1978), 191, see also 182, 231; Carroll Smith-Rosenberg, *Disorderly Conduct: Visions of Gender in Victorian America* (New York: Oxford University Press, 1986), 111–119; Ryan, *Cradle of the Middle Class,* 120–122; Barbara Meil Hobson, *Uneasy Virtue: The Politics of Prostitution and the American Reform Tradition* (New York: Basic Books, 1987), 60; and Gonda, "Strumpets and Angels," 232–243.

8. N.H., "The Importance of Petitions," letter, *Advocate of Moral Reform,* November 15, 1838, 174–175, in Daniel Wright and Kathryn Kish Sklar, eds., *What Was the Appeal of Moral Reform to Antebellum Northern Women, 1835–1841?,* in the online collection *Women and Social Movements in the United States, 1600–2000,* ed. Kathryn Kish Sklar and Thomas Dublin, accessed July 5, 2011, http://womhist.alexanderstreet.com.

9. Warren Burton, *Moral Dangers of the City: To the Clergymen of Various Denominations throughout New England* (Boston: John Wilson, printer, 1848), 2–3.

10. Stephen Robertson, "Seduction, Sexual Violence, and Marriage in New York City, 1886–1955," *Law and History Review* 24, no. 2 (2006), esp. 344–345; Gonda, "Strumpets and Angels," 70–71.

11. Wollstonecraft, *Rights of Woman,* 94.

12. Sarah Connell Ayer to Sarah Kittredge, March 13, 1810, appendix A, *Diary of Sarah Connell Ayer* (Portland, ME: Lefavor-Tower, 1910), 372–373.

13. Lea VanderVelde, "The Legal Ways of Seduction," *Stanford Law Review* 48, no. 4 (1996): 821; Gonda, "Strumpets and Angels," 36–39; Hobson, *Uneasy Virtue,* 58; Michelle J. Anderson, "From Chastity Requirement to Sexuality License: Sexual Consent and a New Rape Shield Law," *George Washington Law Review* 70, no. 1 (2002): 51–162. If a father did not support his daughter, he might not have a claim to lost services. Bartley v. Richtmyer, 4 N.Y. 38 (N.Y. Ct. App. 1850).

14. White v. Nellis, 31 N.Y. 405 (N.Y. Ct. App. 1865); Lawyer v. Fritcher, 7 N.Y.S. 909 (N.Y. Sup. Ct. 1889).

15. Kendrick v. McCrary, 11 Ga. 603, 605–606 (Ga. 1852). On Judge Lumpkin, see *The New Georgia Encyclopedia,* s.v. "Joseph Henry Lumpkin (1799–

1867)," accessed July 5, 2011, www.georgiaencyclopedia.org/nge/Article
.jsp?id=h-636; Peter W. Bardaglio, *Reconstructing the Household: Families,
Sex, and the Law in the Nineteenth-Century South* (Chapel Hill: University of
North Carolina Press, 1995), 37; "The Joseph Henry Lumpkin Family Papers, 1821–1862," Digital Library of Georgia, accessed July 5, 2011, dlg
.galileo.usg.edu/hargrett/lumpkin/.

16. Lawrence M. Friedman, "Name Robbers: Privacy, Blackmail, and Assorted
Matters in Legal History," *Hofstra Law Review* 30, no. 4 (2002): 1093–
1132; Mary Frances Berry, "Judging Morality: Sexual Behavior and Legal
Consequences in the Late Nineteenth-Century South," *Journal of American
History* 78, no. 3 (1991): 835–856.

17. "Irregular Marriages," *New York Times,* July 18, 1873, 4; "District of Co-
lumbia Justice: Remarkable Course of Judge Humphreys—A Case for the
Attention of the Committee to Re-Organize the District Judiciary," *New
York Times,* December 18, 1877, 1. On the unwritten law, see Lawrence
M. Friedman, *Crime and Punishment in American History* (New York: Basic
Books, 1993), 221–222; Amanda Frisken, "Crimes of Passion" (paper pre-
sented at the annual meeting of the Organization of American Historians,
Seattle, March 28, 2009); Hendrik Hartog, "Lawyering, Husbands' Rights,
and 'The Unwritten Law' in Nineteenth-Century America," *Journal of
American History* 84, no. 1 (1997): 67–96; Robert M. Ireland, "Frenzied
and Fallen Females: Women and Sexual Dishonor in the Nineteenth-Century
United States," *Journal of Women's History* 3, no. 3 (1992): 108.

18. Quoted in Laura F. Edwards, *Gendered Strife and Confusion: The Political Culture of Reconstruction* (Champaign: University of Illinois Press, 1997), 203.

19. *St. Louis Globe-Democrat* quoted in "The Press on Maria Barberi," *Woman's
Journal,* August 24, 1895, 268; "The Barberi Trial," *New York Times,* December 13, 1896, 12; Ireland, "Frenzied and Fallen Females," 106–107. See
also Nancy Isenberg, *Sex and Citizenship in Antebellum America* (Chapel
Hill: University of North Carolina Press, 1998), 128–129; *New York Tribune,* reprinted in "Impunity in Crime," *Revolution,* June 10 1869, 362.

20. Lydia Maria Child, in *Advocate of Moral Reform,* quoted in Berg, *The Remembered Gate,* 210; Blanche Hersh, *The Slavery of Sex: Feminist-Abolitionists in
America* (Urbana: University of Illinois Press, 1978), 197; Gonda, "Strumpets
and Angels," 266.

21. "Soliloquy of the Libertine," quoted in Hobson, *Uneasy Virtue,* 56. For
similar arguments from feminists, see C. C. H., "Seduction Law in New
Jersey," *Woman's Journal* 9, no. 39 (1878): 267; and "Impunity in Crime,"
Revolution, June 10, 1869, 362.

22. Matilda Joslyn Gage, *Women, Church and State: A Historical Account of the
Status of Women through the Christian Ages: With Reminiscences of the Matri-
archate* (Chicago: Charles H. Kerr and Co., 1893), 323. See also Catharine
Waugh McCulloch, *Mr. Lex or the Legal Status of Mother and Child* (Chicago: Fleming H. Revell Co., 1899), 25–37; Ireland, "Frenzied and Fallen

Females," 103; Gonda, "Strumpets and Angels," 276. Concerns about the welfare burden of children born out of wedlock could have motivated granting mothers the right to sue, especially if they were widows. VanderVelde, "The Legal Ways of Seduction," 882–884.

23. Smith v. Richards, 29 Conn. 232 (Conn. 1860).
24. Jane E. Larson, "'Women Understand So Little, They Call My Good Nature "Deceit"'": A Feminist Rethinking of Seduction," *Columbia Law Review* 93, no. 2 (March 1993): 385–386; Berry, "Judging Morality," 848; VanderVelde, "The Legal Ways of Seduction," 893; Marshall v. Taylor, 98 Cal. 55, 32 P. 867, 868 (Cal. 1893).
25. VanderVelde, "The Legal Ways of Seduction," 882–883. On the problem of women as individuals in seduction law, see Haag, *Consent,* chap. 2.
26. VanderVelde, "The Legal Ways of Seduction," 884; Kennedy v. Shea, 110 Mass. 147 (Mass. 1872). See also Marshall v. Taylor, 98 Cal. 55, 32 P. 867 (Cal. 1893).
27. Haag, *Consent,* 35.
28. Quoted in Gonda, "Strumpets and Angels," 264; Anonymous, "Seduction a Felony," *Philanthropist,* September 1888, 4.
29. On sexuality as a form of inalienable labor, see Haag, *Consent,* 13, 23.
30. Lori D. Ginzberg, *Women and the Work of Benevolence: Morality, Politics, and Class in the Nineteenth-Century United States* (New Haven, CT: Yale University Press, 1990), 204n70; Larry Howard Whiteaker, "Moral Reform and Prostitution in New York City, 1830–1860" (PhD diss., Princeton University, 1977), 258; Gonda, "Strumpets and Angels," 263–264, 278, 287–289; Isenberg, *Sex and Citizenship,* 25. On male support, see also Eliza B. Duffey, *The Relations of the Sexes* (New York: Wood and Holbrook, 1876), 138–139.
31. Gonda, "Strumpets and Angels," 258–263, 290. Upgraded from a misdemeanor to a felony in 1881, the New York antiseduction law remained in effect well into the twentieth century. Robertson, "Seduction, Sexual Violence, and Marriage," 347.
32. Editorial Notes, *Woman's Journal* 17, no. 26 (1886): 201.
33. Simon Stern, "Remarks upon Dr. Storer's Paper Entitled the 'Law of Rape,'" *Quarterly Journal of Psychological Medicine and Medical Jurisprudence* 2 (1868): 365–366, 367.
34. Larson, "'Women Understand So Little,'" 385; Nathan P. Feinsinger, "Legislative Attack on 'Heart Balm,'" *Michigan Law Review* 33, no. 7 (1935): 988; Robertson, "Seduction, Sexual Violence, and Marriage," 333, 341, 361–362; Gonda, "Strumpets and Angels," 259, 289–291.
35. Brown quoted in VanderVelde, "The Legal Ways of Seduction," 895–896. In New York City between 1886 and 1955, one-third of the seduction charges included physical violence. Stephen Robertson, *Crimes against Children: Sexual Violence and Legal Culture in New York City, 1880–1960* (Chapel Hill: University of North Carolina Press, 2005), 34.

36. Editorial Notes, *Woman's Journal* 17, no. 26 (1886): 201; Robertson, "Seduction, Sexual Violence, and Marriage," 341; VanderVelde, "The Legal Ways of Seduction," 847; Gonda, "Strumpets and Angels," 372. See also Melissa Murray, "Marriage as Punishment," *Columbia Law Review* 112, no. 1 (2012).
37. Croghan v. State, 22 Wis. 444 (Wis. 1868); Block, "'An Accusation Easily to Be Made,'" 89–90.
38. Jones v. State, 16 S.E. 380 (Ga. 1892); VanderVelde, "The Legal Ways of Seduction," 858; Brian Donovan, "Gender Inequality and Criminal Seduction: Prosecuting Sexual Coercion in the Early-20th Century," *Law and Social Inquiry* 30, no. 1 (2005): 61–88. As late as 1947 the Georgia Supreme Court cited Lumpkin's poetic reference in questioning whether a woman might consent even as she resisted (in this case confirming a rape conviction). Davis v. State, 41 S.E.2d 414 (Ga. 1947).
39. Mary Frances Berry, *The Pig Farmer's Daughter and Other Tales of American Justice: Episodes of Racism and Sexism in the Courts from 1865 to the Present* (New York: Vintage Books, 1999), 131–134; Berry, "Judging Morality," 849n51; Parks v. The State, 35 Tex. Crim. 378, 33 S.W. 872 (Tex. Crim. App. 1896). In a sample from 1870 to 1900, none of the seduction reports in the *New York Times* and only four reports in the *Atlanta Constitution* involved African Americans, e.g., "Highly Colored: A Serious Charge against a Well Known Negro," *Atlanta Constitution*, January 5, 1888, 4.
40. Berry, *The Pig Farmer's Daughter*, 133.
41. Augusta H. Howard, "A 'Thinker' Shown to be Unthinking," *Woman's Tribune*, March 19, 1892, 2–3.
42. Editorial Notes, *Woman's Standard*, July 1889, 4.
43. Haag, *Consent*, 4, 30; Genevieve Lee Hawley in *Woman's Journal*, 1888, quoted in "Protection for Girls," *Woman's Standard*, May 1889, 3.
44. People v. Samonset, 32 P. 520 (Cal. 1893).
45. Wood v. State, 48 Ga. 192 (Ga. 1873).
46. McTyier v. State, 18 S.E. 140 (Ga. 1892); People v. Kehoe, 55 P. 911, 912 (Cal. 1898); Charles Curry, "Seduction by a Married Man," *Virginia Law Register* 5, no. 4 (August 1899): 209. See also Berry, *The Pig Farmer's Daughter*, 128–131.
47. For scholarly assessments of the laws and their overlapping concerns for protection and rights, see Gonda, "Strumpets and Angels," 252; VanderVelde, "The Legal Ways of Seduction," 900–901; Haag, *Consent*, chaps. 2–3; and Larson, "'Women Understand So Little.'"

3. Empowering White Women

1. "Impunity in Crime," *Revolution*, June 10, 1869, 362; see also H. A. W., letter to the editor, "Our Natural Protectors," *Revolution*, May 25, 1871, n.p.
2. The phrase appeared in Victoria Woodhull, "The Scare-Crows of Sexual Slavery, an Oration Delivered . . . at Silver Lake, Mass., Camp Meeting on

Sunday, Aug. 17, 1873" (New York: Woodhull and Claflin, 1874); and in August Bebel, *Woman in the Past, Present and Future,* trans. Dr. H. B. Adams Walther (London: Modern Press, 1885), 3.

3. Julia Ward Howe, "The Other Side of the Woman Question," *North American Review,* November 1879, 417–418; M., "Hester Vaughan," *Revolution,* September 17, 1868, 169.

4. In 1890 the two factions united as the National American Woman Suffrage Association (NAWSA). Ellen Carol DuBois, *Feminism and Suffrage: The Emergence of an Independent Women's Movement in America 1848–1869* (Ithaca, NY: Cornell University Press, 1978), chap. 6.

5. Henry B. Blackwell to Lucy Stone, January 3, 1855, in *Loving Warriors: Selected Letters of Lucy Stone and Henry B. Blackwell, 1853 to 1893,* ed. Leslie Wheeler (New York: Dial Press, 1981), 115, 3.

6. "Crimes against Women," *Woman's Journal,* December 18, 1875, 404–405; "Abuse of Women," *Woman's Journal,* August 3, 1872, 247; C. C. H., "Crimes against Women," *Woman's Journal,* December 25, 1875, 413.

7. Blanche Glassman Hersh, *The Slavery of Sex: Feminist-Abolitionists in America* (Urbana: University of Illinois Press, 1978), 196–198; Nancy Isenberg, *Sex and Citizenship in Antebellum America* (Chapel Hill: University of North Carolina Press, 1998), 106–119; Gerda Lerner, "Introduction," in *The Feminist Thought of Sarah Grimké* (Oxford: Oxford University Press, 1998), 37; H. B. B. [Henry Blackwell], "Exceptional Characters—Abuse of Women," *Woman's Journal,* August 8, 1874, 254; "Abuse of Women," *Woman's Journal,* August 3, 1872, 247; H. B. B. [Henry Blackwell], "Crimes of a Single Day," *Woman's Journal,* January 29, 1876, 34.

8. Stories of white male assailants predominated, but of eight stories of seduction or rape reprinted in an 1869 column titled "The Slavery of Women," two accounts from the South reported a revenge rape by a black man against the daughter of his former owner and the lynching of two black men for rape. "The Slavery of Women," *Revolution,* September 9, 1869, 155.

9. "June 3, 1869," *History of Woman Suffrage,* ed. Elizabeth Cady Stanton, Susan B. Anthony, and Matilda Joslyn Gage, vol. 2, *1861–1876* (Rochester, New York: Charles Mann, 1887), 334; Stanton quoted in Michele Mitchell, "'Lower Orders,' Racial Hierarchies, and Rights Rhetoric: Evolutionary Echoes in Elizabeth Cady Stanton's Thought during the Late 1860s," in *Elizabeth Cady Stanton, Feminist as Thinker: A Reader in Documents and Essays,* ed. Ellen Carol DuBois and Richard Cándida Smith (New York: New York University Press, 2007), 137–138; Louise Michele Newman, *White Women's Rights: The Racial Origins of Feminism in the United States* (New York: Oxford University Press, 1999), 64.

10. "Women's Deprivation of Rights the Source of Men's Crimes," *Woman's Journal,* November 13, 1875, 364.

11. Aileen S. Kraditor, *The Ideas of the Woman Suffrage Movement, 1890–1920* (New York: Norton, 1981); Newman, *White Women's Rights;* L. S. [Lucy

Stone], "Crimes against Women," *Woman's Journal,* June 16, 1877, 188; L. S. [Lucy Stone], "Pardoning the Crime of Rape," *Woman's Journal,* May 25, 1878, 164.

12. L. S. [Lucy Stone], "Pardoning the Crime of Rape," *Woman's Journal,* May 25, 1878, 164; Pearl Parsons, "Unpunished Crime in Delaware—A Sign of the Times," *Woman's Journal,* August 20, 1881, 272; "Women Are to Blame," *Woman's Standard,* July 1890, 7. On the denial of suffrage to convicted felons, see Alexander Keyssar, *The Right to Vote: The Contested History of Democracy in the United States* (New York: Basic Books, 2000), 378–384 (table A.15).

13. "State Notes," *Woman's Standard,* May 1894, 4.

14. E. A. A., "Comparative Sentences for Men and Women," *Woman's Exponent,* April 18, 1878, 171; Lucy Stone, "Protective Agencies for Women," in Our Woman's Column, *Christian Recorder,* April 7, 1887, 2; Genevieve Talcott Forbes, letter to the editor, "Something to Think About," *Woman's Standard,* May 1893, 4–5. See also "Unjust Laws—Iowa," *Woman's Standard,* June 1899, 4.

15. "A Case for Women Jurors," *Woman's Journal,* April 24, 1886, 129; "Unjust Courts," *Woman's Standard,* October 1900, 4.

16. "Infanticide," *Revolution,* August 6, 1868, in *The Selected Papers of Elizabeth Cady Stanton and Susan B. Anthony,* ed. Ann D. Gordon (New Brunswick, NJ: Rutgers University Press, 1997), 62–63; E. M. C., "Gen. Cole and Hester Vaughan," *Revolution,* December 31, 1868, 406; E. C. S. (Elizabeth Cady Stanton), "Governor Geary and Hester Vaughan," *Revolution,* December 10, 1868, 354; Gordon, *Selected Papers,* 158–159, 193. The pardon was contingent on Vaughan returning to her native England, which she did in 1869.

17. *History of Woman Suffrage,* ed. Susan B. Anthony and Ida Husted Harper, vol. 4, *1883–1900* (Rochester, NY: Susan B. Anthony, 1902), 182; *Woman's Tribune,* May 13, 1893, 164; "A Legal Outrage on a Woman," *Woman's Tribune,* September 25, 1897, 1.

18. "State Notes," *Woman's Standard,* May 1894, 4; "Safety for Women," *Revolution,* July 22, 1869, 34; H. B. B., "Crimes against Women," 188. The Working Women's National Association memorial in response to the Hester Vaughan case called for the abolition of capital punishment for any crime. "The Case of Hester Vaughan," *Revolution,* December 10, 1868, 358.

19. Robert M. Ireland, "Frenzied and Fallen Females: Women and Sexual Dishonor in the Nineteenth-Century United States," *Journal of Women's History* 3, no. 3 (1992): 106; "The Case of Hester Vaughan," *Revolution,* December 10, 1868, 357; Henry B. Blackwell, "The Case of Maria Barberi," *Woman's Journal,* August 10, 1895, 252. On Canadian women's campaigns to pardon women convicted of murder related to sexual abuse, see Karen Dubinsky, *Improper Advances: Rape and Heterosexual Conflict in Ontario, 1880–1929* (Chicago: University of Chicago Press, 1993), 104–111.

20. Matter of Goodell, 39 Wis. 232 (1876); Mary Ives Todd, "Feminine Logic," letter, *Los Angeles Times,* April 15, 1888, 3; Calhoun, "Chivalry and Reality," letter, *Los Angeles Times,* April 17, 1888, 3. Transcripts of these letters are available at www.csupomona.edu/~reshaffer/Books/LettersToThePeople /contents.htm. See also "Hattie Woolsteen," *Los Angeles Times,* April 14, 1888, 3; "The Woolsteen," *Los Angeles Times,* April 16, 1888, 1.

21. Caroline M. Brown, "Protective Agency for Women and Children," in *Transactions of the National Council of Women of the United States* (Philadelphia: J. B. Lippincott, 1891), 260–262; C. M. Brown, "The Protective Agency for Women and Children, Chicago, Ill.," *Woman's Tribune,* April 3, 1888, 16; Elizabeth Pleck, "Feminist Responses to 'Crimes against Women,' 1868–1896," *Signs* 8, no. 3 (1983): 451–470; Elizabeth Pleck, *Domestic Tyranny: The Making of Social Policy against Family Violence from Colonial Times to the Present* (New York: Oxford University Press, 1987), 95–98. On cross-class reforms, see Sarah Deutsch, *Women and the City: Gender, Space, and Power in Boston, 1870–1940* (New York: Oxford University Press, 2002).

22. Brown, "Protective Agency for Women and Children," 262; Gwen Hoerr Jordan, "'Them Law Wimmin': The Protective Agency for Women and Children and the Gendered Origins of Legal Aid," in *Feminist Legal History: Essays on Women and Law,* ed. Tracy A. Thomas and Tracy Jean Boisseau (New York: New York University Press, 2011), 155–156, 166; D. S. B. Conover, "Chicago Protective Agency for Women and Children," *Charities Review* 8 (1898): 287–288. Caroline M. Brown, "Illinois," in *Report of the Association for the Advancement of Women* (Syracuse: Bardeen, 1892), 96; Fourth Annual Report, quoted in Jordan, "'Them Law Wimmin,'" 162.

23. Jordan, "'Them Law Wimmin,'" 158, 163, 168; Brown, "Protective Agency for Women and Children," 161; Pleck, *Domestic Tyranny,* 98.

24. "Impunity in Crime," *Revolution,* June 10, 1869, 362; T. W. H. [Thomas Wentworth Higginson], "A Terrible Book," *Woman's Journal,* January 17, 1880, 1.

25. Sir Matthew Hale, *The History of the Pleas of the Crown,* ed. W. A. Stokes and E. Ingersoll (Philadelphia: Robert H. Small, 1847), 629.

26. Shaw v. Shaw, 17 Conn. 189 (Conn. 1845); Nancy Isenberg, *Sex and Citizenship in Antebellum America* (Chapel Hill: University of North Carolina Press, 1998), 163; Robert L. Griswold, "The Evolution of the Doctrine of Mental Cruelty in Victorian American Divorce, 1790–1900," *Journal of Social History* 20, no. 1 (1986): 127–148. See also Elaine Tyler May, *Great Expectations: Marriage and Divorce in Post-Victorian America* (Chicago: University of Chicago Press, 1980).

27. Linda K. Kerber, "The Meanings of Citizenship," *Journal of American History* 84, no. 3 (1997): 838. Kerber also points out that if the man was an exiled traitor or in prison, his wife could make a contract because her husband did not have access to her body.

28. Elizabeth Cady Stanton to Susan Brownell Anthony, March 1, 1853, in *Elizabeth Cady Stanton, as Revealed in Her Letters, Diary and Reminis-*

cences, eds. Harriet Stanton Blatch and Theodore Stanton, vol. 2 (New York: Harper and Bros., 1922), 369; Stone quoted in Hersh, *The Slavery of Sex,* 65, 66. By midcentury, states did begin to grant divorces on the grounds of "habitual drunkenness." Isenberg, *Sex and Citizenship,* 158. On nineteenth-century feminist conflicts over the marriage question, see Amy Dru Stanley, *From Bondage to Contract: Wage Labor, Marriage, and the Market in the Age of Slave Emancipation* (New York: Cambridge University Press, 1998), 175–180.

29. Stanton quoted in Hersh, *The Slavery of Sex,* 199, 67; Thomas W. Organ, MD, "Woman Wronged," *Revolution,* April 9, 1868, 214. See also Nancy F. Cott, *Public Vows: A History of Marriage and the Nation* (Cambridge, MA: Harvard University Press, 2002), 67.

30. Miriam Williford, "Bentham on the Rights of Women," *Journal of the History of Ideas* 36 (1975): 170–171; Mill quoted in Martha C. Nussbaum, *Sex and Social Justice* (Oxford: Oxford University Press, 1999), 64. An 1891 British court ruled that a husband did not have the right to confine his wife "in order to enforce restitution of conjugal rights," propelling women's rights advocate Elizabeth Wolstenholme Elmy to distribute one hundred thousand copies of a pamphlet about the decision. Lucy Bland, *Banishing the Beast: Sexuality and the Early Feminists* (New York: The New Press, 1995), 135–138; Rebecca L. Davis, *More Perfect Unions: The American Search for Marital Bliss* (Cambridge, MA: Harvard University Press, 2010), 37.

31. Eliza Bisbee Duffey, *What Women Should Know: A Woman's Book about Women* (1873; repr., New York: Arno Press, 1974), 117; Eliza Bisbee Duffey, *The Relations of the Sexes* (New York: Wood and Holbrook, 1876), 209, quoted in Jesse F. Battan, "The 'Rights' of Husbands and the 'Duties' of Wives: Power and Desire in the American Bedroom, 1850–1910," *Journal of Family History* 24, no. 2 (1999): 166.

32. Linda Gordon, *The Moral Property of Women: A History of Birth Control Politics in America* (Urbana and Chicago: University of Illinois Press, 2002), 55–72; Jill Elaine Hasday, "Contest and Consent: A Legal History of Marital Rape," *California Law Review* 88, no. 5 (2000): 1439; Ellen Carol Dubois and Linda Gordon, "Seeking Ecstasy on the Battlefield: Danger and Pleasure in Nineteenth Century Feminist Sexual Thought," *Feminist Studies* 9, no. 1 (1983): 7–25. On suffragist concerns that forced marital sex led to inferior offspring, see Stanton to Anthony, March 1, 1853, in Blatch and Stanton, *Elizabeth Cady Stanton,* 369.

33. Joanne Ellen Passet, *Sex Radicals and the Quest for Women's Equality* (Urbana: University of Illinois Press, 2003), 11–12; Carl J. Guarneri, *The Utopian Alternative: Fourierism in Nineteenth-Century America* (Ithaca, NY: Cornell University Press, 1991), 142.

34. Cott, *Public Vows,* 69; John D'Emilio and Estelle B. Freedman, *Intimate Matters: A History of Sexuality in America,* 3rd ed. (Chicago: University of Chicago Press, 2012), 112–121, 156–166.

35. T. L. Nichols and Mary S. Gove Nichols, *Marriage: Its History, Character and Results* (New York: T. L. Nichols, 1854), 329–333; Tennessee Claflin Cook, "Which Is to Blame?," *Woodhull & Claflin's Weekly,* January 6, 1872, reprinted in Tennessee Claflin Cook, *Essays on Social Topics* (London: Phoenix, 1898), 123–131.

36. Jean L. Silver-Isenstadt, *Shameless: The Visionary Life of Mary Gove Nichols* (Baltimore: Johns Hopkins University Press, 2002), 26, 215; Thomas Low Nichols, *Human Physiology: The Basis of Social and Sanitary Science* (London: Trubner, 1872), 311, quoted in Silver-Isenstadt, *Shameless,* 213; Nichols and Nichols, *Marriage,* 259, 23, 102. Like some other early supporters of free love, the Nicholses did not stay the course; they eventually converted to Catholicism and embraced more traditional morality.

37. Victoria Woodhull, "Tried as by Fire, or the True and the False, Socially," in *Free Love in America: A Documentary History,* ed. Taylor Stoehr (New York: AMS Press, 1979), 357; Nicola Beisel, *Imperiled Innocents: Anthony Comstock and Family Reproduction in Victorian America* (Princeton, NJ: Princeton University Press, 1997), 79; Amanda Frisken, *Victoria Woodhull's Sexual Revolution: Political Theater and the Popular Press in Nineteenth-Century America* (Philadelphia: University of Pennsylvania Press, 2004), 40.

38. Lillian Harman, "An 'Age-of-Consent' Symposium," *Liberty (Not the Daughter but the Mother of Order)* 10, no. 20 (1895): 2; A. Heywood quoted in Gordon, *The Moral Property of Women,* 65.

39. Heywoods quoted in Beisel, *Imperiled Innocents,* 100, 99.

40. For a summary of the medical literature, see Hasday, "Contest and Consent," 1453–61.

41. Theresa Hughes, "Another Woman's Story of Wrong and Outrage," *Lucifer the Light-Bearer,* May 2, 1890, 1, 4; Jesse F. Battan, "The 'Rights' of Husbands," 170; Dr. W. G. Markland, *Lucifer, Light Bearer* (1886), quoted in Sarah A. Willburn, *Possessed Victorians: Extra Spheres in Nineteenth-Century Mystical Writings* (Burlington, VT: Ashgate, 2006), 74; Jesse F. Battan, " 'In the Marriage Bed Woman's Sex Has Been Enslaved and Abused': Defining and Exposing Martial Rape in Late-Nineteenth-Century America," in *Sex without Consent: Rape and Sexual Coercion in America,* ed. Merrill D. Smith (New York: New York University Press, 2001), 214.

42. Quoted in Battan, "The 'Rights' of Husbands," 17, emphasis in the original; "A Woman's Earnest Plea for Freedom and Justice," *Lucifer the Light-Bearer,* February 12, 1886, 3.

43. Battan, "The 'Rights' of Husbands," 172n39, citing Woodhull, "The Scare-Crows of Sexual Slavery," *Woodhull & Claflin's Weekly,* September 27, 1873, 6–7; and Rachel Campbell, "Sex Ethics, No. 1," *Lucifer the Light-Bearer,* June 24, 1892, 3. See also Ellen Carol DuBois, "Feminism and Free Love," available at www2.h-net.msu.edu/~women/papers/freelove.html, text at n64.

44. Hal D. Sears, *The Sex Radicals: Free Love in High Victorian America* (Lawrence: University Press of Kansas, 1977), 174; Ida Craddock, *The Wedding Night*, reprinted in Vere Chappell, *Sexual Outlaw, Erotic Mystic: The Essential Ida Craddock* (San Francisco: Red Wheel/Weiser LLC, 2010), 213.
45. "Anthony Comstock's Work," *New York Times*, May 4, 1883, 5; Comstock quoted in Beisel, *Imperiled Innocents*, 89–90. See also Helen Lefkowitz Horowitz, *Rereading Sex: Battles over Sexual Knowledge and Suppression in Nineteenth-Century America* (New York: Knopf, 2002), chaps. 16–17.
46. Taylor Stoehr, ed., "Introduction," *Free Love in America*, 67; Ida Craddock, "Ida Craddock's Letter to Her Mother," in *Free Love in America*, 308; Leigh Eric Schmidt, *Heaven's Bride: The Unprintable Life of Ida C. Craddock, American Mystic, Scholar, Sexologist, Martyr and Madwoman* (New York: Basic Books, 2010), chap. 5; Anthony Comstock, "Free-Love Traps," in *Free Love in America*, 382–389; Beisel, *Imperiled Innocents*, 101. On reactions to convictions under the Comstock law, see Horowitz, *Rereading Sex*, chap. 19. In 1899 Henry Blackwell complained about receiving one of Ida Craddock's pamphlets, contributing to Comstock's crusade against her. Schmidt, *Heaven's Bride*, 195.
47. Elizabeth Cady Stanton, "The Christian Church and Woman," *Free Thought Magazine*, November 1896, 673–682 (quote at 680).

4. Contesting the Rape of Black Women

1. "Insult to Injury," *Christian Recorder*, November 5, 1874, 4; and A. H. Newton to Editor, *Christian Recorder*, September 10, 1874, 2; "The Southern Disturbances," *New York Tribune*, August 28, 1874, 8; "The Southern Outbreaks," *New York Tribune*, September 10, 1974, 3; "Tennessee Troubles," *New York Tribune*, October 27, 1874, 3; "Louisiana and the Rule of Terror," *Harper's Weekly*, October 3, 1874, 813; "An Integrating Interview with Governor John [C.] Brown," *Atlanta Constitution*, September 8, 1874, 2.
2. Quoted in Beverly Guy-Sheftall, *Daughters of Sorrow: Attitudes toward Black Women, 1880–1920* (Brooklyn: Carlson, 1990), 52.
3. Important studies of the links among rape, lynching, and rights include: Jacquelyn Dowd Hall, *Revolt against Chivalry: Jessie Daniel Ames and the Women's Campaign against Lynching* (New York: Columbia University Press, 1979); Hannah Rosen, *Terror in the Heart of Freedom: Citizenship, Sexual Violence, and the Meaning of Race in the Postemancipation South* (Chapel Hill: University of North Carolina Press, 2009); and Diane Miller Sommerville, *Rape and Race in the Nineteenth-Century South* (Chapel Hill: University of North Carolina Press, 2004).
4. Quoted in Hannah Rosen, "'Not That Sort of Women': Race, Gender, and Sexual Violence during the Memphis Riot of 1866," in *Sex, Race, Love: Crossing Boundaries in North American History*, ed. Martha Hodes (New York: New York University Press, 1999), 331.

5. Rebecca A. Kosary, "To Degrade and Control: White Violence and the Maintenance of Racial and Gender Boundaries in Reconstruction Texas, 1865–1868" (PhD diss., Texas A&M University, 2006), 87; William D. Carrigan, *The Making of Lynching Culture: Violence and Vigilantism in Central Texas, 1836–1916* (Urbana: University of Illinois Press, 2004), 112.

6. Records of the Assistant Commissioner for the State of Louisiana, Bureau of Refugees, Freedmen and Abandoned Lands, 1865–1869, National Archives Microfilm Publication M1027, roll 34, Records Relating to Murders and Outrages, "Miscellaneous Reports and Lists Relating to Murders and Outrages, Mar. 1867–Nov. 1868," August 1, 1866, accessed May 1, 2012, freedmensbureau.com/louisiana/outrages/outrages4.htm. For a later example of a brother killed for defending his sister from rape by white men, see *Savannah Tribune*, July 24, 1897, 2.

7. Rosen, *Terror in the Heart of Freedom*, 61–61, 69–87.

8. Deborah Gray White, *Ar'n't I a Woman: Female Slaves in the Plantation South* (New York: Norton, 1999), 174–175; Rosen, *Terror in the Heart of Freedom*, 216, 220; Lisa Cardyn, "Sexual Terror in the Reconstruction South," in *Battle Scars: Gender and Sexuality in the American Civil War*, ed. Catherine Clinton and Nina Silber (New York: Oxford University Press, 2006), 147.

9. Records of the Assistant Commissioner for the State of Georgia Bureau of Refugees, Freedmen and Abandoned Lands 1865–1869, National Archives Microfilm Publication M798, roll 32, Reports Relating to Murders and Outrages 1865–1868, List of Freedmen Murdered or Assaulted 1867, August 13, 1868; Records of the Assistant Commissioner for the State of Tennessee Bureau of Refugees, Freedmen, and Abandoned Lands, 1865–1869, National Archives Microfilm Publication M999, roll 34, "Reports of Outrages, Riots and Murders, Jan. 15, 1866–Aug. 12, 1868," July 2, 1867, accessed May 1, 2012, freedmensbureau.com/tennessee/outrages/tennoutrages2.htm.

10. Rosen, *Terror in the Heart of Freedom*, 228.

11. Ibid., 180, 228–230; Eric Foner, *Reconstruction: America's Unfinished Revolution, 1863–1877* (New York: Harper and Row, 1988), 444–455; Evelyn Brooks Higginbotham, "African-American Women's History and the Metalanguage of Race," *Signs* 17, no. 2 (1992): 261.

12. Peter W. Bardaglio, *Reconstructing the Household: Families, Sex, and the Law in the Nineteenth-Century South* (Chapel Hill: University of North Carolina Press, 1995), 191, 196; Laura F. Edwards, *Gendered Strife and Confusion: The Political Culture of Reconstruction* (Urbana: University of Illinois Press, 1997), 199, 206–208.

13. Glenda Elizabeth Gilmore, *Gender and Jim Crow: Women and the Politics of White Supremacy in North Carolina, 1896–1920* (Chapel Hill: University of North Carolina Press, 1996), 74–75. The black men were tried but not convicted for assaulting Jones.

14. In a sample of 752 newspaper accounts of rape in the *New York Times*, the *Atlanta Constitution*, the *Los Angeles Times*, and the *National Police Gazette*

from 1872 to 1897, the proportion of victims who could be identified as white declined from 95 percent in the 1870s, to 88 percent in the 1880s, to 82 percent in the 1890s. Mexican, Asian, and Native women represented 1 percent in the 1870s, 2 percent in the 1880s, and 5 percent in the 1890s. In the 1870s, none of these newspapers published stories about black victims of white rape; in the 1890s, 2.91 percent overall (and 3.94 percent of *Atlanta Constitution* cases) involved white men who assaulted black women or children. On the sample, see Estelle B. Freedman, "'Crimes Which Startle and Horrify': Gender, Age, and the Racialization of Sexual Violence in White American Newspapers, 1870–1900," *Journal of the History of Sexuality* 20, no. 3 (2011): 468n8, 479n35.

15. Edwards, *Gendered Strife and Confusion*, 184, 208; "An Ugly Charge," *Atlanta Constitution*, December 8, 1892, 2; "Man Convicted of Assault," *Atlanta Constitution*, November 20, 1897, 2.

16. State v. Powell, 11 S.E. 191 (N.C. 1890), quoted in Bardaglio, *Reconstructing the Household*, 196. It is not clear if procedural appeals were any more successful in rape cases than for other crimes. On late nineteenth-century technical appeals, see Lawrence Friedman, *Crime and Punishment in American History* (New York: Basic Books, 1993), 256.

17. "Our Women," *New York Freeman*, January 1, 1887, reprinted from the *Scimitar*, in *The Memphis Diary of Ida B. Wells*, ed. Miriam DaCosta-Willis (Boston: Beacon Press, 1995), 185–186.

18. Ibid.

19. On stereotypes, see Crystal N. Feimster, *Southern Horrors: Women and the Politics of Rape and Lynching* (Cambridge, MA: Harvard University Press, 2009), 165; White, *Ar'n't I a Woman*, chap. 1; Sander Gilman, "Black Bodies, White Bodies: Toward an Iconography of Female Sexuality in Late Nineteenth Century Art, Medicine, and Literature," *Critical Inquiry*, 12, no. 1 (1985): 204–242; Evelynn M. Hammonds, "Towards a Genealogy of Black Female Sexuality: The Problematic of Silence," in *Feminist Genealogies, Colonial Legacies, Democratic Futures*, ed. M. Jacqui Alexander and Chandra Talpade Mohanty (New York: Routledge, 1997), 170–182.

20. Bruce quoted in Guy-Sheftall, *Daughters of Sorrow*, 41–42; Thomas quoted in ibid., 55.

21. Mrs. L. H. Harris, letter to the editor, "A Southern Woman's View," *Independent*, May 18, 1899, 1354; Mrs. L. H. Harris, "Negro Womanhood," *Independent*, June 22, 1899, 1687–1689.

22. A Southern Woman, "Experiences of the Race Problem," *Independent*, March 17, 1904, 590. For an exception, see Feimster, *Southern Horrors*, 64–67.

23. A Negro Nurse, "More Slavery at the South," *Independent*, January 5, 1912, 196; A Southern Colored Woman, "The Race Problem—An Autobiography," *Independent*, March 17, 1904, 586, in Gerda Lerner, ed., *Black Women in White America: A Documentary History* (New York: Vintage, 1992), 378.

24. Quoted in Michele Mitchell, *Righteous Propagation: African Americans and the Politics of Racial Destiny after Reconstruction* (Chapel Hill: University of North Carolina Press, 2004), 43.

25. A Southern Colored Woman, "The Race Problem."

26. Daniel Webster Davis, "The Black Woman's Burden," *Voice of the Negro,* July 1904, 308; A Negro Nurse, "More Slavery at the South."

27. Court trials for black-on-black rape had been rare in colonial America, and in the antebellum North they usually involved child victims. Sharon Block, *Rape and Sexual Power in Early America* (Chapel Hill: University of North Carolina Press, 2006), 177–178. Thomas D. Morris found no legal cases concerning the sexual assault of slave women by free blacks in the antebellum South and only rare cases of intraracial rape among slaves. Thomas D. Morris, *Southern Slavery and the Law, 1619–1860* (Chapel Hill: University of North Carolina Press, 1996), 305–306.

28. Peter W. Bardaglio, "Rape and the Law in the Old South: 'Calculated to Excite Indignation in Every Heart,'" *Journal of Southern History* 60, no. 4 (1994): 759; Sommerville, *Rape and Race,* 66. Under Georgia's 1861 code, the sentence for white-on-white rape was two to twenty years, for black-on-white rape the death penalty, and for the rape of a black woman a fine and imprisonment "at the discretion of the court." Bardaglio, *Reconstructing the Household,* 68–69.

29. Records of the Assistant Commissioner for the State of Georgia Bureau of Refugees, Freedmen and Abandoned Lands, 1865–1869, National Archives Publication M798, roll 36, "Unbound Miscellaneous Papers," March 6, 1866, accessed May 1, 2012, freedmensbureau.com/georgia/thadcollins5.htm.

30. Intraracial black rape reports increased from 5 percent to 13 percent in the sample of the *Atlanta Constitution* and from 3 percent to 8 percent in the national sample in this period.

31. "A Brutal Assault," *Atlanta Constitution,* April 28, 1882, 7; "The Days Work," *Atlanta Constitution,* August 9, 1887, 8. See also "Police Paragraphs," *Atlanta Constitution,* June 23, 1887, 5; "A Life Sentence for Rape," *Atlanta Constitution,* April 7, 1887, 4. Only rarely did papers outside the South report intraracial black rape. See, for example, "Outraged by a Negro," *New York Times,* October 3, 1883, 1.

32. "Killed while Attempting an Outrage," *Christian Recorder,* November 29, 1894, 6.

33. Miller, *Crime, Sexual Violence, and Clemency,* 181; Dr. Stimson Lambert quoted in A. C. Tompkins, "The Age of Consent from a Physio-Psychological Standpoint," in "Opposing Views by Legislators on the Age of Consent—A Symposium," *Arena,* July 1895, 209.

34. Quoted in Guy-Sheftall, *Daughters of Sorrow,* 43.

35. Bardaglio, *Reconstructing the Household,* 190–191.

36. Christian v. Commonwealth, 64 Va. 954, 958–959 (Va. 1873).

37. Miller, *Crime, Sexual Violence, and Clemency,* 182–183.

38. Powell quoted in Sommerville, *Rape and Race,* 154 (emphasis in original); Gosha v. State, 56 Ga. 36 (Ga. 1876).
39. Miller, *Crime, Sexual Violence, and Clemency,* 182–183, 191–194, 216.
40. Freedman, " 'Crimes Which Startle and Horrify,' " 492 (table 3).

5. The Racialization of Rape and Lynching

1. "Rape," *Crisis,* May 1919, 12. On moral panic—a reaction based on underlying fears of social change that overdramatize a perceived threat and respond to it in irrational ways—see, e.g., Jeffrey Weeks, *Sexuality,* 3rd ed. (New York: Routledge, 2010), 115; Philip Jenkins, *Moral Panic: Changing Concepts of the Child Molester in Modern America* (New Haven, CT: Yale University Press, 1998); Glenda Gilmore, *Gender and Jim Crow: Women and the Politics of White Supremacy in North Carolina, 1896–1920* (Chapel Hill: University of North Carolina Press, 1996), 84; Karen Dubinsky, *Improper Advances: Rape and Heterosexual Conflict in Ontario, 1880–1929* (Chicago: University of Chicago Press, 1993), chap. 2. On the comparable "black peril" scare in colonial Africa, see Jock McCulloch, *Black Peril, White Virtue: Sexual Crime in Southern Rhodesia, 1902–1935* (Bloomington: Indiana University Press, 2000).
2. Martha Hodes, *White Women, Black Men: Illicit Sex in the Nineteenth-Century South* (New Haven, CT: Yale University Press, 1997), esp. chaps. 7–8; Laura F. Edwards, *Gendered Strife and Confusion* (Urbana: University of Illinois Press, 1997), 200–202; Diane Miller Sommerville, *Rape and Race in the Nineteenth-Century South* (Chapel Hill: University of North Carolina Press, 2004), 120–121, 183. Overviews of historical analyses of the racialization of rape and lynching appear in Sommerville, *Rape and Race,* appendix, 223–259; and in W. Fitzhugh Brundage, introduction to *Under Sentence of Death: Lynching in the South,* ed. W. Fitzhugh Brundage (Chapel Hill: University of North Carolina Press, 1997), 6–13.
3. Frederick Douglass, "Why Is the Negro Lynched?," in *Frederick Douglass: Selected Speeches and Writings,* ed. Philip S. Foner (Chicago: Lawrence Hill Books, 1999), 757. Crystal Feimster suggests that although underreported, these assaults left a deep-seated fear that would fuel postwar reactions to rape. Crystal N. Feimster, *Southern Horrors: Women and the Politics of Rape and Lynching* (Cambridge, MA: Harvard University Press, 2009), 13–27. On fears of rape raised by secessionists, see Stephanie McCurry, *Confederate Reckoning: Power and Politics in the Civil War South* (Cambridge, MA: Harvard University Press, 2010), 27–29.
4. "Brutal Outrage by a Tramp," *New York Times,* August 4, 1878, 7; "Brutal Outrage by Tramps," *New York Times,* October 3, 1878, 2; "A Tramp Lynched in Mississippi," *New York Times,* May 9, 1878, 1. See also "A Tramp's Gross Ingratitude," *New York Times,* August 28, 1884, 5; "Tramp Terror," *National Police Gazette,* March 22, 1879, 1; "Food for Judge Lynch," illustration, *National Police Gazette,* December 21, 1889, 9. For further

discussion, see Estelle B. Freedman, "'Crimes Which Startle and Horrify . . .': Gender, Age, and the Racialization of Sexual Violence in White
American Newspapers, 1870–1900," *Journal of the History of Sexuality* 20,
no. 3 (2011), 465–497.

5. Gilmore, *Gender and Jim Crow,* 82–89.
6. W. Fitzhugh Brundage, *Lynching in the New South: Georgia and Virginia,
1880–1930* (Urbana: University of Illinois Press, 1993), 58; see also Edwards, *Gendered Strife and Confusion,* chap. 6; "Foraker on the Massacre,"
Savannah Tribune, October 13, 1906, 8.
7. Henderson M. Somerville, "Some Co-Operating Causes of Negro Lynching," *North American Review* 177, no. 563 (1903): 506.
8. Leslie K. Dunlap, "The Reform of Rape Law and the Problem of White Men:
Age-of-Consent Campaigns in the South, 1885–1910," in *Sex, Love, Race:
Crossing Boundaries in North American History,* ed. Martha Hodes (New
York: New York University Press, 1999), 356; Peter W. Bardaglio, *Recon-
structing the Household: Families, Sex, and the Law in the Nineteenth-Century
South* (Chapel Hill: University of North Carolina Press, 1995), 189–195.
9. On fears of social equality and intermarriage, see Jane Dailey, *Before Jim
Crow: The Politics of Race in Post-Emancipation Virginia* (Chapel Hill: Uni-
versity of North Carolina Press, 2000), 86–98; Peggy Pascoe, *What Comes
Naturally: Miscegenation Law and the Making of Race in America* (New
York: Oxford University Press, 2009), chap. 1.
10. Hodes, *White Women, Black Men,* 2–6, 178; Pascoe, *What Comes Naturally,* 6.
11. Quoted in Hannah Rosen, "'Not That Sort of Woman': Race, Gender, and
Sexual Violence during the Memphis Riot of 1866," in Hodes, *Sex, Love,
Race,* 193.
12. William D. Carrigan, *The Making of a Lynching Culture: Violence and Vigilantism in Central Texas, 1836–1916* (Urbana: University of Illinois Press,
2006), 149; Ida B. Wells-Barnett, *Southern Horrors and Other Writings: The
Anti-Lynching Campaign of Ida B. Wells, 1892–1900,* ed. Jacqueline Jones
Royster (Boston: Bedford, 1997), 57. On the history of antimiscegenation
laws, see Pascoe, *What Comes Naturally.*
13. Young v. State, 65 Ga. 525 (Ga. 1880). The Appellate Court affirmed the
conviction because the defendant's lawyer did not object to this line from the
prosecutor at the time. On the consequent denial of sexual agency to white
women, see Sommerville, *Race and Rape,* 216.
14. Dorsey v. State, 34 S.E. 135 (Ga. 1899). On the shift from consensual relations, to the image of the Negro Seducer, to the black rapist after the 1880s,
see Carrigan, *The Making of a Lynching Culture,* 150.
15. Philip A. Bruce, *The Plantation Negro as Freeman* (1889), quoted in Sandra
Gunning, *Race, Rape, and Lynching: The Red Record of American Literature, 1890–1912* (New York: Oxford University Press, 1996), 22. On Bruce
and Brinton, see Philip Dray, *At the Hands of Persons Unknown: The Lynching of Black America* (New York: Modern Library, 2002), 101; William Lee

Howard, "The Negro as a Distinct Ethnic Factor," *Medical News* 84, no. 19 (1904): 905. On the use of theories of black degeneracy, see George Fredrickson, *The Black Image in the White Mind: The Debate on Afro-American Character and Destiny, 1817–1914* (Middletown: Wesleyan University Press, 1971), esp. 275–281; and Margot Canaday, *The Straight State: Sexuality and Citizenship in Twentieth-Century America* (Princeton, NJ: Princeton University Press, 2009), 30–31. On constructions of white civilized manliness, see also Gail Bederman, *Manliness and Civilization: A Cultural History of Gender and Race in the United States, 1880–1917* (Chicago: University of Chicago Press, 1995), esp. 49–50.

16. Bruce quoted in Gunning, *Race, Rape, and Lynching*, 22; Thomas Nelson Page, "The Negro: The Southerner's Problem," *McClure's Magazine*, March 1904, 548; Thomas Dixon Jr., *The Clansman: An Historical Romance of the Ku Klux Klan* (New York: Doubleday, 1905). See also Thomas Dixon Jr., *The Leopard's Spots: A Romance of the White Man's Burden, 1865–1900* (New York: Doubleday, 1903).

17. "At Their Own Lips," *Atlanta Constitution*, January 5, 1872, 2; see also "Attempt to Lynch a Negro at Rochester," *New York Times*, January 3, 1872, 8; and Freedman, " 'Crimes Which Startle and Horrify.' "

18. "British Anti-Lynchers," *New York Times*, August 2, 1894, 4; "The Negro Crime," *National Police Gazette*, September 2, 1879, 3. See also "The Negro Crime," *National Police Gazette*, May 4, 1878, 3; "The Negro Crime," *National Police Gazette*, May 21, 1878, 5; "A Travesty of Justice," *National Police Gazette*, May 18, 1878, 2. Although white men dominated in the rape stories in this paper, the graphics reinforced the racialization of rape by representing black men as rapists more frequently than white men. Amanda Frisken, "Obscenity, Free Speech, and 'Sporting News' in 1870s America," *Journal of American Studies* 42, no. 3 (2008): 560–565.

19. Dray, *At the Hands of Persons Unknown;* Christopher Waldrep, *The Many Faces of Judge Lynch: Extralegal Violence and Punishment in America* (New York: Palgrave Macmillan, 2002), esp. chap. 3; William D. Carrigan and Clive Webb, "The Lynching of Persons of Mexican Origin or Descent in the United States, 1848 to 1928," *Journal of Social History* 37, no. 2 (2003): 414–416, 420; Sommerville, *Rape and Race*, 49; Thomas G. Dyer, "A Most Unexampled Exhibition of Madness and Brutality: Judge Lynch in Saline County, Missouri," in Brundage, *Under Sentence of Death*, 98–99.

20. Carrigan, *Making of a Lynching Culture*, 83, 153.

21. On the racialization of lynching, see Waldrep, *Many Faces of Judge Lynch;* Sommerville, *Rape and Race*, 158–165; Joel Williamson, *The Crucible of Race: Black-White Relations in the South since Emancipation* (Oxford: Oxford University Press, 1984); Stewart E. Tolnay and E. M. Beck, *A Festival of Violence: An Analysis of Southern Lynchings, 1882–1930* (Urbana: University of Illinois Press, 1995); Wells-Barnett, *Southern Horrors;* Brundage, *Lynching in the New South;* Hodes, *White Women, Black Men;* Robyn Weigman,

"The Anatomy of Lynching," *Journal of the History of Sexuality* 3, no. 3 (1993): 445–467; and Jacqueline Goldsby, *A Spectacular Secret: Lynching in American Life and Literature* (Chicago: University of Chicago Press, 2006).

22. Sommerville, *Race and Rape*, 159–166. While Martha Hodes points out that owners no longer had an incentive to protect their property, Lisa Lindquist Dorr found that in the early twentieth century some white men did continue to champion black men convicted of rape. Hodes, *White Women, Black Men*, 158; Lisa Lindquist Dorr, *White Women, Rape, and the Power of Race in Virginia, 1900–1960* (Chapel Hill: University of North Carolina Press, 2004), esp. 175–176. See also Nell Irvin Painter, "'Social Equality' and 'Rape' in the Fin-de-Siècle South," in *Southern History across the Color Line* (Chapel Hill: University of North Carolina Press, 2002), esp. 123; and Carrigan, *Making of a Lynching Culture*, 83.

23. Data derived from Robert L. Zangrando, *The NAACP Crusade against Lynching, 1909–50* (Philadelphia: Temple University Press, 1980), 6–7 (table 2); Painter, "'Social Equality' and 'Rape,'" 131, 117; Brundage, *Lynching in the New South*, xii. See also Jacquelyn Hall, *Revolt against Chivalry: Jessie Daniel Ames and the Women's Campaign against Lynching* (New York: Columbia University Press, 1979), 134 (table 1). Tolnay and Beck found that lynchings resulting from accusations of rape or rape/murder declined from 38.1 percent in 1882–1899 to 24.8 percent in 1900–1930. They concluded that lynching correlated most directly with falling cotton prices and the need to control the black labor force, rather than with political competition between Republicans and Democrats. Tolnay and Beck, *A Festival of Violence*, 47–50. On women as victims of lynching, see Debra Gray White, *Ar'n't I a Woman: Female Slaves in the Plantation South* (New York: Norton, 1999), 177; on the lynching of both black and white women, see Feimster, *Southern Horrors*, chap. 6.

24. Felton quoted in Feimster, *Southern Horrors*, 127, 143; see also 128–134.

25. Feimster, *Southern Horrors*, 145–152; "She Called for the Torch," *New York Times*, February 22, 1892, 5; Wells-Barnett, *Southern Horrors*, 57.

26. *Savannah Tribune*, September 23, 1899, 2; Bardaglio, *Reconstructing the Household*, 190. Only nine of the forty-seven appellate rape or attempted-rape cases in Georgia from 1865 to 1900 involved black men. Catherine Clinton, "Bloody Terrain: Freedwomen, Sexuality, and Violence during Reconstruction," *Georgia Historical Quarterly* 76, no. 2 (1992): 315–316. In the South, lynchings slightly outnumbered legal executions in the late nineteenth century. William J. Bowers et al., *Executions in America* (Lexington, MA: D. C. Heath, 1974), 40.

27. Johnson v. State, 63 Ga. 356 (Ga. 1879); Gaskin v. State, 105 Ga. 631 (Ga. 1898). See also Dorsey v. State 108 Ga. 477 (GA. 1899).

28. Michael J. Pfeifer, *Rough Justice: Lynching and American Society, 1874–1947* (Urbana: University of Illinois Press, 2004), 119; Brundage, *Lynching in the New South*, 67. "Girl Murdered in the Woods," *New York Times*, July 14, 1897, 2. On lynching outside the South, see Jean F. Riss, "The Lynching of

Francisco Torres," *Journal of Mexican American History* 2 (1972): 90–121; William Dean Carrigan, "Between South and West: Race, Violence, and Power in Central Texas, 1836–1916" (PhD diss., Emory University, 1999); and Waldrep, *Many Faces of Judge Lynch,* 215n26. On female victims, see Kerry Segrave, *Lynchings of Women in the United States: The Recorded Cases, 1851–1946* (Jefferson, NC: McFarland, 2010).

29. Inter- and intraracial lynching of blacks peaked around 1892–1893, but black-on-black lynching declined more sharply after 1900 than did white-on-black lynching. E. M. Beck and Stewart E. Tolnay, "When Race Didn't Matter: Black and White Mob Violence against Their Own Color," in Brundage, *Under Sentence of Death,* 136–142.

30. "Negroes Lynch One of Their Race," *New York Times,* June 5, 1900, 11; "Negroes Lynch a Negro," *New York Times,* August 19, 1900, 4; "A Black Mob Lynches a Criminal," *Atlanta Constitution,* November 16, 1897, 3.

31. Brundage, *Lynching in the New South,* 89–95, and 270–280 (appendix A, table 22); Dorr, *White Women, Rape, and the Power of Race,* 17; Beck and Tolnay, "When Race Didn't Matter," 144–148.

32. The *New York Times* considered the case notable as "the first in which a white man was lynched by negroes for assaulting a colored girl." "Lynched by Negroes," *New York Times,* July 12, 1888, 5. See also Bruce E. Baker, "Lynch Law Reversed: The Rape of Lula Sherman, the Lynching of Manse Waldrop, and the Debate over Lynching in the 1880s," *American Nineteenth Century History* 6, no. 3 (2005): 273–293.

33. "Vardaman Answers Questions," *Savannah Tribune,* September 29, 1906, 8.

34. *New Orleans Times-Democrat* quoted in Pfeifer, *Rough Justice,* 116–117; Atticus G. Haygood, "The Black Shadow in the South," *Forum,* October 1893, 167–175; Graves quoted in Hall, *Revolt against Chivalry,* 147.

35. Waldrep, *Many Faces of Judge Lynch,* 128; "Vardaman Answers Questions," *Savannah Tribune,* September 29, 1906, 8; "Lynching in Georgia," *New York Times,* September 16, 1897, 6; *Savannah News,* quoted in "The Indiana Lynching," *Atlanta Constitution,* September 20,1897, 4f; Edward L. Ayers, *Vengeance and Justice: Crime and Punishment in the 19th-Century American South* (New York: Oxford University Press, 1984), 240.

36. Virginia and St. Louis papers quoted in "Nothing Sectional in It," *Atlanta Constitution,* June 12, 1897, 7; "Southern Lynchings," *Atlanta Constitution,* May 13, 1892, 4. See also "The Mob's Protection," *Los Angeles Times,* September 28, 1897, 6; "Anti-Lynching Movement," *Chautauquan,* November 1894, 230.

37. Hall, *Revolt against Chivalry,* 150; "At the Stake," *Los Angeles Times,* February 21, 1892, 1; "Chained to Stake and Torch Applied," *Atlanta Constitution* August 12, 1901, 1; "Another Coon to Roast," *National Police Gazette,* January 30, 1886, 7.

38. "Outrages on Women and Children," *National Police Gazette,* February 11, 1882, 3; "He Will Be Lynched," *Atlanta Constitution,* February 29, 1892,

1; Waldrep, *Many Faces of Judge Lynch,* 96. On the acquittal of a black man who killed a black assailant, see "Killed by One of His Color," *Atlanta Constitution,* August 19, 1897, 1.
39. Baker, "Lynch Law Reversed," 286.

6. African Americans Redefine Sexual Violence

1. Ida B. Wells, *A Red Record,* reprinted in *Southern Horrors and Other Writings: The Anti-Lynching Campaign of Ida B. Wells, 1892–1900,* ed. and intro. Jacqueline Jones Royster (Boston: Bedford, 1997), 78, 80. On Wells's anti-lynching career, see Paula J. Giddings, *Ida: A Sword among Lions* (New York: HarperCollins, 2009).
2. Glenda Elizabeth Gilmore, *Gender and Jim Crow: Women and the Politics of White Supremacy in North Carolina, 1896–1920* (Chapel Hill: University of North Carolina Press, 1996), xix.
3. Cleveland, Ohio, *Gazette,* May 12, 1888, quoted in Allen W. Jones, "The Black Press in The 'New South': Jesse C. Duke's Struggle for Justice and Equality," *Journal of Negro History* 64, no. 3 (1979): 220. See also Jacqueline Goldsby, *A Spectacular Secret: Lynching in American Life and Literature* (Chicago: University of Chicago Press, 2006), 66–67.
4. Jones, "Black Press in the 'New South,'" 221–225; Philip Dray, *At the Hands of Persons Unknown: The Lynching of Black America* (New York: Random House, 2002), 125–126. See also Martha Hodes, *White Women, Black Men: Illicit Sex in the Nineteenth-Century South* (New Haven, CT: Yale University Press, 1997), 178–193; and Gilmore, *Gender and Jim Crow,* 105–113.
5. Ida B. Wells, *Southern Horrors: Lynch Law in All Its Phases,* reprinted in Royster, *Southern Horrors and Other Writings,* 66, 61; Mia Bay, *To Tell the Truth Freely: The Life of Ida B. Wells* (New York: Hill and Wang, 2009), 6. See also Patricia A. Schechter, *Ida B. Wells-Barnett and American Reform, 1880–1930* (Chapel Hill: University of North Carolina Press, 2001); and Goldsby, *A Spectacular Secret,* 48–49.
6. Crystal N. Feimster, *Southern Horrors: Women and the Politics of Rape and Lynching* (Cambridge, MA: Harvard University Press, 2009), 87; Royster, introduction to *Southern Horrors and Other Writings,* 3–4; Ida B. Wells, *Crusade for Justice: The Autobiography of Ida B. Wells,* ed. Alfreda M. Duster (Chicago: University of Chicago Press, 1970), 64.
7. Wells, *Southern Horrors,* 52, 66; Royster, introduction to *Southern Horrors and Other Writings,* 1; Ida B. Wells-Barnett, *On Lynchings* (1892; New York: Humanity Books, 2002), 29–31; "British Anti-Lynchers," *New York Times,* August 2, 1894, 4, pt. 2; J. W. Mans and John S. Durham, letter to the editor, "Not Representative of Her Race," *New York Times,* April 30, 1894, 2.
8. Wells, *Southern Horrors,* 61. See also Richard M. Perloff, "The Press and Lynchings of African Americans," *Journal of Black Studies* 30 no. 3 (2000): 315–330; and Goldsby, *A Spectacular Secret,* chap. 2. Subsequent scholars confirmed Wells's finding that only a minority of lynchings involved accusa-

tions of sexual assaults. Stewart Tolnay and E. M. Beck, *A Festival of Violence: An Analysis of Southern Lynchings, 1882–1930* (Urbana: University of Illinois Press, 1995).

9. Mia Bay, *To Tell the Truth Freely*, 127; Dray, *At the Hands of Persons Unknown*, 67; Wells, *Southern Horrors*, 53–54.

10. Wells, *Southern Horrors*, 70; "About Southern Lynchings," *Baltimore Herald*, October 20, 1895, Temperance and Prohibition Papers microfilm (1977), sec. 3, reel 42, scrapbook 70, frame 153.

11. From Our Editor, *Savannah Tribune*, July 29, 1899, 2; "Colored Press on Lynchings," *Savannah Tribune*, June 19, 1897, 2; M. A. Majors, MD, "A Swipe at Bishop Haygood: The Light Turned On—Short but Caustic and to the Point," *Christian Recorder*, November 30, 1893, 1. On Wells's radicalism, see Giddings, *Ida: A Sword among Lions*, 228–229, 318, 348–349.

12. "The Manager's Weekly Letter," *Christian Recorder*, June 24, 1897, 3; "Lynching Unlawful," *Savannah Tribune*, July 28, 1894, 2; R. B. Brooks, "Race Trouble from Key West, Florida," letter to the editor, *Christian Recorder*, July 22, 1897, 1.

13. Booker T. Washington, "The South and Lynch Law," *Congregationalist*, August 31, 1893, 282; Rev. J. G. Robinson, "Rape and Lynching," *Christian Recorder*, July 22, 1897, 1.

14. "Let Colored Men Be on Their Guard . . . ," *Christian Recorder*, July 29, 1897, 2; Gilmore, *Gender and Jim Crow*, 62–63; Thomas B. Lillard, "Communicated," *Savannah Tribune*, 1904, 2. On ideas about black manhood, see Gilmore, *Gender and Jim Crow*, chap. 3; and Martin Summers, *Manliness and Its Discontents: The Black Middle Class and the Transformation of Masculinity, 1900–1930* (Chapel Hill: University of North Carolina Press, 2004).

15. Mary Church Terrell, "Lynching from a Negro's Point of View," *North American Review*, June 1904, 853; Booker T. Washington, "The South and Lynch Law," *Congregationalist*, August 31, 1893, 282. On racial uplift, see Kevin K. Gaines, *Uplifting the Race: Black Leadership, Politics, and Culture in the Twentieth Century* (Chapel Hill: University of North Carolina Press, 1996).

16. "Editor T. Thomas Fortune . . . ," *Savannah Tribune*, October 16, 1897, 2; "Murderers Burn the Body," *Savannah Tribune*, December 7, 1895, 1.

17. *Florida Sentinel* quoted in "Colored Press on Lynchings," *Savannah Tribune*, June 19, 1897, 2; *Savannah Tribune*, June 6, 1896, 2. On the rhetoric of civilization, see Gail Bederman, *Manliness and Civilization: A Cultural History of Gender and Race in the United States, 1880–1917* (Chicago: University of Chicago Press, 1995).

18. "Message on Lynch Law," *Savannah Tribune*, November 9, 1895, 2; *Savannah Tribune*, June 6, 1896, 2, and December 12, 1896, 2; Wells, *A Red Record*, 155; "For the Investigation of Acts of Unlawful Violence," *Woman's Era* 1, no. 8 (November 1894), reprinted online at Emory Women Writers Resource Project, Women's Advocacy Collection, http://womenwriters .library.emory.edu/advocacy/ (all further citations to the *Woman's Era* appear in this source); Robert L. Zangrando, "The NAACP and a Federal

Antilynching Bill, 1934–1940," *Journal of Negro History* 50, no. 2 (1965): 108; Linda O. McMurry, *To Keep the Waters Troubled: The Life of Ida B. Wells* (New York: Oxford University Press, 2000), 230.

19. Wells, *Southern Horrors,* 61 (emphasis in original); Terrell, "Lynching from a Negro's Point of View," 853–854.
20. Wells, *A Red Record,* 107; "Foes at Home and Friends Abroad," *Christian Recorder,* May 25, 1893, 4; Terrell, "Lynching from a Negro's Point of View," 861.
21. "The Negro Question," *Independent: Devoted to the Consideration of Politics, Social and Economic Tendencies, History, Literature, and the Arts,* October 1, 1903, 2308.
22. "Last Week Our Morning Contemporary . . . ," *Savannah Tribune,* October 21, 1893, 2; *Savannah Tribune,* October 28, 1899, 2; Leslie K. Dunlap, "The Reform of Rape Law and the Problem of White Men: Age-of-Consent Campaigns in the South, 1885–1910," in *Sex, Love, Race: Crossing Boundaries in North American History,* ed. Martha Hodes (New York: New York University Press, 1999), 356.
23. Feimster, *Southern Horrors,* 137–141; Edward L. Ayers, *Vengeance and Justice: Crime and Punishment in the 19th-Century American South* (New York: Oxford University Press, 1984), 248; "Southern Lynching," *Nation,* November 2, 1893, 322–323.
24. "Our Women," *New York Freeman,* January 1, 1887, reprinted in *The Memphis Diary of Ida B. Wells,* ed. Miriam DaCosta-Willis (Boston: Beacon Press, 1995), 185–186.
25. Evelynn M. Hammonds, "Towards a Genealogy of Black Female Sexuality: The Problematic of Silence," in *Feminist Genealogies, Colonial Legacies, Democratic Futures,* ed. M. Jacqui Alexander and Chandra Talpade Mohanty (New York: Routledge, 1997), 175–176; Darlene Clark Hine, "Rape and the Inner Lives of Black Women in the Middle-West: Preliminary Thoughts on the Culture of Dissemblance," *Signs* 14, no. 4 (1989): 912–920.
26. Anna J. Cooper, *A Voice from the South* (Xenia, OH: Aldine Printing House, 1892), 24–25; A Southern Colored Woman, "The Race Problem—An Autobiography," *Independent,* March 17, 1904, 586; Hazel Carby, *Reconstructing Womanhood: The Emergence of the Afro-American Woman Novelist* (New York: Oxford University Press, 1987), 130–133; Sandra Gunning, *Race, Rape, and Lynching: The Red Record of American Literature, 1890–1912* (New York: Oxford University Press, 1996), 96ff.
27. "A Charge to Be Refuted," *Woman's Era* 2, no. 3 (June 1895). In a letter to the Anti-Lynching Society of England, Jacks, who was the president of the Missouri Press Association, made charges that Ruffin considered "so sweeping and so base" that the *Woman's Era* asked male and female race leaders to reply. See also Bay, *To Tell the Truth Freely,* 221.
28. Josephine St. P. Ruffin, "Address of Josephine St. P. Ruffin, President of Conference," *Woman's Era* 2, no. 5 (August 1895); Mary Church Terrell,

"In Union There Is Strength," in Beverly Eliza Jones, *Quest for Equality: The Life and Writings of Mary Eliza Church Terrell* (Brooklyn: Carlson, 1990), 133–138.

29. Terrell, "Lynching from a Negro's Point of View," 865; Pauline Elizabeth Hopkins, *Contending Forces: A Romance Illustrative of Negro Life North and South* (1900; repr., Oxford: Oxford University Press, 1988), 271 (emphasis in original); Carby, *Reconstructing Womanhood,* 141.

30. Sylvanie Francaz Williams, "The Social Status of the Negro Woman," *Voice of the Negro,* July 7, 1904, 299.

31. "Our Women," 186; Wells, *A Red Record,* 80.

32. "Mob Law in Detroit," *Christian Recorder,* March 14, 1863, 2; "The Case Dismissed," *Savannah Tribune,* September 9, 1893, 3; "Scipio Americanus," *Savannah Tribune,* September 9, 1893, 2. See also "Communicated," *Savannah Tribune,* June 20, 1896, 3.

33. Wells, *Southern Horrors,* 58–59; Wells, *A Red Record,* 80.

34. Wells, *A Red Record,* 127; Ridley quoted in Mary E. Odem, *Delinquent Daughters: Protecting and Policing Adolescent Female Sexuality in the United States, 1885–1920* (Chapel Hill: University of North Carolina Press, 1995), 30; Burroughs quoted in Christina Simmons, *Making Marriage Modern: Women's Sexuality from the Progressive Era to World War II* (New York: Oxford University Press, 2009), 22.

35. "Report: The National Colored Woman's Congress," *Woman's Era* 2, no. 9 (January 1896); see also "Report: Separate Car Law," *Woman's Era* 2, no. 10 (February 1896).

36. Addie Hunton, "Negro Womanhood Defended," *Voice of the Negro: An Illustrated Monthly Magazine,* July 1904, 281.

37. "Report: The National Colored Woman's Congress"; Fannie Barrier Williams, "A Northern Negro's Autobiography," *Independent,* July 14, 1904, 96; Hine, "Rape and the Inner Lives of Black Women," 918; Michelle Mitchell, *Righteous Propagation: African Americans and the Politics of Racial Destiny after Reconstruction* (Chapel Hill: University of North Carolina Press, 2004), 198.

38. Hine, "Rape and the Inner Lives of Black Women."

39. Victoria Earle Matthews quoted in Carby, *Reconstructing Womanhood,* 118; *A Brighter Coming Day: A Frances Ellen Watkins Harper Reader,* ed. Frances Smith Foster (New York: Feminist Press, 1990), 345–346. See also Dunlap, "Reform of Rape Law," 354.

40. Burroughs quoted in Crystal Nicole Feimster, "Ladies and Lynching: The Gendered Discourse of Mob Violence in the New South, 1880–1930," (PhD diss., Princeton University, 2000), 277.

41. Frances E. Willard, "The Lynching Question," *Fraternity,* October 1, 1895, Temperance and Prohibition Papers microfilm (1977), sec 3, reel 32, scrapbook 13, frame 213.

42. A. S. Blackwell, "The Penalty for Rape," *Woman's Column,* August 22, 1903, 3; Schofield quoted in Dunlap, "Reform of Rape Law," 363.

43. Bay, *To Tell the Truth Freely*, 186–187; Jane E. Larson, "'Even a Worm Will Turn at Last': Rape Reform in Late Nineteenth-Century America," *Yale Journal of Law & the Humanities* 9, no. 1 (1997): 51; Wells, *A Red Record*, 67. See also Vron Ware, *Beyond the Pale: White Women, Racism and History* (London: Verso, 1992), 205–208; Wells, *Crusade for Justice*, 111–112.

44. Frances Elizabeth Caroline Willard, "President's Address," in *Minutes of the National Woman's Christian Temperance Union, at the Twenty-first Annual Meeting, Held in Cleveland, Ohio, 16–21 November, 1894* (Chicago: Woman's Temperance Publication Association, 1894).

45. "Miss Willard in Boston" and "Miss Willard and the Colored People," *Woman's Era* 1, no. 4 (July 1894); "Lady Somerset and Miss Willard Confess of Themselves Apologists for Lynching," *Woman's Era* 2, no. 5 (August 1895). For detailed accounts of the feud between Wells and Willard, see Ware, *Beyond the Pale*, chap. 4; Bay, *To Tell the Truth Freely*, 206–210; Feimster, *Southern Horrors*, 108–109.

46. Bederman, *Manliness and Civilization*, 65–66.

47. Wells, *Southern Horrors*, 53–54.

48. Gunning, *Race, Rape, and Lynching*, 11.

7. Raising the Age of Consent

1. Pounds v. State, 20 S.E. 247 (Ga. 1894). Earlier Georgia Supreme Court rulings had affirmed convictions of men for the rape of girls aged seven through thirteen—e.g., Dunn v. State, 56 Ga. 401 (Ga. 1876). See also Johnson v. State, 61 Ga. 35 (Ga. 1878); Joiner v. State, 62 Ga. 560 (Ga. 1879). The Georgia Supreme Court reversed in other cases, such as Simmons v. State, 99 Ga. 699 (Ga. 1896), which invoked Lord Hale to overturn a conviction for the rape of a young girl.

2. "To Protect Young Girls," *Chicago Daily Tribune*, February 17, 1905, 6.

3. Mary E. Odem, *Delinquent Daughters: Protecting and Policing Adolescent Female Sexuality in the United States, 1885–1920* (Chapel Hill: University of North Carolina Press, 1995), table 1, 14–15.

4. Mary R. Block, "'An Accusation Easily to Be Made': A History of Rape Law in Nineteenth-Century State Appellate Courts, 1800–1870" (master's thesis, University of Louisville, 1992), 14–15, 43–45, 62–76; Mary R. Block, "'An Accusation Easily to Be Made': A History of Rape Law in Nineteenth-Century America" (PhD diss., University of Kentucky, 2001), 43–45, 161–162; Constance Backhouse, "Nineteenth-Century Canadian Rape Law, 1800–92," in *Essays in the History of Canadian Law*, ed. D. Flaherty vol. 2 (Toronto: University of Toronto Press, 1981), 201; Diane Miller Sommerville, *Rape and Race in the Nineteenth-Century South* (Chapel Hill: University of North Carolina Press, 2004), 45, 70.

5. Timothy J. Gilfoyle, *City of Eros: New York City, Prostitution, and the Commercialization of Sex, 1790–1920* (New York: Norton, 1992), 349n34; Ste-

phen Robertson, *Crimes against Children: Sexual Violence and Legal Culture in New York City, 1880–1960* (Chapel Hill: University of North Carolina Press, 2005), 237 (table 2); Sharon E. Wood, *The Freedom of the Streets: Work, Citizenship, and Sexuality in a Gilded Age City* (Chapel Hill: University of North Carolina Press, 2005), 139.

6. Block, "'An Accusation Easily to Be Made'" (PhD diss.), 126–128.

7. Estelle B. Freedman, "'Crimes Which Startle and Horrify': Gender, Age, and the Racialization of Sexual Violence in White American Newspapers, 1870–1900," *Journal of History of Sexuality* 20, no. 3 (2011): 493 (table 3).

8. "Fiendish Outrage on a Child," *New York Times,* September 16, 1882, 5; "Two Rapists Lynched," *National Police Gazette,* September 13, 1879, 5; "A Brute Told to Move On," *New York Times,* August 14, 1888, 8; "Cowhided by Women," *Los Angeles Times,* June 2, 1892, 8; "Attempted Rape," *Atlanta Constitution,* May 19, 1877, 1; "Lynching Barely Prevented," *New York Times,* September 2, 189, 6; "Wild Scene before Judge McGuire," illustration, *National Police Gazette,* September 17, 1892, 5; "Fifty Years," *Los Angeles Times,* November 6, 1887, 3; "Justice in California," *New York Times,* April 15, 1872, 2; see also "A Depraved Wretch," *Los Angeles Times,* May 23, 1892, 8.

9. "A Negro's Brutal Crime," *New York Times,* August 24, 1883, 1; Victor Jew, "'Chinese Demons': The Violent Articulation of Chinese Otherness and Interracial Sexuality in the U.S. Midwest, 1885–1889," *Journal of Social History* 32, no. 2 (2003): 389–410.

10. Michael Ryan, *A Manual of Medical Jurisprudence* (Philadelphia: Cary and Lea, 1832), 162; Susan Gonda, "Strumpets and Angels: Rape, Seduction, and the Boundaries of Consensual Sex in the Northeast, 1789–1870" (PhD diss., UCLA, 1999), 172.

11. Gonda, "Strumpets and Angels," 173; Jerome Walker, "Reports, with Comments, of Twenty-One Cases of Indecent Assault and Rape upon Children," *Archives of Pediatrics* 3, no. 5 (May 1886): 277; Lynn Sacco, *Unspeakable: Father-Daughter Incest in American History* (Baltimore: Johns Hopkins University Press, 2009), 83, 106.

12. Sacco, *Unspeakable,* 104, 78–86. See also Robertson, *Crimes against Children,* 43.

13. Tubervile v. State, 4 Tex. 128 (Texas 1849); Taylor v. State, 35 S.E. 161, 164 (GA 1900). Taylor was also charged with intent to murder because he tried to procure an abortifacient for his stepdaughter.

14. "San Bernardino County . . . The Incest Fiend Let Off with a Very Light Punishment," *Los Angeles Times,* May 13, 1892, 7; Peter W. Bardaglio, *Reconstructing the Household: Families, Sex, and the Law in the Nineteenth-Century South* (Chapel Hill: University of North Carolina Press, 1995), 48; Sacco, *Unspeakable,* 35; Vivien M. L. Miller, *Crime, Sexual Violence, and Clemency: Florida's Pardon Board and the Penal System in the Progressive Era* (Gainesville: University Press of Florida, 2000), 212.

15. Smith v. State 12 Ohio St. 466, 466–468 (Ohio 1861); Block, "'An Accusation Easily to Be Made'" (master's thesis), 55–61. See also O'Meara v. State 17 Ohio St. 515, 519–520 (Ohio 1867); State v. Connelly, 59 N.W. 479, 486 (Minn. 1894), quoted in Susan Estrich, *Real Rape* (Cambridge, MA: Harvard University Press, 1987), 44.

16. Dunn v. State, 56 Ga. 401 (Ga. 1876); Joiner v. State, 62 Ga. 560 (Ga. 1879). See also Jones v. State. 68 Ga. 760 (Ga. 1882); Jones v. State, 34 S.E. 174, 175 (Ga. 1899). In dissent, Judge Lumpkin wrote that the evidence shows "too strongly both physical and mental capacity on the part of the female to consent to sexual intercourse . . . she did not really resist the accused, and her conduct amounted to consent." Jones, 34 S.E. at 176.

17. E.g., Johnson v. State, 76 Ga. 76 (Ga. 1885); Brown v. State, 76 Ga. 623 (Ga. 1886); Gaines v. State, 26 S.E. 760 (Ga. 1896); Seymour v. State, 30 S.E. 263 (Ga. 1898). The Georgia Supreme Court reversed convictions of rape charges brought by girls under the age of fourteen at about the same overall rate of reversals in the late nineteenth century (about half), but at a lower rate (one-fourth, compared to 30 percent of all rape cases) in the early twentieth century.

18. Block, "'An Accusation Easily to Be Made'" (PhD diss.), 156; Holly Brewer, *By Birth or Consent: Children, Law, and the Anglo-American Revolution in Authority* (Chapel Hill: University of North Carolina Press, 2007), 332.

19. Stephen Robertson, "'Boys, of Course, Cannot Be Raped': Age, Homosexuality, and the Redefinition of Sexual Violence in New York City, 1880–1955," *Gender & History* 18, no. 2 (2006): 360; Elizabeth Pleck, *Domestic Tyranny: The Making of Social Policy against Family Violence from Colonial Times to the Present* (New York: Oxford University Press, 1987), chap. 4; Linda Gordon, *Heroes of Their Own Lives: The Politics and History of Family Violence* (New York: Viking, 1988), chap. 7; Sherri Broder, *Tramps, Unfit Mothers, and Neglected Children: Negotiating the Family in Nineteenth-Century Philadelphia* (Philadelphia: University of Pennsylvania Press, 2002), 120.

20. Judith R. Walkowitz, *Prostitution and Victorian Society: Women, Class, and the State* (New York: Cambridge University Press, 1980); David J. Pivar, *Purity Crusade: Sexual Morality and Social Control, 1868–1900* (Westport: Greenwood Press, 1973); Stephen Robertson, "Age of Consent Law and the Making of Modern Childhood in New York City, 1886–1921," *Journal of Social History* 35, no. 4 (2002): 784.

21. Judith R. Walkowitz, *City of Dreadful Delight: Narratives of Sexual Danger in Late-Victorian London* (Chicago: University of Chicago Press, 1992), 101–105; Odem, *Delinquent Daughters,* 12; Leslie K. Dunlap, "The Reform of Rape Law and the Problem of White Men: Age-of-Consent Campaigns in the South, 1885–1910," in *Sex, Love, Race: Crossing Boundaries in North American History,* ed. Martha Hodes (New York: New York University Press, 1999), 360–362.

22. Ruth Bordin, *Woman and Temperance: The Quest for Power and Liberty, 1873–1900* (Philadelphia: Temple University Press, 1981), 3–14.

23. "Petition of the Woman's Christian Temperance Union for the Protection of Women to Congress," quoted in Odem, *Delinquent Daughters*, 9.

24. Odem, *Delinquent Daughters*, 16; J. E. Rowen, "Protection for Immature Girlhood," in "Opposing Views by Legislators on the Age of Consent: A Symposium," *Arena*, July 1895, 217–218; Helen H. Gardener, "What Shall the Age of Consent Be?," in "The Shame of America—The Age of Consent Laws in the United States: A Symposium," *Arena*, January 1895, 201. Gardener became vice president of the National American Woman Suffrage Association in 1917. Adelaid Washburn, "Helen Hamilton Gardner," *Notable American Women: A Biographical Dictionary*, vol. 2, ed. Edward T. James (Cambridge, MA: Belknap Press, 1971), 11–13.

25. Senator G. W. Granberry, "The 'Age-of-Consent' Act in the General Assembly of the State of Arkansas," *Arena*, November 1895, 405; "Oregon," *Arena*, October 1895, 210; "Protection for Immature Girlhood," *Arena*, July 1895, 218.

26. Jane E. Larson, "'Even a Worm Will Turn at Last': Rape Reform in Late Nineteenth-Century America," *Yale Journal of Law & the Humanities* 9, no. 1 (1997): 33–40, 47; Dorcas James Spencer, *A History of the Woman's Christian Temperance Union of Northern and Central California* (Oakland: West Coast Printing Co., 1913), 112; Susan B. Anthony and Ida Husted Harper, eds., *The History of Woman Suffrage*, vol. 4 (Rochester: Susan B. Anthony, 1902), 687. Calls to include castration as a punishment generally failed. See, e.g., Dr. R. B. Leach, "A Physician's Standpoint," *Arena*, April 1895, 285; Block, "'An Accusation Easily to Be Made'" (PhD diss.), 208–210.

27. P. P. "Decision Diabolical!," *Revolution*, July 29, 1869, 56–57.

28. Augusta H. Howard, "A 'Thinker' Shown to Be Unthinking," *Woman's Tribune*, March 19, 1892, 2–3; Charles K. Whipple, "Twenty-One the Age of Consent," *Woman's Journal*, April 10, 1886, 118–119; Henry B. Blackwell, "Equal Suffrage vs. Prostitution," in *The National Purity Congress: Its Papers, Addresses, Portraits*, ed. Aaron Macy Powell (New York: American Purity Alliance, 1896; repr. New York: Arno Press, 1976), 425. Not all male supporters favored suffrage—e.g., Leach, "A Physician's Standpoint," 282–285.

29. "Protection for Girls," *Woman's Standard*, May 1889, 3.

30. Ibid.

31. Helen H. Gardener, "A Battle for Sound Morality," *Arena*, November 1895, 402 (emphasis in original); Alexander Keyssar, *The Right to Vote: The Contested History of Democracy in the United States* (New York: Basic Books, 2000), 131–132. See also Jeff Manza and Christopher Uggen, *Locked Out: Felon Disenfranchisement and American Democracy* (New York: Oxford University Press, 2006).

32. "Unjust Laws—Iowa," *Woman's Standard*, June 1899, 28; "An Important Judicial Decision," *Woman's Tribune*, December 17, 1887, 1; S. E. B., "The

Outlook on Age of Consent," *Woman's Journal,* April 20, 1895, 122. See also Vie H. Campbell, "Why an Age of Consent?," *Arena,* April 1895, 285–288; and Frances E. Willard, "Arousing the Public Conscience," *Arena,* January 1895, 198–202. On the metaphors of property in liberal discourse, see Pamela Haag, *Consent: Sexual Rights and the Transformation of American Liberalism* (Ithaca, NY: Cornell University Press, 1999), 35–36

33. Dunlap, "Reform of Rape Law," 358–359; Larson, "'Even a Worm Will Turn,'" 29.

34. Campbell, "Why an Age of Consent?"; Larson, "'Even a Worm Will Turn,'" 42; Gardener, "Battle for Sound Morality," 409; Will Allen Dromgoole, "The Age of Consent in Tennessee," in "The Shame of America—The Age of Consent Laws in the United States: A Symposium," *Arena,* January 1895, 212.

35. Emily Blackwell, MD, "Another Physician Speaks," in "The Shame of America," 212; "Laws Passed in American Suffrage States," *International Women's News,* December 12, 1913, i, ii, iv; Spencer, *A History,* 112.

36. Dunlap, "Reform of Rape Law," 358; *The Woman Citizens Library: A Systematic Course of Reading in Preparation for the Larger Citizenship* (Chicago: Civics Society, 1913), 1948; Crystal N. Feimster, *Southern Horrors: Women and the Politics of Rape and Lynching* (Cambridge, MA: Harvard University Press, 2009), 198–202.

37. Tompkins in "Opposing Views by Legislators on the Age of Consent," 220; C. C. Mapes, "Higher Enlightenment Versus 'Age of Consent,'" *Medical Age* 14 (February 26, 1896): 105–108; Robinson in "Opposing Views by Legislators on the Age of Consent," 211; Dromgoole, "Age of Consent in Tennessee."

38. The revised Colorado law treated consensual underage sex as third-degree rape, punished less harshly than forcible rape. Larson, "'Even a Worm Will Turn,'" 36, 61; Dunlap, "Reform of Rape Law," 360; Mary E. Bates, "The Law on Rape in Colorado," *Woman's Medical Journal* 15, no. 1 (January 1905): 9–12; Gardener, "Battle for Sound Morality," 208.

39. State v. White, 25 P. 33, 33 (Kan. 1890), quoted in "Constitutional Law Statute Crimes and Punishments: Rape," *Central Law Journal* 31, no. 24 (December 12, 1890): 478. For other examples of equality arguments, see Larson, "'Even a Worm Will Turn,'" 56–59.

40. G. W. Granberry, "The 'Age-of-Consent' Act in the General Assembly of the State of Arkansas," in Gardener, "Battle for Sound Morality," 403–405; "Opposing Views by Legislators on the Age of Consent," 216; Tennessee legislator quoted in Dunlap, "Reform of Rape Law," 360.

41. Dunlap, "Reform of Rape Law," 361; "Opposing Views by Legislators on the Age of Consent," 223; Neil R. McMillen, *Dark Journey: Black Mississippians in the Age of Jim Crow* (Urbana: University of Illinois Press, 1989), 18. On Texas, see Helen M. Stoddard, "Review of the Age-of-Consent Legislation in Texas," in Gardner, "Battle for Sound Morality," 408–411.

42. Dunlap, "Reform of Rape Law," 362.
43. Ibid., 362–364; Odem, *Delinquent Daughters,* 28; Larson, " 'Even a Worm Will Turn,' " 48.
44. Dunlap, "Reform of Rape Law," 353; Gilmore, *Gender and Jim Crow,* 45–50; see, for example, Rev. R. A. Adams, *The Negro Girl* (Kansas City: Independent Press, 1915), esp. 76, 84–85.
45. Lillian Harman, "An 'Age-of-Consent' Symposium," *Liberty (Not the Daughter but the Mother of Order)* 10, no. 20 (February 9, 1895): 2; Larson, " 'Even a Worm Will Turn,' " 59; Joanne E. Passet, *Sex Radicals and the Quest for Women's Equality* (Urbana: University of Illinois Press, 2003), 138; T., "Anarchy and Rape," *Liberty (Not the Daughter but the Mother of Order)* 5, no. 7 (March 31, 1888): 4.
46. Lillian Harman, "Another 'Age-of-Consent' Symposium," *Liberty (Not the Daughter but the Mother of Order)* 11, no. 2 (June 1, 1895): 6; Harman, "An 'Age-of-Consent' Symposium," 3.
47. Harman, "An 'Age-of-Consent' Symposium," 2; Harman, "Another 'Age-of-Consent' Symposium," 6.
48. T., "Anarchy and Rape," 4.
49. Larson, " 'Even a Worm Will Turn,' " 20.
50. Ibid., 63, 66; Dunlap, "Reform of Rape Law," 353. For other evaluations of the laws, see Backhouse, "Nineteenth-Century Canadian Rape Law, 1800–92"; Odem, *Delinquent Daughters;* Kathleen R. Parker, " 'To Protect the Chastity of Children Under Sixteen': Statutory Rape Prosecutions in a Midwest County Circuit Court, 1850–1950," *Michigan Historical Review* 20, no. 1 (1994): 57; and for a broader critique, see Steven Schlossman and Stephanie Wallach, "The Crime of Precocious Sexuality: Female Juvenile Delinquency in the Progressive Era," *Harvard Educational Review* 48, no. 1 (1978): 65–94.

8. From Protection to Sexualization

1. People v. Lee, 51 P. 22, 22 (Cal. 1897); People v. Edwards, 127 P. 58, 60 (Cal. 1912). See also People v. Benc, 62 P. 404, 405 (Cal. 1900), and People v. Vann, 61 P. 776 (Cal. 1900); People v. Verdegreen, 39 P. 607, 609 (Cal. 1895); People v. Totman, 67 P. 51, 52 (Cal. 1901); People v. Vann, 61 P. 776, 777 (Cal. 1900); People v. Babcock, 117 P. 549, 549 (Cal. 1911).
2. California increased the age of consent to sixteen in 1897 and to eighteen in 1913. Thirty percent of rape convictions considered by the California Supreme Court from 1870 to 1899 involved girls between the ages of eleven and eighteen. After 1905 the newly established Court of Appeal handled most rape cases. Sixty-five percent of the rape convictions reviewed in both courts between 1890 and 1909 involved girls aged eleven to eighteen. All data for California, New York, and Georgia appellate courts are based on calculations from Lexis-Nexis database searches of state court rulings.

3. Kathleen R. Parker, "'To Protect the Chastity of Children Under Sixteen': Statutory Rape Prosecutions in a Midwest County Circuit Court, 1850–1950," *Michigan Historical Review* 20, no. 1 (1994): 75 (table 1); Kathleen Ruth Parker, "Law, Culture, and Sexual Censure: Sex Crime Prosecutions in a Midwest County Circuit Court, 1850–1950" (PhD diss., Michigan State University, 1993), 471 (table 2), 470 (table 1). The increase in the number of cases far exceeded population growth in the county.

4. Lynn Sacco, *Unspeakable: Father-Daughter Incest in American History* (Baltimore: Johns Hopkins University Press, 2009), 50; Parker, "Law, Culture, and Sexual Censure," 488 (table 20) (an increase from four to twelve cases).

5. The New York Court of Appeals and Supreme Court ruled on one incest case prior to 1888 and on eight between 1896 and 1917, affirming all but three convictions. California appellate courts reviewed twenty-three incest cases between 1850 and 1930 (excluding intrafamilial rape charges not identified as incest). After passage of the Georgia statutory rape law in 1918, incest appeals declined precipitously, suggesting that the wave of interest may have passed by the time the state raised the age of consent.

6. "Rape—Evidence—Sufficiency—State v. Katon, 91 Pac. (Wash.) 250," *Yale Law Journal* 17, no. 3 (1908): 212. The Georgia law incorporated a corroboration requirement, and the appellate court reversed convictions for lack of evidence of resistance. J. B. Pratt, "The Demise of the Corroboration Requirement: Its History in Georgia Rape Law," *Emory Law Journal* 26 (1977): 805–839; Davis v. The State, 152 Ga. 320, 110 S.E. 18 (Ga. 1921); Sacks v. United States, 41 App. D.C. 34 (U.S. App. 1913).

7. People v. Verdegreen, 39 P. 607, 608 (Cal. 1895).

8. People v. Kuches, 52 P. 1002 (Cal. 1898). See also Sharon Ullman, *Sex Unseen: The Emergence of Modern Sexuality in America* (Berkeley: University of California Press, 1997), 29–31, on the original 1896 cases. Other state appellate courts also upheld convictions when a girl over the legal age of consent seemed immature. Mary R. Block, "'An Accusation Easily to Be Made': A History of Rape Law in Nineteenth-Century America" (PhD diss., University of Kentucky, 2001), 199–200.

9. People v. Williams, 142 P. 124, 125 (Cal. App. 3 Dist. 1914); People v. Parrish, 143 P. 546 (Cal. App. 3 Dist. 1914); Lawrence M. Friedman and Robert V. Percival, *The Roots of Justice: Crime and Punishment in Alameda County, California, 1870–1910* (Chapel Hill: University of North Carolina Press, 1981), 207.

10. For the New York Supreme Court, appellate rape cases involving girls under age eighteen increased from one-third of the six appeals between 1870 and 1889 to two-thirds of the thirty appeals between 1890 and 1909. In both periods the court reversed convictions at a higher rate for statutory than for forcible rape.

11. People v. Dohring, 59 N.Y. 374, 375, 382 (N.Y. 1874).

12. People v. Connor, 27 N.E. 252, 253–254 (N.Y. 1891).

13. Sarah Deutsch, *Women and the City: Gender, Space, and Power in Boston, 1870–1940* (New York: Oxford University Press, 2000), chap. 3; Joanne J. Meyerowitz, *Women Adrift: Independent Wage Earners in Chicago, 1880–1930* (Chicago: University of Chicago Press, 1987); Kathy Lee Peiss, *Cheap Amusements: Working Women and Leisure in Turn-of-the-Century New York* (Philadelphia: Temple University Press, 1986); Mary E. Odem, *Delinquent Daughters: Protecting and Policing Adolescent Female Sexuality in the United States, 1885–1920* (Chapel Hill: University of North Carolina Press, 1995), 53–56.

14. Joan Jacobs Brumberg, *The Body Project: An Intimate History of American Girls* (New York: Random House, 1997), 3–5.

15. "San Diego County," *Los Angeles Times,* October 19, 1897, 11; People v. Vann, 61 P. 776 (Cal. 1900).

16. People v. Derbert, 138 Cal. 467, 71 P. 564 (Cal. 1903). See also Jones v. State, 106 Ga. 365, 34 S.E. 174, 175 (Ga. 1899); McCombs v. State, 148 Ga. 304 (Ga. 1918); "Courthouse Notes," *Los Angeles Times,* October 23, 1904, A6.

17. People v. Mayne, 118 Cal. 516, 50 P. 654 (Cal. 1897); People v. Howard, 143 Cal. 316, 76 P. 1116 (Cal. 1904). See also New York v. Benjamin Lammes, 208 A.D. 533; 203 N.Y.S. 736 (N.Y. App. Div. 1924); NY v. Marks, 146 A.D. 11, 130 N.Y.S. 524 (N.Y. App. Div. 1911).

18. People v. Costa, 142 P. 508, 509 (Cal. App. 2 Dist. 1914).

19. Sharon E. Wood, *The Freedom of the Streets: Work, Citizenship, and Sexuality in a Gilded Age City* (Chapel Hill: University of North Carolina Press, 2005), 132–151.

20. "Crime and Criminals," *Los Angeles Times,* May 24, 1892, 3; "Price Prosecuted," *Los Angeles Times,* April 14, 1900, 7; "Big Bad Girl Committed to Whittier," *Los Angeles Times,* April 13, 1900, 10.

21. "A Terrible Tale," *Los Angeles Times,* September 23, 1897, 12; "A Rape Case Dismissed," *Los Angeles Times,* June 20, 1897, 24; "A Bad Bad Girl," *Los Angeles Times,* September 3, 1897, 14; "Led Gypsy Lives," *Los Angeles Times,* May 17, 1897, 7; "Lack of Morality," *Los Angeles Times,* May 18, 1897, 8; "Plotsam [*sic*] and Jetsam," *Los Angeles Times,* May 28, 1897, 9; and Parker, " 'To Protect the Chastity of Children,' " 66–67.

22. People v. Fong Chung, 91 P. 105, 108 (Cal. App. 1 Dist. 1907). The court also reversed the conviction of Ah Lean on similar grounds. People v. Ah Lean, 95 P. 380 (Cal. App. 1 Dist. 1908) but affirmed a conviction for consensual relations between a Chinese man and a white girl in People v. Ah Lung, 83 P. 296, 298 (Cal. App. 3 Dist. 1905).

23. New York v. Specks and Shearer, 173 A.D. 440, 159 N.Y.S. 308 (N.Y. App. Div. 1916).

24. Edward O. Janney, *The White Slave Traffic in America* (New York: National Vigilance Committee, 1911), 66, 60; "Mob Seeks Murderer," *Los Angeles Times,* December 6, 1920, 4; Kevin K. White, *The First Sexual Revolution:*

The Emergence of Male Heterosexuality in Modern America (New York: New York University Press, 1993), 90–94.

25. Steven Schlossman and Stephanie Wallach, "The Crime of Precocious Sexuality: Female Juvenile Delinquency in the Progressive Era," *Harvard Educational Review* 48, no. 1 (1978): 72–73; Estelle B. Freedman, *Their Sisters' Keepers: Women's Prison Reform in America, 1830–1930* (Ann Arbor: University of Michigan Press, 1981), 80–85, 37; Susan K. Cahn, *Sexual Reckonings: Girls in a Troubling Age* (Cambridge, MA: Harvard University Press, 2007), 88; Odem, *Delinquent Daughters,* 65–74.

26. Elizabeth Lunbeck, " 'A New Generation of Women': Progressive Psychiatrists and the Hypersexual Female," *Feminist Studies* 13, no. 3 (1987): 513–543. Max Huhner, "Rape and Satyriasis," *American Journal of Urology and Sexology* 14, no. 18 (1918): 362; Elizabeth Lunbeck, *The Psychiatric Persuasion: Knowledge, Gender, and Power in Modern America* (Princeton, NJ: Princeton University Press, 1994), 212. See also Carol Groneman, *Nymphomania: A History* (New York: W. W. Norton, 2000), chap. 4.

27. Estelle B. Freedman, " 'Uncontrolled Desires': The Response to the Sexual Psychopath, 1920–1960," *Journal of American History* 74, no. 1 (1987): 83–106; Lunbeck, " 'A New Generation of Women,' " 516, 535–536.

28. Elizabeth Pleck, *Domestic Tyranny: The Making of Social Policy against Family Violence from Colonial Times to the Present* (New York: Oxford University Press, 1987), 150–154; John E. B. Myers, *Evidence in Child Abuse and Neglect Cases,* 3rd ed., vol. 3 (New York: Wiley Law, 1997), 165–166; John Henry Wigmore, *A Supplement to a Treatise on the System of Evidence in Trials at Common Law* (Boston: Little, Brown, 1915), 202; John Henry Wigmore, *Supplement, 1923–1933: To the Second Edition (1923) of A Treatise on the System of Evidence in Trials at Common Law* (Boston: Little, Brown, 1934), sec. 924a at 379.

29. Travis Gibb, "Criminal Aspect of Venereal Diseases in Children," *Medical Record* 71, no. 16 (1907): 644; William Isaac Thomas, *The Unadjusted Girl: With Cases and Standpoint for Behavioral Analysis* (Boston: Little, Brown, 1923), 99, 125–126.

30. Gurney Williams, MD, "Rape in Children and in Young Girls," *International Clinics,* 23rd ser. (1913): 2:245–247, 259, 3:245–267.

31. Frank Winthrop Draper, "Rape," in *A Textbook of Legal Medicine* (Philadelphia: W. B. Saunders, 1905), 119–120, 123, 125.

32. Dr. F. R. Bronson, "A Case of Rape on a Young Girl," *American Journal of Urology and Sexology* 14, no. 2 (1918): 490–494; Bronson, "False Accusations of Rape," *American Journal of Urology and Sexology* 14, no. 2 (1918): 509–510; Bronson, "Miscellaneous Cases of Rape," *American Journal of Urology and Sexology* 15, no. 14 (1919): 151–160.

33. Gibb, "Criminal Aspect of Venereal Diseases," 645. See also Charles Gilbert Chaddock, "Sexual Crimes," in *A System of Legal Medicine,* vol. 2, ed. Allan McLane Hamilton and Lawrence Godkin, (New York: E. B. Treat and Co., 1894), 548;

34. Dr. J. L. Casper, "Daughter Accuses Her Own Father of Rape—Father Acquitted," *American Journal of Urology and Sexology* 15, no. 3 (1919): 104; Casper, "False Accusation of Rape: Young Girl Her Father's Regular Mistress," *American Journal of Urology and Sexology* 15, no. 16 (1919): 279. See also Dr. Jerome Walker, "Policeman Wrongly Accused of Rape" *American Journal of Urology and Sexology* 15, no. 16 (1919): 106.

35. Sacco, *Unspeakable*, 189–192.

36. Ibid., 136, 139; Linda Gordon, *Heroes of Their Own Lives: The Politics and History of Family Violence—Boston, 1880–1960* (Urbana: University of Illinois Press, 2002), 219; Jacob A. Goldberg and Rosamond W. Goldberg, *Girls on City Streets: A Study of 1400 Cases of Rape* (New York: American Social Hygiene Association, 1935; repr., New York: Arno Press, 1974), 295 (table 6). On women's studies of delinquent girls during the Progressive era, see Freedman, *Their Sisters' Keepers,* chap. 6.

37. Gordon, *Heroes of Their Own Lives,* 22; See also Lunbeck, *The Psychiatric Persuasion;* Pamela Haag, *Consent: Sexual Rights and the Transformation of American Liberalism* (Ithaca, NY: Cornell University Press, 1999), 164, 167–172.

38. Anonymous, "Seduction a Felony," *Philanthropist,* September 1888, 4; E. D. K. Jr., "History of the Changes in the Law on the Age of Consent," *Virginia Law Review* 11, no. 1 (1924): 83.

39. State v. White, 25 P. 33 (Kan. 1890), quoted in Weems v. United States, 217 U.S. 349 (1910); People v. Derbert, 138 Cal. 467, 71 P. 564 (Cal. 1903).

40. Odem, *Delinquent Daughters,* 77 (table 5); Stephen Robertson, *Crimes against Children: Sexual Violence and Legal Culture in New York City, 1880–1960* (Chapel Hill: University of North Carolina Press, 2005), 132. See also Ullman, *Sex Unseen,* 36.

41. Ullman, *Sex Unseen,* 40–41; Odem, *Delinquent Daughters,* 80–81 and 77 (table 5) ; Bonni Kay Cermak, "In the Interest of Justice: Legal Narratives of Sex, Gender, Race and Rape in Twentieth Century Los Angeles, 1920–1960" (PhD diss., University of Oregon, 2005), 89–94.

42. Pablo Mitchell, *Coyote Nation: Sexuality, Race, and Conquest in Modernizing New Mexico, 1880–1920* (Chicago: University of Chicago Press, 2005), 68–75. For examples of appellate courts overturning convictions of Mexican Americans for rape, see Pablo Mitchell, *West of Sex: Making Mexican America, 1900–1930* (Chicago: University of Chicago Press, 2012), 26–33.

43. Cermak, "In the Interest of Justice," 54–59, 84–89, 98, 104, 110–118; Mitchell, *West of Sex,* 33; Mae M. Ngai, *Impossible Subjects: Illegal Aliens and the Making of Modern America* (Princeton, NJ: Princeton University Press, 2004), 113–114. On Filipinos, see also Rick Baldoz, *The Third Asiatic Invasion: Empire and Migration in Filipino America, 1898–1946* (New York: New York University Press, 2011), 120–129; Dawn Bohulano Mabalon, "Life in Little Manila: Filipinas/os in Stockton, California, 1917–1972," (PhD diss., Stanford University, 2003), chap. 1.

44. Ullman, *Sex Unseen,* 41; Bendel v. Nagle, 17 F.2d 719 (9th Cir. 1927).

45. The reversal rate for statutory rape cases for the New York Supreme Court increased from approximately one-third from 1890 to 1909 to over two-thirds between 1910 and 1929.
46. People v. Feldman, 77 A.D. 639 (N.Y. App. Div. 1, 1902); People v. Swasey, 77 A.D. 185 (N.Y. App. Div. 1, 1902). Other reasons for reversal included admissibility of medical testimony, insufficient proof of a girl's age, or failure to report a rape promptly.
47. Between 1891 and 1910, twenty-six out of twenty-nine complainants in rape appeals were under age eighteen; between 1911 and 1930, eight complainants out of twenty-six appellate rape cases in New York State were under age eighteen. Robertson, *Crimes against Children*, 132; Stephen Robertson, "Signs, Marks, and Private Parts: Doctors, Legal Discourses, and Evidence of Rape in the United States, 1823–1930," *Journal of the History of Sexuality* 8, no. 3 (1998): 386, 47; Philip Jenkins, *Moral Panic: Changing Concepts of the Child Molester in Modern America* (New Haven: Yale University Press, 1998), 77, 45.
48. Quoted in Kathleen R. Parker, "'To Protect the Chastity of Children,'" 71.
49. Ben B. Lindsey and Wainwright Evans, *The Companionate Marriage* (New York: Boni and Liveright, 1927), 352–353.
50. In California, for example, statutory rape cases displaced forcible rape against adult women in the appellate courts, and violent rapes were often prosecuted as assault rather than rape. Ullman, *Sex Unseen*, 32–36, 59n57.
51. State v. Johnson, 133 N.W. 115, 116 (Iowa 1911); "Admissibility of Evidence as to Unchastity of Alleged Victim of Rape to Show Probability of Consent," *Virginia Law Review* 3, no. 6 (1916): 448, 451. See also Michelle J. Anderson, "From Chastity Requirement to Sexuality License: Sexual Consent and a New Rape Shield Law," *George Washington Law Review* 70, no. 1 (2002): 51–162.
52. "Admissibility of Evidence as to Unchastity," 450.
53. John D'Emilio and Estelle B. Freedman, *Intimate Matters: A History of Sexuality in America* (Chicago: University of Chicago Press, 1997), 241.
54. On Robinson, see Gordon, *Heroes of Their Own Lives*, 173–178, and Kevin J. Mumford, "'Lost Manhood' Found: Male Sexual Impotence and Victorian Culture in the United States," *Journal of the History of Sexuality* 3, no. 1 (1992): 54–55; Bronson, "False Accusations of Rape," 539, 552; William J. Robinson, *Woman: Her Sex and Love Life* (New York: Eugenics, 1929), 309; Robinson, *America's Sex and Marriage Problems* (New York: Eugenics, 1928), 307–339.

9. The Sexual Vulnerability of Boys

1. Sharon Ullman, *Sex Unseen: The Emergence of Modern Sexuality in America* (Berkeley: University of California Press, 1997), 63–64; Paul A. Herman, "American Homophobia: 'The Homosexual Menace' in Twentieth-Century American Culture" (PhD diss., Stanford University, 2005), 67, 77–94, 102;

Peter Boag, *Same-Sex Affairs: Constructing and Controlling Homosexuality in the Pacific Northwest* (Berkeley: University of California Press, 2003), 122.

2. C. C. Mapes, "Higher Enlightenment versus 'Age of Consent,'" *Medical Age* 14, no. 4 (February 25, 1896): 106; Jane E. Larson, "'Even a Worm Will Turn at Last': Rape Reform in Late Nineteenth-Century America," *Yale Journal of Law & the Humanities* 9, no. 1 (1997): 58; Helen H. Gardener, "A Battle for Sound Morality, or the History of Recent Age-of-Consent Legislation in the United States: Part II. The Victory in Colorado, Nebraska, and Missouri," *Arena*, September 1895, 7.

3. Anna Garlin Spencer, "The Age of Consent and Its Significance," *Forum*, April 1913, 417; Helen H. Gardener, "A Battle for Sound Morality. Part III," *Arena*, October 1895, 208.

4. Ex parte Rankin, 183 P. 686, 686 (Cal. App. 1 Dist. 1919); William N. Eskridge, *Dishonorable Passions: Sodomy Laws in America, 1861–2003* (New York: Viking, 2008), appendix, 388–407; Jonathan Ned Katz, *Love Stories: Sex between Men before Homosexuality* (Chicago: University of Chicago Press, 2001), 71.

5. Jonathan Ned Katz, *Gay American History: Lesbians and Gay Men in the U.S.A.* (New York: Crowell, 1976), 508–512; Katz, *Love Stories;* Leila J. Rupp, *A Desired Past: A Short History of Same-Sex Love in America* (Chicago: University of Chicago Press, 1999), 19–22; Lynn Sacco, *Unspeakable: Father-Daughter Incest in American History* (Baltimore: Johns Hopkins University Press, 2009), 83; Philip Jenkins, *Moral Panic: Changing Concepts of the Child Molester in Modern America* (New Haven, CT: Yale University Press, 1998), 27; Gurney Williams, MD, "Rape in Children and in Young Girls," *International Clinics*, 23rd ser., vol. 2 (1913): 257. Some judges also cleared the courtroom in rape cases, a practice ruled allowable in Reagan v. United States, 202 F. 488 (9th Cir. 1913), in which a judge felt that many were in the courtroom "out of morbid curiosity."

6. Michael Lynch, "New York City Sodomy, 1796–1873" (paper presented at the New York University Institute for the Humanities, New York City, February 1985), 3; "Police Statistics," *National Police Gazette*, November 28, 1846, 90; Eskridge, *Dishonorable Passions*, 22–23.

7. Katz, *Love Stories*, 73; Eskridge, *Dishonorable Passions*, 50; Patricia Cline Cohen, Timothy J. Gilfoyle, and Helen Lefkowitz Horowitz, *The Flash Press: Sporting Male Weeklies in 1840s New York* (Chicago: University of Chicago Press, 2008), 60–62. Historian Greg Robinson located only twenty-four sodomy reports in nineteenth-century American newspapers available online through the ProQuest and NewspaperArchive.com databases (2007); most of these articles had been published between 1870 and 1900 (Greg Robinson, letter to the author, September 2007). A search of the expanded ProQuest newspaper database (accessed February 17, 2013) produced 103 references to sodomy, three-quarters of which had been published between 1870 and 1900.

8. Eskridge, *Dishonorable Passions*, 20. See also Brief of Professors of History George Chauncey, Nancy F. Cott, John D'Emilio, Estelle B. Freedman, Thomas C. Holt, John Howard, Lynn Hunt, Mark D. Jordan, Elizabeth Lapovsky Kennedy, and Linda P. Kerber as Amici Curiae in Support of Petitioners, Lawrence v. Texas, 539 U.S. 558 (2003); Margot Canaday, *The Straight State: Sexuality and Citizenship in Twentieth-Century America* (Princeton, NJ: Princeton University Press, 2009), 84.

9. Katz, *Love Stories*, 70; Mary R. Block, "'An Accusation Easily to Be Made': A History of Rape Law in Nineteenth-century America" (PhD diss., University of Kentucky, 2001), 158n29; Michael Lynch, "New York City Sodomy," 17; Stephen Robertson, "Shifting the Scene of the Crime: Sodomy and the American History of Sexual Violence," *Journal of the History of Sexuality* 19, no. 2 (2010): 223–242; Louis Dwight, "The Sin of Sodom Is the Vice of Prisoners . . ." (1820), in Katz, *Gay American History*, 27. See also Mark E. Kann, "Sexual Desire, Crime, and Punishment in the Early Republic," in *Long before Stonewall: Histories of Same-Sex Sexuality in Early America*, ed. Thomas A. Foster (New York: New York University Press, 2007), 279–302.

10. Greg Robinson, letter to the author, September 2007. Reports of sodomy with boys included: "Superior Criminal Court, Mason J.," *Fitchburg Sentinel* (MA), August 17, 1889, 2; "The Courts: James Kelly Acquitted of an Unnatural Crime," *Los Angeles Times*, June 2, 1893, 5; "Miller Has Confessed," *Los Angeles Times*, May 10, 1899, 7; and "Crime of an Unmentionable Nature Is Charged against Geo. Pague," *Lima Daily News* [OH], April 2, 1898, 1. My sample of 752 rape reports in four white newspapers during the late nineteenth century identified only two articles about boy victims: "Vice's Varieties," *National Police Gazette*, May 18, 1878, 15; and "Boy Burglars," *Los Angeles Times*, December 28, 1892, 5.

11. Eskridge, *Dishonorable Passions*, 20; Katz, *Love Stories*, 71. The case is Mascolo v. Montesanto, 23 A. 714 (Conn. 1891).

12. See John D'Emilio and Estelle B. Freedman, *Intimate Matters: A History of Sexuality in America*, 3rd ed. (Chicago: University of Chicago Press, 2012), pt. 3; Katz, *Love Stories;* George Chauncey, *Gay New York: Gender, Urban Culture, and the Making of the Gay Male World, 1890–1940* (New York: Basic Books, 1994); Kevin J. Mumford, *Interzones: Black/White Sex Districts in Chicago and New York in the Early Twentieth Century* (New York: Columbia University Press, 1997).

13. Herman, "American Homophobia," 1. On the construction of the homosexual, see also Katz, *Love Stories;* D'Emilio and Freedman, *Intimate Matters;* Chauncey, *Gay New York;* Jennifer Terry, *An American Obsession: Science, Medicine, and Homosexuality in Modern Society* (Chicago: University of Chicago Press, 1999). On the emergence of modern homosexuality, see Mary McIntosh, "The Homosexual Role," *Social Problems* 16, no. 2 (1968): 182–192; Jeffrey Weeks, *Sex, Politics, and Society: The Regulation of Sexuality since 1800* (London: Longman, 1981), chap. 6; and Michel Foucault, *The*

History of Sexuality, vol. 1, *An Introduction,* trans. Robert Hurley (New York: Pantheon, 1978).

14. Jenkins, *Moral Panic,* 27; Eskridge, *Dishonorable Passions,* 44; Terry, *An American Obsession,* 118; Chauncey, *Gay New York,* 141, 185; Boag, *Same-Sex Affairs,* 72–76, 186. See also Don Romesburg, "'Wouldn't a Boy Do?': Placing Early-Twentieth-Century Male Youth Sex Work into Histories of Sexuality," *Journal of the History of Sexuality* 18, no. 2 (2009): 367–392.

15. Stephen Robertson, *Crimes against Children: Sexual Violence and Legal Culture in New York City, 1880–1960* (Chapel Hill: University of North Carolina Press, 2005), 59; Stephen Robertson, "'Boys, of Course, Cannot Be Raped': Age, Homosexuality, and the Redefinition of Sexual Violence in New York City, 1880–1955," *Gender & History* 18, no. 2 (2006): 361; Herman, "American Homophobia," 49.

16. Boag, *Same-Sex Affairs,* 275, 195; "Would Bar Newspapers," *Morning Olympian,* January 11, 1910, 257. The 1909 Washington State law forbade public reporting of rape, seduction, adultery, sodomy, "or any other sexual crime." Washington State, *Session Laws of the State of Washington* (Olympia: E. L. Boardman, 1909), sec. 209, p. 952.

17. Portland (OR) Vice Commission, *Report to the Mayor and City Council of the City of Portland, Oregon,* vol. 4 (Portland: Henry Russell Talbot, 1913), 136. A search of articles that included the term *sodomy* in the ProQuest national newspaper database (conducted October 1, 2012) showed an increase from fifty-five in the 1920s, to seventy in the 1930s, to two hundred in the 1940s.

18. "Nameless Crimes Out West," *National Police Gazette,* May 11, 1895, 6.

19. Eskridge, *Dishonorable Passions,* 77 (fig. 3.1). This fivefold increase in sodomy arrests far outpaced the growth of the New York City population, which less than doubled between 1900 and 1920. Campbell Gibson, "Population of the 100 Largest Cities and Other Urban Places in the United States: 1790 to 1990," U.S. Census Bureau, June 1998, www.census.gov/population/www/documentation/twps0027/twps0027.html.

20. Katz, *Love Stories,* 73–74; Boag, *Same-Sex Affairs,* 204; Ullman, *Sex Unseen,* 154–155, 155n87. On sexual liberalism and the separation of reproduction and sexuality, see D'Emilio and Freedman, *Intimate Matters,* chap. 11. For an example of sodomy law applied to heterosexuals, see Comer v. State, 21 Ga. App. 306, 94 S.E. 314 (Ga. 1917), upholding the conviction of a woman who allowed a man to have oral sex with her.

21. Terry, *An American Obsession,* 80–82; Boag, *Same-Sex Affairs,* 207–214. In 1909, California passed the first state sterilization law to include sexual perverts. The law applied to any person convicted of two or more offenses if they showed evidence of being a "moral or sexual pervert." Eskridge, *Dishonorable Passions,* 55; Frederick W. Brown, "Eugenic Sterilization in the United States," *Annals of the American Academy of Political and Social Science* 149 (May 1930): 23. A 1922 Nebraska law allowed sterilization for second convictions for rape or incest if the victim was under age eleven. By 1930, California,

Indiana, Kansas, Maine, Minnesota, Nebraska, North Dakota, Oregon, Utah, and Washington allowed criminal sterilization of inmates for sexual perversion or moral degeneracy. Brown, "Eugenic Sterilization," 23–28, and 29 (table 1). For a summary of the laws and on the justification of sterilization as a means of protecting the innocence of children and youth, see Marie E. Kopp, "Surgical Treatment as Sex Crime Prevention Measure," *Journal of Criminal Law and Criminology* 28, no. 5 (January–February, 1938): 692–706. For a critique of eugenic sterilization for rape, see Mickle v. Henrichs, 262 F. 687 (U.S. Dist. 1918).

22. Eskridge, *Dishonorable Passions,* 49–50 (the increase in the prison population greatly exceeded general population growth); Lawrence M. Friedman and Robert V. Percival, *The Roots of Justice: Crime and Punishment in Alameda County, California, 1870–1910* (Chapel Hill: University of North Carolina Press, 1981), 207; Boag, *Same-Sex Affairs,* 205.

23. Robertson, *Crimes against Children,* 63; Chauncey, *Gay New York,* 140.

24. Robertson, *Crimes against Children,* 62–63; Harry E. Smoot, *Illinois Manual of Laws Affecting Women and Children* (Chicago: Juvenile Protective Association of Chicago, 1922), 44–46.

25. Because a 1902 New York ruling made the person submitting to sodomy an accomplice, it was necessary for boys to show they had resisted, lest they be guilty of the crime. Robertson, *Crimes against Children,* 64. In People v. Troutman, 187 Cal. 313, 201 P. 928 (Cal. 1921), the court affirmed that it was irrelevant whether the fourteen-year-old boy who had sex with a thirty-eight-year-old man had been an "accomplice" or had "suggested the commission of the act charged."

26. Hodges v. State, 19 S.E. 758 (Ga. 1894); Wharton v. State, 198 S.E. 823 (Ga. App. 1938); People v. Deschessere, 74 N.Y.S. 761 (N.Y.A.D. 1 Dept. 1902); Lafray v. The State, 48 Ga. App. 133, 172 S.E. 115 (Ga. App. 1933).

27. People v. Harrison, 112 P. 733 (Cal. App. 2 Dist. 1910).

28. Nayan Shah, "Between 'Oriental Depravity' and 'Natural Degenerates': Spatial Borderlands and the Making of Ordinary Americans," *American Quarterly* 57, no. 3 (2005): 707.

29. William J. Eskridge Jr., *Gaylaw: Challenging the Apartheid of the Closet* (Cambridge, MA: Harvard University Press, 1999), 375 (appendix C2: "Reported 'Sodomy' Cases, 1880–1995").

30. Robertson, " 'Boys, of Course, Cannot Be Raped,' " 366–367. Although indictments increased, the conviction rates fell. Robertson, *Crimes against Children,* 240–241 (appendix, table 4).

31. Robertson, *Crimes against Children,* 158, 69–70; Robertson, " 'Boys, of Course, Cannot Be Raped,' " 355–356.

32. William H. Walker, "The Rape of the Sabine Men," *Life,* March 13, 1913, 534.

33. Gail Bederman, *Manliness and Civilization: A Cultural History of Gender and Race in the United States, 1880–1917* (Chicago: University of Chicago Press, 1995). See also Kevin White, *The First Sexual Revolution: The Emer-*

gence of Male Heterosexuality in Modern America (New York: New York University Press, 1993), 11–12.

34. Honoré Willsie, "American Race-Control," *Woman's Journal,* June 3, 1922, 15. On the racialization of the homosexual, see Siobhan B. Somerville, *Queering the Color Line: Race and the Invention of Homosexuality in American Culture* (Durham, NC: Duke University Press, 2000). See also Matthew Frye Jacobson, *Whiteness of a Different Color: European Immigrants and the Alchemy of Race* (Cambridge, MA: Harvard University Press, 1998), 77–78; and Mae Ngai, *Impossible Subjects: Illegal Aliens and the Making of Modern America* (Princeton, NJ: Princeton University Press, 2005), 19–20.

35. Tomás Almaguer, *Racial Fault Lines: The Historical Origins of White Supremacy in California* (Berkeley: University of California Press, 1994), 160–162; Henry Yu, "Mixing Bodies and Cultures: The Meaning of America's Fascination with Sex between 'Orientals' and 'Whites,'" in *Sex, Love, Race: Crossing Boundaries in North American History,* ed. Martha Hodes (New York: New York University Press, 1998), 449; Victor Jew, "'Chinese Demons': The Violent Articulation of Chinese Otherness and Interracial Sexuality in the U.S. Midwest, 1885–1889," *Journal of Social History* 32, no. 2 (2003): 389–410; Mary Ting Yi Lui, *The Chinatown Trunk Mystery: Murder, Miscegenation, and Other Dangerous Encounters in Turn-of-the-Century New York City* (Princeton, NJ: Princeton University, 2005), 67–80. A study of thirty-three cases of sexual assault in California by Chinese men between 1851 and 1912 concluded that they were feared more as bearers of disease than as violent threats. Beth Lew [Williams], "Rape across Another Color Line: California Court Cases against Chinese Men, 1850–1915" (unpublished paper, Department of History, Stanford University, 2006).

36. "Race Fights Spreading: Filipinos Beaten in Bay City," *Los Angeles Times,* January 29, 1930, 1. On interethnic conflicts between Filipinos and European immigrants over dance halls and dating, see Mumford, *Interzones,* 67–68.

37. Edward O. Janney, *The White Slave Traffic in America* (New York: National Vigilance Committee, 1911), 31; Clifford Roe, *The Prodigal Daughter: The White Slave Evil and the Remedy* (Chicago: L. W. Walter, 1911), 101, 104. In Roe's book *Panders and Their White Slaves,* 36 percent of the references to panders identified them as immigrants, contrasted with only 8 percent of the references to panders in Jane Addams's *A New Conscience and an Ancient Evil.* Brian Donovan, *White Slave Crusades: Race, Gender, and Anti-Vice Activism, 1887–1917* (Urbana: University of Illinois Press, 2006), 70 (table 4.1).

38. Najia Aarim-Heriot, *Chinese Immigrants, African Americans and Racial Anxiety in the United States, 1848–1882* (Urbana: University of Illinois Press, 2003), 136; Boag, *Same-Sex Affairs,* 59; Alfred J. Zobel, "Primary Gonorrhea of the Rectum in the Male," *Physician and Surgeon* 31, no. 8 (August 1909): 356; Canaday, *The Straight State,* 29.

39. Watson quoted in Sally Steinberg-Brent, "The Leo Frank Murder Case," in *Jews on Trial*, ed. Bruce Afran and Robert A. Garber (Jersey City: Ktav, 2005), 131. On the case, see Leonard Dinnerstein, *The Leo Frank Case*, rev. ed. (Athens: University of Georgia Press, 2008), 19; Nancy MacLean, "The Leo Frank Case Reconsidered: Gender and Sexual Politics in the Making of Reactionary Populism," *Journal of American History* 78, no. 3 (1991): 917–948; Kristoff Kerl, "The Pure and the Sodomite: Masculinity, Sexuality and Antisemitism in the Leo Frank Case," *Gender Forum: An Internet Journal for Gender Studies* 32 (2011), accessed September 21, 2011, www.genderforum.org/issues/historical-masculinities-as-an-intersectional-problem/the-pure-and-the-sodomite. On images of Jewish perversion, see Sander L. Gilman, *Inscribing the Other* (Lincoln: University of Nebraska Press, 1991), 200; and Sander L. Gilman, *The Jew's Body* (New York: Routledge, 1991).

40. Chauncey, *Gay New York*, 74–75; Rupp, *A Desired Past*, 21; Nicola Beisel, *Imperiled Innocents: Anthony Comstock and Family Reproduction in Victorian America* (Princeton, NJ: Princeton University Press, 1997), 59.

41. Vivien M. L. Miller, *Crime, Sexual Violence, and Clemency: Florida's Pardon Board and the Penal System in the Progressive Era* (Gainesville: University Press of Florida, 2000), 151–154; Boag, *Same-Sex Affairs*, 61, 45–52.

42. Boag, *Same-Sex Affairs*, 22–34, 72–76; Chauncey, *Gay New York*, 140, 88–96. See also Regina Kunzel, *Criminal Intimacy: Prison and the Uneven History of Modern American Sexuality* (Chicago: University of Chicago Press, 2008), 65–67.

43. Canaday, *The Straight State*, 29, 34, 36, 40, 42–44, 50; Boag, *Same-Sex Affairs*, 59.

44. Gordon Brent Ingram, "Returning to the Scene of the Crime: Uses of Trial Dossiers on Consensual Male Homosexuality for Urban Research, with Examples from Twentieth-Century British Columbia," *GLQ: A Journal of Lesbian and Gay Studies* 10, no. 1 (2003): 91.

45. Shah, "Between 'Oriental Depravity' and 'Natural Degenerates,'" 703, 707; Lew [Williams], "Rape across Another Color Line," 20–21.

46. Quoted in Boag, *Same-Sex Affairs*, 57.

47. State v. Robbins, 154 P. 317, 321 (Cal. 1915); Shah, "Between 'Oriental Depravity' and 'Natural Degenerate,'" 711; Lew [Williams], "Rape across Another Color Line," 20.

48. On the shift from "fairy" to "homosexual," see Chauncey, *Gay New York*, esp. chap. 2.

49. Canaday, *The Straight State*, chap. 2; Allan Bérubé, *Coming Out Under Fire: The History of Gay Men and Women in World War Two* (New York: Free Press, 1990).

50. Romesburg, "'Wouldn't a Boy Do?'"; "Hunt Man in Murder Vicinity," *Los Angeles Times*, December 16, 1920, 1. See also Boag, *Same-Sex Affairs*; D'Emilio and Freedman, *Intimate Matters*; Christina Simmons, "Compan-

ionate Marriage and the Lesbian Threat," *Frontiers* 4, no. 3 (1979): 54–59; Estelle B. Freedman, "The Prison Lesbian: Race, Class, and the Construction of the Aggressive Female Homosexual, 1915–1965," *Feminist Studies* 22, no. 2 (1996): 397–423.

51. Reuben Oppenheimer and Lulu L. Eckman, *Laws Relating to Sex Offenses against Children*," Children's Bureau Publication no. 145 (Washington, DC: U.S. Department of Labor, 1925), 18–19; Eskridge, *Dishonorable Passions*, 55, and appendix, 388–407. In 1917 Florida made "unnatural and lascivious acts" a misdemeanor; in 1919 Connecticut passed a law against "lewdness"; and in 1921 California criminalized "oral copulation." Eskridge, *Dishonorable Passions*, 388, 396.

52. Eskridge, *Gaylaw*, 55–56, 66, 374 (appendix C1); Chauncey, *Gay New York*, 140.

53. M. Hamblin Smith and Anne Fairweather, "The Case of Richard Loeb and Nathan Leopold," *Journal of Mental Science* 71, no. 292 (1925): 82; Herman, "American Homophobia," 86–94; Canaday, *The Straight State*, 101; Vito Russo, *The Celluloid Closet: Homosexuality in the Movies* (New York: Harper and Row, 1981), 3–59.

54. Robertson, " 'Boys, of Course, Cannot Be Raped,' " 357; Robertson, *Crimes against Children*, 146; Estelle B. Freedman, " 'Uncontrolled Desires': The Response to the Sexual Psychopath, 1920–1960," *Journal of American History* 74, no. 1 (1987): 94; Terry, *An American Obsession*, 277.

55. Freedman, " 'Uncontrolled Desires,' " 97–99. Prior to the psychopath laws, white men were likely to be seen as intellectually deficient and "incapable of making appropriate sexual object choices," rather than impulsively harmful. By the late 1930s, however, the new laws viewed the deviant sexual predator as intending the harm of young victims. Bonni Kay Cermak, "In the Interest of Justice: Legal Narratives of Sex, Gender, Race and Rape in Twentieth Century Los Angeles, 1920–1960" (PhD diss., University of Oregon, 2005), 140–154.

56. Jack Frosch and Walter Bromberg, "The Sex Offender: A Psychiatric Study," *American Journal of Orthopsychiatry* 9 (1930): 20–24, quoted in Terry, *An American Obsession*, 460n15; Mayor's Committee of New York, *Report,* cited in California Legislative Assembly, Interim Committee on Judicial System and Judicial Process, Subcommittee on Sex Crimes, *Preliminary Report* (Sacramento, March 8, 1950), 34; Freedman, " 'Uncontrolled Desires,' " 101. See *Report of Mayor's Committee for the Study of Sex Offenses* (New York: 1940).

57. Jenkins, *Moral Panic*, 67 (table 3.1). See also Robertson, *Crimes against Children*, 244 (table 8).

10. "Smashing the Masher"

1. " 'Mashers' Must Go," *Washington Post,* July 4, 1910, 14; "Police Inaugurate War on 'Mashers,' " *San Francisco Call,* November 23, 1910, 18.

2. Martha Hodes, *White Women, Black Men: Illicit Sex in the Nineteenth-Century South* (New Haven, CT: Yale University Press, 1997), 203; Nayan Shah, *Stranger Intimacy: Contesting Race, Sexuality, and the Law in the North American West* (Berkeley: University of California Press, 2011), 37.

3. John J. Jennings, *Theatrical and Circus Life: Or Secrets of the Stage, Green-Room and Sawdust Arena* (St. Louis: Sun, 1882), 55.

4. "Mash" and "Masher," in John Stephen Farmer and W. E. Henley, *Slang and Its Analogues Past and Present*, vol. 4 (London, 1906), 287, 288. The *Oxford English Dictionary* defines *masher* as slang that is "orig. and chiefly U.S.," referring historically to a Victorian or Edwardian dandy "fond of the company of women" and in the United States to "a womanizer; a man who makes indecent sexual advances towards women, esp. in public places." *Oxford English Dictionary*, 3rd ed. (Oxford: Oxford University Press, 2011), OED Online, accessed March 6, 2012, www.oed.com. The distinction between "gentlemanly" and "crude" mashers appears in George Augustus Sala, *Living London: Being "Echoes" Re-echoed* (London: Remington and Co., 1883), 529.

5. "The Masher," 1905 illustrated postcard in possession of the author; Keith Tester, *The Flâneur* (New York: Routledge, 1994); Elisabeth Wilson, "The Invisible Flâneur," *New Left Review* 191 (1992): 90–110; Elizabeth Wilson, *The Sphinx in the City: Urban Life, the Control of Disorder, and Women* (Berkeley: University of California Press, 1992), 55–56; Lauren Rabinovitz, *For the Love of Pleasure: Women, Movies, and Culture in Turn-of-the-Century Chicago* (New Brunswick, NJ: Rutgers University Press, 1998), 8, 26–28; Brent Shannon, *The Cut of His Coat: Men, Dress, and Consumer Culture in Britain, 1860–1914* (Athens: Ohio University Press, 2006), 129–132.

6. In England the masher survived the public concerns about homosexuality that followed the trials of Oscar Wilde in 1895–1896, when the Aesthete and the dandy merged with the deviant homosexual. Shannon, *The Cut of His Coat*, 137–159. A small subgenre of newspaper articles described female mashers, sometimes associated with emancipated women and, in the twentieth century, lesbians. See "Female Mashers," *New York Times*, September 3, 1883, 5; "The Emancipated Female," *Puck*, April 16, 1884, 371; "The Exposition," *Atlanta Constitution*, March 22, 1885, 11; "She Had Charm and Beauty: She Wolf but She Preyed on Her Own Sex," *Baltimore Afro-American*, November 17, 1934, 24.

7. "More Than He Bargained For," *National Police Gazette*, March 26, 1881, 37, 183; "Squelched: How a Susceptible Man Was Cured of His Disposition for 'Mashing,' Variety Actresses," *National Police Gazette*, January 8, 1881, 12; "What a Masher Found Out," *Atlanta Constitution*, August 18, 1885, 4; Farmer and Henley, *Slang and Its Analogues*, 288; "The Masher," in Charles Godfrey Leland, *Brand-New Ballads* (London: "Fun" office, 1885), 116.

8. Katherine Jorgensen Gray, "Mixed Company: Elite Youth and Heterosociability in Philadelphia, 1750–1815" (PhD diss., Johns Hopkins University, 2011), 142–147.

9. Mary P. Ryan, *Women in Public: Between Banners and Ballots, 1825–1880* (Baltimore: Johns Hopkins University Press, 1990), 68; Augustine E. Costello, *Our Police Protectors: History of the New York Police* (New York: Charles F. Roper, 1885), 116; Christine Stansell, *City of Women: Sex and Class in New York, 1789–1860* (New York: Knopf, 1986), 96–100. On the heterosexual male "sporting culture" in New York, see Helen Lefkowitz Horowitz, *Rereading Sex: Battles over Sexual Knowledge and Suppression in Nineteenth-Century America* (New York: Knopf, 2002), chap. 6.

10. Elaine S. Abelson, *When Ladies Go A-Thieving: Middle-Class Shoplifters in the Victorian Department Store* (New York: Oxford University Press, 1989), 20; Ryan, *Women in Public*, 78; Patricia Cline Cohen, "Safety and Danger: Women on American Public Transport, 1750–1850," in *Gendered Domains: Rethinking the Public and Private in Women's History*, ed. Dorothy O. Helly and Susan M. Reverby (Ithaca, NY: Cornell University Press, 1987), 109–122. On the efforts of African American women to gain admission to first-class railroad cars, see Barbara Y. Welke, "When All the Women Were White, and All the Blacks Were Men: Gender, Class, Race, and the Road to Plessy, 1855–1914," *Law and History Review* 13, no. 2 (Autumn 1995): 261–316.

11. Ryan, *Women in Public*, 79–82; Kathy Lee Peiss, *Cheap Amusements: Working Women and Leisure in Turn-of-the-Century New York* (Philadelphia: Temple University Press, 1986), esp. chap. 5; Joanne Meyerowitz, *Women Adrift: Independent Wage Earners in Chicago, 1880–1930* (Chicago: University of Chicago Press, 1987); "A Curious Creature at Coney Island," *Puck*, July 19, 1882, 314. Films include *The Masher's Waterloo* (1900), *Lovers Interrupted* (1903), *How the Masher Was Punished* (1907), *Chimmie Fadden* (1915), *A Man's Man* (1918), and *A Man's Man* (1923). American Film Institute Catalogue of Feature Films, www.afi.com/members/catalog/.

12. Mrs. Charles Henrotin quoted in "Leading Women Hope to Arouse Sentiment That Will Put an End to the Growing Evil," *Chicago Daily Tribune*, February 4, 1906, F3.

13. Guy Szuberla, "Ladies, Gentlemen, Flirts, Mashers, Snoozers, and the Breaking of Etiquette's Code," *Prospects: An Annual of American Cultural Studies* 15 (1990): 171–177; Georgina Hickey, "From Civility to Self-Defense: Modern Advice to Women on the Privileges and Dangers of Public Space," *Women's Studies Quarterly* 39, nos. 1–2 (2011): 77–94; A Working Girl from Detroit, "Women's Blank Expression," *New York Times*, December 4, 1909, 10. See also Judith R. Walkowitz, "Going Public: Shopping, Street Harassment, and Streetwalking in Late Victorian London," *Representations* 62 (1998): 5–7, 12–15.

14. "Tries Love Powder," *Los Angeles Times*, July 20, 1911, 16; "Broadway Swell Poses as Masher," *Los Angeles Herald*, July 30, 1905, 6. The distinction between insults and enticements appeared in "The Girl Who Travels Alone," *Medical Times*, January 1907, 26–29.

15. Theodore Dreiser, *Sister Carrie* (New York: Doubleday, 1900), 3–4.

16. "Dago Masher," *Atlanta Constitution,* February 22, 1901, 10; Gates, "The Girl Who Travels Alone," *Cosmopolitan,* December 1, 1906, 166–167; "One of Buck's Beauties," *Atlanta Constitution,* May 16, 1890, 7; "A Colored Masher," *Atlanta Constitution,* April 26, 1895, 3; "Insulted White Woman," *Graham* (Arizona) *Guardian,* June 15, 1895 (first page, unnumbered); "Would Be Negro Masher Jailed for 30 Days," *Syracuse Journal,* June 1, 1911, 1; "Negro Masher Is Fined and Jailed," *Spokane Daily Chronicle,* February 5, 1914, 19. "To Chain Gang Goes 'Masher,'" *Los Angeles Times,* August 5, 1909, 12. A rare racialized image of mashers appeared in an evolutionary theory presented by Jules Dunnaire, "The 'Masher' Is but a Type of the Lower Vertebrate," *Chicago Daily Tribune,* January 15, 1905, F2.

17. State v. Rollins, 83 N.W. 141 (Minn. 1900); Thomas C. Mackey, *Pursuing Johns: Criminal Law Reform, Defending Character, and New York City's Committee of Fourteen, 1920–1930* (Columbus: Ohio State University Press, 2005). For later accounts of street flirtations leading to rape and sexual delinquency, see Lee Alexander Stone, "Present Day Social Hygiene Problems," *Modern Medicine* 2, no. 12 (January–June 1920): 835; and Jacob A. Goldberg and Rosamond W. Goldberg, *Girls on City Streets: A Study of 1400 Cases of Rape* (New York: American Social Hygiene Association, 1935; repr., New York: Arno Press, 1974), esp. 108–111.

18. "Suppressing the Street 'Masher,'" *Chicago Daily Tribune,* May 8, 1901, 12; Peiss, *Cheap Amusements,* 54–55, 108–111.

19. "Women Applaud War on Mashers," *Chicago Daily Tribune,* May 8, 1901, 9.

20. Eleanor Gates, "The Girl Who Travels Alone," *Cosmopolitan,* January 1907, 308; Gates, "The Girl Who Travels Alone" (1906), 166, 170.

21. "The Girl Who Travels Alone," *Medical Times,* January 1907, 26–29.

22. Ibid.; Another Worker, "The Single Woman Knows the Courtesy of Men," *New York Times,* December 15, 1909, 10. On the role of "street conversations" and "glad-eyeing" in working-class courtship in London, see Walkowitz, "Going Public," 16–19.

23. Preface and J. Sanderson Christison, "The "Confessions" of Ivens: A Character Study and Analysis of the Case" (1906), in Richard G. Ivens, *The "Confessions" of Ivens: A Character Study and Analysis of the Case* [N.p., 1906?], 17, Harvard Law School Library, accessed January 21, 2012, nrs.harvard.edu/urn-3:HLS.Libr:1043101.

24. "Leading Women Hope to Arouse Sentiment"; "Terror Due to Murders," *Chicago Daily Tribune,* January 14, 1906, 3; W. C. H. Keough, "Hunting Women Is Favorite Sport of Chicago Men," *Chicago Daily Tribune,* February 1, 1906, F4; "24 Women Killed; Record of Year," *Chicago Daily Tribune,* January 21, 1906, 3. The latter article also acknowledged that the list excluded "the many women who were killed by their husbands." Chicagoans may have been particularly concerned about this crime wave, given the publicity over the murders of women during the 1893 World's Fair in their city.

Karen Abbott, *Sin in the Second City: Madams, Ministers, Playboys, and the Battle for America's Soul* (New York: Random House, 2007).

25. "Demand Police Protect Women," *Chicago Daily Tribune,* January 15, 1906, 1; "Terror Due to Murders"; "The Kind of Man Who Mashes and How He Insults His Victims," *Chicago Daily Tribune,* February 4, 1906, F2.

26. "Demand Police Protect Women," 4; Catharine Waugh McCulloch, "Let Women Vote in Self Defense," *Chicago Daily Tribune,* April 1, 1906, B5.

27. Rabinovitz, *For the Love of Pleasure,* 33; "Girl Knocks Out Masher," *Chicago Daily Tribune,* May 22, 1905, 5; "'Masher' Given Deserts," *Chicago Daily Tribune,* July 16, 1905, 4; "Japanese Woman Throws Masher Over Her Head," *Chicago Daily Tribune,* October 11, 1905, 5; "Woman Who Knocked Down Masher Wants Society for Suppression of Ilk," *Chicago Daily Tribune,* August 26, 1905, 2. See also "Saved by Hair's Breadth and Also by Hairspring," *Los Angeles Times,* January 7, 1910, 8; "Girls' Word Holds Rowdy," *Los Angeles Times,* September 23, 1910, 1; "Slips Through Police Dragnet," *Los Angeles Times,* November 1, 1910, 3.

28. Arney H. Ritchie, "How a Masher Was Punished," *Chicago Daily Tribune,* March 17, 1907, E4; "Girl Knocks Out Intrusive Masher," *Chicago Daily Tribune,* February 21, 1906, 6.

29. "Chicago Women Train for Defense," *Chicago Daily Tribune,* July 1, 1906, F2. On the New Woman and physicality, see Susan Cahn, *Coming on Strong: Gender and Sexuality in Twentieth-Century Women's Sport* (Cambridge, MA: Harvard University Press, 1995). For a rare report of the dangers of fighting back, see "Flee Mashers' Bullets," *Chicago Daily Tribune,* November 6, 1920, 2.

30. "Leading Women Hope to Arouse Sentiment."

31. "Urges War on Mashers," *Chicago Daily Tribune,* December 17, 1906, 3; W. L. Bodine, "How the Board of Education Is Trying to Protect School Girls from the Pest," *Chicago Daily Tribune,* January 27, 1907, F3.

32. Keough, "Hunting Women"; "Dress Cause of Evil," *Washington Post,* August 4, 1912, 11.

33. Beginning in 1907, prosecutor Clifford Roe began to target prostitution, which became the dominant focus of the discourse on sexual danger, culminating in the 1911 publication of *The Social Evil in Chicago* (Chicago: The Vice Commission of the City of Chicago). See Eric Anderson, "Prostitution and Social Justice: Chicago, 1910–1915," *Social Service Review* 48, no. 2 (1974): 203–228.

34. Hickey, "From Civility to Self-Defense," 81; Esther Andrews, "'Smash the Masher! Cry Gotham Women in Crusade to Rid Streets of Flirts,'" *The Day Book* (Chicago), September 8, 1916, 14; "President's Niece Insulted by Masher, Causes His Arrest; He Gets Ten Days," *Washington Post,* October 20, 1914, 3; "President's Niece Says 500 Men Have Tried to Flirt with Her; Sends Doctor to Jail as Masher," *Washington Post,* October 21,1914, 5; "Wants 'Masher' Held," *Washington Post,* October 29, 1914, 9. (Howe's husband was a nephew of President Woodrow Wilson.)

35. Janice Appier, *Policing Women: The Sexual Politics of Law Enforcement and the LAPD* (Philadelphia: Temple University Press, 1998), 9–10, 29, 127–128; Dorothy Moses Schulz, "From Policewoman to Police Officer: An Unfinished Revolution," *Police Studies: The International Review of Police Development* 16, no. 3 (1993): 93; Nixola Greeley-Smith, "Says More Policewomen Will Rid Streets of Mashers Who Pester Young Girls," *The Daybook* (Chicago), February 10, 1914, 9; "Smashing the 'Masher'—A Nation-Wide Crusade," *Atlanta Constitution*, December 31, 1916, D5; "Chicago Rejoices in Policewomen," *New York Times*, August 6, 1913, 7; "Trapped as Masher by Woman Detective," *New York Times*, September 29, 1922, 5. On policewomen in Canada who posed as widows or matrons to entrap mashers, see Greg Marquis, "The Police as a Social Service in Early Twentieth-Century Toronto," *Social History* 15, no. 50 (1992): 354.

36. "Women in the Police Department," *Chicago Defender*, March 13, 1915, 8; "Man with Brute Nature Arrested," *Chicago Defender*, October 26, 1918, 11; "City Briefs (Girl Accuses Jackson)," *Chicago Defender*, March 19, 1921, 7. "Charged with Rape," *Chicago Defender*, December 16, 1922, 8; Megan M. Everett, "Extra! Extra! Tracing the Chicago Defender's Campaign for African American Policewomen in the Early 20th Century," *Explorations: An Undergraduate Research Journal* 12 (2009), accessed April 2, 2012, ue.ucdavis.edu/explorations/2009/chicagoDefender.pdf. "D.C. Policewoman Nabs White Masher," *Baltimore Afro-American*, November 16, 1929, 1.

37. "The Changing World," *Chicago Daily Tribune*, May 12, 1919, 1.

38. P. C. Mason and Harry Rogers, "Wouldn't You Like to Flirt with Me?" (New York: Hamilton S. Gordon, 1906) and Jerome Kern and M. E. Rourke, "Come Along Pretty Girl" (New York: T. B. Harms and Francis, Day, and Hunter, 1909), UCLA Digital Archive of Popular American Music, accessed August 26, 2011, http://digital.library.ucla.edu/apam/; "The Rival Mashers (1914)," *Chaplin, The Collection: Comedy Classics from the World's Favorite Tramp*, vol. 3 (St. Laurent, Québec, Canada: Madacy Entertainment Group, 1998), DVD. On the heterosexual urban culture, see Elaine Tyler May, *Great Expectations: Marriage and Divorce in Post-Victorian America* (Chicago: University of Chicago Press, 1980); Lewis Erenberg, *Steppin' Out: New York City Nightlife and the Transformation of American Culture, 1890–1930* (Chicago: University of Chicago Press, 1984); Peiss, *Cheap Amusements;* John D'Emilio and Estelle B. Freedman, *Intimate Matters: A History of Sexuality in America,* 3rd ed. (Chicago: University of Chicago Press, 2012).

39. Marsha Orgeron, "Making 'It' in Hollywood: Clara Bow, Fandom, and Consumer Culture," *Cinema Journal* 42, no. 4 (2003): 76–97. On new ideals of masculinity, see Gail Bederman, *Manliness and Civilization: A Cultural History of Gender and Race in the United States, 1880–1917* (Chicago: University of Chicago Press, 1995); E. Anthony Rotunda, *American Manhood: Transformations in Masculinity from the Revolution to the Modern Era*

(New York: Basic Books, 1993); Kevin White, *The First Sexual Revolution: The Emergence of Male Heterosexuality in Modern America* (New York: New York University Press, 1993), 164 and chap. 3.

40. "Winifred Black Writes about Good Women Who Dress 'Bad,'" *Washington Post,* December 10, 1920, 8; "How to Mash the Masher" (K. H. to editor, in Voice of the People), *Chicago Daily Tribune,* April 16, 1920, 6; "She Leads Masher to Gotham Jail," *Chicago Daily Tribune,* January 4, 1915, 11; "Winnie Winkle, the Breadwinner," *Chicago Daily Tribune,* March 13, 1924, 21.

41. E.g., "Slaps and Holds Masher for Police," *Boston Daily Globe,* June 21, 1922, 13; "Movie Masher Is Jailed," *New York Times,* January 24, 1929, 56; "Crowd in Panic at Movie as Cop Battles Masher," *Chicago Daily Tribune,* November 14, 1927, 2; "Movie Masher Is Fined $25 after Woman Testifies," *Chicago Daily Tribune,* September 21, 1934, 10. On the space of the "darkened theatre," see Tom Gunning, "Weaving a Narrative: Style and Economic Background in Griffith's Biograph Films," in *Early Cinema: Space, Frame, Narrative,* ed. Thomas Elsaesser (London: BFI, 1990): 338–339.

42. Beth L. Bailey, *From the Front Porch to the Back Seat: Courtship in Twentieth-Century America* (Baltimore: Johns Hopkins University Press, 1988); Lisa Lindquist Dorr, "Walking Home and Mad Money: Chivalry, Sexual Danger, and Dating in the South in the Twentieth Century" (paper presented at the annual meeting of the American Studies Association, Oakland, California, October 13, 2006). See also Lisa Lindquist Dorr, "The Perils of the Back Seat: Date Rape, Race and Gender in 1950s America," *Gender & History* 20 (2008): 27–47; White, *The First Sexual Revolution,* 91; "Father of Two Children Fined as Oak Park 'Masher,'" *Chicago Daily Tribune,* December 20, 1936, 5; "Collins Warns Women against Motor Morons," *Chicago Daily Tribune,* August 18, 1925, 1; "Girls Help Police War on Mashers," *Los Angeles Times,* August 30, 1925, B1.

43. "The 'Flirt Cop' Beaten," *Washington Post,* September 2, 1911, 6. On the abuse of masher arrests, see "Poses as Policewoman; Demands $5 Bribe; Seized," *Chicago Daily Tribune,* July 27, 1938, 2, and "Man Accused as Flirt Freed; Accuser Held," *New York Times,* January 26, 1922, 10; "Trapping of Mashers Denounced by Fenning," *Washington Post,* July 24, 1925, 1. For exceptional articles for this period, see "Crack Masher Gets Mashed by Expert Female Masher," *Chicago Daily Tribune,* July 31, 1929, 3, and "Womanly Art of Self Defense," *Chicago Daily Tribune,* August 14, 1938, G6; "Flirt Case Lost by Policewoman," *Chicago Daily Tribune,* February 12, 1915, 1.

44. Anna Cadogan Etz, "Chicago Is No Longer the Happy Hunting Ground for the Masher," *Judge* 70 (1916): n.p.; "The Masher," *Chicago Defender,* August 7, 1920, 12. The few earlier masher stories in the *Defender* were also humorous—e.g., "Discomfited Masher," *Chicago Defender,* April 6, 1912, 6; "Preacher Aids Bashful to Meet Future Wives," *Chicago Defender,* September 7, 1912, 7; [untitled], *Chicago Defender,* March 1, 1919, 20. See also *Baltimore Afro-American,* August 8, 1925, 14.

45. Stone, "Present Day Social Hygiene Problems," 835; Virginia Scharff, *Taking the Wheel: Women and the Coming of the Motor Age* (Albuquerque: University of New Mexico Press, 1992), 140; "Lonely Masher Didn't Know It Was a Policewoman," *Chicago Daily Tribune*, July 18, 1926, 14.

46. "Race Discrimination in Chicago," *Chicago Defender*, October 3, 1914, 8. For an early comic reference to a stylish young black "masher" in the southern black press, see Glenda Elizabeth Gilmore, *Gender and Jim Crow: Women and the Politics of White Supremacy in North Carolina, 1896–1920* (Chapel Hill: University of North Carolina Press, 1996), 76. The closest male character in urban black communities may have been the "sweetback," an unemployed man who dressed well, loafed in pool halls or on street corners, and lived off the earnings of women. Martin Summers, *Manliness and Its Discontents: The Black Middle Class and the Transformation of Masculinity, 1900–1930* (Chapel Hill: University of North Carolina Press, 2004), 178–179. On black dandies who adopted the latest elite clothing as a performative act of resistance to racial stereotypes, see Monica L. Miller, *Slaves to Fashion: Black Dandyism and the Styling of Black Diasporic Identity* (Durham, NC: Duke University Press, 2009).

47. "Plucky Elevator Girl Fights Off White Masher," *Baltimore Afro-American*, November 1, 1918, 1; "Woman Spills White Collector on Front Steps," *Baltimore Afro-American*, October 21, 1921, 12; "Actress 'Bawls Out' White Stage Door Johnnie," *Baltimore Afro-American*, December 10, 1927, 1. See also "White Masher Embarrassed by Young Girl," *Pittsburgh Courier*, December 27, 1924, 11; "White Mashers Whipped by Two Girls," *Baltimore Afro-American*, October 27, 1928, 5.

48. "Bold Flirt Is Taken to Jail," *Chicago Defender*, April 12, 1924, 3; "White Masher Fined $100," *Baltimore Afro-American*, December 27, 1930, 5; "Masher Fined $25," *Baltimore Afro-American*, November 24, 1928, 2; "Ofay Masher, Accused by Young Woman, Is Fined $5 and Costs," *Baltimore Afro-American*, April 18, 1936, 15. Violent episodes include "Flirt Gets Knife in Breast," *Chicago Defender*, March 29, 1924, 3, and "White Sailor Masher Cut Fifteen Times," *Chicago Defender*, April 28, 1928, 1.

49. "Slays Masher," *Chicago Defender*, June 3, 1916, 1; "White Mashers Whipped by Two Girls"; "Cut by 'Masher' Who Annoyed Wife," *Baltimore Afro-American*, September 5, 1925, 16; A Reader, "Why Do Some Men Fail to Resent Insults Offered to Our Women," *Baltimore Afro-American*, February 15, 1930, 6. On black responses to harassment in the 1950s, see Lisa Lindquist Dorr, *White Women, Rape, and the Power of Race in Virginia, 1900–1960* (Chapel Hill: University of North Carolina Press, 2004), 241.

50. Elliott Freeman, "The Whirling Hub," *Baltimore Afro-American*, May 7, 1938, 18, August 10, 1940, 22, and March 1, 1941, 22; "Ofay Masher Escapes thru Back Door," *Baltimore Afro-American*, October 22, 1932, 11; "White Masher Gets Only a Reprimand," *Baltimore Afro-American*, August

6, 1938, 24; "Ofay Flirt Escapes Being Lynched," *Baltimore Afro-American,* July 8, 1933, 19; "Two More Ofay Mashers Get Beatings," *Baltimore Afro-American,* July 15, 1933, 9; Freeman, "The Whirling Hub," August 6, 1938, 18.

51. "Mashers and Auto Cruisers Infect City Streets, Is Claim," *Baltimore Afro-American,* August 1, 1925, 20; "People We Can Get Along Without," *Chicago Defender,* August 13, 1921, 16, and September 15, 1923, 12.

52. Only a handful of reports of intraracial black mashers appeared in the Chicago, New York, Pittsburgh, and Baltimore black papers. In the absence of studies of the prosecution of mashers in police records, it is not possible to compare news reports with arrests. On the primacy of race over sex oppression for the "New Negro," see Erin D. Chapman, *Prove It on Me: New Negroes, Sex, and Popular Culture in the 1920s* (New York: Oxford University Press, 2012), 117–118, 148–151.

53. *Chicago Defender* 1922, quoted in Everett, "Extra! Extra!," 84.

11. After Suffrage

1. Anne Harbottle Whittic, "New York Denies Jury Service to Women," *Equal Rights* 17, no. 7 (1931): 53.

2. "Concerning Women," *Woman's Standard,* 20, no. 10 (1921): 2; "Spring Styles in Legislature," *Woman Citizen* 5, no. 42 (1921): 1088; Lorraine Gates Schuyler, *The Weight of Their Votes: Southern Women and Political Leverage in the 1920s* (Chapel Hill: University of North Carolina Press, 2006), 166, 169–171.

3. "Answers to Suffrage Queries," *Chicago Daily Tribune,* August 10, 1913, E5.

4. "What Do You Know about Your Government? Women's Legal Status," *Woman Citizen* 6, no. 7 (1921): 22; "Laws Every Woman Should Know," *Woman Citizen* 4, no. 30 (1920): 862; Shailer Matthews, *The Woman Citizen's Library: A Systematic Course of Reading in Preparation for the Larger Citizenship* (Chicago: Civics Society, 1913–1914), 3141. For other examples of citizenship education, see George James Bayles, Sallie Joy White, and William Herbert Carruth, *American Women's Legal Status* (New York: Collier, 1905), and Harry Edward Hunt, *Michigan Laws Relating to Women and Girls: A Comprehensive Digest of the Statutory Law and Amendments Thereto as They Relate to Women and Girls: Also, Pointed Decisions of the Supreme Court of Michigan Affecting Same* (Detroit: Michigan Equal Suffrage Association, 1911).

5. Linda Kerber, *No Constitutional Right to Be Ladies: Women and Obligations of Citizenship* (New York: Hill and Wang, 1998), 134, 137, 180–181; Barbara A. Babcock, "A Place in the Palladium: Women's Rights and Jury Service," *University of Cincinnati Law Review* 61, no. 4 (1993): 1167; Rose M. Palmer quoted in New York State Bar Association, *Proceedings of the Forty-Second Annual Meeting,* vol. 42, January 17–18, 1919 (Albany: Argus Co., 1919), 609; Whittic, "New York Denies Jury Service to Women," 52.

6. "Women Jurors," *Oregon Voter: Magazine of Citizenship,* April 2, 1921, 23–24.

7. G. M. Farley, "Women on Washington Juries," *Independent,* July 3, 1913, 50–54.

8. Ex parte Mana, 178 Cal. 213 (1918).

9. Joanna L. Grossman, "Women's Jury Service: Right of Citizenship or Privilege of Difference?," *Stanford Law Review* 46 (1994): 1152; Nancy F. Cott, *The Grounding of Modern Feminism* (New Haven, CT: Yale University Press, 1987), 121–122; Holly J. McCammon, Soma Chaudhuri, Lyndi Hewitt, Courtney Sanders Muse, Harmony D. Newman, Carrie Lee Smith, and Teresa M. Terrell, "Becoming Full Citizens: The U.S. Women's Jury Rights Campaigns, the Pace of Reform, and Strategic Adaptation," *American Journal of Sociology* 113, no. 4 (2008): 1121–22.

10. Grossman, "Women's Jury Service," 1152n219; Ex parte Mana, 178 Cal. 213 (1918); Barbara Babcock, *Woman Lawyer: The Trials of Clara Foltz* (Stanford: Stanford University Press, 2011), 52–53. On the responses of the international suffrage movement to this argument, see *International Woman Suffrage News* 16, no. 5 (1922): 70–71.

11. Grossman, "Women's Jury Service," 1144; Catharine Waugh McCulloch, address before the Michigan Constitutional Convention, January 9, 1908, and *Illinois Laws Concerning Women* (Chicago: Illinois Equal Suffrage Association, [1912]), both microformed in Catherine Gouger (Waugh) McCulloch Papers, 1862–1945, ser. 6, in *Women's Studies Manuscripts from the Schlesinger Library, Radcliffe College, Part E: The Midwest and Far West;* "Women Jurors," 24.

12. "The Breslau Scandal," *International Women's News,* December 1, 1913, 34.

13. Crystal N. Feimster, *Southern Horrors: Women and the Politics of Rape and Lynching* (Cambridge, MA: Harvard University Press, 2009), 133–135, 186–188, 196, 204; "Crime of Mob Violence Unpunished in Georgia, Declares Mrs. Felton," *Atlanta Constitution,* January 13, 1920, 8; Leslie K. Dunlap, "The Reform of Rape Law and the Problem of White Men: Age-of-Consent Campaigns in the South, 1885–1910," in *Sex, Love, Race: Crossing Boundaries in North American History,* ed. Martha Hodes (New York: New York University Press, 1999), 363; "A Lynching in the Making," *National Business Woman,* January 1935, 33.

14. "Women Jurors," 24; State v. Chase, 211 P. 920 (Ore. 1922); Burnita Shelton Matthews, "The Status of Women as Jurors: Article IV. Equal and Unequal Exemptions from Jury Service," *Equal Rights* 16, no. 19 (1930): 148–149.

15. Kerber, *No Constitutional Right,* 130–139; Jessica Weiss, "The Feminine Point of View: California Women's Struggle for a Voice in the Legal System" (BA honors thesis, University of California at Berkeley, 1986), 20–21; Grossman, "Women's Jury Service"; Florence E. Allen, "Tried and Approved— The Woman Juror," *Woman Citizen* 6, no. 1 (1921): 8–9; "The First Ten Years," *Woman's Journal* 15, no. 8 (1930): 5–7, 30–32.

16. McCammon et al., "Becoming Full Citizens," 1107–9; Kerber, *No Constitutional Right*, 136–147; Grossman, "Women's Jury Service," 1137; Beverly B. Cook, "Women Judges: A Preface to Their History," *Golden Gate University Law Review* 14, no. 3 (1984): 576 (table 1).

17. "Charles Locke Weller," in *History of the Bench and Bar of California*, ed. J. C. Bates (San Francisco: Bench and Bar, 1912), 548; "From the Churches," *Pacific Unitarian* 23, no. 2 (1914): 54; "Weller, Charles Locke," *Who's Who on the Pacific Coast: A Biographical Compilation of Notable Living Contemporaries West of the Rocky Mountains*, ed. Franklin Harper (Los Angeles: Harper, 1913), 596; "Police Inaugurate War on 'Mashers,'" *San Francisco Call*, November 23, 1910, 17; "Woman's New Status," *Los Angeles Times*, December 10, 1911, 25; "Separate Courts for Women Urged by Club Members," *San Francisco Call*, March 7, 1912, 10; "The First Judicial Recall," *Independent*, May 8, 1913, 1014.

18. Gayle Gullett, "City Mothers, City Daughters, and the Dance Hall Girls: The Limits of Female Political Power in San Francisco, 1913," in *Women and the Structure of Society: Selected Research from the Fifth Berkshire Conference on the History of Women*, ed. Barbara J. Harris and JoAnn McNamara (Durham, NC: Duke University Press, 1984), 152–153; "Findings of the Legislative Committee and Board of Directors of the San Francisco Center on the Question of the Recall of Judge Weller," February 21, 1913, 2–3, League of Women Voters of San Francisco Records, California Historical Society (hereafter LWVSF), box 4, folder 1.

19. "Findings of the Legislative Committee," 3–4; Charles L. Weller to the Board of Directors of the San Francisco Center, March 4, 1913, LWVSF, box 4, folder 1; "Women Agitate Judge's Recall," *San Francisco Chronicle*, January 8, 1913, 8; "Fugitive Indicted by Grand Jury," *San Francisco Chronicle*, January 10, 1913, 5; "Charge Perjury in Recall Case," *Los Angeles Times*, January 14, 1913, 3.

20. Neil Larry Shumsky, "Vice Responds to Reform: San Francisco, 1910–1914," *Journal of Urban History* 7, no. 1 (1980): 31–47.

21. "Clubwomen Aid Recall Movement," *San Francisco Call*, January 9, 1913, 4.

22. "Threaten to Recall Police Judge Weller," *San Francisco Call*, January 8, 1913, 5; "Weller's Recall Urged in Meeting," *San Francisco Chronicle*, January 15, 1913, 5.

23. "Charge Perjury in Recall Case"; Weiss, "Feminine Point of View," 14; E. A. Walcott, "Initiative, Referendum and Recall," in *National Municipal Review*, vol. 2, ed. Clinton Rogers Woodruff (Baltimore: Williams and Wilkins, 1913), 468–469; "Vent Ire on Judge," *Los Angeles Times*, January 15, 1913, 1; "Women at Helm in Recall Fight: Alice Best to Direct the Campaign," *San Francisco Chronicle*, January 19, 1913, 64.

24. Susan Englander, "'We Want the Ballot for Very Different Reasons': Clubwomen, Union Women, and the Internal Politics of the Suffrage Movement, 1896–1911," in *California Women and Politics: From the Gold Rush to the*

Great Depression, ed. Robert W. Cherney, Mary Ann Irwin, and Ann Marie Wilson (Lincoln: University of Nebraska, 2011), 225; "Women at Helm in Recall Fight"; "Crusaders Plan Reform of Bench," *San Francisco Chronicle,* February 21, 1913, 5; "The First Judicial Recall," *Independent,* May 8, 1913, 1014.

25. "Recall League Clears Deck for Action: 'All's Well That Ends Weller' Is Slogan," *San Francisco Chronicle,* January 21, 1913, 1; "Recall Petition Gets New Signers," *San Francisco Chronicle,* January 26, 1913, 42; "No Candidate in View, Say Women," *San Francisco Chronicle,* January 28, 1913, 1; "Women Name Candidate: Select Man to Beat Weller," *San Francisco Chronicle,* March 5, 1913, 1; Weiss, "Feminine Point of View," 25; "Recall League to Extend Its Scope," *San Francisco Call,* March 26, 1913. See also Gullett, "City Mothers, City Daughters," 150–153.

26. "Crist's Election Credited to Men," *San Francisco Chronicle,* May 2, 1913, 7; "Judge Crist Seated," *Los Angeles Times,* May 3, 1913, 3; "Judge Weller Is Recalled," *Los Angeles Times,* April 23, 1913, 3; "First Judicial Recall," *Independent,* May 8, 1913, 1014; "Say Women's Votes Ousted Weller," *San Francisco Chronicle,* May 4, 1913, 41; "The Woman's Vote in California," typescript, June 1913, 10–11, LWVSF, box 4, folder 1.

27. "Recall Workers Form a New Club," *San Francisco Chronicle,* May 6, 1913, 2; "Doings of Women's Clubs: Recall League Is Given New Birth," *San Francisco Chronicle,* June 5, 1913, 7; "Club Women Will Ask Removal of Chief White," *San Francisco Chronicle,* August 6, 1913, 5; "Question of Women on Grand Jury Discussed," *San Francisco Chronicle,* January 14, 1914, 9.

28. Weiss, "Feminine Point of View," 26; Gullett, "City Mothers, City Daughters," 153; San Francisco Center of the California Civic League, "Report of the Committee Investigating Police Court Procedures in San Francisco," typescript, 1913, LWVSF, box 4, folder 2.

29. Cott, *Grounding of Modern Feminism,* 117–142.

30. Alice Paul, *Outline of the Legal Position of Women in Pennsylvania, 1911(Including Changes Made in the Law by the 1911 Legislature)* (Philadelphia: Pennsylvania State Woman Suffrage Association, 1911), 25, 29–30, 33–34; "News from the Field," *Equal Rights* 1, no. 10 (1923): 78–79; Kathryn Miller, "Equal Rights Bills in Albany," *Equal Rights* 15, no. 6 (1929): 43–45; Anonymous, "The Legal Dependence of Women," *Equal Rights* 12, no. 14 (1925): 6–7; Press Comment, "Inequalities in the Law," *Equal Rights* 14, no. 28 (1927): 222–224; "Equal Rights Measures in the States," *Equal Rights* 14, no. 51 (1929): 407; "Blackstone and Women," *Equal Rights* 11, no. 21 (1924): 167.

31. "Comments of the Press," *Equal Rights* 1, no. 5 (1923): 38–39; Lessie Stringfellow Read, "What Club Women Want," *Woman Citizen* 8, no. 15 (1923): 23; "A Specious Question," *Equal Rights* 12, no. 4 (1925): 28; Ethel M. Smith, *Toward Equal Rights for Men and Women* (Washington, DC: Committee on the Legal Status of Women, National League of Women Voters, 1929), 31.

32. Lady Willie Forbus, "The Lucretia Mott Amendment," *Equal Rights* 11, no. 11 (1924): 85–86.
33. Dorothy Dunbar Bromley, "Breach of Promise—Why?," *Woman Citizen* 12, no. 4 (1925): 8–9, 40; Dorothy Dunbar Bromley, "Feminist—New Style," *Harper's*, October 1927, 552–560; C[atherine] Gasquoine Hartley, *The Truth about Woman* (London: E. Nash, 1913), 364–365; Hartley, *Women's Wild Oats: Essays on the Re-Fixing of Moral Standards* (New York: Frederick A. Stokes Co., 1920), 167.
34. H. W. Humble, "Seduction as a Crime," *Columbia Law Review* 21, no. 2 (1921): 144–154; Mary Coombs, "Agency and Partnership: A Study of Breach of Promise Plaintiffs," *Yale Journal of Law and Feminism* 2, no. 1 (1989): 12n77; Jane E. Larson, " 'Women Understand So Little, They Call My Good Nature "Deceit"': A Feminist Rethinking of Seduction," *Columbia Law Review* 93, no. 2 (1993): 395–398. See also Michael Grossberg, *Governing the Hearth: Law and Family in Nineteenth Century America* (Chapel Hill: University of North Carolina Press, 1985); and on the ideal of individual liberty within modern constructions of sexual rights, see Pamela Haag, *Consent: Sexual Rights and the Transformation of American Liberalism* (Ithaca, NY: Cornell University Press, 1999), esp. 82–99.
35. See Coombs, "Agency and Partnership," 14–15.
36. Rebecca Ryan, "The Sex Right: A Legal History of the Marital Rape Exemption," *Law and Social Inquiry* 20, no. 4 (1995): 942–943.
37. "Note of Explanation," *International Socialist Review* 5 (1905): 451 (this is an abstract of an article by Isador Ladoff). See also Wenonah Stevens Abbot, "Capitalism and Womanhood," *Machinists' Monthly Journal* 15, no. 9 (1903): 799.
38. Ellen Key, *Love and Marriage* (New York: G. P. Putnam's Sons, 1911), 386–387; Havelock Ellis, *Studies in the Psychology of Sex*, vol. 6, *Sex in Relation to Society* (Philadelphia: F. A. Davis Co., 1910), 473–475.
39. Emma Goldman, "The Traffic in Women," in *Red Emma Speaks: Selected Writings and Speeches by Emma Goldman,* comp. and ed. Alix Kates Shulman (New York: Vintage Books, 1972), 145.
40. Charlotte Perkins Gilman, *Herland* (1915; New York: Pantheon Books, 1979), 132–133.
41. Christina Simmons, *Making Marriage Modern: Women's Sexuality from the Progressive Era to World War II* (New York: Oxford University Press, 2009), 197–199; Dr. Horch Mainz, "Sexual Causes of Divorce," *American Journal of Urology and Sexology* 12, no. 4 (April 1916): 154; Sherwood Eddy, *Sex and Youth* (Garden City, NY: Doubleday, Doran and Co., 1932), 319.
42. William English Carson, *The Marriage Revolt: A Study of Marriage and Divorce* (New York: Hearst's International Library, 1915), 160–161; Maurice Chideckel, *The Single, the Engaged, and the Married* (New York: Eugenics, 1936), 248–249.

43. Joseph Warren Madden, *Handbook of the Law of Persons and Domestic Relations* (St. Paul, MN: West, 1931), 227, 264.

44. Jill Elaine Hasday, "Contest and Consent: A Legal History of Marital Rape," *California Law Review* 88, no. 5 (2000): 1467–1471; Elaine Tyler May, *Great Expectations: Marriage and Divorce in Post-Victorian America* (Chicago: University of Chicago Press, 1980), 105–109.

45. Cott, *Grounding of Modern Feminism*. On the recurrence of paradox in feminist history, see Joan Wallach Scott, *Only Paradoxes to Offer: French Feminists and the Rights of Man* (Cambridge, MA: Harvard University Press, 1996).

12. The Anti-Lynching Movement

1. C. Vann Woodward, *The Strange Career of Jim Crow* (New York: Oxford University Press, 1955), chap. 3.

2. "Speech of Senator Benjamin R. Tillman, March 23, 1900," *Congressional Record*, 56th Congress, 1st Sess., 3223–24, reprinted in *Document Sets for the South in U.S. History*, ed. Richard Purday (Lexington, MA: D. C. Heath, 1991), 147; Blease quoted in Christopher Waldrep, *The Many Faces of Judge Lynch: Extralegal Violence and Punishment in America* (New York: Palgrave Macmillan, 2002), 121.

3. Theodore Roosevelt, "Message Communicated to the Two Houses of Congress at the Beginning of the Second Session of the Fifty-Ninth Congress, December 3, 1906," *Presidential Addresses and State Papers*, vol. 5, April 14, 1906–January 14, 1907 (New York: Review of Reviews Co., 1910), 911; Philip Dray, *At the Hands of Persons Unknown: The Lynching of Black America* (New York: Modern Library, 2002), 101, 197–198; Thomas Dixon Jr., *The Clansman: An Historical Romance of the Ku Klux Klan* (New York: Doubleday, Page and Co., 1905); *The Birth of a Nation*, directed by D. W. Griffith (Los Angeles: Epoch Film, 1915).

4. Dray, *At the Hands of Persons Unknown*, 101, 166; Jacquelyn Dowd Hall, *Revolt against Chivalry: Jessie Daniel Ames and the Women's Campaign against Lynching* (New York: Columbia University Press, 1979), 134 (table 1); Roberta Senechal de la Roche, *In Lincoln's Shadow: The 1908 Race Riot in Springfield, Illinois* (Carbondale: Southern Illinois University Press, 2008); Walter White, *Rope and Faggot: A Biography of Judge Lynch* (New York: Alfred A. Knopf, 1929), 264–266.

5. Robert L. Zangrando, *The NAACP Crusade against Lynching, 1909–1950* (Philadelphia: Temple University Press, 1980), chap. 3; Thomas Sugrue, *Sweet Land of Liberty: The Forgotten Struggle for Civil Rights in the North* (New York: Random House, 2008), 8–10; Erin D. Chapman, *Prove It on Me: New Negroes, Sex, and Popular Culture in the 1920s* (New York: Oxford University Press, 2012), esp. 4–7, 23–27.

6. W. E. Burkhart Du Bois, "Georgia: Invisible Empire State," *Nation*, January 21, 1925, 67.

7. Jacquelyn Dowd Hall, "'The Mind That Burns in Each Body': Women, Rape and Racial Violence," in *Powers of Desire: The Politics of Sexuality,* ed. Christine Stansell, Ann Snitow, and Sharon Thompson (New York: Monthly Review Press, 1983), 330.

8. "Horrible Memphis Lynching Astounds Civilized World: Millions Prepare to Leave the South following Brutal Burning of Human," *Chicago Defender,* May 26, 1917, 1; Patrick S. Washburn, *The African American Newspaper: Voice of Freedom* (Evanston, IL: Northwestern University Press, 2006), 83, 126, 140. See also James R. Grossman, *Land of Hope: Chicago, Black Southerners, and the Great Migration* (Chicago: University of Chicago Press, 1989), 74–88.

9. W. E. B. Du Bois, "Intermarriage," *Crisis,* February 1913, 181; Peggy Pascoe, *What Comes Naturally: Miscegenation Law and the Making of Race in America* (New York: Oxford University Press, 2009), 71–72, 170, 178; "Definition of a Southern Gentleman," *Chicago Defender,* February 13, 1915, 8; "White Lady of Georgia Defends Her Colored Sisters," *Chicago Defender,* January 6, 1912, 1; "Jackass Club Takes African in Its Ranks," *Chicago Defender,* July 21, 1923, 13; Booker T. Washington, "Gods of Hemp Rope Indicted," *Chicago Defender,* March 30, 1912, 1; W. E. B. Du Bois, *Darkwater: Voices from within the Veil* (New York: Harcourt, Brace, and Howe, 1920), 172.

10. Pascoe, *What Comes Naturally,* chap. 5, 172–180; "About Miscegenation," *Chicago Defender,* December 24, 1927, A2.

11. "The Deadly Parallel," *Baltimore Afro-American,* November 12, 1920, 9. Data based on a sample of two hundred rape reports in the *New York Times,* the *Atlanta Constitution,* and the *Los Angeles Times* in 1910, 1920, and 1930. Two-thirds of the men in the rape accounts were black; for Atlanta, that figure rose to 85 percent.

12. For example: "Surgeon Faces Serious Charges," *Pittsburgh Courier,* June 11, 1927, 1; "Pastor Faces Serious Charge," *Pittsburgh Courier,* January 21, 1928, 1. In the 1920s through the 1940s, intraracial black assaults declined as a proportion of rape reports in the *Baltimore Afro-American* (from 40 percent to 36 percent) and in the *Chicago Defender* (from 51 percent to 16 percent). Jessica Moore, "Rape, Race, and Reporting: Press Coverage of Sexual Violence in Black and White American Newspapers, 1920–1945" (undergraduate honors thesis, Stanford University, 2012), 17 (table 1).

13. E.g., "Southern Newspaper Rot," *Baltimore Afro-American,* April 2, 1904, 4; "D. H. Chamberlain Flayed," *Savannah Tribune,* November 26, 1904, 2; *Savannah Tribune,* October 6, 1906, 4; "Morons," *Savannah Tribune,* September 28, 1922, 4; *Chicago Defender,* October 7 1911, 1; Milton Pope Fuller, "Fifty Years of Unequaled Progress," *Chicago Defender,* January 2, 1915, 7; "Oklahoma a Little Hell," *Chicago Defender,* October 29, 1910, 1; "The World Coming to an End," *Chicago Defender,* December 10, 1910, 1.

14. "Southern White Gentleman Rapes Colored Lady, Is Killed By Husband," *Chicago Defender*, November 4, 1911, 1; "Report of Lynchings Past Year Submitted," *Chicago Defender*, January 5, 1918, 9; "White Man Tries to Rape Small Girl in Washington Pk," *Chicago Defender*, July 25, 1914, 2; "White Man Charged with Rape of Eight-Year-Old Girl," *Chicago Defender*, October 23, 1915, 1; "White Man Rapes Six-Year-Old Girl," *Chicago Defender*, May 31, 1919, 1; "White Man Attempts Rape," *Chicago Defender*, December 13, 1919, 3; "White Man Assaults Young Negro Girl," *Savannah Tribune*, August 19, 1922, 1; "White Held for Rape," *Baltimore Afro-American*, June 30, 1922, 4; "Philly Aroused over Epidemic of Assaults by Nordic Morons," *Pittsburgh Courier*, August 25, 1928, 10; "White Man Rapes Six-Year-Old Girl," *Chicago Defender*, May 31, 1919, 1.

15. "Mother at Fifteen, November 30th: Is Fate of Little Mator McFerrin," *Chicago Defender*, November 9, 1912, 1; Cynthia M. Blair, *I've Got to Make My Livin': Black Women's Sex Work in Turn-of-the-Century Chicago* (Chicago: University of Chicago Press, 2010), 188–218; "White Man Tries to Rape Small Girl"; "White Man Charged with Rape of Eight-Year-Old Girl"; "Did the Janitor Mistreat This Little Girl, Club Women Should Get Busy," *Chicago Defender*, September 25, 1915, 1; "White Married Man Is Given 20 Years for Rape," *Chicago Defender*, January 31, 1925, 1. Black victims in the *Baltimore Afro-American* during the 1920s were almost three years younger than white victims; the average age was similar for the two races in the *Chicago Defender*. Moore, "Rape, Race, and Reporting," 45 (table 5).

16. "A Dastardly Outrage," *Baltimore Afro-American*, August 1, 1908, 4; "Attempted Rape by White Interne Causes His Arrest; Victim 17-Year-Old Girl," *Chicago Defender*, March 2, 1918, 1; "White Doctor Held on Charge of Rape," *Chicago Defender*, August 4, 1918, 1; "Woman Is Attacked by Officer," *Pittsburgh Courier*, February 16, 1924, 2; "Threatens Mother and Babes with Ax," *Chicago Defender*, September 11, 1920, 1; "Accuser," *Chicago Defender*, February 9, 1924, 3. On police officers, see "Uncalled for Outrage," *Savannah Tribune*, June 10, 1893, 3; "And yet,—They Say the White Man Doesn't Commit Rape," *Pittsburgh Courier*, February 7, 1925, 20; "Officer Accused of Attack on Girl," *Pittsburgh Courier*, May 16, 1925, 9.

17. "Pretty Girl Assaulted by a Lawyer Finds Injustice Reluctant to Prosecute," *Pittsburgh Courier*, September 6, 1924, 13; "Cases," *Pittsburgh Courier*, April 24, 1926, 16; "Crimes against Human Nature," *Baltimore Afro-American*, January 27, 1922, 7; "Hoodwinking Justice," *Baltimore Afro-American*, August 22, 1908, 4; "Girls Reveal Story of Brutal Crime," *Chicago Defender*, March 6, 1926, 1; "Kentucky's Chance," *Chicago Defender*, March 13, 1926, A8; "Kentucky Is Watched on Testing Law," *Chicago Defender*, March 20, 1926, 1; "Four White Youths Held on Statutory Charges," *Chicago Defender*, December 3, 1927, 3; "Other Papers Say," *Chicago Defender*, October 29, 1927, A2.

18. "White Man Sentenced to Penitentiary for High Crime," *Savannah Tribune,* October 12, 1922, 1, 6; "Southern 'Gentleman' Is Sentenced to Die for Rape," *Pittsburgh Courier,* October 31, 1925, 1; "It Wasn't Our Race This Time in Beastly Role," *Chicago Defender,* July 8, 1922, 2.

19. Patricia Bernstein, *The First Waco Horror: The Lynching of Jesse Washington and the Rise of the NAACP* (College Station: Texas A&M University Press, 2005), 133; Dray, *At the Hands of Persons Unknown,* 224; "Report of Lynchings Past Year Submitted," *Chicago Defender,* January 5, 1918, 9; "1924 Lynching Report Shows Lowest Record," *Chicago Defender,* January 3, 1925, 8.

20. "False Charges Stir Camp Grant Soldiers," *Chicago Defender,* May 25, 1918, 1; "Nab Dining Car Waiter on Bogus Rape Charge," *Chicago Defender,* July 8, 1922, 3; "'I'll Scream If You Don't,' Ruse of Girl Bandit," *Chicago Defender,* January 13, 1923, 1; "Mob Quiet; Rape Case Fizzles Out," *Baltimore Afro-American,* August 24, 1929, 5. In a sample of rape reports in the *Chicago Defender* and the *Baltimore Afro-American* between 1920 and 1945, almost 40 percent of the reports of black-on-white rape emphasized that the charges were false. Moore, "Rape, Race, and Reporting," 56.

21. Khalil Gibran Muhammad, *The Condemnation of Blackness: Race, Crime, and the Making of Modern Urban America* (Cambridge, MA: Harvard University Press, 2010), 86; Waldrep, *Many Faces of Judge Lynch,* 128–129; Rev. Amory H. Bradford, "Our Nation's Shame," *Outlook* 49 (June 23, 1894): 25; "Southern Protests against Lynching," *Outlook,* July 30, 1919, 493; Jane Addams, "Respect for Law," *Independent,* January 3, 1901, 18–20. On barbarism, see Gail Bederman, *Manliness and Civilization: A Cultural History of Gender and Race in the United States* (Chicago: University of Chicago Press, 1996).

22. Walter H. Page, "The Last Hold of the Southern Bully," *Forum* 16 (November 1893): 303; *Montgomery Journal* quoted in "Southern Protests against Lynching," 493.

23. "The Mob Spirit," *Chautauquan,* September 1903, 11–13; L. E. Bleckley, "Negro Outrage No Excuse for Lynching," *Forum* 16 (November 1893): 300–302; "Governor Atkinson of Georgia on the Question of Lynching," *American Lawyer* 6, no. 2 (January–December 1898): 52; "Gov. Longino on Mobs," *Christian Recorder,* March 14, 1901; Anonymous, "Suggested Prevention of Lynching," *Woman's Tribune,* May 14, 1904, 58; Lew A. Chase, "Law and Lynching," *Outlook,* January 18, 1902, 197.

24. "White Lady of Georgia Defends Her Colored Sisters"; Crystal Nicole Feimster, *Southern Horrors: Women and the Politics of Rape and Lynching* (Cambridge, MA: Harvard University Press, 2009), 196–197, 203; "Crime of Mob Violence Unpunished in Georgia, Declares Mrs. Felton," *Atlanta Constitution,* January 13, 1920, 8.

25. Juliette V. Harring to W. E. B. Du Bois, August 14, 1922, W. E. B. Du Bois Papers (MS312), Special Collections and University Archives, UMass Amherst

Libraries, oubliette.library.umass.edu/view/full/mums312-b019-i311; Juliette V. Harring, "A Lynching," September 14, 1922, NAACP Papers, pt. 7: The Anti-Lynching Campaign, 1912–1955, series B: Anti-Lynching Legislative and Publicity Files, 1916–1955, Library of Congress (microfilm, reel 3, frame 291), included in "How Did Black Women in the NAACP Promote the Dyer Anti-Lynching Bill, 1918–1923?," documents selected and interpreted by Angelica Mungarro under the supervision of Karen Anderson, in the online collection *Women and Social Movements in the United States, 1600–2000,* ed. Kathryn Kish Sklar and Thomas Dublin (hereafter cited as WASM; accessed March 27, 2012, http://womhist.alexanderstreet.com).

26. "Open Letters from the University Commission on Southern Race Questions to the College Men of the South," *Minutes of the University Commission on Southern Race Questions* (Lexington, Va., n.d.), 45–46 (appendix A); "Law and Order League Suppress Crime," *Savannah Tribune,* March 9, 1918, 1; Tillett quoted in "The Liberal South," *Crisis,* March 1918, 234.

27. George P. Upton, "The Facts about Lynching," *Independent,* September 29, 1904, 719–721; "The Lynching Record," *Outlook,* February 28, 1914, 434; "Lynchings in Six Months," *Chautauquan,* September 6, 1913, 15; "A Contagious Social Disease," *Independent,* February 7, 1916, 178; Herbert L. Stewart, "The Casuistry of Lynch Law," *Nation,* April 24, 1916, 173–174; "Southern Protests against Lynching," 493; "The Mob Spirit and Lynching," *Outlook,* August 7, 1918, 542; Mary White Ovington, "The White Brute," *Masses* 6 (October–November 1915): 87–89.

28. Jeffrey Melnick, *Black-Jewish Relations on Trial: Leo Frank and Jim Conley in the New South* (Jackson: University Press of Mississippi, 2000), 56, also 47–87. See also Leonard Dinnerstein, *The Leo Frank Case* (Athens: University of Georgia Press, 2008); and Nancy MacLean, "The Leo Frank Case Reconsidered: Gender and Sexual Politics in the Making of Reactionary Populism," *Journal of American History* 70, no. 3 (1991): 932.

29. The *Times* editorial was reprinted in the *Chicago Defender:* "The South at the Bar," *Chicago Defender,* August 8, 1915, 8; "Tidal Wave of Leo Frank Pleas into Georgia," *Chicago Daily Tribune,* May 29, 1915, 7; "A Regrettable Incident," *New York Times,* August 19, 1915; 8; "Lying of Leo Frank a Reproach to Georgia," *Los Angeles Times,* August 18, 1915, 12. On the sexual implications of the case, see MacLean, "Leo Frank Case Reconsidered."

30. "Germany Suppresses 'Black Horror Film,'" *New York Times,* August 24, 1921, 9; F. P. Wilhelm, "Correspondence: A Hymn of Hate," *Nation* 112 (June 8, 1921): 815; Carrie Chapman Catt, "The Truth about the Black Troops on the Rhine," *Woman's Journal,* March 5, 1921, 1038. W. E. B. Du Bois also investigated and refuted the claims. On the controversy, see Keith L. Nelson, "The 'Black Horror on the Rhine': Race as a Factor in Post–World War I Diplomacy," *Journal of Modern History* 42, no. 4 (1970): 606–627.

31. Anonymous, "Kept Together by Cohercion [*sic*]," *Woman Patriot,* September 1, 1922, 9.

32. Feimster, *Southern Horrors*, 214–217; Dray, *At the Hands of Persons Unknown*, 220–221, 172–176; Zangrando, *NAACP Crusade against Lynching*, 20; Booker T. Washington, "Lynchings and International Peace," *Outlook*, March 9, 1912, 554; "Damages for Lynching," *Nation*, December 8, 1910, 546.

33. Mark Curriden and Leroy Phillips Jr., *Contempt of Court: The Turn of the Century Lynching That Launched a Hundred Years of Federalism* (New York: Anchor Books, 1999).

34. United States v. Shipp, 214 U.S. 386, 29 S. Ct. 637, 53 L. Ed. 1041 (U.S. 1909).

35. Feimster, *Southern Horrors*, 120–121; "Six Women," *Crisis*, May 1914, 22; "Lynching," *Crisis*, September 1915, 227–228; "The Burning Question," *Crisis*, September 1916, 223; "Progressive Oklahoma," *Crisis*, June 1916, 94; "Legal Defense," *Crisis*, March 1922, 212.

36. Mary White Ovington, "The National Association for the Advancement of Colored People," *Journal of Negro History* 9, no. 2 (1924): 107–116; Mary White Ovington, *The Walls Came Tumbling Down* (1947; New York: Schocken Books, 1970), 112.

37. Zangrando, *NAACP Crusade against Lynching*, 22–28; "Lynching," *Crisis*, January, 1914, 125; "Where Does Your Congressman Stand: A Questionnaire," *Crisis*, November 1914, 22.

38. Roy Nash, "Memorandum for Mr. Philip G. Peabody on Lynch-Law and the Practicability of a Successful Attack There On," Boston, May 22, 1916, Papers of the NAACP, pt. 7, ser. A, reel 20. On the NAACP and Waco, see Bernstein, *The First Waco Horror*, 166–170.

39. Bernstein, *The First Waco Horror*, 69–77, 138–158; "British Suffragist Here in War on Lynching Due to Burning of Boy at Waco," *Detroit Journal*, July 21, 1916, 1; "Women in Seattle Hiss Miss Freeman," *New York Times*, October 14, 1916, 8. "Columbus, Ohio NAACP Branch to Franklin County Woman Suffrage Association, 16 May 1916" and "Agnes V. Sawyer to the Columbus Branch of the NAACP, 23 June 1916," Elisabeth Freeman Collection of Margaret Johnston, included in "How Did Elisabeth Freeman's Publicity Skills Promote Woman Suffrage, Antilynching, and the Peace Movement, 1909–1919?," pt. 2, documents selected and interpreted by Thomas Dublin and Margaret Johnston, in WASM, accessed March 27, 2012.

40. Walter White, *A Man Called White: The Autobiography of Walter White* (New York: Viking Press, 1948), 42; "The Anti-Lynching Conference," *Crisis*, June 1919, 92.

41. Dray, *At the Hands of Persons Unknown*, 257; "Johnson Addresses the League," *Chicago Defender*, February 21, 1920, 12; James Weldon Johnson, "Lynching—America's National Disgrace," *Current History* 19 (January, 1924): 596–601; William Pickens, "More White Rapists in America Than Colored, Says Dr. Wm. Pickens," *Baltimore Afro-American*, December 30, 1921, 12; William Pickens, *Lynching and Debt-Slavery* (New York: American Civil Liberties Union New York, 1921), Papers of the ACLU, reel 7, vol. 69, 7.

42. Pickens, *Lynching and Debt-Slavery,* 7–8; Glenda Gilmore, *Defying Dixie: The Radical Roots of Civil Rights, 1919–1950* (New York: W. W. Norton, 2008), 97–99.

43. Dray, *At the Hands of Persons Unknown,* 229; "The Shame of America," *Nation,* July 19, 1919, 89.

44. Dray, *At the Hands of Persons Unknown,* 269, 282; Neil R. McMillen, *Dark Journey: Black Mississippians in the Age of Jim Crow* (Urbana: University of Illinois Press, 1990), 235; "Favors Anti-Lynching Bill," *Savannah Tribune,* March 9, 1922, 1; J. Blaine Poindexter, "Chicagoans Hear Congressman on Dyer Lynch Bill," *Chicago Defender,* June 2, 1923, 3; "Mob Spirit and Lynching"; Barbara Holden-Smith, "Lynching, Federalism, and the Intersection of Race and Gender in the Progressive Era," *Yale Journal of Law and Feminism* 8, no. 31 (1996): 39–40; Lisa Lindquist Dorr, *White Women, Rape, and the Power of Race in Virginia, 1900–1960* (Chapel Hill: University of North Carolina Press, 2004), 30.

45. Congressman John Rankin quoted in McMillen, *Dark Journey,* 235; Senator Caraway of Arkansas, on November 29, 1922, 67th Cong., 3rd sess., *Congressional Record* 63, pt. 1, 400; Senator Heflin of Alabama, on May 8, 1928, 70th Cong., 1st sess., *Congressional Record* 75, pt. 8, 8054; "Heflin Denounced by Maryland Colleague," *Chicago Defender,* June 2, 1928, 7; Senator Bilbo of Mississippi, on January 21, 1938, 75th Cong., 3rd sess., *Congressional Record* 83, pt. 1, 873.

46. Herbert J. Seligman, letters dated October 15–20 and responses, in "Rape Statistics, October–November, 1919," NAACP Papers, pt. 7, ser. A, reel 21; Mark Robert Schneider, *"We Return Fighting": The Civil Rights Movement in the Jazz Age* (Boston: Northeastern University Press, 2002), 29–31, 360–361.

47. William Pickens, "Bess Paramour of Woman Who Tricked Him," *Baltimore Afro-American,* August 4, 1928, 7; N. J. Frederick to Walter White, October 16, 1929, Papers of the NAACP, pt. 12, Selected Branch Files, 1913–1939, ser. A: The South, reel 19; "Fearing Death, White Woman's Confession Gives Man Freedom; Admits Lie after Innocent Victim Serves 13 Years of 30-Year Stretch," *Baltimore Afro-American,* May 12, 1928, 1; "Southern Justice," *Chicago Defender,* May 19, 1928, A2. Collins revoked her recantation, setting in motion a battle over whether the governor could revoke his pardon. "Ben Bess Again Freed by the S.C. Court," *Baltimore Afro-American,* October 19, 1929, A1.

48. Field Secretary to George B. Kelley, June 30, 1920; William T. Francis to George W. Kelley [*sic*], June 21, 1920; G. B. Kelley to Mr. Bagnall, April 12, 1930; all in Duluth Branch File, Papers of the NAACP, pt. 12, Selected Branch files, 1913–1939, ser. C: The Midwest, reel 15.

49. "Meharry Students Said to Be Victim of 'Hello Girl' Plot," *Pittsburgh Courier,* April 26, 1924, 9; "Medical Student Is Given New Trial," *Pittsburgh Courier,* June 6, 1925, 14; "From the Defender Files: 15 Years Ago," *Chi-*

cago Defender, June 10, 1939, 14. Although the state supreme court ordered a new trial, the case was not re-prosecuted. "Unusual Endings to the Usual Crime Told by NAACP," *Atlanta Daily World,* August 1, 1934, 6.

50. White, *Rope and Faggot,* 260–263.
51. On black women and politics in the 1920s, see Rosalyn Terborg-Penn, "Discontented Black Feminists: Prelude and Postscript to the Passage of the Nineteenth Amendment," in *Decades of Discontent: The Women's Movement, 1920–1940,* ed. Lois Scharf and Joan M. Jensen (1983; Boston: Northeastern University Press, 1987), 261–278.
52. "Mrs. Mossell Griffin's Lynch Bill as a Model" [1922], NAACP Papers, pt. 7: The Anti-Lynching Campaign, 1912–1955, ser. B: Anti-Lynching Legislative and Publicity Files, 1916–1955, reel 3, frame 672; Mr. Storey's Secretary to Mrs. C. J. Walker, May 10, 1919, NAACP Papers, pt. 7: The Anti-Lynching Campaign, 1912–1955, ser. B: Anti-Lynching Legislative and Publicity Files, 1916–1955, reel 1, frame 284, included in Mungarro, "How Did Black Women in the NAACP Promote the Dyer Anti-Lynching Bill, 1918–1923?" WASM; Feimster, *Southern Horrors,* 224.
53. Feimster, *Southern Horrors,* 228; Zangrando, *NAACP Crusade against Lynching,* 78; "The Anti-Lynching Crusaders: The Lynching of Women" [1922], NAACP Papers, pt. 7: The Anti-Lynching Campaign, 1912–1955, ser. B: Anti-Lynching Legislative and Publicity Files, 1916–1955, Library of Congress (microfilm, reel 3, frames 570–573), WASM doc. 7; Mary E. Jackson, "Suggestions from Miss Jackson" [1922], NAACP Papers, pt. 7: The Anti-Lynching Campaign, 1912–1955, ser. B: Anti-Lynching Legislative and Publicity Files, 1916–1955, Library of Congress (microfilm, reel 3, frame 553); doc. 11A, Mary B. Talbert, Letter to State Director [1922], NAACP Papers, pt. 7: The Anti-Lynching Campaign, 1912–1955, ser. B: Anti-Lynching Legislative and Publicity Files, 1916–1955, Library of Congress (microfilm, reel 3, frames 550–551). Doc. 14, Mary B. Talbert et al., Minutes of the Executive Committee of the Anti-Lynching Crusaders [1922], NAACP Papers, pt. 7: The Anti-Lynching Campaign, 1912–1955, ser. B: Anti-Lynching Legislative and Publicity Files, 1916–1955, Library of Congress (microfilm, reel 3, frames 565–566), in Mungarro, "How Did Black Women in the NAACP Promote the Dyer Anti-Lynching Bill, 1918–1923?," WASM.
54. "The Anti-Lynching Crusaders," *Woman Citizen,* December 16, 1922, 23; Feimster, *Southern Horrors,* 230; Paula J. Giddings, *Ida: A Sword among Lions—Ida B. Wells and the Campaign against Lynching* (New York: Amistad, 2008), 644.
55. Evelyn Brooks Higginbotham, *Righteous Discontent: The Women's Movement in the Black Baptist Church, 1880–1920* (Cambridge, MA: Harvard University Press, 1993), 197–199; Charlotte Hawkins Brown, October 8, 1920, in *Black Women in White America: A Documentary History,* ed. Gerda Lerner (New York: Vintage Books, 1973), 467–472; Feimster, *Southern Horrors,* 227–228.

56. Doc. 7, "Southern Negro Women and Race Co-operation," June 28–30, 1921, Commission on Interracial Cooperation Papers, Atlanta University Center, Robert W. Woodruff Library (microfilm, reel 14, no. 476–80); Feimster, *Southern Horrors*, 228.

57. Hall, *Revolt against Chivalry*, 45–46, 55, 59, 107, 111–112, 124.

58. Jessie Daniel Ames, "Southern Women and Lynching," October 1936, Association of Southern Women for the Prevention of Lynching Papers, Atlanta University Center, Robert W. Woodruff Library (microfilm, reel 4, no. 1816), in Dublin, Sklar, and Vill, "How Did Black and White Southern Women Campaign to End Lynching, 1890–1942?," WASM; doc. 10, "History of Movement" [November 1930], Commission on Interracial Cooperation Papers, Atlanta University Center, Robert W. Woodruff Library, Southern Regional Council collection (microfilm, reel 43, no. 1168). "Suggested Points in Presenting Purposes of A.S.W.P.L." [1931], Association of Southern Women for the Prevention of Lynching Papers, Atlanta University Center, Robert W. Woodruff Library (microfilm, reel 4, no. 43), from Dublin, Sklar, and Vill, "How Did Black and White Southern Women Campaign to End Lynching, 1890–1942?," WASM.

59. Quoted in Hall, *Revolt against Chivalry*, 156.

60. Jessie Daniel Ames, "Southern Women Look at Lynching," Atlanta, Association of Southern Women for the Prevention of Lynching, February 1937, 4–5, 8–9, 11; doc. 16, Jessie Daniel Ames, "Southern Women and Lynching," October 1936, Association of Southern Women for the Prevention of Lynching Papers, Atlanta University Center, Robert W. Woodruff Library (microfilm, reel 4, no. 1816). Hall, "'The Mind That Burns in Each Body,'" 337; Lewis T. Nordyke, "Ladies and Lynchings," *Survey Graphic* 28 (November 1939): 683–686. On Ames's views on the Dyer act, see also Zangrando, *NAACP Crusade against Lynching*, 149.

61. Quoted in Hall, "'The Mind That Burns in Each Body,'" 331, 339.

62. Nancy J. Weiss, *Farewell to the Party of Lincoln: Black Politics in the Age of FDR* (Princeton, NJ: Princeton University Press, 1983), 119.

63. Quoted in Dorr, *White Women*, 28. See also Adam Fairclough, *Race and Democracy: The Civil Rights Struggle in Louisiana, 1915–1972* (Athens: University of Georgia Press, 1995), 31; Marilynn S. Johnson, "Gender, Race, and Rumors: Re-examining the 1943 Race Riots," *Gender and History* 10, no. 2 (1998): 252–277; Zangrando, *NAACP Crusade against Lynching*, 6–7 (table 2), 148; Dorr, *White Women*, 30, 206, 44, 12; and "Memphis Stages 'Legalized' Lynching," *Pittsburgh Courier*, February 27, 1926, 1.

13. Scottsboro and Its Legacies

1. Dan T. Carter, *Scottsboro: A Tragedy of the American South*, rev. ed. (Baton Rouge: Louisiana State University Press, 2007), 3–6; James Goodman, *Stories of Scottsboro* (New York: Vintage Books, 1995), 3–5. The accused were

between the ages of thirteen and twenty; the youngest received a sentence of life imprisonment.

2. Hugh T. Murray Jr., "The NAACP versus the Communist Party: The Scottsboro Rape Cases, 1931–1932," *Phylon* 28, no. 3 (1967): 276–287; Glenda Gilmore, *Defying Dixie: The Radical Roots of Civil Rights, 1919–1950* (New York: W. W. Norton, 2008), 98–99, 118–119, 126–137; James A. Miller, Susan D. Pennybacker, and Eve Rosenhaft, "Mother Ada Wright and the International Campaign to Free the Scottsboro Boys, 1931–1934," *American Historical Review* 106, no. 2 (2001): 387–420. On changing interpretations of Scottsboro, see Carroll Van West, "Scottsboro and Its Interpreters," *South Atlantic Quarterly* 80 (1981): 36–48.

3. Hugh T. Murray Jr., "Changing America and the Changing Image of Scottsboro," *Phylon* 38, no. 1 (1977): 82–92. See also Gilmore, *Defying Dixie,* 127–128, 207–208; and James A Miller, *Remembering Scottsboro: The Legacy of an Infamous Trial* (Princeton, NJ: Princeton University Press, 2009).

4. Powell v. Alabama, 287 U.S. 45 (1932); Norris v. Alabama, 294 U.S. 587 (1935). Precedents include Strauder v. West Virginia (1880), Neal v. Delaware (1881), and Moore v. Dempsey (1923). Goodman, *Stories of Scottsboro,* 252.

5. Quoted in Goodman, *Stories of Scottsboro,* 5, 15, 116.

6. Ibid., 222.

7. Quoted in Jacquelyn Dowd Hall, *Revolt against Chivalry: Jessie Daniel Ames and the Women's Campaign against Lynching* (New York: Columbia University Press, 1993), 208; Goodman, *Stories of Scottsboro,* 6, 53–57. After the convictions, an ASWPL member alerted "responsible citizens" in Scottsboro to "watch for any lawless movement." Mary M. McCoy to Jessie Daniel Ames, April 21, 1931, ASWPL Papers, reel 5, file 97.

8. Goodman, *Stories of Scottsboro,* 249, 120–122, 250; "Scottsboro Ruling Got Colored on 27 Juries, Survey Shows," *Baltimore Afro-American,* November 9, 1935, 12.

9. Goodman, *Stories of Scottsboro,* 257, 304–313, 380–381. Patterson died in a Michigan prison serving time for manslaughter. See also Haywood Patterson and Earl Conrad, *Scottsboro Boy* (Garden City, NY: Doubleday, 1950).

10. Jessica Moore, "Rape, Race, and Reporting: Press Coverage of Sexual Violence in Black and White American Newspapers, 1920–1945" (undergraduate honors thesis, Stanford University, 2012), 86 (table 7). See also Felecia G. Jones Ross, "Mobilizing the Masses: The Cleveland *Call and Post* and the Scottsboro Incident," *Journal of Negro History* 84, no. 1 (1999): 48–60.

11. "Scottsboro Principle Is Applied to Jess Hollins' Case by U.S. High Court," *Chicago Defender,* May 18, 1935, 2. On retrial an all-white jury reconvicted Hollins, who died in prison awaiting parole. Charles H. Martin, "Oklahoma's 'Scottsboro' Affair: The Jess Hollins Rape Case, 1931–1936," *South Atlantic Quarterly* 79, no. 2 (1980): 175–188.

12. "New 'Scottsboro' Case Hinted in Jersey Town," *Baltimore Afro-American,* October 12, 1935, 6; "New 'Scottsboro Case' Brought to

Light in Arkansas," *Baltimore Afro-American,* October 5, 1935, 10; "Army Scottsboro Case Victims Refused Freedom," *Chicago Defender,* February 24, 1945, 4; Catherine Roth, "'California's 'Scottsboro': The Forgotten Case of Festus Coleman" (master's thesis, San Francisco State University, 2011). The national NAACP declined to take on the case, which was championed by the local branch as part of the Coleman Defense Coordinating Committee.

13. Adam Fairclough, *Race and Democracy: The Civil Rights Struggle in Louisiana, 1915–1972* (Athens: University of Georgia Press, 1995), 120, 125–132; Mark V. Tushnet, *Making Civil Rights Law: Thurgood Marshall and the Supreme Court, 1936–1961* (New York: Oxford University Press, 1994), 29; Steven F. Lawson, David R. Colburn, and Darryl Paulson, "Groveland: Florida's Little Scottsboro," *Florida Historical Quarterly* 65, no. 1 (1986): 1–26 (the two surviving defendants were paroled after spending twelve and sixteen years in prison, respectively); Lisa Lindquist Dorr, *White Women, Rape, and the Power of Race in Virginia, 1900–1960* (Chapel Hill: University of North Carolina Press, 2004), 220–223.

14. Eric W. Rise, "Race, Rape and Radicalism: The Case of the Martinsville Seven, 1949–1951," *Journal of Southern History* 58, no. 3 (1992): 484; Eric W. Rise, *The Martinsville Seven: Race, Rape, and Capital Punishment* (Charlottesville: University Press of Virginia, 1995); Dorr, *White Women,* 206, 213, 211; Stuart Banner, *The Death Penalty: An American History* (Cambridge, MA: Harvard University Press, 2003), 246; Furman v. Georgia, 408 U.S. 238 (1972); Coker v. Georgia, 433 U.S. 584 (1977).

15. Quoted in Goodman, *Stories of Scottsboro,* 330.

16. Martha Hodes, *White Women, Black Men: Illicit Sex in the Nineteenth-Century South* (New Haven, CT: Yale University Press, 1997); Dorr, *White Women,* 109, 113–114.

17. Goodman, *Stories of Scottsboro,* 22, 43.

18. Carter, *Scottsboro,* 105; (Mrs. I[saac]) Daily F. Morris to Mrs. Jessie Daniel Ames, April 27, 1931, "State Councils: Alabama, 1930–Dec 18, 1940, n.d.," ASWPL Papers, reel 5, file 97; Miller, Pennybacker, and Rosenhaft, "Mother Ada Wright," 70.

19. Quoted in Goodman, *Stories of Scottsboro,* 43, 56, 125–126, 134, 147. In a sign of the partial fraying of white southern solidarity, one of the physicians who testified for the state told Horton in the men's room that he didn't believe Price and Bates but that he feared testifying for the defense. Goodman, *Stories of Scottsboro,* 175–176.

20. Quoted in Carter, *Scottsboro,* 269, and Goodman, *Stories of Scottsboro,* 177–179.

21. Quoted in Goodman, *Stories of Scottsboro,* 227.

22. Kathryn McGarr, "'Nine Negroes' v. 'Mrs. Price' v. 'The Bates Girl'" (undergraduate paper, Stanford University, 2005); Goodman, *Stories of Scottsboro,* 167.

23. Langston Hughes, "Southern Gentlemen, White Prostitutes, Mill-Owners, and Negroes," *Contempo,* December 1, 1931, reprinted in *Good Morning Revolution: Uncollected Social Protest Writings by Langston Hughes,* ed. Faith Berry (New York: Lawrence Hill, 1973), 49; John Spivak, "Victoria's Brazen Words Abash the Newspaper Reporters," *Baltimore Afro-American,* April 15, 1933, 2. For another interpretation of the accusations as the result of growing southern white poverty, see Ben Cothran, "South of Scottsboro," *Forum and Century* 93, no. 6 (June 1935): 323–329. See also Goodman, *Stories of Scottsboro,* 188–190.

24. Hollace Ransdell, "Report on the Scottsboro, Ala. Case," mimeographed report to the American Civil Liberties Union, May 27, 1931, New York Public Library, Humanities and Social Sciences Library, in Sara L. Creed, "How Did Women Shape the Discourse and Further Interracial Cooperation in the Worldwide Mass Movement to 'Free the Scottsboro Boys'?," in the online collection *Women and Social Movements in the United States, 1600–2000,* ed. Kathryn Kish Sklar and Thomas Dublin, accessed March 27, 2012, http://womhist.alexanderstreet.com; Mary Heaton Vorse, "How Scottsboro Happened," *New Republic,* May 10, 1933, 356–358; Ames quoted in Hall, *Revolt against Chivalry,* 203.

25. Jessie Daniel Ames to Mrs. L. P. Donovan, July 7, 1931, ASWPL Papers, reel 5, file 97; (Mrs. J. F.) Nellie G. Hooper to Jessie Daniel Ames, April 28, 1931, ASWPL Papers, reel 5, file 97; and Goodman, *Stories of Scottsboro,* 57.

26. Dorr, *White Women,* 48–49. Not all efforts to invoke female immorality and duplicity worked. In Oklahoma the jury convicted Jess Hollins despite testimony from both black and white witnesses that the accuser had a reputation for dancing lewdly with black men. Martin, "Oklahoma's 'Scottsboro' Affair," 180, 183.

27. Goodman, *Stories of Scottsboro,* 167; Susan Brownmiller, *Against Our Will: Men, Women, and Rape* (New York: Simon and Schuster, 1975), 229–230; Hall, *Revolt against Chivalry,* 203; Leigh B. Bienen, "A Question of Credibility: John Henry Wigmore's Use of Scientific Authority in Section 924a of the Treatise on Evidence," *California Western Law Review* 19, no. 2 (1983): 235–268; "Forcible and Statutory Rape: An Exploration of the Operation of Objectives of the Consent Standard," *Yale Law Journal* 62 (December 1952): 55. Harper Lee, *To Kill a Mockingbird* (Philadelphia: Lippincott, 1960); film adaptation by Universal International Films, 1963. For a psychosexual interpretation of white men's relationships with black women, originally published in 1949, see Lillian Smith, *Killers of the Dream* (New York: W. W. Norton, 1994), chap. 3.

28. Brownmiller, *Against Our Will,* 230; Leigh Ann Wheeler, *How Sex Became a Civil Liberty* (New York: Oxford University Press, 2012), 180–184. On the continuing importance of a woman's character, see Dorr, *White Women,* esp. chap. 4.

29. Charles H. Martin, "The Civil Rights Congress and Southern Black Defendants," *Georgia Historical Quarterly* 71, no. 1 (1987): 25–52; Leandra Zarnow, "Braving Jim Crow to Save Willie McGee: Bella Abzug, the Legal Left, and Civil Rights Innovation, 1948–1951," *Law & Social Inquiry* 33, no. 4 (2008): 1003–41; Stephen J. Whitfield, *A Death in the Delta: The Story of Emmett Till* (New York: Free Press, 1988).

30. Quoted in Fairclough, *Race and Democracy,* 244. See also William Peters, *The Southern Temper* (New York: Doubleday, 1959), 202.

31. Miller, Pennybacker, and Rosenhaft, "Mother Ada Wright"; Creed, "How Did Women Shape the Discourse?" On continuing limitations on female jury service in the South, see Linda Kerber, *No Constitutional Right to Be Ladies: Women and the Obligations of Citizenship* (New York: Hill and Wang, 1998), 359n158. Before the 1960s the black press sometimes referred to "all-white, all-male" juries, rather than "all-white" juries—e.g., "Jury Fails to Agree in Attack Case," *Baltimore Afro-American,* June 1, 1940, 15; and "Judge Blasts 'Biased' Jury," *Chicago Defender,* August 11, 1951, 1.

32. Brownmiller, *Against Our Will,* 245; Hall, *Revolt against Chivalry,* 206. For a comparison of arguments in favor of black and female jurors, see Joanna L. Grossman, "Women's Jury Service: Right of Citizenship or Privilege of Difference?," *Stanford Law Review* 46, no. 5 (1994): 1115–60.

33. Roy Wilkins to James J. McClendon, March 8, 1940, and March 18, 1940, Papers of the NAACP, pt. 6: The Scottsboro Case, 1931–1950, reel 19, group 1, box H-5, Scottsboro Defense Committee, January–May 1940.

34. "Woman Charges Attack," *New York Times,* July 28, 1940, 20; "Scottsboro Case Man Freed," *New York Times,* August 1, 1940, 19; "Scottsboro Boy Held in Attack," *Los Angeles Sentinel,* August 1, 1940, 1; "Montgomery Free of Detroit Charge," *Baltimore Afro-American,* August 10, 1940, 3. The *Pittsburgh Courier* and the *Chicago Defender* also covered the story. Most historians state that the NAACP succeeded in keeping the story out of the press, citing Carter, *Scottsboro,* 401.

35. E.g., "Young Wife Tells of Brutal Attack," *Baltimore Afro-American,* August 30, 1930, A20; "Mother in Jail Cell; Roomer Rapes Child," *Baltimore Afro-American,* August 16, 1930, A20; "Rev. W. W. Henry, Facing Rape Charge, Missing," *Baltimore Afro-American,* January 26, 1935, 1; Moore, "Rape, Race, and Reporting," 35–36, 38, 17 (table 1), 23 (table 3).

36. White-on-black assaults reported in the *Chicago Defender* increased from one-fourth to one-third of sampled rape stories between the 1920s and the 1940s. Moore, "Rape, Race, and Reporting," 17 (table 1) ; "Dixie Cop, Ousted in Rape Scandal, Arrested Again," *Chicago Defender,* September 15, 1945, 1; "S.C. Cop Held in Assault on Minor," *Baltimore Afro-American,* April 14, 1945, 1; "White Attack Suspects Indicted; Girl Bonded," *Baltimore Afro-American,* March 23, 1940, 15; "Offer of Job Lured Girl: Miss Creech Sobs as She Tells of Abuses," *Baltimore Afro-American,* May 25, 1940, 24. See also Dorr, *White Women,* 235–236.

37. Dorr, *White Women*, 233–244; "N. Carolinian Speaks Out . . . Judge Blasts 'Biased' Jury Ashamed, He Says of Rape Verdict," *Chicago Defender*, August 11, 1951, 1.

38. "New Rape Case Reported in Alabama," *Chicago Defender*, February 3, 1945, 10; Dorr, *White Women*, 236–242.

39. Danielle L. McGuire, *At the Dark End of the Street: Black Women, Rape, and Resistance—A New History of the Civil Rights Movement from Rosa Parks to the Rise of Black Power* (New York: Knopf, 2010), xix, 8, 31, 34, 17–19, 25–26.

40. Ibid., 53–64.

41. Ibid., 192–195. Cannon appealed, but the Mississippi Supreme Court upheld the conviction. Cannon v. State of Mississippi, 190 So. 2d 848 (Miss. 1966).

42. On race differences in criminal justice procedures, see Marvin E. Wolfgang and Marc Riedel, "Race, Judicial Discretion, and the Death Penalty," *Annals of the American Academy of Political and Social Science* 407 (1973): 119–133; Gary Kleck, "Racial Discrimination in Criminal Sentencing: A Critical Evaluation of the Evidence with Additional Evidence on the Death Penalty," *American Sociological Review* 46, no. 6 (1981): 788, 792–793, 798; and Samuel R. Gross and Robert Mauro, "Patterns of Death: An Analysis of Racial Disparities in Capital Sentencing and Homicide Victimization," *Stanford Law Review* 37, no. 1 (1984): 38–39n45, 39n47.

14. The Enduring Politics of Rape

1. Mark V. Tushnet, *Making Civil Rights Law: Thurgood Marshall and the Supreme Court, 1936–1961* (New York: Oxford University Press, 1994), 65; Dawn Rae Flood, *Rape in Chicago: Race, Myth, and the Courts* (Urbana: University of Illinois Press, 2012), 56, 69–70, 162; Danielle L. McGuire, *At the Dark End of the Street: Black Women, Rape, and Resistance—A New History of the Civil Rights Movement from Rosa Parks to the Rise of Black Power* (New York: Knopf, 2010), 51–52, 198.

2. Leigh Ann Wheeler, *How Sex Became a Civil Liberty* (New York: Oxford University Press, 2012), 287n3.

3. Flood, *Rape in Chicago*, 75–80, 98–109; Dawn Rae Flood, " 'They Didn't Treat Me Good': African American Rape Victims and Chicago Courtroom Strategies during the 1950s," *Journal of Women's History* 17, no. 1 (2005): 41, 47–48, 52, 61n95.

4. Wheeler, *How Sex Became a Civil Liberty*, 181; "Corroborating Charges of Rape," *Columbia Law Review*, 67, no. 6 (1967): 1138; Catherine Jacquet, "Responding to Rape: Contesting the Meanings of Sexual Violence in the United States, 1950–1980" (PhD diss., University of Illinois–Chicago, 2012), chap. 2.

5. Menachem Amir, "Victim Precipitated Forcible Rape," *Journal of Criminal Law, Criminology & Police Science* 58, no. 4 (1967): 493; Jacquet, "Responding to Rape," chap. 2; "The Resistance Standard in Rape Legislation,"

Stanford Law Review 18 (1966): 682; Susan Estrich, *Real Rape* (Cambridge, MA: Harvard University Press, 1987), 38.

6. Louis B. Schwartz, "Morals Offenses and the Model Penal Code," *Columbia Law Review* 63 (1963); 674; American Law Institute, *Model Penal Code: Changes and Editorial Correction in May 5, 1962 Proposed Official Draft* (Philadelphia: American Law Institute, 1962), 144–147.

7. Quoted in Susan Estrich, "Teaching Rape," *Yale Law Journal* 102, no. 2 (1992): 510–511n8.

8. Maria Bevacqua, *Rape on the Public Agenda: Feminism and the Politics of Sexual Assault* (Boston: Northeastern University Press, 2000), 89; Michelle J. Anderson, "From Chastity Requirement to Sexual License: Sexual Consent and a New Rape Shield Law," *George Washington Law Review* 70 (2002): 52n2, quoting People v. Fryman, 22 N.E.2d 573, 576 (Ill. 1954); Estrich, "Teaching Rape," 510–511n8. For other degrees of rape recommended in the Code, see Richard H. Kuh, "A Prosecutor Considers the Model Penal Code," *Columbia Law Review* 63, no. 4 (1963): 611–612; Elizabeth H. Pleck, *Domestic Tyranny: The Making of Social Policy against Family Violence from Colonial Times to the Present* (New York: Oxford University Press, 1987), 171. The Code included both vaginal and anal assault in its definition of rape.

9. Estrich, *Real Rape*.

10. Estelle B. Freedman, "'Uncontrolled Desires': The Response to the Sexual Psychopath, 1920–1960," *Journal of American History* 74, no. 1 (1987): 83–106. Newspaper data based on ProQuest searches of the *Chicago Defender* and the *Baltimore Afro-American* from 1900 to 1970.

11. Samuel D. Warren and Louis D. Brandeis, "The Right to Privacy," *Harvard Law Review* 4 (1890): 193, 196; Vivien M. L. Miller, *Crime, Sexual Violence, and Clemency: Florida's Pardon Board and the Penal System in the Progressive Era* (Gainesville: University Press of Florida, 2000), 186; Elizabeth M. Koehler, "Emergence of a Standard: The Rape Victim Identification Debate prior to 1970" (master's thesis, University of Washington, 1995), 117–122; Stuart Gullickson, "Constitutional Law—Standard of Certainty in Criminal Statute—Freedom of Press—Presumption of Unconstitutionality—State v. Ejvue," *Wisconsin Law Review* 1949, no. 2 (March 1949): 362–364; Wheeler, *When Sex Became a Civil Liberty*, 180.

12. Cox Broadcasting Corp. v. Cohn, 420 U.S. 469 (1975); Susan Brownmiller, *Against Our Will: Men, Women, and Rape* (New York: Simon and Schuster, 1975), 217–218; Marcia M. Gallo, "The Parable of Kitty Genovese, the *New York Times*, and the Erasure of Lesbianism," *Journal of the History of Sexuality* (forthcoming).

13. Sara Evans, *Personal Politics: The Roots of Women's Liberation in the Civil Rights Movement and the New Left* (New York: Knopf, 1979); McGuire, *Dark End of the Street*, chaps. 4–5; Mary Aickin Rothschild, "White Women Volunteers in the Freedom Summers: Their Life and Work in a Movement for Social Change," *Feminist Studies* 5, no. 3 (1979): 483–485; Alice Walker, "Advanc-

ing Luna—and Ida B. Wells," in *You Can't Keep a Good Woman Down* (New York: Harcourt Brace Jovanovich, 1981), 85–104; Nancy (Shaw) Stoller, "Lessons from SNCC—Arkansas 1965," in *Arsnick: The Student Nonviolent Coordinating Committee in Arkansas,* ed. Jennifer Jensen Wallach and John A. Kirk (Fayetteville: University of Arkansas Press, 2011), 136–138.

14. Susan Griffin, "Rape: The All-American Crime," *Ramparts* 10, no. 3 (1971): 26–35; Susan Brownmiller, *Against Our Will: Men, Women, and Rape* (New York: Simon and Schuster, 1975). See also Diana Russell, *The Politics of Rape: The Victim's Perspective* (New York: Stein and Day, 1975).

15. Bevacqua, *Rape on the Public Agenda,* 54–55.

16. Ibid., 50–57, 130–131; Susan Brownmiller, *In Our Time: A Memoir of a Revolution* (New York: Dial Press, 1999), 253; Georgina Hickey, "From Civility to Self-Defense: Modern Advice to Women on the Privileges and Dangers of Public Space," *Women's Studies Quarterly* 39, nos. 1–2 (2011): 86–89; Cynthia Grant Bowman, "Street Harassment and the Informal Ghettoization of Women," *Harvard Law Review* 106, no. 3 (1993): 517–580.

17. Laura R. Woliver, "Feminism at the Grassroots: The Recall of Judge Archie Simonson," *Frontiers: A Journal of Women Studies* 11, nos. 2–3 (1990): 111–119; Winifred Breines, *The Trouble between Us: An Uneasy History of White and Black Women in the Feminist Movement* (New York: Oxford University Press, 2006), 166–167.

18. On women jurors, see Linda K. Kerber, *No Constitutional Right to Be Ladies: Women and the Obligations of Citizenship* (New York: Hill and Wang, 1998), chap. 4. On the influence of women jurors in rape cases, see Charles Elliot, "Juries, Sex, and Emotional Affect," *Law and Psychology Review* 35, no. 37 (2011): 45–46.

19. Bevacqua, *Rape on the Public Agenda,* 129; Estrich, *Real Rape,* 81.

20. Angela Davis, "Forum: Joanne Little—The Dialectics of Rape," *Ms.,* June 1975, 106; Walker, "Advancing Luna"; Bevacqua, *Rape on the Public Agenda,* 38–42; Breines, *The Trouble between Us,* 157, 167–168; Nancy A. Matthews, *The Feminist Anti-Rape Movement and the State* (London: Routledge, 1984), 32, 136.

21. Angela Davis, *Women, Race, and Class* (New York: Random House, 1981), chap. 11; Bettina Aptheker, introduction to "Lynching and Rape: An Exchange of Views by Jane Addams and Ida B. Wells," in *Occasional Papers* (New York: American Institute for Marxist Studies, 1977), 19–20; Brownmiller, *In Our Time,* 244–250; Bettina Aptheker, *Woman's Legacy: Essays on Race, Sex, and Class in American History* (Amherst: University of Massachusetts Press, 1982), 53.

22. Wheeler, *How Sex Became a Civil Liberty,* 181–193.

23. Corey Rayburn, "Better Dead Than R(ap)ed?: The Patriarchal Rhetoric Driving Capital Rape Statutes," *St. John's Law Review* 78, no. 4 (2004): 1134; Andrea Dworkin, *Letters from a War Zone* (New York: Dutton, 1989), 201; Estelle B. Freedman and Barrie Thorne, "Introduction to 'The Sexuality Debates,'" *Signs: Journal of Women in Culture and Society* 10, no. 1 (1984):102–106.

24. Rebecca M. Ryan, "The Sex Right: A Legal History of the Marital Rape Exemption," *Law and Social Inquiry* 20, no. 4 (1995): 941–1001; Wheeler, *How Sex Became a Civil Liberty*, 190–191; J. E. Hasday, "Contest and Consent: A Legal History of Marital Rape," *California Law Review* 88, no. 5 (2000): esp. 1491–98; Diana E. H. Russell, *Rape in Marriage* (New York: Macmillan, 1982); Ruth Rosen, *The World Split Open: How the Modern Women's Movement Changed America* (New York: Viking, 2000), 184.

25. Florence Rush, *The Best Kept Secret: The Sexual Abuse of Children* (Englewood Cliffs, NJ: Prentice-Hall, 1980); Judith Lewis Herman with Lisa Hirschman, *Father-Daughter Incest* (Cambridge, MA: Harvard University Press, 1981); Sandra Butler, *Conspiracy of Silence: The Trauma of Incest* (San Francisco: New Glide, 1978); Toni Morrison, *The Bluest Eye* (New York: Plume Book, 1994); Dorothy Allison, *Bastard out of Carolina* (New York: Dutton, 1992); Jane Smiley, *A Thousand Acres* (New York: Knopf, 1991); Louise Armstrong, *Kiss Daddy Goodnight: A Speak-Out on Incest* (New York: Hawthorn Books, 1978). See also Diana E. H. Russell and Nicole Van de Ven, comps. and eds., *Proceedings of the International Tribunal on Crimes against Women* (Millbrae, CA: Les Femmes, 1976).

26. Peggy Reeves Sanday, *A Woman Scorned: Acquaintance Rape on Trial* (New York: Doubleday, 1996), 189; Robin Warshaw, *I Never Called It Rape* (New York: Harper and Row, 1988); Jackson Katz, *The Macho Paradox: Why Some Men Hurt Women and How All Men Can Help* (Naperville, IL: Sourcebooks, 2006).

27. Deborah L. Rhode, *Justice and Gender: Sex Discrimination and the Law* (Cambridge, MA: Harvard University Press, 1989), 246–252; Carol Groneman, *Nymphomania: A History* (New York: W. W. Norton, 2000), 114–119; Kimberle Crenshaw, "Mapping the Margins: Intersectionality, Identity Politics, and Violence against Women of Color Women at the Center," *Stanford Law Review* 43 (July 1991): 1241–99.

28. Katie Roiphe, *The Morning After: Sex, Fear, and Feminism on Campus* (Boston: Little, Brown, 1993); Carrie N. Baker, *The Women's Movement against Sexual Harassment* (Cambridge: Cambridge University Press, 2008).

29. Wendy McElroy, *Sexual Correctness: The Gender-Feminist Attack on Women* (Jefferson: McFarland, 1996), 16–17.

30. Catharine A. MacKinnon, "Feminism, Marxism, Method, and the State: Toward Feminist Jurisprudence," *Signs* 8, no. 4 (1983): 647; Robin West, "Sex, Law, and Consent," in *The Ethics of Consent: Theory and Practice,* ed. Franklin G. Miller (New York: Oxford University Press, 2009), 229–230; Dorothy E. Roberts, "Rape, Violence, and Women's Autonomy," *Chicago-Kent Law Review* 69 (1993): 371.

31. Nancy Whittier, *The Politics of Child Sexual Abuse: Emotion, Social Movements, and the State* (New York: Oxford University Press, 2009), 90–93, 133–166; Roger N. Lancaster, *Sex Panic and the Punitive State* (Berkeley: University of California Press, 2011), esp. 46–59.

32. Angela Y. Davis, "Violence against Women and the Ongoing Challenge to

Racism," (Latham, NY: Kitchen Table: Women of Color Press, 1985), 10; Matthews, *Feminist Anti-Rape Movement,* esp. 6–8, 66, 72. See also Whittier, *Politics of Child Sexual Abuse.*

33. Rivka Gewirtz Little, "Rage before Race: How Feminists Faltered on the Central Park Jogger Case," *Village Voice,* October 16–22, 2002; Crenshaw, "Mapping the Margins," 1267–69.

34. Bevacqua, *Rape on the Public Agenda,* 169–172.

35. Julie Goldschied, "*United States v. Morrison* and the Civil Rights Remedy of the Violence against Women Act: A Civil Rights Law Struck Down in the Name of Federalism," *Cornell Law Review* 86 (2000): 114–119. Establishing the economic consequences of violence helped justify the law as an exercise of congressional authority to regulate commerce.

36. *Violence against Women Act: Hearings on H.R. 3355, before the Comm. on the Judiciary,* 103d Cong. (1993) (prepared statement of Elizabeth Symonds, legislative counsel, American Civil Liberties Union and Women's Rights Project, ACLU), reprinted as doc. 11B in "How Have Recent Social Movements Shaped Civil Rights Legislation for Women? The 1994 Violence against Women Act," ed. Kathryn Kish Sklar and Suzanne Lustig, in the online collection *Women and Social Movements in the United States, 1600–2000,* ed. Kathryn Kish Sklar and Thomas Dublin, accessed October 26, 2012, http://womhist.alexanderstreet.com.

37. United States v. Morrison, 529 U.S. 598 (2000); "Reauthorize the Violence against Women Act," *Washington Post,* April 23, 2012. Congress reauthorized the VAWA in March 2013. For a feminist critique of expanding state powers in the name of protecting women from sexual violence, see Renee Heberle, "Deconstructive Strategies and the Movement against Sexual Violence," *Hypatia* 11 (1996): 63–76.

38. "Critical Resistance—INCITE! Statement: Gender Violence and the Prison Industrial Complex" (2001), accessed July 31, 2012, http://incite-national.org/index.php?s=92; *The Color of Violence: The Incite! Anthology* (Boston: South End Press, 2006); Kristin Bumiller, *In an Abusive State: How Neoliberalism Appropriated the Feminist Movement against Sexual Violence* (Durham, NC: Duke University Press, 2008), 140–146.

39. Holly Kearl, *Stop Street Harassment: Making Public Places Safe and Welcoming for Women* (Santa Barbara, CA: Praeger, 2010); Christie Thompson, "Taking Slut for a Walk," *Ms.,* Summer 2011, 14; Molly M. Ginty, "Court-Martialing the Military," *Ms.,* Spring 2012, 36–39; N. Bruce Duthu, "Broken Justice in Indian Country," *New York Times,* August 11, 2008, A17; Estelle B. Freedman, *No Turning Back: The History of Feminism and the Future of Women* (New York: Ballantine Books, 2002), chap. 12.

40. From Amicus Brief, U.S. vs. Morrison. On Writ of Criteria to the United States Court of Appeals for the Fourth Circuit. Brief of Law Professors as Amici Curiae in Support of Petitioners, reprinted as doc. 18 in Sklar and Lustig, "How Have Recent Social Movements?"

Acknowledgments

In 1975, when I was completing my doctoral training in U.S. social history and beginning to teach the history of women, I read journalist Susan Brownmiller's book *Against Our Will: Men, Women, and Rape.* At the time I wondered why professional historians had not explored the topic of sexual violence, but I left that task to other scholars as I wrote about women's prison reform. A decade later, surveying the exploding historical literature on sexuality for the book *Intimate Matters,* I noticed again how little had been written about rape, even as topics such as prostitution and homosexuality were attracting scholarly attention. After my initial foray into the field, an article on the sexual psychopath scare, I returned to prison reform. Eventually, though, both academic and personal shifts drew me to the study of sexual violence. By the late 1990s a new generation of scholars had begun to mine local court and police records to construct the social history of rape. As the references in this book attest, these historians and legal scholars made it possible for me to grasp the contours of this subject. Equally important, offering a course on interdisciplinary feminist studies taught me about the extent of child abuse and sexual assault, as well as their effects on the lives of my students. That realization in turn forced me to come to terms with my own experience of nonconsensual sex and the ways I had relabeled it over time. Only then did I determine to find a way to study sexual violence.

Once I had made this commitment, a story about a protest song triggered my curiosity about social movements that had attempted to redefine rape. I learned that in 1977, near the end of her life, the indomitable singer-songwriter Malvina Reynolds had been performing in Madison, Wisconsin, when Judge Archie Simonson justified his lenient sentencing of several young men convicted of sexual assault on the grounds that "rape is a normal reaction," given the way women dress. At her next stop, in Chicago, Reynolds wrote and recorded the song "The Judge Said," in which she envisioned a petition campaign to recall Simonson. Reynolds sent the tape to feminists in Madison, who followed up on her suggestion and launched a successful campaign to recall the judge. That story prompted me to ask how feminists in the past had mobilized to protest the treatment of rape. I began by looking at the suffrage press and then expanded my research to include both feminist and racial justice movements. Parallel and intersecting

373

political histories began to unfold, and what I expected to be a short book on the late nineteenth century turned into a more sweeping account of political contestations over gender, race, and rape in American history.

It took far longer to write this book than I could have imagined when I started the research over a decade ago. The generous aid provided by several fellowships, the extensive help of research assistants, and the critical support of those close to me made this task possible. An internal faculty fellowship at the Stanford Humanities Center in 2004–2005 allowed me to complete a large part of the research for this project and to benefit from the feedback of my colleagues there. I was extremely fortunate to spend the 2009–2010 academic year at the Center for Advanced Studies in the Behavioral Sciences at Stanford (CASBS), with additional funding from the American Council on Learned Societies. At CASBS, an incomparable academic haven, I drafted most of the chapters, enabled by the supportive staff and the literal fellowship of my colleagues, particularly the participants in the Gender Lunch Group. A Guggenheim Memorial Foundation Fellowship in 2012 gave me the opportunity to complete and then revise the manuscript. During each of these critical years, supplementary funding from the School of Humanities and Sciences at Stanford permitted me to take time away from teaching to concentrate on the book. I thank Dean Richard Saller and Associate Dean Debra Satz for providing this assistance. The Faculty Fellows Program at the Clayman Institute for Gender Research at Stanford offered interdisciplinary insights and welcome research funds during 2010–2011, as well as an ongoing feminist scholarly community.

None of these fellowships would have been possible without the multiple recommendations generously provided by historians for grant applications, whether lost or gained. I am deeply grateful to Nancy F. Cott, George Fredrickson, Ramón Guttiérrez, Jacquelyn Dowd Hall, Linda K. Kerber, Gerda Lerner, Elaine Tyler May, and Kathryn Kish Sklar for taking the time to write letters and to improve my proposals with their comments. I am also indebted to Barbara Babcock, Sharon Block, Laura Carstensen, Shelley Fisher Fishkin, Thomas A. Foster, Lawrence M. Friedman, Ramón Guttiérrez, Allyson Hobbs, Renee Romano, Esther Rothblum, Penny Sablove, and Eve Sweetser for their invaluable comments on individual chapters and papers related to the book. For sharing material from their own work I thank Bonni Cermak, Frances Dinkelspiel, Lisa Dorr, Brenda Frink, Marcia Gallo, Katie Gray, Catherine Jacquet, Adrienne Johnson, Kathryn McGarr, Jessica Moore, Greg Robinson, Lillian Robinson, Jessica Weiss, and Leigh Ann Wheeler. Peggy Pascoe always encouraged this project in our conversations and I know that this would have been a far better book had she lived to read the manuscript.

I had the opportunity to present parts of this work to a number of academic audiences. The Stanford Gender History Workshop provided bountiful feedback, especially commentary from Matt Sommer, Laura Stokes, Caroline Winterer, and Kari Zimmerman. I also benefited from responses and conversations during invited talks at the University of Michigan Institute for Research on Women and

Gender; the Gender, Sexuality, and Feminist Studies Institute at Oberlin College; the Ethnic Studies Program at the University of Oregon; the Princeton University Program in the Study of Women and Gender; and the joint Stanford–University of California–Berkeley History colloquium. I thank the *Journal of the History of Sexuality* for allowing me the opportunity to develop my ideas on some of these subjects at a conference held at the University of California, San Diego and in an article, "'Crimes Which Startle and Horrify': Gender, Age, and the Racialization of Sexual Violence in White American Newspapers, 1870–1900," published in the journal in September 2011.

The students who enrolled in my course on the history of sexual violence repeatedly helped me clarify my understandings of the subject. The Stanford history department staff, so ably led by Monica Wheeler, supported my work at every step. At Stanford's Green Library, Benjamin Stone acquired and explained the databases that were critical to my research. Sam Ablao and Troy Hernandez from Stanford Information Technology Services and Ravi Shivanna at CASBS resolved multiple technical problems over the years. Thanks to Marilyn Meeker, Estelle Carol, and Margaret Johnston for responding to requests for images. Brian Distelberg at Harvard University Press did a careful and graceful job of troubleshooting production. Wendy Nelson and Melody Negron provided expert copyediting. A generation of research assistants located sources, entered data, cleaned up the citations, and proofed chapters, allowing me to focus on reading and writing. I thank Adelina Acuña, Samantha Barbas, Caley Horan, Michael Hunter, Erin Lichtenstein, Casey Lindberg, Natalie Marine-Street, Sara Mayeux, Kellea Miller, Camille Ricketts, Jacqui Shine, Patricia Tirada, and Kyla Wazana Tomkins for their help. Annelise Heinz greatly facilitated the reproduction of illustrations. Katherine Marino deserves special praise for her prompt, professional, and meticulous assistance during the final three years of this project.

My greatest intellectual debts are to the scholars who read my manuscript in progress. Elaine Tyler May, Elizabeth Hafkin Pleck, and Nancy Stoller showed the depth of their friendship by plowing through the first, raw draft of the study and offering pointed critiques along with warm encouragement. The revised manuscript benefited greatly from another round of careful readings by Linda Kerber, Judith Walzer Leavitt, Leila Rupp, Kate Torrey, and a very astute anonymous reader for Harvard University Press, all of whom helped me move from manuscript to book. I am especially grateful to my editor, Joyce Seltzer, who left her legendary mark throughout these pages, making them clearer, leaner, and more to the point. My lifelong friend and collaborator John D'Emilio commented wisely at each stage of the project, enriched every chapter of the book, and for years patiently counseled me as I navigated the ups and downs of research, writing, and revising. Ricki Boden, Ilene Levitt, Jenna Moskowitz, and Mickey Zemon followed my progress, cheered me on, and provided welcome and sometimes joyous distractions. I am deeply appreciative for all of their support.

As always, I thank Susan Krieger, who listened to every word of this book, showed me how to improve it, and helped me maintain focus while keeping me grounded in our daily lives and excursions. For over three decades Susan has been a model to me as a writer and a comfort to me as a loving partner. I dedicate this book to her with deep gratitude for her insights and for our life together.

Index

Abbott, Robert, 232–233
Abbott, Sukie, 29
Abzug, Bella, 264, 265
Acquaintance rape, 283–285, 287
Addams, Jane, 161, 238, 243
African American women. *See* Black women
Against Our Will (Brownmiller), 264, 278, 280
Age-of-consent movement, 125–167; temperance movement, prostitution, and chastity, 126–127, 133–136; opponents' criticisms of, 127, 139–145; press and, 128–129, 132, 154–155; medical and legal questioning of accounts of statutory rape, 129–132; incest and, 130–131, 148, 158, 159–161; changing meaning of childhood, 132–133; suffragist movement, equal rights, and women's virtue, 136–139; reforms, and initially increased prosecutions, 147, 148–152; changing understanding of female sexuality, 151–157; courts' balancing of protection of girls and of accused men, 153–154; class and, 155–156; race and, 155; medical and psychiatric opinions and, 157–161; victimized men and, 161–165; adult women and accusations of rape, 165–167; boys and, 169–170
Age of female victims in press, 87, 128–129. *See also* Boys, and age of consent laws; Children
"Agreeable Rape, The" (poem), 14
Ah Soon, 184
Allen (California judge), 177–178

Allen, Florence, 216
Allison, Dorothy, 282–283
Alva, Ricardo, 163
American Bar Association (ABA), 279
American Civil Liberties Union (ACLU), 245, 256, 260; rights of accused men and discrediting of accusers, 272–273; sexual privacy of women and, 281; marital rape and, 282; Women's Rights Project of, 287
American Journal of Urology and Sexology, 159, 166
American Law Institute, Model Penal Code of, 274–275, 281
American Woman Suffrage Association (AWSA), 54, 59
Ames, Jessie Daniel, 250–251, 262, 263, 265
Anthony, Susan B., 54, 64
Anti-Lynching Conference, 244
Anti-Lynching Crusaders, of NAACP, 248–249
Anti-lynching movement, 208, 230–252; initial white supremacist context, 230–232; blacks' migration north, 232–233; press reporting of rape and, 232–238; consensual interracial relations, 233–234; exposing of white men as threat to black women, 234–236; female duplicity, 236–237, 247–248; critique of lynching as crime itself and as ineffective preventive, 236–241; public officials held responsible for actions of lynch mobs, 241–247; black women's clubs and, 248–251. *See also* Lynching, racialization of rape and

377